HANGMAN'S BEACH

HANGMAN'S BEACH

Thomas H. Raddall

NIMBUS
PUBLISHING

Nimbus Publishing Limited
P O Box 9301, Station A
Halifax, N.S.
B3K 5N5

Cover design by Arthur Carter, Halifax
Printed and bound in Canada by
Gagné Printing
Published by arrangement with
McClelland and Stewart Inc.

Canadian Cataloguing in Publication Data

Raddall, Thomas H., 1903-

        Hangman's beach

        ISBN 1-55109-014-7

I.   Title.

PS8535.A27H36 1992   C813'.54   C92-098546-7
PR9199.3.R23H36 1992

CONTENTS

HANGMAN'S BEACH

PART ONE

McNAB'S ISLAND

1

When Peter McNab—Peter the First, as some called him afterwards—came to Halifax, the island lay in the harbor entrance like
a green cork in the neck of a green bottle; a cork twisted in a crude
8 and somewhat shrunken in width, so that it did not pretend to
stop the mouth of the bottle but left passage for a stream of salt
water on both sides. The eastern passage was shallow, crooked,
narrow, used by a few fishermen on the Dartmouth shore. Merchantmen and His Majesty's men-o'-war sailed the west channel,
which ran deep and straight, with fair room for tacking. It was over
a mile wide, except where a stony spit ran out from the island
like a lean grey finger pointed at the steep bluff across the water.
The spit was a beach of shingle flung up by southeasterly gales
during God knew how many centuries. Some of the stones were
mere pebbles, some as big as powder kegs, and all rounded and
polished in the rough and tumble of that long chapter in God's
time.

The finger stretched a good half-mile, and made a natural break-
water for the outer anchorage, except in hurricane weather when
a wild surf dashed over it and tossed driftwood and tangles of
kelp and wrack into McNab's cove. Seamen called it simply The
Beach. A long time before English settlers founded the town in
1749, some wandering Biscayan fishermen had built huts on the
island shore and dried their codfish on the beach for shipment
home to France. Indians came there to chaffer with them over
furs and brandy, and somewhere by the cove was the lost grave
of a French priest, the first missionary in those parts.

All these were a legend in 1754 when Peter the First came and

set up as a merchant in this new British outpost on the edge of
French Canada. He brought a stock of English manufactured
goods to trade for pine boards and salt codfish, which in turn he
shipped to the West Indies, taking his pay there in rum, sugar,
molasses, and a balance in Spanish dollars.

The town was four miles up the harbor from The Beach. When
Peter came, Halifax was just five years old, a small huddle of
crude wooden hovels, stores and barracks on part of the harbor
slope, shut in by dark green woods that came down to the shore
as far as the eye could scan. Gradually as the years went by he
watched the hill behind the town become a citadel whose guns
looked over the town and anchorage, with other batteries on the
little hump in the harbor called George's Island, and at wooded
Point Pleasant, and far out on the steep bluff called York Redoubt,
directly opposite The Beach. The passage of time and imperial
affairs produced a busy naval yard, a swarm of redcoated soldiers,
and a town sprawling along the harbor shore, with handsome
wooden mansions for the great merchants and officials.

McNab's interest in the wooded island at the harbor mouth
was first confined to the stony spit where fishermen dried their
catch, and where he went to buy it. His fortunes grew like the
town, slowly in time of peace, spurting in the wars, when the magnificent haven running into the land for almost ten miles became
the chief British army and sea base in North America. Here he
sold supplies in '58 to the British forces on their way to the con-
quest of Louisburg, and again in '59 when Wolfe took them on to
Québec. He had a good share in commissary contracts at Halifax
during the long war of the American Revolution. Ten years after
that was done the wars of the French Revolution began, and
were just getting into their full Napoleonic fury when he died.

While his children were young, and when the squalid little town
baked and stank in summer weather, Peter liked to take his family
by sailboat out to the island. They landed in the west cove, near
the shore end of The Beach, and spent a whole day in clean sea
air, digging clams, gathering lobsters among the weedy rocks at
low tide, and feasting on them in the shade of the trees.

As the summers went by, the short Nova Scotia summers, Mc-
Nab had a growing itch to own this pleasant retreat in the harbor
mouth. Not just the beach or the cove. The whole island. It was

three miles long and its twisted shape contained a good thousand acres, covered with virgin forest. The notion was a back-throw to young days in Perthshire, where his father was a close relation of the clan chief but with little property, in fact that common figure in the Highlands after the Forty-Five, a poor gentleman. Now that Peter began to see money for luxuries there came this longing for an estate, a domain of land and forest all his own at a clean remove from the town but handy enough for his business affairs. He would build there a good house for himself, and cottages for servants and tenants. His retainers would clear away the woods, a little every year, and plant food crops in loamy places sheltered from the sea winds; but mostly the clearings would make pasture for sheep, great flocks of sheep, as he had seen them grazing on the lands of gentry in Scotland. And in this delightful scene he would wear the kilt and play the laird in the good old Highland fashion, with a warm fire and a hearty board for friends and visitors.

Such dreams come easily. Fulfillment is another matter. In McNab's case it took many years. Cornwallis, the first Governor at Halifax, granted the big green cork in the harbor neck to English nephews of his name, who never came across the sea. After some years, seeing a growth in the town's importance, Cornwallis agents offered the island for sale at a price of one thousand pounds sterling, a sum beyond Peter's grasp for many a day, indeed a fantastic price for a wild island so far from town. Nobody offered to buy, but the price remained, and in the meantime the distant owners leased the island to a Halifax official named Bulkeley.

When at last McNab had saved up the Cornwallis price, he found that he must now pay for what Bulkeley called his "improvements." This was polite robbery, of course. Bulkeley had made no effort to clear and cultivate the island. His "improvements" meant felling the best trees and rafting them up the harbor to sawmills and the naval yard. He had made a pretty profit at this, especially during the rebellion of the Americans, when His Majesty's dockyard at Halifax paid a fat price in gold for all the timber it could get.

The American war was at an end, and so was Bulkeley's easy profit, on a day in 1783 when Peter walked into the man's office with a canvas bag and astonished him by paying out the full ex-

tortion, £1313 in Bank of England notes and gold. In the true
spirit of a Highland gentleman McNab was too proud to haggle
with this greedy Englishman over a matter so close to his heart.
He came away joyfully with a receipt, and eventually received
a deed that gave him all of "the Island situate in the Bay and Road
of Halifax, with small islands annexed with stony beaches to the
same, the whole commonly called Cornwallis Island, containing
one thousand acres more or less."

As Peter fingered the deed his mind went to the son who would
inherit all this and, please God, play the laird after him. Long
ago he had determined that his heir should be educated in Scotland; and so at the age of eleven Peter the Second had gone to
Glasgow in the care of a sea captain, and thence to the care of
an uncle McNab in Perthshire. During the next five years young
Peter attended a school in Perth town, and spent the holidays
sometimes with the uncle at Dundrum and sometimes with The
McNab himself, laird of Killen. What his mother thought of this
long separation from her son nobody ever knew. Perhaps, being
Scotch herself, she bore it with McNab's own fortitude.

During young Peter's absence the war of the American Revolution was in full broil, and Halifax merchants were busy dipping
hands in a stream of gold that flowed from London in the wake
of British ships and armies. Some of McNab's profit went back
across the sea to Mr. Colquhoun, his agent in Britain; and in return McNab received neatly detailed accounts for Master Peter
from 1778 through 1783, listing such matters as jackets, plaids,
kilts, bonnets, hose, and what Colquhoun's clerk spelled "brogs,
best quality," as well as receipted bills for board and lodging, for
schooling in the general way, and for special tuition in dancing
and in French. At the end of that time young Peter was put aboard
a little coaster at Leith for London, to get a year's final polish in
an English school.

Thus he returned to Nova Scotia an accomplished Highland
gentleman at the age of seventeen. But still his education was not
complete. He had to learn yet what few Highland gentlemen understood, the art of turning bawbees into guineas, without which
he could not maintain himself as the proprietor of a thousand acres
in North America, with a swarm of servants and tenants. His father
took him into the countinghouse of the business in Halifax, put

up a new sign, PETER-MCNAB & SON, and began to teach him the mysteries of trade.

At intervals they sailed down the tide to the island, where Mc-Nab had axmen clearing the woods and a gang of masons and joiners busy with his house. For the site he had chosen a knoll by the west cove, with views over The Beach and the western passage, up the harbor to the town, and into the harbor's northwest arm, which thrust a blue sleeve through the woods behind the town. Later on, when his workmen had stripped the trees from the island's south end, he could look past The Thrum Cap and Devil's Island to the broad Atlantic, on a line of latitude that touched nothing dry between North America and the Landes de Gascogne on the coast of France.

With his memories of Tayside in winter he had a dour view of the wooden houses favored in America. When you lived with a sea on the east, where all the wild weather came from, you wanted a "muckle hoose" about you. So he sent a ship up the coast to the ruined French fortress at Louisburg, and fetched tons of cut stone that the diligent French had quarried over the sea at Caen in Normandy. Other stone he fetched from Scotland, as ballast in his returning timber ships; and these solid walls he roofed with good thick Ballachulish slates that only a rain of cannonballs could penetrate.

Inside, he drew the ceilings low to give his rooms the full warmth of stoves and hearths in cold weather, so that it was not a tall house but rather one that sat long and low on the knoll, like an outcrop of bedrock. Yet none of the chambers lacked room or finish, and the drawing room especially was large, with panels of polished bird's-eye maple and finely carved moldings. The doors were of rich mahogany fetched north from the Caribbean in his trading ships, and so were the handsome staircase and banisters; and the floors were of Nova Scotia birchwood planed and rubbed to a smooth finish. Under the mantelpieces gaped fireplaces made to burn four-foot logs with space at their ends for a good round blaze. The thickness of the stone walls gave deep embrasures to the windows, like those of a fortress.

Across the sea busy Mr. Colquhoun was hunting about London, Bristol, and Glasgow for choice furniture, carpets, draperies, pictures, ornaments, silver, and chinaware. Also he recruited Scots and Irish tenant families and sent them over the sea to be housed in neat cottages on McNab's island, where they would plant crops for themselves and tend the laird's sheep on the green slopes where the woods had been. For the "muckle hoose" and its own fields and gardens came servants from Scotland, including a bagpiper; and in the easy way of a Highland chief McNab took into his board and pay one or two old soldiers from the Halifax garrison, more fond of rum than work, a sailor discharged with a crippled hand, and others quite nondescript, who came and went as they felt inclined.

At first this fancy of McNab's seemed mad to his merchant friends in the town. They could not fit together the spendthrift dreamer and the canny man of business they had known so long; but they came to see McNab as a man of two sides, both worth knowing. To them, to the garrison officers and their ladies, and a flow of naval visitors, the hospitality of McNab on his island became a feature of Halifax life. To be sure some in the little official circle, nearly all English-born, were inclined to look down their noses at anyone "in trade"; but in 1794 a son of King George came to Halifax as commander of the garrison, and in his six years' duty at this colonial outpost Prince Edward and his charming little French mistress came often to visit McNab in that scene so pleasantly remote from the town.

It put a royal seal on the laird. He might have become that worst of snobs, the merchant whose money has got him favor among the toplofty; but there was no chance of that in Peter McNab. Gay parties of gentry and ladies continued to sail down to the island, step ashore in the cove, and receive the welcome of a host whose manner was simply that of a Highland gentleman among equals.

Sometimes they feasted at McNab's board in the house. At other times they were entertained in a wooded nook by the shore, where the laird's men gathered lobsters and clams and fish for the great iron pot over a driftwood fire, and McNab himself watched over the cooking of chowder and the serving of wine whose bottles had been kept cool in the old French spring. When his guests sailed back to the town they chattered of these adventures as if they had voyaged to the back of the world and called on the Great Cham.

When young Peter—"Peter the Second"—fell in love with the daughter of an Irish settler, they got a blessing from old Peter, and a great concourse of Halifax fashionables came to their wedding. Old Peter was then failing in health, and he turned over the island house to the young couple and lived the rest of his days with one of his merchant friends in Halifax. His wife was long dead, and in 1799 he rattled out his last breath in a town changed immensely from the one that he had first seen forty-five years before.

Thus "young Peter" became laird of the island and master of the business that Halifax knew as Peter McNab & Son. He was thirty-two, a dark stocky Highlandman like his father, with the same shrewd ability in affairs and the same gift for friendship. His wife Joanna was—in contrast to himself on every point—tall, blonde, Irish, Catholic, yet their marriage was a happy one; in the common phrase they were made for each other; and that, too, became a legend in the town.

By the year 1800 McNab's men had cleared the woods and underbrush from a great part of the island, and seamen passing saw flocks of sheep in the pastures. The long war with France, which had become a total war against "Boney," put a high price on such things as wool and mutton in the busy Halifax market, and what carping folk before the war had dubbed "McNab's folly" was now a profitable venture, despite the cost of hired hands and lazy dependents and the constant flow of guests to be entertained.

During the winter season Halifax trade was quiet, and the laird could leave the business in the hands of his factor and spend weeks away on his island. The ships of the naval squadron went south in November to the sunshine of Bermuda and Jamaica, not to return until next summer; the garrison troops shivered and kept to their winter quarters; and there was scant merchant shipping. In the bitter months of January and February there was so little stir in the harbor that it sometimes froze across; and when spells of polar weather lasted calm and cold for several days on end the ice grew thick enough to bear horse and sleigh parties between Halifax and Dartmouth. Sometimes the hard white floor extended seaward as far as McNab's island.

Then, in the fickle habit of the seaboard winter, a wind danced up from the south with warm airs and rains, the ice thawed, and the town's snowbanks turned to slush. At such times Peter and his boatmen rowed and poked their way through broken ice-pans to the town, and the laird turned man of business for a time, going over ledgers and inventories with his factor in the counting-house on Water Street, and returning to the island with letters and newspapers and little notions and luxuries for his people there.

McNab loved the close life of winter, especially when snow-storms whistled about the sturdy house and shut off all view of the town. His cellar and barns were well stocked with supplies for all his dependents, whether they went on two legs or four. The woodsheds were piled to their roofs with maple and birch logs sawn, split and dried in last summer's sun, and another shed had a black heap of coal from shallow pits up the coast at l'Indienne. Nothing was lacking for this cosy siege.

Occasionally naval or merchant ships made a winter run to Halifax, and came in from the sea with hulls and deck gear iced like the fancy cakes of the town confectioners. As they passed the beach their crews could see McNab's chimney smoke, and wondered why anyone chose to dwell on such a place when the company and comfort of a town lay just a few miles up-tide.

In the spring of 1803 Britain's brief experimental peace with Napoleon came to a foredoomed end, and the great war flared up again with more violence than ever. French naval cruisers and a swarm of nimble privateers slipped into the Atlantic to harry British trade, and again McNab's islanders saw processions of merchantmen sailing past The Beach under convoy of His Majesty's frigates and sloops-of-war.

Armed from the naval stores at Halifax, a little fleet of Nova Scotia privateers went south to cruise against the French and Spaniards in the Caribbean. From time to time their prizes, with strange and charming names, came under McNab's spyglass as they sailed in past The Beach, and he hurried up to town to examine them and find what was in their holds. When the Court of Vice-Admiralty had ruled them legal captures, to be sold at public "vendue," the sale was usually held in the Prussian Arms tavern on Water Street, an inn known to seamen as the "Split Crow" from its double-eagle sign; and at the Split Crow the laird McNab would be ready with a shrewd figure at the bidding.

The victualling of all these ships, naval and merchant, and the daily needs of the townsfolk, the garrison, and the growing swarm of French and Spanish prisoners of war, all made a hungry demand for provisions. Doomed cattle and sheep pattered continually along the track through the forest between the farms of the Annapolis Valley and the bustling town, and wagons groaned or sleds whined under loads of pork and poultry, vegetables, grain, and fruit. In all ways the war made a great business in the town; and in the countinghouse of Peter McNab & Son there was never such a cheerful chinking of coins, and in such variety—guineas, crowns, florins, shillings, guilders, Johannes and "half joes," doubloons, moidores, napoleons, pistareens, pieces-of-eight—the coinage of half the world. There was another side to all this, and some Halifax gentry had begun to envy McNab his quiet retreat on the island. The tide of money had floated into the town a raffle of swindlers, thieves, and whores from the Devil knew where. At the foot of the Citadel, Barrack Street and its noisome alleys had become a colonial Whitechapel; along the harborside seamen found Water Street a match for it; and between them lay the offices of business and government, the churches, the homes of townsfolk of the middle class and many of the great merchants. When gangs of sailors trotted up the slope to test the delights on Barrack Street, or when the redcoats trooped down to Water Street, there were lusty encounters in the middle streets which often turned to bloody riots.

The town's night watch was useless in such affairs—a handful of men in civilian clothes, including battered top hats, and armed with staves and rattles. A squad of soldiers mounted guard on Grand Parade with ceremony every morning and evening, but their chief duty was to drag sodden redcoats up the hill in time for roll call in the Citadel. The only naval patrols were press gangs, roving the streets to a screaming chant of "Press! Press! Press!" from angry females in upper windows.

The press gangs reached a supreme arrogance in the spring of 1805, when their admiral told them to seize men, not only in the streets but in lodginghouses, stews, and grogshops—even in the stores and warehouses. This aroused the guild of merchants. As much as the admiral despised "those dam' fellers in trade" the traders had power in the civil courts, where even so formidable an admiral as Sir Andrew Mitchell, K.B., could be brought to the book of British law. The merchants chose a case at random, a

press gang forcing their way into the store of a Scotch firm, Forsyth
& Company. They haled the admiral into court, where he got a
scolding on the rights of British citizens within their walls, even in
this far province of His Majesty. Sir Andrew heard it with disdain;
but the scolding went on to a sharp fine, a stab at his most sensitive part, the purse in which he tucked away his fat portion of
the squadron's prize money. For this he sought revenge under the
law of another court, and his eye fell on Peter McNab, a leading
member of the merchants' guild. McNab happened to be vulner-
able in a way that suited the admiral's humor.

On a soft summer morning in 1805 the laird sailed up to town
in a pretty little sloop, newly built and named *Bonnie Jo* for his
wife. His crew was an old sailor, Gahagan, whose maimed right
hand had got him out of the naval service years before. The admiral's squadron lay anchored between the dockyard and the small
hump of George's Island, which marked the inner roadstead, a
line of black hulls striped with yellow along the gun decks, and
showing a chequer pattern of square black gunports in the yellow
bands. Their masts and precisely squared yards and tightly furled
canvas arose like scaling ladders to the blue dome of the morning.

Somewhere in the blue immensity of the North Atlantic were
the sails of Napoleon's fleet under Villeneuve, and Nelson's ships
in search of them. Other British men-o'-war were posted in stra-
tegic places on the watch. As part of this vast chess game of ships
and guns the Lords of Admiralty had strengthened the squadron
at Halifax, giving Sir Andrew a vast new sense of his importance.

As the *Bonnie Jo* skimmed like a white tern past George's Island the laird and Gahagan heard a shrilling of boatswains' whis-
tles and saw men in a great scurry about the decks and rigging
of the men-o'-war.

"Hark at them Spit Head nightingales!" Gahagan said. "That's
the tune of *All hands to witness punishment* or I'm a Dutchman.
And every ship's astir. They'll be floggin' a man around the fleet
today, God pity him."

"Wait a bit," said McNab. "See the yellow flag at the flagship's
mizzen topmast."

"So! It's hangin!"

"Ay."

The laird turned his gaze away, but he could not turn his mind.

He detested the harsh rules and punishments of the Navy as he despised a high-handed admiral. As the sloop nosed in to the steps of the market dock he looked back to the flagship, and hated himself for it. A gun spat noise and smoke from the upper deck, and as its soiled white cloud blew away a tiny figure soared in swift jerks from the deck toward the fore yardarm. At this distance the hangrope was invisible. The mannikin leaped, stood a moment on air, leaped again, and at last dangled just below the yardarm, swaying a little in the sunshine.

McNab's tongue made a click at his teeth, and he stalked away up the wet stone steps toward his place of business. Ever since the mutinies of '97 the Lords of Admiralty had been haunted by the thought of more, and passed their bogy to every officer in His Majesty's sea service. They had to be sharp, of course, McNab admitted to himself. With thousands of pressed men in the lower decks the whole fleet had a leaven of jailbirds and ruffians picked up in ports around the world. But was it all necessary, or even useful, this continual flogging and frequent hanging in His Majesty's ships? So many of McNab's naval friends had confessed that the cat ruined a good seaman and made a bad one worse. And the hangings! Since '97 any seaman who blurted a wrong word or made a wrong gesture, even in drink, could be charged with "mutiny and contempt" and yanked off the ship's muster sheet with a one-gun salute and a stretch of hemp.

Tach! snapped McNab to himself. A merchant skipper who couldn't make a voyage without catting half his men and hanging one or two to frighten the others would soon find himself out of employ. And no half-pay to ease his idleness! Within his countinghouse the laird dived into much more sensible matters, which had to do with invoices, bills of lading, letters, and ledgers. He could not see the blue gleam of the harbor from his place of business, only the whirligig of people and carts on Water Street, and the topmasts of merchant ships and fishing schooners poking above the flat roofs of the warehouses on the harbor side. Like every other space about the harbor those roofs were spread with codfish split, gutted, salted, and set out in the sun to dry, and the reek of them hung in the street below.

In the store of Peter McNab & Son however there was a more interesting scent, a blend of sugar, molasses, rum, wine, spices, lamp oil, rope, candles, canvas and cloth bolts, and a multitude of other things in stock. These made an air to join in the counting-house with the smell of ink and paper, and of old leather-covered daybooks and ledgers that went back to the days of Peter the First. To the merchant in Peter the Second all this was incense, just as the other side of him rejoiced in the smell of firwoods, kelp on the shore, sheep, cattle, wet collies rubbing at his kilted knees, and the sweet reek of wood smoke from tenant cots and the "muckle hoose."

At the bang of the noon gun on Citadel Hill the chief merchants put on their hats and sauntered down the plank walk on George Street, to chat and later to dine together in the Merchants' Exchange coffeehouse, where over meat and ale they compared news of the town and the world, and did much business with each other before returning to their countinghouses.

When the clock on his own countinghouse wall sounded the last stroke of six o'clock McNab arose, bade a good evening to his factor and clerks, and marched away with his quick step to the market slip, where gnarled Gahagan and the sloop awaited him. The evening breeze was brisk down the harbor and they made good sailing past George's Island and into the outer reach. As the *Bonnie Jo* drew near to his island the laird's eye caught a speck at the far end of The Beach. A fine sunset made a huge red splash over the western sky, and cast on the harbor channel the growing black shadow of York Redoubt. Things close to the water were indistinct, with no apparent relation of distance, shape or size.

"What's that yon?" he said, pointing. In the illusory light the old sailor's eyes were no better than his own, and Gahagan shook the grey locks that ringed his bald head, and made a puzzled mouth.

"Shift your helm," ordered McNab. "I'll tend the sheet. Something's odd there, and I want a glim of it."

2

Some time and distance before McNab set foot on the sea-polished stones at the tip of the point he saw the object of his curiosity well enough, but he went on and stepped ashore to note the details. A tall post of eight-by-eight-inch timber had been set up, with a massive cairn of beach stones piled about the foot to hold it against any wind that blew. At the top of the post, a height of two fathoms, a short arm of the same timber jutted at a right-angle, and from it hung the naked body of a man, daubed with tar from head to foot. A few links of chain and an iron collar about his neck held him to the beam. His wrists were shackled together, and so were his ankles. The wood was new, with fresh chips lying about, and tar spattered on the stones. The feathery ashes of a driftwood fire showed where the tar pot had been heated.

Just then, from the rocky height across the channel, sprang the flash and puff of the sunset gun in York Redoubt, followed by a thunderclap delayed at half a mile. Then fainter claps far up the harbor, as if in echo, from the town batteries on George's Island and the Citadel. The laird stood as rigid as the post in the rocks, glaring at the silent intruder as if to stare him down and out of sight. Inside he was cursing, and in Gaelic, a language vastly more expressive than mere English. Gahagan spoke in a musing voice, full of old memories. "Must be the poor divil that danced the hornpipe at a rope's end this morning, sor. The tar's for to hold off the crows an' seagulls for a while, so he'll hold together like, an' show better to passin' ships. A proper sight for a bad dream, ain't he now? Minds me of an old song the sailors used to bawl at their grog pots, The Black Joke."

"Why here—here of all places?" snapped McNab.

"Och, 'tis common other places, sor. I've see 'em strung up just like this on beachy p'ints along the mouth o' Thames, an' Chatham, an' Spit Head, an' places abroad like the Palisadoes where ye pass into Kingston harbor in Jamaiky. It's for an example, d'ye see, sor, a warnin' to ivery seaman goin' by."

"Bah! Whatever he hanged this puir devil for, the Admiral stuck him up here, in sight of my hoose, to wipe the eye of McNab, who backed Forsyth against him in the courts! Aweel, tomorrow the Admiral shall take doon his black joke, or I'll haul him into court for a prettier penny than e'er Forsyth got out of him. Now shove us off and away from this carrion."

Stamping ashore at the head of the cove he was the picture of a dark Highlandman in a rage, lacking only kilt and claymore to be on a march to battle instead of the pleasant walk up the hillside to his house. Joanna had been watching for him and came to meet him with her boys. She was wearing a high-waisted gown of some cool white stuff, and flat silk shoes tied with tapes about her fine ankles.

Only six years younger than McNab, she looked younger by a dozen. Her hands clasped the arms of the two boys as they sauntered together down the path. At thirteen James—"Sheamus" to McNab's Gaelic servants—promised to be tall and fair like his mother. At eleven the boy Peter—"Para"—was the laird all over again, with the same black hair and darkling eyes and sturdy build. The lads were dressed alike in shirt and kilt, stockings and brogues, the rig that McNab ordained for wear at home.

At the moment the laird himself was dressed for the counting-house and the Merchants' Exchange, in broadcloth breeches, silk stockings, and buckled shoes. Over a plain white shirt he wore what he called "my tanny weskit" and a blue coat very short in front, with tails to the back of his knees. A vast cravat came up to his ears, and his tall beaver hat had been jammed well nigh down to them for the breezy run down the harbor. Indeed with his hat set thus, his thick muscular legs planted well apart at every step, the deep chest thrust forward, the fists clenched and swinging, and the chin like a prow cleaving the air before him, McNab seemed in trim for a hurricane.

He failed to kiss his wife and tousle the boys, as he always did on homecoming. Instead he halted abruptly and threw out a hand towards that obscene object far in the distance.

"D'ye ken what's yon—at the beach end?"

Joanna said mildly, "We noticed a pair of boats out there this afternoon. Man-o'-war boats according to the shepherds. The sailors stayed an hour or two, and had a fire. A chowder party, I suppose. What's the matter?"

McNab gazed sternly along the beach to the point in the channel. At half a mile the gibbet and its uncanny tenant could be seen only as a speck, an illusion almost, now there, now gone, like the eye motes of a bad digestion. *Wheesht,* he told himself, *ye're in a stew about a trifle.* But he could not convince himself of that, nor cease his rage.

He said loudly, "The matter? We'll discuss the matter atween ourselves and the bedpost, woman; it's no tale for young ears. And you lads—you'll keep off the beach from now on, mind that—and never mind why!"

At the supper table his household regarded him carefully. They consisted of his wife and boys, his great-aunt Frances McNab, and his ward Ellen Dewar, another of the family connections, who had been sent across the sea as an orphan of ten just when the old laird was faltering to his grave. McNab sat dour, drinking a great depth of Madeira from the decanter at his elbow, but making a poor touch at the food. All of which was unusual. Joanna could not attempt to get the matter out of him until their bedroom door closed for the night. Then he told her, in a low and shaking voice more violent than a shout. At first she felt as outraged as himself. Then, seeing the black depth of his anger, she tried to tease him out of it.

"Peter! Peter! This isn't you, getting yourself in a tirravee about a scarecrow on a pole. Ah, sure, I feel sorrow for the poor man hanged, but that's past mending. Tomorrow as you say the Admiral must take him off your property. You've only to mention it, surely? Sir Andrew's a gentleman."

"Sir Andrew's naething of a gentleman, and I doot much of an admiral! A weevil swollen wi' importance in his own sma' biscuit, ever since Monsieur Villeneuve got away into the Atlantic and the Lords of Admiralty sent an extra ship or two to bolster the Halifax squadron. Why, gel, this Knight of the Bath is chust a bag of wind wi' one pipe set in it, a pipe that screams 'Who-are-ye-damn-ye' whenever he meets a man in trade. Naething's in him but wind and arrogance, the arrogance o' the de'il himself."

The laird was pulling on his nightshirt as he said this, and speak-

ing in the broad Scots that came upon him always in emotion.
Half his words were muffled in the flannel, and Joanna had a nervous impulse to laugh; but as she blew out the candle she foresaw
a wakeful and uncomfortable night. So it was. McNab was up most
of it, prowling belowstairs, sipping brandy which did him no good
whatever, and staring from one of the deep window embrasures
towards the beach hidden in the night.

Years back, when Halifax people twitted Peter the First about
his house so far from the town, the old laird used to smile and say,
"Oh ay, but I'm a man from the braes by Firth of Tay, and I sleep
better where I hear the sea brawl. There's no sleep like that to
be had in toon."

Tonight the sea was just a murmur on the stones of the long
point, but the sound came clearly in the dark, as if water kelpies
were at whisper over the dead man there. Anon the laird peered
at an eastern window, wishful for daylight, but never in all his life
was daylight so long coming. He made a scant breakfast, and at
last he was off to town in a pelter of rain. Thunder crackled up
from the southward to chime with his mood as the *Bonnie Jo*
arrived at the market steps. He passed the cherished sign PETER
MCNAB & SONS without a glance and stalked on, a wet boat-
cloak hanging about him, until he came to the office of his friend
Cogswell the lawyer. Cogswell was a craggy man with thick hairy
eyebrows and a nutcracker face, a sprig of the shrewd Yankee
folk who came to settle in Nova Scotia after the fall of Louisburg.
He had made a fortune at the law, chiefly in prize cases and other
matters of the sea.

He listened to McNab's indignant tale in silence, with a brooding eye and a growing twist of mouth. At the end he got up from
his desk and walked to a window where he could see the harbor
and the hornet-striped warships in the anchorage. Then, over
his shoulder, "So you want to put another dash of salt on the Admiral's tail, eh? Wasn't one enough?"

"That was another matter," Peter snapped. "So let's have
no bauchle about this. I want a writ, or whatever's required, to
make this damned admiral take away his gibbet and corpse afore
another day's oot."

"And if he ignores the writ?"

"Then I want a suit for trespass, insult, nuisance to public health—ye're a lawyer, man, ye can drum a dozen things."

Cogswell thrust his lean hands under his coattails and moved up and down the floor. He had a slow long-legged wary step, like a bittern stalking frogs in a swamp. "Well, let's take one at a time and start with trespass—all you say stems from trespass, McNab. What makes you think the beach is yours, or any stone there, for that matter?"

Astonished, McNab sputtered, "Why—why it says so in my father's deed from the Cornwallis heirs across the sea. Must I show ye that? Ye know verra weel the beach is mine and every stone on it. All Halifax knows it. So does the Admiral. That's why he hanged his carrion there."

"Um! The Admiral, to be sure. The Admiral got himself a bride in town last spring, did he not?"

"Och, ay, a gel young enough to be his daughter. No doubt the title and the gold tassies on his shoulders caught her fancy—no one could love the man himself. Why, at the wedding some of the market women waited outside St. Paul's to show the bridegroom their esteem, and pelted him wi' curses and hard chunks o' salt codfish, the way they pelt his press gangs in the streets. But, *tach!* What the de'il has the Admiral's bride to do wi' what I'm here about?"

"She happens to be a daughter of Richard Uniacke, who happens to be Attorney General of this province and—must I remind you?—a power in the Vice-Admiralty court."

"Bah! That didn't save his son-in-law a smart fine in the civil court!"

"True, but I suspect the Admiral's taken advice of Uniacke since that affair at Forsyth's, my friend. He knows now what he can't do here ashore—and what he can. And the sad fact is, McNab, he can put up a gibbet anywhere about the shore that he's a mind, so long as it's seaward of the town and 'tween high water mark and low."

Cogswell stepped to his bookshelves, laden with tomes in scuffed leather covers, and snatched one down. He flicked over pages rapidly, wetting a long forefinger with his tongue from time to time. "The High Court of Admiralty, you understand, wields power over all that has to do with ships and the sea . . . and that's anywhere . . . let's see now . . . come to it in a moment

. . . um! . . . here we are . . . *all rivers, nooks and places overflown whatsoever within the ebbing and flowing of the sea, and high water mark, or upon any of the shores or banks adjacent from any of the first bridges towards the sea, throughout Britain and Ireland or elsewhere beyond the seas."*

He shut the book with a bang. "You see? The Admiralty Court is Almighty God over everything wet between Hell, Hull, and Halifax. That beach of yours may be dry during common tides at any time of year; but with a long gale from the southeast and a flood tide, the seas leap clean over it. I saw proof of that whenever I was your guest out there, McNab. Old wreckage from the outer reefs, washed in and flung over the beach into the very shadow of the trees by the old French spring. Where else would you get the driftwood for your chowder pots?"

The laird's eyebrows lifted in angry arches. "D'ye mean to say that makes my beach a Tom Tiddler's ground for anybody's mischief?"

"Mischief or not, it makes the beach a ground for Tom Tiddler's use, and certainly the use of an admiral with the Vice-Admiralty Court behind him and the Honorable Richard Uniacke under his lee. His gibbet's a lawful fixture whether you like it there or no."

"Fixture! I'll have my men throw the damned thing in the sea."

"Do that, McNab, and you'll find yourself in the Vice-Admiralty Court for willful damage to His Majesty's naval property, *videlicet* one gibbet and attachments thereto, including a felon condemned to death and exposure under the laws of the High Court of Admiralty. And don't forget the Judge of Vice-Admiralty here in Halifax—another high cockaloram with nothing but contempt for people like you and me."

Cogswell now dived his fingers into an untidy heap of papers on the window shelf. "The Lords of Admiralty have such matters printed and sent about the ports at home and abroad for public notice. Saw one a few days back. Here somewhere. Not that . . . nor that . . . nor that . . . where the deuce is the thing? . . . ah!" He plucked out a broadsheet and read aloud. *"At a Court Martial assembled and held on board H.M.S. So-and-so, et cetera . . . um! . . . the charges of mutiny being fully proved, the Court do therefore adjudge that the prisoner be hanged by the neck until dead, at the yardarm of H.M.S. So-and-so . . .* and here's the important thing, McNab . . . final paragraph . . . mark it well . . . *As further example to deter others from such evil courses, his body shall be hung in chains upon a gibbet, on such a conspicuous point or headland as the Commanding Officer may choose."*

Cogswell thrust the sheet under Peter's nose. "Read it, man! Read it for yourself!"

"Away wi' it!"

"So you see, my friend, if you remove that gibbet, or even chop it down, you're flouting the High Court of Admiralty, not just Mitchell. What's more, you're flouting the rules of Admiralty in time of war—and as it happens a very dangerous time of war. The French fleet in the Atlantic, free to strike anywhere, even here. Boney at the Strait of Dover waiting with his army for the ships to take him across. All the rest of the bad news and worse prospects. Fancy how the Honorable Dick Uniacke would pile all that on, in the Vice-Admiralty Court . . . Dick standing well over a fathom in his silk stockings and pumps, shaking his wig like Britannia herself insulted, and stabbing a finger at you there in the box like a thief caught stealing the Crown jewels. And Judge Croke on the dais above, perched like a fish hawk marking a tom-cod in shallow water. And the little silver oars on the desk before him in sign of his authority. Why, it'd cost the Mint to keep you out of jail!"

"What if it did?"

"Ah! There speaks the proud Scot! And what if it did? Surely even you, my stubborn friend, can see an inch ahead of your nose. In another week, or fortnight, or a month . . . a tyrant like Mitchell will surely find another man to hang by then . . . you'd find another gibbet on your beach, with another pretty fruit to ripen on it . . . and you'll have another chance to make a fool of yourself for the Admiral and Croke."

McNab bent his head and shook it fiercely, as if the lawyer's words were mosquitoes at his ears. Cogswell put a hand on his shoulder.

"Peter, there's just one course for you. Swallow your pride and yield the point . . . and I don't mean an idle pun. Just run your mind ahead a bit. Tar or no tar, that poor devil on your beach

can't hang there forever. The tar may hold off the birds but it
can't stop natural decay; and once the flesh is gone what's to hold
the bones?"

"Mebbe, mebbe," growled McNab. "But the Admiral wins
his point, ye say. He can dangle a dead man under my nose whenever he feels inclined?"

"Tut! Your nose indeed! The beach tip's a half mile from the
main island shore, and your house tucked inside the cove. You're
making too long a nose, McNab. It's your pride that catches the
whiff. Well pocket your pride, man, pocket it! Things can change
quickly in time of war. Mitchell's commanded the North American
squadron four years now, a long time as such appointments go.
Who's to say where he'll be in another six months or six weeks?
For that matter where's Monsieur Villeneuve this minute? He
can't stay at sea forever. He must make for France or Spain to
store and refit; in fact he's got to do that soon, and nobody knows
it better than the Lords of Admiralty. I venture they've sent dis-
patches already, calling home every ship-of-the-line and frigate
they can muster. That means Sir High-and-Mighty Mitchell must
part soon with his biggest guns and learn to sing small again."

"Ah! May the guid God let me hear that tune!"

The summer slipped by as fine summers do. Parties from Halifax
came sailing out to McNab's island, and usually steered close
enough to the beach to give the ladies a glance and a shudder at
the grim exhibit there. Nobody spoke a word of this in the hearing
of McNab, of course, for it was well known to be a sore matter.
On her own part Joanna made sure that her youngsters, and those
of the servants and tenants, never set foot on the beach, not even
the shore end of it, where the shallow lagoon flowed into McNab's
Cove.

Every morning McNab poked a spyglass from his bedroom
window to inspect the object on the gibbet. True to Cogswell's
guess the thing shrank to skin and bones in a few weeks; but tough
sinews at the neck kept it dangling from the iron collar until August waned. Then the first fall hurricane blew up from the West
Indies, with gusts that set the island trees cowering and hurled
waves of the North Atlantic right across the beach into the harbor.

At some hour between dark and morning the long-awaited disappearance came to pass. In the wild yellow light of a stormy sunrise the gibbet leaned precariously in a shaken pile of stones, and its branch was as bare as a winter thorn.

Soon after that a despatch from London, long on the passage in the teeth of the westerlies, commanded the Admiral to send home his sail-of-the-line. The laird watched them moving ponderously past the empty gibbet on their way to sea, and in his patriotic heart he wished them well. All summer there had been delayed reports of Villeneuve's raid to the Caribbean, with Nelson in vain pursuit. Then a Nova Scotia brig, homeward bound from a West Indies voyage, reported the French fleet steering east.

Like every other merchant in Halifax the laird was in good cheer at this turn of events. He could even doff his beaver, with a twitch of irony, to the admiral's carriage as it trotted along Barrington Street on a drear wet autumn afternoon. There was a glimpse of a cocked hat, a hard face and a pair of frosty eyes, no more, and no sign of recognition whatever. All through the roaring gales of October and November, grey with rain or white with snow, with an interlude of Indian summer as magical as a rosebush in a desert, the sea-wise folk of Halifax awaited word from Europe. Where had Villeneuve made for? And where was Nelson?

It was not until Christmas of that stormy year 1805 that they learned the answer to all their questions in one tremendous tale. Peter McNab carried it home to the island in a London newspaper fifty days old, and he gathered the family and servants about him in the drawing room and read out in a shaking voice the tidings of Trafalgar. They heard him in silence, and when he finished his eyes were wet and so were theirs. Nelson dead! It was as if the sun had fallen in the Spanish sea and left a cold darkness on the world.

Joanna said hopefully at last, "But it means the end of Napoleon's fleet."

"The end of one fleet, ay, and a big one, French and Spanish —the biggest Boney had. But mind, he's still the master of Europe, and he'll have more ships built, depend on't, if only a swarm of cruisers to slip out and harry the British sea trade. And when it comes to ships we must give the devil his due. The French can design and build a better ship than we, 'specially in the lower rates.

Their frigates and corvettes are clean lined and cleverly sparred and rigged . . . which means they're fast . . . and when it comes to shifting tacks or wearing they can spin about like dancers. If their seamen were half as good as their ships . . . but let's thank God they're not. Ah no, we're not done wi' Frenchmen on the sea, not by a verra long shot. All we can say from this news is that Boney canna cross the Channel a while yet. The rogue does miracles with armies but he canna conjure up sail-o'-the-line in a fortnight nor even a twelve-month. Tae build and equip a ship that size takes a lot more time. And what about crews? Ye canna sail a ship without a crew. This paper says the enemy lost nigh twenty-three thousand men. Think on't! Three-an'-twenty thousand seamen wiped off Boney's muster sheet in one sweep, like a sum from a schoolboy's slate! A lot of 'em now prisoners in England, an' the rest dead as pickled herrings. Ah! Boney may take young clodhoppers from the farms an' make soldiers of 'em in a few weeks; but he canna make an able seaman short of a year in active service, ay, an' two years at the least if they're to stand a chance wi' ours."

"How long have ours been in active service?" Ellen Dewar said, with the black eyes large in her thin face.

"Many men in the fleet havena set foot to shore in years."

"And when will they see their folk again?"

"When Boney's beat."

"That may take for aye."

The laird gave her a look of superior wisdom, of pity for her ignorance, as if Ellie were still an orphan of ten and not a woman grown.

"Boney," he said profoundly, "can't last for aye, gel. All men come to an end, and so do wars and winters."

The girl nodded and turned her eyes away to the cove, and then to the far end of the beach where the empty gibbet leaned in the stones.

"And women," she said.

3

In the stark white January of 1807 the English mail arrived by a naval ten-gun brig via Bermuda, the usual practice in winter, when the North American squadron was cruising in warm southern waters. Hearing the brig's salute to York Redoubt in the first light of morning, McNab roused out four strong-armed Highlandmen for a boat's crew and embarked for the town. The *Bonnie Jo* was hauled up on the cove shore for the winter, dismasted and snug under canvas. For these winter journeys the laird kept a four-oared shallop, easy to launch over the ice if the cove was frozen, and no great work for the oarsmen when the wind was light and the harbor open.

The snow lay deep on the harbor slopes, and in the town the shoveled walks were like trenches in a siege. People scurried, well muffled, to the post office, and when anyone spoke his mouth fumed like a pistol. A boat's crew from the brig, after delivering the precious sacks from England, dived into the nearest tavern bawling for rum, that bottled sunshine of the West Indies. The brig had reached the harbor just in time, for the breeze was dying fast and the thermometer outside the Exchange was dying faster still. The harbor would have a skin of ice by tomorrow morning and a hard grey floor by afternoon. The narrow streets, the very houses, seemed to huddle closer against the cold, and the town had a canopy of chimney smoke that barely wavered in the sharp air.

Returning to the island at the end of the short winter afternoon, McNab's boatmen rowed mightily for warmth as much as speed. The laird, crouching over the tiller, felt a chill to his bones in spite of his caped greatcoat and thick Scotch bonnet. When they reached the "muckle hoose" he commanded whiskey all round before turning to the letters and newspapers.

The family and servants had gathered with an expectant air. Ever since that tremendous news at Christmas 1805 they had come to look on the winter mail from England as a package of excite-

ment far beyond anything that came in summer. They watched
the laird's face as he made a swift scan of the newspapers, and saw
it change from eagerness to a glum indifference. At last he said,
"Tach! There's naething but one o' Boney's pompous decrees.
This time he's ordering British trade shut out from all of the Continent that's under his fist, or frightened of it anyhow. And London's hit him back tit-for-tat. Orders in council forbid anyone
trading with France or any country under French direction. A
business of thumbing noses at each other."

The boatmen drank another generous dram and trooped away.
The servants disappeared. Even old Aunt Frances went off to her
knitting by the fireside in her chamber. Joanna remained, peeping
over the laird's shoulder as he turned to his letters, and Ellen Dewar
holding her hands out to the blaze on the great hearth.

The letters appeared to be matters of business mostly, but there
was one from Admiral Berkeley, who had replaced the outrageous
Mitchell last year. It was nothing much, a polite note from Bermuda, written in the beautiful elliptical hand of the Admiral's secretary and signed with the scrabble of Berkeley himself. The
squadron had weathered a hard gale of wind and snow off Cape
Sable on the way south in November, otherwise the passage had
been excellent and the ships were now at anchor in the harbors
of Hamilton and Saint George. He asked to be remembered to
Mrs. McNab and to his merchant friends at Halifax.

McNab passed it over his shoulder to his wife and broke the
seal on another. It was marked New York and superscribed *via
His Majesty's Mail, Bermuda.*

> Peter McNab, esq.,
> at Water Street,
> Halifax in Nova Scotia,
> North America.
> Dear Mr. McNab,
>   Although we have done much business with each
> other, we have never met, and since you never come to
> New York I intend the pleasure of calling upon you
> with the first fine weather. I shall come in my brig Mon-
> tauk, Captain Phips, on a spring voyage to the Provinces.
> Should anything prevent, I shall let you know by the

first ship direct to Halifax. I send these lines via Bermuda and the post office brig and trust they find you and your family well and prosperous, as they leave me and mine at the present.

> With my compliments &c, &c,
> Malachi Sparling,
> Sparling, son, & Company

Joanna passed back to him the note from Admiral Berkeley. "These decrees of Napoleon, will they mean anything to us, on this side of the ocean?"

"Nothing to us in Nova Scotia, my dear. Our trade over there is with Britain, not the continent, except maybe some dry fish to Italy and a stop at Iviza for salt and Cádiz for wine on the way back. The fur traders up in Canada will be hurt, of course—the Hudson Bay fellows and the Nor'westers. Europe's the best fur market in the world, and Hamburg's the chief port for it, right under Boney's thumb. For that matter he can shut any entry on the Continent, any time he likes."

"And what about the orders in council from London?"

"They won't hurt anyone but Boney in the end, though they may upset some American trade with the Continent. No concern of ours at any rate."

His wife turned to join Ellen and put her own hands out to the fire.

"What a blessing to live as we do, where nothing ever happens!" Ellie Dewar stared on into the flames.

Spring came at last, with its cat-and-mouse weather; rains and suns to melt the winter's snow, chill sea fogs, warm airs from the south, icy winds from Labrador, sudden northeasters hurling snow upon the land again, and so the dreary round.

Captain Luke Phips of the *Montauk* brig brought his owner into Halifax on a chill day of early May, and after mooring at the McNab wharf they lost no time in calling on Peter in his store on the other side of Water Street. The captain had a chunky body like McNab's own, but perched on very long legs that moved with a

sea gait, wide apart for the ship's roll, like a pair of compasses
stalking point by point across a chart. He had sharp grey eyes and
black side-whiskers with the mouth and chin shaved clean, and
he wore a blue jacket and brass buttons, a squat glazed billycock
hat with a narrow brim curled inward, and brown nankeen trousers
held taut by loops under the insteps of his boots.

Malachi Sparling was a very different personage. His was a lean
and scholarly face, shaven clean, and with short locks of pepper-
and-salt hair brushed forward over the brow. He was old-fashioned
like McNab in clinging to breeches, silk stockings and buckled
shoes in a time when fashion had run to trousers and boots, but
he wore a tremendous cravat of the fashionable size, and a beaver
top hat shaped rather like the captain's but without the waterproof
glaze. His eyes were large and of a dark grey, and their gaze was
serious.

Captain Phips introduced him to McNab and they withdrew to
the small inner office, where a fire of Cape Breton coals flickered
and murmured in an iron basket on the hearth. Mr. Sparling began to talk at once, in a voice that was light and rather high in key,
like a boy's, yet crisp in every word and phrase.

"I've come on business, Mr. McNab, very important business,
too, I'll tell you that right off. I didn't mention it in my letter because, um, letters go astray sometimes, and this was a matter best
not written down. A delicate matter, sir. Delicate indeed. By way
of opening I'll refer to this war. I mean to say France and your
country at hammer-and-tongs, and my country neutral and trying
to do business abroad. You know the difficulties, I'm sure. Last
year Napoleon shut the door on British trade with Europe—
bang!—like that!" And Mr. Sparling slapped a white hand on the
table top with a force and noise that startled the clerks outside.

"There's no denying Boney gives the orders on the continent of
Europe nowadays. That's a fact. So your government in London
slaps an embargo on *anybody's* trade with Europe—unless the
ships undergo British inspection and clearance. Then Napoleon
again. Any ship submitting to British clearance will lose all claim
to neutrality. She'll be snapped up by any French privateer or
man-o'-war that comes her way. Pretty kettle of fish! I mean
to say neither of 'em seems to think the American nation has a right
of free trade anywhere that we've a mind. Yet they both want our

supplies of timber, flour, tobacco, and so forth. So far we've been able to deliver the goods in our own ships, neutral, quiet, and reliable. Now all of a sudden England and France decide to cut off their nose to spite their face—and our nose into the bargain."

Mr. Sparling raised a finger and rubbed his own nose with a wounded air.

"Well, sir, I tell you nothing new when I mention Boney was getting plenty of American supplies, run through the British blockade, up to the time his navy got that almighty thrashing at Trafalgar. That left the British with ships to spare for a long reach over the sea. To our American coast, d'you see. Off New York, and the Delaware and Chesapeake waters anyhow, for that's where most of our French exports hail from. It amounts to a British blockade. They're actually stopping American ships within sight of our own coast, and searching 'em for stuff that may be bound for France or any country under Boney's thumb. Mind you, it's not a declared blockade, nor an effective blockade—not really—not yet anyhow. The British men-o'-war have to work out of Halifax and Bermuda to watch our ports, and that's a mighty long haul for repairs and victualling and watering and what not. Still, it's annoying, Mr. McNab."

"It's a dam' outrage!" cried his skipper.

Mr. Sparling held up a white forefinger of arresting length. With fascination McNab estimated more than four inches stabbing the air like the sharply steeved bowsprit of the *Montauk*.

"No language, please!" the New Yorker said severely. Turning to McNab he resumed the voice and manner of a schoolmaster explaining step by step a problem in geometry. "A bad matter, sir, as you see. I now come to something worse. When your men-o'-war overhaul an American merchant ship and bring her to, it isn't only the ship's papers and cargo they want to see. No indeed! The boarding party wants a muster of the crew. And certain ones are ordered to pack their duds and get into the man-o'-war's boat. Deserters from His Majesty's Navy—or so the boarding officer declares—and his party's well armed in case the Americans make a fuss. When they get those men aboard His Majesty's ship there's a cat-o'-nine-tails waiting for anyone that balks His Majesty's duty. So they've no choice, whether they're British, American, or anything else. It's a monstrous tyranny any way you look at it."

"I agree," said the laird. "Indeed I dislike many things about His Majesty's sea service in these times. I clashed with an admiral myself not long ago. But on this point, isn't it true that hundreds of British seamen run off to American ports and American ships for the better pay?"

"And better treatment, sir."

"Treatment, then. And isn't it true that real American seamen nowadays carry a paper to prove it?"

Captain Luke Phips broke in with his tops'l-yard voice. "Ah, but your Navy officers just larf at that. They say a British deserter can buy one o' those papers for a dollar or two, anywhere from N'Orleans up to Bawston. Could be true, at that. Someone's always out to make an easy dollar, and nothin's easier than pen and paper. But papers or none, your Navy captains are always short o' men and out to grab able seamen anywhere, no matter who they are or where they come from. Why, sir, a few months back I had five men pressed out o' my ship by a British frigate cruisin' well inside the Delaware Capes. Americans, every man o' the five. One was an American Injun, even—one o' the Gay Head tribe that go to sea in Nantucket whalers and learn to hand, reef, and steer. The British lootenant couldn't understand his talk but he swore the feller was a sunburnt Welshman, and he went off with all five of 'em, larfin' fit to kill hisself."

McNab's mouth drooped in glum lines. "We've had our own troubles here with the press, as I've told you. I might add that a lot of our trade's with the West Indies, and on those voyages our crews are picked over by naval boarding parties all the way from Halifax to Demerara and back again. More than once I've seen a ship creep in past my island with her crew reduced to a few hands old or sick, and one or two boys—barely enough to handle a few sails and keep her off the rocks." He shrugged. "We protest, of course, and have the backing of our Governor. And now and again we get a few men released. But on the whole we canna do a thing. Fortunately for us the present flag officer's quite a gentleman, and very serviceable and obliging in the matter of convoys. And since we do have the benefit of His Majesty's convoys we canna say verra much about the way His Majesty gets his seamen."

The New Yorker did not seem to hear a word of this. He went on with his discourse in the same precise voice. "Now, sir, men like Captain Phips and me don't like your nation's sea manners a bit. That goes without saying. On the other hand, we trust Napoleon no further than your 'prentice boy could heave an anchor down the street. Since this war began we've done business with the French nation, one way or another, and found 'em a slippery crew. Like master, like man. If it came right down to a single choice I guess we'd rather trade with the British. People like yourself, sir. Fair and square dealing. No trumped-up claims for damage or shortage or bad quality in the cargo—none of the tricks the French get up to, once our goods are in their hands. And all debts paid when the bills come due. In short, just good plain business."

Mr. Sparling paused, with his hands on the table, the hands of a man of business, slim and white and capable. He closed them to fists, put the thumbs together, and opened the long forefingers so that the tips touched. They pointed straight across the table at McNab like a ship's prow at a seamark.

"Everything I've said so far is serious enough, mark you, Mr. McNab; but now I come to the *almighty* serious part. Our American nation's grown and spread a long way inland since the war for independence. New states like Tennessee, Kentucky, Ohio; new territories like Louisiana, Indiana, Michigan, Mississippi; all filling up with people and more pushing westward all the time. That's the point you've got to understand if you're to see the rest. All those people want land. Land! More land! That's the great cry. Only us people on the coast care anything about the sea."

"Those freshwater fellers," grumbled Captain Phips, "just know the sea ain't fit to drink, and anything they can't drink don't signify."

"Ah!" Mr. Sparling said quickly, "but right now their politicians are showing a sudden interest in what they can't drink."

"I'm afraid I don't understand," McNab murmured politely.

"Their notions happen to fit right in with Long Tom Jefferson's ideas—and he's the President. 'Free Trade and Sailors' Rights'— that's the way they're putting it. Fact is, the freshwater people don't care a straw for sea trade or seamen. They're after more land, and they see a way of getting it. They've grabbed most of the Indian lands east of the Mississippi. Now they're looking north. They want Canada."

"Canada? You're joking!"

"I'm dead serious. They're hoping to start a war between the
United States and England so they can march up and take Canada.
And they figure now's the time while the British are up to their eyes
in war with Napoleon. Easy as rolling off a log. Matter of marching a few muskets along the Canadian shore of Lake Ontario and
down the river to Québec. The Canadians are mostly French,
they won't fight for King George, and so on. I'm giving it to you
just the way we hear it from men like Henry Clay."

"It all comes o' shiftin' our gov'ment into the backwoods,"
roared Captain Phips. "So long as the Congress set in Philadelphy
they was bound to take a saltwater view o' things. Stands to reason. There it was, right afore their noses all the time. But what
happened a few years ago? Why, they took'n moved their whole
crew back into the woods, place called Washington—a parcel o'
fancy foreign-sort buildin's stuck up in a Virginia swamp. Got
their heads turned round—can't see anywhere but inland, freshwater everywhere they look—the Great Lakes, the Ohio, the
Mississippi, and all that. What's the ocean? Just somethin' you
can't mix whiskey with, like you can good branch water."

"But," said the laird, getting back to the point, "surely your
President won't listen to this dangerous nonsense about war? I've
always understood Mr. Jefferson was set on keeping your nation
out of foreign wars."

"Right!" said Malachi Sparling. "But Mr. Jefferson's got a notion that the way to keep out of foreign wars is to cut out foreign
trade. He wants to roll up the map of the world and pretend there's
no place but America."

McNab's stubby fingers plucked hard at his side-whiskers. It
was all very hard to understand. In his dealings with Americans
he had found them shrewd and sensible—almost as good as Scots,
which was saying a great deal. The notion of such folk planning a
war to take Canada made no sense whatever. What the deuce was
Canada? He scraped his memory for things he had heard. A jabber
of Frenchmen between Québec and Montreal; a few stump farmers
grumbling in English by the shore of Lake Ontario; west of that
nothing but a wilderness haunted by wild Indians and a scatter
of frost-bitten ragamuffins in the fur trade! Remote as China, most
of it. Not worth a pinch of anybody's powder. And on the other
hand this strange suggestion of President Jefferson cutting off the

whole American sea trade, like a man sawing off his leg, because of some arrogant British captains!

"Ye canna be serious, Mr. Sparling. What!"

"I'm dead serious, sir. It can happen, all right. In fact all that's required to *make* it happen is something real outrageous on the part of your men-o'-war off our coast. Something the newspapers and broadsheet printers can get a hold of. Something the backwoods politicians can talk up big and get the freshwater people all excited about. I don't say war, mind. Not war right away, anyhow. War takes a lot of talking up and getting ready for. If the war-hawks try to force his hand Mr. Jefferson will plump for an embargo on foreign trade."

Again the American merchant made that ship's-bow gesture of thumb and forefingers across the table. "Now, Mr. McNab, let's assume your naval captains do tread on American toes next week, next month, next year—it makes no difference. Then, sure as thunder, we'll have more uproar about Free Trade and Sailors' Rights, and demands for a war against Canada; and suddenly we'll have Long Tom Jefferson's compromise, the embargo on sea trade. Now, my friend, what should we do about that—I and all the other Americans engaged in foreign trade? We're saltwater men. The sea's our life. We can't just tie up our ships, leave 'em to rot, and tramp off to shoot Indians in the Mississippi woods."

Mr. Sparling leaned over the table, pushing the miniature prow before him until the fingertips almost touched the laird's waistcoat.

"So we must plan a course to steer when Jefferson slaps on his embargo. Chiefly it's a course towards England. England can't keep up this everlasting war against Napoleon without American provisions, masts, timber, tobacco for the soldiers and sailors, and so forth—specially now that Boney's cut off the Baltic timber trade. That's where we come in. And let me say here that I'm not interested in profit alone. I'm thinking as a patriotic American who dislikes tyranny, English or French or whatever, but chiefly wants to see his country stay out of war."

McNab stared him hard in the eyes. In the American's calm gaze he saw nothing but a firm sincerity. The man believed what he was saying.

"The embargo, when it comes," Sparling went on, "will give His Majesty's government a jolt. Then they'll see they've got to have the American supplies, and they'll order the Lords of Admiralty to pull their warships off the American coast. With a bit of common sense the Admiralty will even command their captains to give civil usage to American ships, and help 'em on their way, if help they need. That will kill all the fuss about Free Trade and Sailors' Rights, and won't leave our war-hawks a thing to start a fight about."

Mr. Sparling leaned back and clasped his hands together on the table edge. There was a long silence, broken only by Captain Phips, who drew a small round horn box from a waistcoat pocket, snapped the lid open, made a thin roll of snuff with an expert twist of thumb and fingers, inserted it inside his lower lip, and snapped the box shut again.

"Your sentiments do ye credit, sir, and I respect them," McNab said at last. "War between your country and mine would be a disaster any way we look at it. But ye havena come all the way here from New York just to tell me that. What's special in your mind?"

Mr. Sparling gazed out of the window at the masts and spars of merchantmen showing above the warehouse roofs on Water Street.

"Mr. McNab, I'm told you're a leader among the merchants here. So you must have a powerful influence with all the men who count for something in this province, including the Admiral and Governor."

"Oh not all that!" the laird protested. "Ye mustn't let the name of Nova Scotia deceive ye, sir. We Scots here have influence, ay, but we're a minority by far. Most of the Nova Scotians are American by origin. Their fathers and grandfathers were settlers from New England."

"Bluenoses!" grinned Captain Phips, in a tone that implied some sort of tattooed savages.

"Some say whitewashed Yankees," returned McNab amiably.

"Call 'em what you like," said Malachi Sparling sharply, turning his gaze to Phips. "The Nova Scotians are good seamen, and as traders they live up to what they bargain for. People like ourselves, the kind we can do business with. Now, Mr. McNab, a minute or two ago you asked me how we'll get around Long Tom's embargo when it comes. I'll tell you plump and plain. We intend to go on loading our ships with goods we can sell to the British; but we'll make out the ships' papers to New Orleans or some place else far down the coast that takes a considerable voyage there and back. Then we'll put to sea. Where for? Not England, that's sure. Nor New Orleans. No, sir, we'll slip away to the nor'east as far as Nova Scotia."

"Eh!"

"And that's where you come in, sir, you and your Nova Scotiamen. With a nod from your Governor and a wink from your Admiral we'll transfer our cargoes to ships of your own, and you can take 'em to England or anywhere else that suits your fancy. That's up to you and makes no difference to us, so long as it's you we're dealing with. For pay we'll accept bills at six months' sight, drawn on neutral merchants in the West Indies, for preference the Swedes at Saint Bartholomew."

"Not so fast, not so fast my dear Sparling, if you please!" The laird found it hard not to gape like a stranded sculpin at low tide. Malachi Sparling had not come six hundred miles in the *Montauk* merely to talk nonsense; but even so his proposal was fantastic. Even a third of the present American trade to Britain would take every ship the Nova Scotians owned or could charter in a world at war, and more seamen than they could coax into their forecastles—certainly more than they could keep free of the Royal Navy's press gangs, unless of course the Lords of Admiralty had a change of heart.

"A tremendous undertaking!" he muttered in a whirl of mental arithmetic. In the back of his head was a notion that this whole conversation was something dreamed after a late supper and too much wine.

"There's a tremendous profit," suggested Sparling primly.

"Ay, nae doot," falling into broad Scots at last. "But we'd hae to go canny aboot it, verra canny indeed. I'd hae tae see the Governor fairst, and get him to talk tae the Admiral, for they must write tae the government in London an' put the matter verra thoroughly—free trade, the rights of American sailors, the proposed embargo, the danger of war wi' the United States—a thing that'd give a great glee to Boney—an' so on. There'll be letters back and forth the ocean. All that—it'll take a lot o' time."

"Ah yes! Time to be sure. That's why I'm here now, my friend, to get the matter started while there's time."

"There's something else," McNab said carefully. "Ye canna transfer heavy cargo at sea. Not the kind o' sea we get in this latitude, except on rare days in summer. What aboot that?"

Mr. Sparling's lean white hands went up to the lapels of his coat, holding them delicately. "We'll make the transfers in port, here on your own coast, Mr. McNab. Captain Phips tells me you've got all kinds of sheltered anchorage, in out-of-the-way places where nobody lives, or nobody's likely to tell tales, anyhow. Why, you yourself, sir, could handle your own share right out there at your island, with the ships coming in after dark and slipping out by morning."

"What!"

"That p'int o' yours was made for it," boomed the skipper of the *Montauk*. "I mean that beachy p'int we passed on our way into the harbor, stickin' out like a yardarm from the island. I bet many's the smuggler dropped anchor in the lee o' that beach in times gone by, eh? What with the port doctor an' tide-waiters an' all such posted miles up the harbor to George's Island, hard by the town, eh?"

McNab ventured a dour smile. "Smugglers? Ay, there used to be smugglers afore my father's time. Notably a rogue named Mauger who dealt in every evil business from Negro slaving to trade wi' the enemy at Louisburg. Made his fortune, went off to England, and lived like a lord the rest o' his days. Folk in Halifax still twist his name and call the place Major's Beach, though the beach has been McNab's for more than fifty years. And verra respectable, too, I assure ye!"

Suddenly they smiled, all three of them, and then they were laughing aloud, as if McNab had told the joke of the year. But under the laughter McNab was thinking of the whole strange conversation. It reminded him somehow of old wives and gaffers sitting at a hearth on Halloween, with candles doused and no light but the fire, and telling tales of witches, bogles, and forerunners. Especially forerunners, those visions of evil to come. You could put yourself in the mood and accept the whole nonsense, knowing comfortably that next morning's daylight would abolish it.

Malachi Sparling jumped up briskly and put out a hand. "Well, there's no more to say now. Will you shake hands on what's been said so far?"

"Why not?" said the laird, and shook hands firmly with Sparling and Phips. "Now ye must come with me to my island, and visit a few days while your brig's unloading and taking on new cargo at the wharf. After all," with a pawky smile, "it may be the last time she does that."

Mr. Sparling looked at his skipper. "I'm afraid we can't stay a moment, Mr. McNab. Eh, Luke?"

"That's right," the skipper said. "We've got no cargo, either way."

"Ye mean tae say ye came all the way up here in ballast?"

"Yes!" said Malachi Sparling. "This talk was too important for any delay by cargo matters, at home or here. Admirals can use a frigate or a sloop-of-war for their express messages. I use the *Montauk*. And now she must get me home again as fast as possible. As for you, sir, don't lose a moment either. Start your Governor writing to London. And your Admiral, who should be back from the West Indies any week now. And talk over the whole matter with your friends here in the shipping trade—all in strict confidence, you understand. Meanwhile keep your eyes and ears open for news from the States. Things are warming there, and may get hot any time; and when a pot gets hot, it's apt to boil over awful quick."

With that the visitors clapped on their hats, shook McNab's hand, and went out at a skipping pace, as if they would run the whole way back to New York. As they whisked out of sight beyond the warehouses of the waterfront McNab turned from the window, passed a hand over his face as if to make sure he was awake and not in a dream, and said aloud, to nobody at all, "Guid God Almighty—and I say't in all reverence—what the de'il next?"

4

A sloop entered the cove, dropped her sails, and tied up at the end of the boat-wharf. Although Joanna lacked Peter's unerring eye for water craft she recognised this one with ease, the stubby and stiffly rigged thing called *Rob Roy,* in which for years Captain MacDougal had made his rounds from town to dockyard, to Dartmouth, to the hulks in Bedford Basin, and lately to the experimental prison in the Northwest Arm. In another minute she recognised Rory MacDougal's lame step as he came along the wharf. And the tall black-robed figure at his side could be nobody but Father Burke, who was likely to turn up any time, in anything from a fishing shallop to McNab's own immaculate *Bonnie Jo*.

She walked out to meet them as they drew to the house, and put out one hand to priest and the other to the Agent for Prisoners.

"Welcome!" she said, smiling, and to MacDougal, "What brings you so far off your course for Melville Island, Rory?"

"Ye know verra well the answer, ma'am. I was pressed—waylaid and pressed—by the Father here. I was going doon in all innocence from my lodging to the wharf, and there he was. Says he, 'Are ye by any chance going around to the Arm for a look at those poor Frenchmen confined in the fish-house?' And of course I was. And of course he says, 'Then 'tis only a mite out o' your way to run down to McNab's and put me ashore in the cove. The wind's hauled east and a bit southerly, so ye'll get a slant from McNab's right up the Arm.' Ye see? No use making professional objections —he knows the lingo and gets his jib hauled first."

MacDougal's blue eyes blinked and twinkled as candles flutter blue in a draft, and he uttered his low-pitched chuckle, like the bubble of a pot.

"What he means," Father Burke laughed, "is he's glad of any excuse to come away here, for a sip of McNab's prime Jamaica and a bit of conversation that hasn't a word about prisoners, rations, paroles, escapes, or orders from the Transport Office. Confess now, Captain, like a man."

"As a guid Presbyterian I'll confess naething to ye, sir. But as a man I'll admit I never need persuasion to come away here."

The easterly turn of the breeze had fetched a low scud of cloud, a grey blanket wrinkled in deep folds and drawn loosely across the sky, with a promise of showers for McNab's gardens after weeks of dry weather. They passed into the house and Joanna called a servant for refreshments. MacDougal soon had a tumbler in his big fist and a decanter of rich black Jamaica at his elbow, while Joanna and Father Burke sipped at small glasses of Madeira.

The priest was an Irishman from Kildare, a tall lean man in his fifties, with a thin straggle of beard at the tip of his chin. He had studied in Paris, crossed the sea to teach in the French seminary at Québec, and then spent fourteen years as a missionary in the wilderness of Upper Canada. His charges there were mostly Indians, with some French Canadians, and scattered groups of Irish and Scotch Catholics, veterans of the British Army who had settled in Canada after the American war. From that tough and varied experience he had been transferred eastward in 1801, to act as vicar-general in Nova Scotia for the diocese of Québec. At Halifax his Catholic flock was far outnumbered by the Protestants; but Edmund Burke combined in his tall stooped figure an urbane and witty townsman along with the man of learning and the dedicated priest, and before long he had the respect and friendship of the Protestants as much as the Catholics.

Indeed his friendship with the McNabs was symbolic; Peter McNab was Scotch Presbyterian, body and soul. His wife was a devout Catholic and so were many of his servants and tenants. Joanna McNab had never questioned the laird's assumption, as master in his house, that the children should be educated in his way, although he was no bigot. When he could sail up to the town early on Sabbath mornings he attended Presbyterian service at wee St. Matthew's kirk; and like most of the Scotch merchants he kept a pew also in St. Paul's, the Church of England—symbol of the very faith of which King George was crowned Defender. To a merchant who looked for commissary contracts with His Majesty's forces that was wise policy; but Peter saw it in a further light as a mark of loyalty to the Crown, which in no way impaired the plain faith of his fathers. And in the same light he saw Jo's faith, and her visits to the little chapel of St. Peter whenever she came to town. He admired her devotion and the inborn goodness, which led his servants to refer to her in their conversations as "The Saint."

So in the run of a year the McNabs were generous to St. Matthew, St. Peter, and St. Paul—"our three apostles" as Peter used to say—and visitors to the island were used to finding in the McNab drawing room, singly and sometimes together, the Catholic vicar, the Anglican bishop, and the Presbyterian minister, not to mention other clerics and preachers from the world outside.

For a time the talk in the drawing room played over the affairs of the season, notably the great wedding of the year, and the false alarm of a French invasion fleet. They could laugh now over the alarm; the warning guns from York Redoubt; the urgent flutter of bunting going up and down the telegraph masts; the hasty muster and marching of redcoats and militia; McNab turning out his own little clan of manservants and tenants, armed with anything from his own expensive Manton fowling guns to Gahagan's rusty cutlass, ready to defend their island to the death; the laird himself watching with a spyglass from the red clay knoll of the Thrum Cap; and at last the strange sails fading away like wraiths in the rain to the southeast, never to be seen again, whatever they were.

The fashionable wedding had been in St. Paul's, and, like every woman in Halifax, Jo was delighted with the romance of Sir Thomas Hardy—Captain Tom Hardy, in whose gallant arms Nelson had died less than two years ago—taking to wife the very-much-alive Miss Berkeley. Hardy was thirty-eight—time he married!—and his bride a slip of a girl, daughter of the admiral on the North American station. Both had been guests at parties on McNab's island, and Jo liked to think their romance had begun like so many others in the pleasant groves beyond the "muckle hoose."

Rory MacDougal paid due attention to McNab's rum as well as the conversation. Of the false alarm he chuckled, "Och, those Army fellas here have aye the hope that Boney will come chapping at their door. It gripes 'em to sit and twirl their thumbs when a war's on and the Navy getting all the glory."

And of the wedding, "Captain Tom Hardy! D'ye mind what Nelson murmured to him at the last? Kiss me, Hardy—kiss me, Hardy! Deleerious, o' course. But the saying's famous now, like England Expects and a' that. So what is Hardy's bride to say? The puir gel canna even whisper't, ever, for fear o' sounding in his ear like Nelson's ghost!"

With this he arose, bobbed his head politely to the lady and the priest, rumbled "I think I'll take a bit exercise in the air," and limped away outdoors and disappeared.

Joanna and Father Burke glanced at each other with humor. One never knew what Rory might say, especially with a dram under his belt.

With all this light chatter past Father Burke could come to the point of his visit, and he wasted no time. "My dear lady, I'm after money again—I always am, to be sure."

"That," said Joanna, "is because your heart's as big as all outdoors, and every pagan beggar in Halifax knows it—white, black, or Indian."

"Um! Well, I wouldn't say that by any means. When bodies are famished one doesn't ask if they're Catholic or what, or notice a shade of skin one way or the other. There's a lot of hunger up there," he said with a flick of his lean hand towards the town. "The war's to blame, I suppose, though there's money enough for swords and guns and uniforms. Your husband knows how it is of course, and does what he can. The Scotch merchants are always the most generous. However it's not the poor I've come about this time. It's my schools."

"Oh!"

"I'm up against the law, as you know. Times change, of course, and so do laws—in time. It used to be that Catholics in Halifax couldn't have a church. That changed twenty years or so ago, after the American war, when a lot of Catholics came here in the British and Loyalist regiments. They'd done their duty to the King. So when they asked to do their duty to God in a church of their own, they got it. Long before my time here, of course. So we have our chapel of St. Peter. Soon after I came I saw need of schools for our children. The law said No, but our Protestant friends were sympathetic. So I went ahead, law or no law. As you know, I've established a school for girls, and I teach classes of boys myself in the glebe house. The Governor and Council know I'm breaking the rule, but like Nelson they put their dim eye to the spyglass. It's a matter for ourselves. That means we ourselves must find the money for it."

"Have you spoken to Mr. McNab?" Jo said.

"Of course. And you can guess what he said. 'Reverend sir, I'll give with both hands to your poor, but not a lift of finger for your schools. I'm a contractor to His Majesty's forces and I can't go thumbing my nose at His Majesty's laws.' That, mind you, with a face as hard as one of His Majesty's own sea biscuits, which by all accounts are sawn out of oak plank. And then the warm smile in the eyes—the Highlander behind the mask. 'O' course, Father Burke, if you should go to my wife, and she should give you money for anything under the sun, it's no business of mine whatever.'"

Joanna put back her fair head and laughed, a sound like the merry trill of silver bells.

"I can see that look and hear him saying it."

"We're all God's creatures," the priest went on, with his grave smile, "but next to the Irish I'd rate the Highland Scots the finest in the world."

"Even Protestants?"

"Why not?"

Peter's wife arose. "I find them so myself. Will you let me have your purse, please?" He fetched it promptly from a stoutly sewn pocket inside his robe. Joanna knew it well, a big shabby leather pouch with a draw-string, familiar to at least half the poor of Halifax. The cabinet by her drawing-room fireplace was not locked, nor was the little mahogany chest inside, where Peter kept the working cash for his island estate. In that house nothing ever was locked. She counted out gold and silver to the amount of twenty pounds and slipped the coins into the purse. It was fat now, and heavy, and when she passed it to him Father Burke tucked it away in his robe with care, murmuring, "As we say in the Irish, a thousand thanks and a thousand thousand blessings, lady of the good heart."

"I only wish . . ." Jo said and halted.

"Yes?"

"I only wish my own boys could have your schooling, Father. But that's a path we never tread upon, my husband and I. Mind you, it's not in itself a matter of religion. It's McNab's obsession to see the boys educated just as he was, in all ways."

"You don't mean over the sea in Scotland?"

"And England. Peter himself was sent away over the sea, in a time of war, and kept at schools there from the age of eleven to seventeen. What his poor mother must have felt! I know how I'd feel myself—indeed what I fear myself."

"But why?" he said. "My dear good lady, when your husband was young there wasn't a decent school in this province, the American war had cut off schools in the older colonies, and the only place for education was across the sea. But things are different now—for Protestant boys anyhow. I mean they've a good grammar school in Halifax, and after that an easy day's carriage drive to King's College at Windsor.

"Ah yes. And for that matter, here on our own island we've had Peter's great-aunt McNab, as you know, a lady of the best education, who came from Scotland when our boys were small to stay with us and teach them. I doubt if any two boys in the Halifax grammar school have better accomplishments. But now my husband begins to talk of giving them a 'final polish' over the sea."

Father Burke noted her rueful face and tone, and wondered what to say.

"No doubt I'm weak and foolish-fond," she sighed. "A hen that can't bear her chicks out of sight. It's selfishness, and that's a sin, isn't it?"

The priest frowned. "The masters of the Halifax grammar school are men well qualified in every way. So are those at King's. They come from the best colleges—Oxford, Edinburgh, Aberdeen, one or two from Trinity in Dublin—what would your boys get in Britain that they couldn't get here?"

"Polish!" Joanna cried the word with all the feeling in her. "Polish! As far as I can see, it isn't what boys learn at schools across the sea, it's just that people should know they went there. Oh, Peter doesn't put it that way, but he's mad on the notion. I've asked him more than once the very question you just asked me."

"And what does he say?"

"He looks blank for a moment, and then seizes on the French language and goes on about it at great length. A language every gentleman should have, and with a good accent and fluency—all the polite people in England make a point of conversing in French from time to time, and even mix it with their English speech, a word here and a sentence there. It's a mark of what they call the *ton*—the people of the best breeding and manners. Besides, there's this eternal war with Boney, likely to go on for years and years. If either of our boys should decide to enter His Majesty's service, why, an officer fluent in French is bound to forge ahead. Didn't Nelson himself, as a young man, study the language in France?

"If I mention my hope that neither of our boys will go to war, then he's off on the other tack—the business. If the boys choose to stay with the firm, remember we're in the West Indies trade, and pretty soon Britain will have the principal French islands there, Guadeloupe, Martinique, even Haiti, which used to be the richest colony of France, where even the black people speak French in their fashion. And always he comes back to the same thing." Jo put on Peter's face and air and spoke in his very accent. "Ye canna lairn tae speak French in the best manner anywhere this side the sea."

"Not in Québec?" the priest said.

"Least of all there—he thinks the Canadians speak a peasant dialect, though he's never been up the St. Lawrence in his life. During his young years over the sea he got French poked at him by Scotch and English schoolmasters—part of his 'polish'—and scarcely remembers a word of it today. What French he learned, I suspect, was in an accent no Frenchman, peasant or whatever, could understand for a minute. I could mention a very good teacher close to home—yourself—who learned the language in Paris, with the best accent in the world. But you teach a Catholic school and make no bones about it, nor about the law. So, as I say, I hold my tongue."

"And you can do nothing more?"

Joanna looked away and pinched her lips together. "A wife can get a lot of her own way, even with a stubborn Scot, if she knows how to ca' canny, as Peter himself would say. And in the matter of sending my boys abroad for polish, especially French polish, I intend to be the canniest wife in the whole of King George's empire!"

Rory MacDougal stumped away along the path through the fir wood, and not for exercise nor air. His knee made walking awkward, even on the easy going of a street, and in sailing his boat around the peninsula from Bedford Basin to the tip of the Northwest Arm he breathed all the air that one man could conveniently use. He had first wandered along this island path a year or two before, when a sudden gale forced him to spin out a visit, while the old *Rob Roy* bobbed safely at moorings in the lee. The island here was nipped to a slim waist by McNab's cove on the west and Back Cove on the east. A path crossed over from one cove to the other, a distance of maybe four hundred yards. It made a favorite stroll for McNab's guests; the winding path brown and soft with fallen needles from the firs, the warm scent of balsam in sunny patches, the friendly green shelter from an east wind, and then the water of Back Cove glittering like the blue steel of a dress sword thrust into the land, and shielded by another island called Lawlor's, shaggy and picturesque with woods of spruce and fir, and beyond that a glimpse of the waves and whitecaps in Eastern Passage.

The path wandered on around Back Cove, following the shore of McNab's island to its northern tip, a trail beaten by the laird and his sportsmen friends, gunning for snipe and wild duck. Other than these autumn hunting parties, rarely a foot traveled that side of the island except the light pair Rory had come to meet.

He sat on the bleached butt of a ship's mast, broken by the force of the seas and flung up high and dry with other raffle in a tremendous gale long ago. Tufts of salt grass and the clinging green tendrils and blue flowers of the beach pea grew amongst the old wreckage. Between these and the shade of the woods ran a border of wild rose bushes covered with bloom. Bees were busy there, and green hummingbirds and grey hawk-moths darting from flower to flower, like pigmy Don Juans in a world of pink petticoats. Overhead the wind soughed in the fir tops. Terns flitted like sea swallows over the shallows of the cove, hovering now and then with a swift flutter of white wings, and then plunging and splashing after fish.

It was a pleasant place to sit on a summer day, and Rory sat contentedly for half an hour. He would be late at Melville Island, but that did not matter. A fair wind into the Arm meant a foul wind for coming out, and he would have to stay the night in the British officers' quarters at the prison. They would be glad to see him. The guard of redcoats lived a bored life, removed from the pleasures of the town to watch over a batch of French prisoners in that lonely place. He wondered if Father Burke would come along. The priest was permitted to visit the prisoners and converse with them, but they showed small interest in his vocation. They had grown up under the republic, with a contempt for all such matters, and in any case they regarded with suspicion this *Irlandais* who came amongst them wearing the black robe and speaking like a Parisian. Was he a spy for the English, sent to find out their various little plots for escape?

MacDougal chuckled when he thought of that. In a long experience of captured Frenchmen he had come to regard them as a lot of mischievous monkeys caged and put into his charge. They were amusing always with their chatter and capering and their gestures of hands and fingers but you never quite knew what they might be up to, and it didn't pay to be off your guard.

But now appeared the person he had been watching for, a slight figure in a gown of some thin brown stuff that swayed about her, and clung for a moment and swayed again as she moved with her springing step along the stony path around the cove. Ellen Dewar had the grace of a doe, but she was too thin for beauty. MacDougal had first seen her as a child of ten, an orphan sent out from Scotland to the care of her McNab kin, a scrawny thing, all bones and huge mysterious black eyes; and although she was tall and in her twenties now, it seemed to Rory that she was still the elfin child.

As she drew near he saw on her feet the battered brogues she used for these excursions. The gown was an old one too, with inserts of faded ribbon at the short sleeves and throat. She wore no hat—she never did except in rain or winter weather—and the face under the coiled black hair was tanned as if to match the gown. The fashionable women of Halifax, young and old, prized a pale complexion above all else, even virtue; and here was this young female, the ward of Peter McNab, Esquire, with the complexion of a fish-girl. In the crook of her right arm lay a bundle of flowers, plucked in a strip of swamp beyond the cove, the long juicy stems and green sword leaves of iris, and their bright blue flowers.

Rory knew she had noticed him as soon as she turned the corner of the cove path, but she gave no sign of it until she was almost up to him. Then, "Och! What do you here, Mr. MacDougal?"

"Just enjoying a bit air and a stretch o' leg," said Rory carelessly. "Ye weren't aboot the house, so I guessed ye'd be on one o' your strolls aboot the shore, and here we are. I see ye've been gathering the bonnie blue flags."

"Yes."

"And where are ye bound with 'em—the house, I daresay?"

The girl gave him one of her dark looks but no answer.

"It's none o' my business," MacDougal said.

"I'm taking them to the Thrum Cap."

"Away oot there?" He was astonished. "What the de'il for?"

"Have you ever been on the Cap?"

"Wi' a gammy leg like mine? Ha! I've seen it often enough, mind, sailin' into the harbor. It's a good sea mark, the Cap."

"It's the burying place for shipwrecked sailors—the ones that drown and wash up on the island shore. It's been so from the time of the old laird, the one who bought the island. There are no gravestones, just the mounds, for nobody knew who they were. They seem so lonely away there—the poor lost men, with no one to care for them. So in the time of the flowers I gather some and take them to strew about the graves."

MacDougal wagged his head. "That must be all o' two mile from here, the way ye have to go—the shore to the Cap's as crooked as a fishhook—and hard going, too, for all ye travel like a deer."

"I like the walk. And it's pleasant to sit there on a summer day, and watch the ships and fishing boats, and the birds. The Mother Carey's chickens nest there, in burrows in the clay; and so do the bank swallows."

"Weel, there's no hurry for that, gel. Sit down and rest yourself a bit, an' talk to me."

Ellen Dewar seated herself on the mast, with the flowers in her lap, and gazed with half-closed eyes at the glitter of the cove. Rory eyed her sidelong. Under the sun's tan the girl had a skin as clear as silk, and long black lashes, and glossy hair like the folded wings of a blackbird. She had good Scots marrow in those bones, but not enough flesh upon them. A jimp lass. Too jimp by half. And shy as a wild bird.

She was silent, and Rory waited. At last she murmured, "How long were you on the sea, Mr. MacDougal?"

"Eh? Oh, four-and-twenty years."

"And why did you leave?"

"This leg. In a fight wi' the French frigate *Ambuscade,* back in '93, I was hit in the face and knee. Spoiled my beauty a bit, but that was no matter. 'Twas the knee put me on the beach."

"And you were captain in this fight?"

MacDougal's eyes put forth their merry twinkle. "Not at all. People call me Captain hereabouts, but truth to say, I never got ayont lieutenant's rank. In His Majesty's Navy ye need money and influence to get a captaincy, and I had neither. But as a lamester, though, I was luckier than some that get winged in His Majesty's service. They found a post for me ashore at Halifax, in the dock-yard; and later the Transport Office made me Agent for Prisoners of War here. So I have the *Rob Roy,* a command o' my own at last, an' the charge o' five hundred to a thousand men—all French. The captain of a ship-o'-the-line in Boney's Navy couldna say more."

"I don't see how you can be so blithe, after your hard service and pains. What a dreadful life it is—the Navy."

"I wouldna say that, Ellie."

"All those years on the sea. Were you married?"

"Ay, once. But she died at home of the pneumonia while I was away to the India station, and we'd no bairns to greet for her—or me."

"What was she like?"

MacDougal took off his hat and pushed thick fingers through the grizzled brown hair that retreated from his forehead. "She was like you, summat. About the hair and eyes. The mouth, too, it seems to me. But not near as tall as yourself, nor sae—sae jimp. She was the sonsy kind. Young and sonsy as a partridge. But that's all long ago. She's been under a Portsmouth gravestone seven-and-twenty years. Och! How did we get on this?"

"Graves!" Ellen Dewar said, rising quickly, "I must be on my way to the Cap or I'll be late for supper. Are you staying the night?"

"No. I must be on my way, too. That's to Melville."

"Goodbye then, Captain." She was moving already, with her face towards the Thrum Cap, as if she could see it through the trees.

"I'll see ye again afore long," Rory said, and watched her out of sight. Something about her, about the way she looked and

moved, the dream on her face and the swift vitality of the slender
body, awakened a ghost in him that had not stirred in seven-and-
twenty years.

"Tach!" he growled. "Ye're auld enough to be her father.
More! Are ye daft, Rory Mac?" And he limped away back over
the path to McNab's house.

Father Burke was sitting in the garden with tall white-haired
Miss McNab, Peter's great-aunt and the teacher of his children.

MacDougal gave the lady one of his awkward little bows and
turned to the priest. "I must be off, sir. Will ye come along to Melville? It'll mean staying the night wi' the guard officers, the wind
the way it is."

"I guessed that," the priest said. "And there's little good I can
do there, with the guard or with the prisoners, as you know. Miss
McNab tells me there's a bed made ready for me here, so I'll return
to town with Mr. McNab in the morning. My thanks, Captain,
for your help this far."

Without further ado MacDougal was off. The languid youth
who was his crew aroused from a doze in the cuddy, and together
they cast off the lines and got the sails up. In five minutes the *Rob
Roy* was out of the cove with a fair wind pushing her across the
western passage and into the harbor's northwest arm. The tide
was making and the Arm ran like a salt river for three miles
through steep wooded ridges on either hand, with here and there a
fisherman's hut or cottage by the shore. Near the crest on the east
side of the fiord the woods opened in various places, where well-
to-do Halifax merchants and officials had mansions and parks like
lords in the old country, with long carriage drives winding away
through the trees towards the town.

Near the Arm's end, a round cove opened in the woods on the
western side, and there like a small green duck in a pond swam
Melville Island. On a grassy knoll at one end stood the British
officers' quarters, a plain wooden dwelling house, with the soldiers'
quarters farther down. On the duck's back sat the prison, an old
warehouse surrounded by a tall fence of sharp pickets, with sentry
boxes here and there about the circumference. There was a small
wharf, and a wooden bridge crossed a salt creek between the
island and the shore.

MacDougal steered the sloop in to the wharf as the boy doused the sails. With the pride of a seaman under the eyes of soldiers he liked to come in neatly, fetching up to the wharf with scarcely a jar. Already the grey sky was letting fall a drizzle of rain. Bored heads peered from the shelter of sentry boxes outside the palisade, and there was little of the usual babble of French in the prison yard.

A debonair young man was just crossing the bridge from the cove shore, clad in a loose duck frock and trousers, with a broad-brimmed chip hat of the kind the prisoners wove from strips of maple wood. MacDougal recognised Lieutenant Thorpe, commander of the guard. He carried a fishing rod and had a well-laden creel slung by a strap from his shoulder.

"Well, my old Square-Foot," he called out, "you've come at a good time. Fried trout for supper, and Burton ale to wash it down."

"Well enough!" said Rory. "This is the place for high living. How d'ye do it?"

"The Burton came by merchant ship from Liverpool; and just in time—the regimental mess was running dry, let alone this lousy post out here."

"And the trout?"

"From a brook a half-mile walk away. Flows into the Arm from a chain of small lakes in the woods. Plenty of good runs and pools. An angler's dream. And don't ever let anyone tell you trout won't bite in an east wind. I could have filled a canoe."

"It has some compensation, then—this lousy post?"

Thorpe grinned. He had merry grey eyes and a head of curly brown hair.

"Oh, I keep a nag in a stable across the bridge, so I can jog into town of an evening now and then for a dinner in the mess and then a bit of feminine company. And in the days there's trout fishing, and some quite good shooting—grouse and hares—in those scrub woods by the shore. It's a dam' sight better than keeping guard aboard a hulk in Bedford Basin, I can tell you that. Not that it's proper work for soldiers, any of it. Are you going to visit my Frogs now, or put it off till the morning?"

"I might as well do't in the morning," Rory said. "There'll be no getting out of the Arm on this wind. I suppose our lodgers have the usual complaints?"

"No doubt of it. Funny how they can't understand English when

I try to lay down the rules about this and that. When the Agent for Prisoners turns up there are Frogs by the dozen whining in English about being shut up in a fishhouse, and the food they have to eat, and all the rest of it. Bah! The ones left in the hulks are a dam' sight worse off, and these Frogs know it, but don't ever expect a Frenchman to be grateful. How long d'you intend to keep on with this experiment?"

"That depends on the Transport Office in London. As far as I'm concerned the experiment's a success. The sick-and-death rate here's away lower than the hulks. I'm trying to persuade the Admiral to recommend a proper barrack for prisoners here at Melville. Something big enough to house the whole lot, except the officers on parole of course, and do away wi' the hulks altogether."

"Um! If it's anything like getting the Army to do anything, even for our own troops, I wish you luck. And now, my dear Mac, let's go in and drink to the bull Frog of all the world—and may he swell up big enough to bust."

5

Sir John Wentworth listened to McNab with his own mouth held tight and his hands fidgeting with the papers on his desk. They were sitting in the library of Government House, a handsome room at the rear—"the quiet side" as Wentworth liked to remark, pointing up the slope to the old town burial ground.

The Governor was in his seventies, a very different personage from the brisk brown man of McNab's earliest memories, when he was plain John Wentworth and a busy surveyor of the King's woods. He sat slumped in a high-backed velvet chair, with a paunch bulging his waistcoat, the attitude and figure of a man who had given up hard marching long ago and since found no zest in life. His hair was thin and white, his mouth drooped at the corners as if dragged down by the sallow jowls, and the once keen grey eyes were faded and morose. Long ago he and his wife had been driven from their New Hampshire home by the Tory-baiting mobs of '75. He had spent years adrift and idle in England, and many more in a petty post in Nova Scotia, before the wheel of fortune came around again and awarded him another Governor's seat and then the baronetcy, the climax of his up-and-down career.

When the laird's tale was finished, Sir John remained silent for a time, his dry wrinkled hands thrusting amongst the papers, his gaze through the window at the rows of tombstones tottering like a drunken regiment under the trees. At last he said heavily, "All this—doesn't surprise me really, you know. I know my own Americans, McNab. And I've been in trade myself. From Harvard College I went straight into my father's timber business in New Hampshire. Ship masts and yards for the great part. Our best market was in England—and always had been—from a very early time. So I know something of export trade, and I understand what it means to the people in the seaboard states."

Another shuffle of the papers. "I also have a shrewd idea of what's brewing to the south and west of us. For several years now I've objected to the naval gentlemen searching American ships, taking seamen out of them, and bringing them in here as pressed hands in the lower decks; just as I've objected to the arrogance of their press gangs ashore in Halifax. Remember Admiral Mitchell? —but of course you do—the Forsyth affair. I told Mitchell plump and plain that he must curb his pressing habit, afloat and ashore, or one day we'd have insurrection in this province and war with the United States. I wrote that to London too—though in a more diplomatic vein, of course."

His thin lips opened and closed with a wry twist as if they tasted something sour. "The Admiral said Stuff. A lot of stuff and nonsense. Nova Scotia was a province in His Majesty's realm, and when it came to manning His Majesty's ships why should these provincial fellows be exempt, any more than Cork or Bristol men, or for that matter London men? As for the Yankees—Stuff again. What had they got to make war with? Not a single ship-of-the-line. Just a few frigates and brigs and a litter of worthless gunboats in the harbors. Not much of an army either, by all accounts. The Sons of Liberty don't trust each other enough to allow an effective standing army—afraid some Yankee Napoleon might arise and take over the country with it. So what can they do? Just make a noise.

The Americans are good at that. So are certain other people to the north of Yankeedom. And he looked me right in the eye."

A parched laugh. "Nowadays we have other faces under the cocked hats and a more suave turn of speech. Admiral Berkeley, eh? But the same arrogance. More! Ever since Trafalgar our naval gentlemen have assumed that no one dare face them on the sea, and so they do as they please with any ship they meet, whatever flag it flies. Precisely the attitude of Napoleon on land."

The Governor turned his old disillusioned eyes from the window to McNab.

"Do you remember the American Revolution?"

"Not much, sir. I was just a boy then, sent to Britain for schooling. People over there seemed to have small knowledge or concern about America. Their minds were on France, Holland, Spain, the siege of Gibraltar and all that. America? America was like the man in the moon, too far to be heard, and only dimly to be seen."

"Humph! Well, I was on the moon, McNab. Indeed I was a native of the moon, and Governor of my own New Hampshire slice of it. In that position I saw the trouble coming and did my part to forestall it. Begging London to conciliate. Begging my own people to stay cool and patient. No good, of course. When the rebellion came my wife and I were driven out of the country with the other Loyalists—"Tories" as they called us. All that's long ago and far away. I wouldn't mention it except for one thing—the attitude of His Majesty's government and His Majesty's Army and Navy gentlemen. Their notion now is just what it was away back in '74. The Yankees wouldn't fight, and couldn't anyhow, without an army or a fleet."

Sir John came out of his slouch and sat up, looking strangely fierce and almost tall, a momentary resurrection of the man he once had been.

"But they *did* fight, McNab, didn't they? And kept on fighting, and got the French into the war on their side, and then the Spaniards and the Dutch. And in the end who got licked? Not the Yankees!" Again the gesture at the papers. "And what do we see today? The same attitude, and the same damned situation bobbing up again, only it's turned end-for-end. I mean today we're already fighting France and the French puppet nations in Europe, while His Majesty's sea officers do their damnedest to stir up a war with the United States. And now here's the first consequence. I've alarming news from the States. D'you know Captain Humphreys—Humphreys of the *Leopard* frigate?"

"I've met him, once, back in June. I remember the *Leopard* sailing out past my beach the next day."

"A zealous fellow, this Humphreys. Too zealous for his country's good. He took his station, cruising between the Capes of Virginia, on the lookout for ships bound to France with contraband of war, and somehow or other he got wind of some British deserters aboard an American ship coming out of Norfolk roads. Ran alongside and ordered her to stop for search. When she didn't, fired a broadside into her. Killed or wounded twenty-one of her crew."

Wentworth sniffed in a long breath and held it, like a swimmer who sees a great wave bearing down. His sallow face turned red and then purple before the breath rushed out in words.

"D'you know what she was? A frigate of the United States Navy!"

"No!"

"Oh, yes!"

"So there was a fight!"

"Not at all. The *Chesapeake* hadn't a chance to fight. She was taken by surprise, like a ship beset by pirates in an unexpected place. After all there was no war with England, no reason to expect attack by an English ship, especially in American waters. Not a single gun ready to fire. And the *Leopard* alongside, following her cannon blast with a swarm of armed boarders ready to cut down any resistance. Humphreys seized four of her crew as British deserters, and sailed off as blithe as a boy after sparrows with a fowling piece."

"Um!" the laird cried. He was looking at the Governor, but seeing Malachi Sparling, and hearing Sparling's voice in that brisk interview in the countinghouse on Water Street.

"*Leopard!*" Sir John snapped. "That's what Napoleon calls our whole nation—'the English leopards.' Ha! Well, this particular English leopard has stuck his paw into a bees' nest, I can tell you. Since the *Chesapeake* sailed back to port with her dead and wounded, and her damages and her story, there's been an angry buzz all over the United States. Crowds of people at the sailors' funerals. Every newspaper cramming up excitement." Another thrust at the papers on the desk. "I have all sorts of reports, and I note especially a hasty despatch, sent forward by Admiral Berkeley. It's from Mr. Erskine—the British envoy-extraordinary to the United States—warning me that this affair may lead to war and I must take precautions here."

"What d'you think yourself, sir?"

"Well of course if our naval gentlemen don't make amends for this rash business we'll deserve to have war, won't we? Though I think not right away. The war party in the United States lives mostly in the south and west. They'll gain a lot of followers over this *Chesapeake* affair, depend on it; but their nation's unready for war, and the nation knows it. Nobody knows it better than Mr. Jefferson, who's kept their armed forces low. He's nearing the end of his second term and he wants peace in his time."

"At any cost?" McNab said.

"That remains to be seen. One thing seems clear. Once he retires, the war hawks will get into power as sure as thunder comes in June."

"And what then?"

"They'll prepare for war and keep an eye on Europe, where Napoleon rides farther every year. The day will come when Bonaparte can muster the whole of the Continent against England. That will be the Americans' time to strike."

"And meanwhile they'll do nothing?"

"Oh, Mr. Jefferson will have to do something in the face of this *Chesapeake* affair. He'll delay as long as he can, and he'll probably try an embargo on American goods to Europe, which means chiefly England. That won't work, if your New York merchant friend knows what he's talking about. So our affairs in North America will go on drifting like a log above Niagara."

The Governor suddenly poked a finger to the east. "Those gentlemen in the cabinet in London, who see nothing but the war in Europe—they've got to wake up and move quickly if they don't want war on both sides of the Atlantic. Call the Royal Navy off the coast of the United States, restore the prisoners, offer apologies, pay the damages. Yes! Are four runaway seamen worth the risk of a new war, or short of that a stoppage of American supplies, just when we're at full strain against Bonaparte?"

McNab stayed mum. Sir John seemed to be addressing the invisible gentlemen across the sea in Whitehall and Downing Street. But at last the Governor came back to the library and McNab, saying in a dour voice, "Admiral Cochrane—Sir Alexander Cochrane—is on his way here from the West Indies with a squadron including two ships-of-the-line. Undoubtedly he'll pause off the Capes of Virginia to confer with Berkeley's frigates cruising there. That means he'll bring along those four deserters for court martial in this port. Another zealous man. His brother was killed by an American shell at Yorktown, away back in '81, and Sir Alex never forgot it. Hates the Yankees like poison."

As Wentworth talked the laird was regarding Wentworth's books, rising shelf above shelf all about the room, and scenting the air with a pleasant aroma of paper and buckram and leather. From the tops of the bookcases rose small plaster busts of Shakespeare and other literary worthies, whose blank eyes and pallid faces looked like heads exposed on Traitors' Gate.

"To get back to the matter of an embargo," Sir John went on grimly. "I suppose you've discussed it with the Committee on Trade here. The proposal to carry American goods to Britain, I mean."

"Yes, sir. And they're agreed it's a thing we should do, provided we have your consent—and the Admiral's of course."

"You have my own, McNab. I can't vouch for the Admiral's until I've talked to him; but I think he'll see it's in the interest of fighting Napoleon. The main trouble, as always, will be to keep his press gangs off your own crews, as well as the Americans'. Do you intend to take a leading part in this business?"

"I shall take some part, sir," McNab said cautiously. "If our naval people keep their hands off, I could transfer American cargoes in the lee of the beach at my island. However, most of our trading gentlemen plan to make their transfers in harbors elsewhere along the coast—places they'll keep secret, not only on account of Mr. Jefferson, but mainly to make sure they get no visits from His Majesty's fleet tenders and their gangs. Once at sea, of course, our ships will have to take their chance of naval overhaul and press, and still more when they reach a British port. But all trade's chancy nowadays. On the whole, I suppose carrying American goods to Britain in these times is no more risky than the West Indies trade, what with French and Spanish privateers swarming out of every creek from Cuba to the Spanish Main, and His Majesty's West India squadrons always on the prowl and short of men. Um! Well, sir, may I say to the Committee of Trade that we have your verbal consent; that you'll urge the same upon the Admiral; and that you're writing London in secrecy to clear the passage there?"

"Yes, you may say that, McNab. Of course you understand the peculiar nature of my own position here. A lot of our provincial folk don't like their Governor a bit. They say I'm too much the old Tory, stiff in the neck and deaf to the people—exactly what Americans used to say of royal governors long ago. On the other hand our naval gentlemen think I'm too much of a Yankee."

Again the sour twist of lips. During their long exile in England his wife, young and beautiful then, had mingled eagerly with the fashionable caste who called themselves the *ton* and ruled the empire by their influence. She had studied their snobbery, their caprices, their very accents, and learned them so well that when her husband became Sir John Wentworth, Baronet, she was able to play a titled lady to the manner born. She was ageing and ailing now, her beauty gone, but still she played the *grande dame* in the English fashion. On the other hand, whatever else had changed about him since he left New Hampshire, John Wentworth had never lost his Yankee turn of speech.

"So you see," he said, "I've enemies in and out of uniform, at home and abroad. For some time past I've heard tattle that London intends replacing me with a younger man—that I'm to be transferred to the governorship of some petty West Indian island or put away on half pay like an old horse to grass. Well, McNab, there might be something in it. Nova Scotia's no important post in time of peace, far from it; but in time of war it's vital to His Majesty's domains. The key to Canada, you know. Wolfe proved that. This is where he mounted his attack upon Québec. And since Wolfe's time we've had the American Revolution, which left His Majesty with just one ice-free naval base on the whole continent —this port of Halifax. That being the case, His Majesty's government daren't risk the loss of Halifax any more than, say, Gibraltar. If things really begin to look like war with the United States, London will send troops and warships this way fast, and maybe a younger man for Governor. But tcha!—let's not think of that. This

matter of American supplies to Britain is quite enough for the
present. And now I must call in my secretary and begin composing
letters. Letters! Ecod, before we're done with this American affair,
whichever way it turns, there'll be acres of paper marred with ink,
and pens worn out, ay, and clerks and governors too. Good day
to you, McNab, and good luck in your ventures."

Towards the end of August, as the summer waned and the
nights began to cool, Admiral Cochrane's men-o'-war swam in a
stately column past McNab's island and into the anchorage. Sir
Alexander had indeed stopped off the Virginia coast to confer
with Admiral Berkeley, and what he thought of the *Chesapeake*
affair was soon apparent. Every captain in his squadron was ordered to make his ship ready for war at once. At the same time
the Admiral made a demand on the dockyard and the Halifax
contractors for a three-month supply of victuals and stores. The
victuallers were worried men. Three-months' food for several thousand men, on top of the demands for Admiral Berkeley's cruisers,
the garrison, and the French prisoners in the hulks and at Melville
Island, not to mention the needs of nine thousand civilian mouths
old and young, within the town!

However the work began at once, with postriders off to the
farms of Windsor and the Annapolis Valley. Small droves, and
then large droves of cattle and swine came in to the Halifax
slaughterhouses, emerged still warm as chunks of beef and pork,
and plunged into brine in new oak casks that all the coopers of the
town were busy hammering together. The chimneys of the bake-
houses smoked day and night, and out of doors rolled barrels of
ship biscuit, to be rattled away in drays to the King's Wharf. A
thousand other matters, from vinegar to gunpowder, passed to the
ships from the warehouses of the contractors, the stores at the
dockyard, and the magazine on George's Island.

As always these demands made a profitable bustle, especially
for merchants with commissary contracts like Peter McNab. The
laird had no time now for sailing between his island and the town,
and his merchant friend Ross, another Scot, offered the hospitality
of his great house in Argyle Street. "Bring your family too," insisted Ross. "The women and boys will enjoy a holiday in town,

ye know they will. It's never so lively as when a fleet's in. Something stirring every minute of the day and half the night."

And so the laird moved up to town, and brought Joanna and her boys, and Ellen Dewar. Ellie came with reluctance; but once they were settled in the Ross house and free to roam about the streets, the air of excitement in the town infected them all. Argyle was the fashionable street, lined with homes of well-to-do merchants and officials, and shaded in the summer weather by fine old willows, pollarded to make the branches spread over sidewalks and the road. The mansions were nearly all of wood, built and ornamented by carpenters skilled in shipwork, and kept shining with paint.

Some had flat roofs and belvederes, from which the merchants and their guests could look over the lower town and watch the busy waterfront and anchorage. There were handsome pillared porticos and entrances, approached by wide stone steps; and inside, the rooms and apartments were tall, with great windows, elaborate landscape wallpapers, and fine gesso work about the upper walls and ceilings. Compared with these, the laird's "muckle hoose" on the island seemed a cottage.

But McNab's folk had no mind for comparisons. Their minds were all for the shops; the playhouse where gentlemen of the garrison put on London comedies; the Grand Parade where regimental bands played on fine evenings; the streets alive with redcoats and bluejackets, townsfolk in fine clothes and townsfolk in rags, and young countrymen up for the cattle market with a sharp eye for the press gangs; and the constant flash and rattle of smart carriages, coaches, curricles, and gigs, weaving amongst the stolid drays and carts and wagons.

For wider excursions Mr. Ross lent his own smart carriage and four, with a Negro coachman in livery. They traveled out of town and along the Basin road, where the forest came down to the salt rim of the great inner anchorage. The drive was beautiful, and the *pièce de résistance* was the "Lodge" where Prince Edward and his "little French lady" had lived and loved not many years before. Edward's busy soldiers and engineers had trimmed the woodland behind the Lodge to a natural park, laid out a long walk of intricate windings through the trees to spell the letters of Julie's name, led a brook in a series of pretty waterfalls down to a pond dug in the shape of a heart, and planted it with water lilies. On the hill above stood the tower and flagstaff of the military telegraph, which had enabled the soldier prince to keep in touch with the garrison while spending pleasant hours at the Lodge with his *chère amie.* And there was the little round bandstand, looking out on the water, where Army musicians had played for the pleasure of their guests. The happy pair had removed to England a few years back, and the Lodge was now the summer residence of Governor and Lady Wentworth; but the aura of royal romance still clung to the house and the grounds, like the ghost of "that French woman's" perfume.

On another day they followed a favorite jaunt of Halifax folk, by carriage or afoot, along the road that ran from the town to Point Pleasant. Near the edge of the Point Pleasant woods the road passed over a wide brook on a rustic bridge, a haunt of lovers on summer afternoons and evenings, and well known as the Kissing Bridge. The name was a mockery to the seamen of Admiral Cochrane's squadron, who came in a continual flow of boats, laden with casks to be filled with fresh water just below the bridge, where the brook tumbled into the tide. Among the strollers from the town were many girls of the poor class, drawn by the magic presence of sailors in this romantic scene; but alas for them and the sailors there was no chance of mingling, even for a chat.

The men, brown from the West Indian sun, and wearing nothing but frayed duck trousers in the summer weather, were allowed to skylark amongst themselves; but a line of redcoated marines, with loaded muskets and fixed bayonets, stood watchfully between them and the roadway. It was comical to hear the remarks of the seamen, and of the more saucy girls, but the marines were stolid under this cheerful insult. If a sailor escaped they got a flogging themselves, and they took no chance on that. And this scene at the Kissing Bridge went on day after day, as the ships poured away the last foul dregs of their West Indian water, scoured the casks, and sent them ashore to be filled with the bright fresh water of the northern stream.

On yet another day the McNab ladies traveled by carriage inland to the Dutch Village on the isthmus, and thence by a narrow lane winding through the woods around the tip of Northwest Arm to Melville Cove. They were curious to see where Rory kept his

Frenchmen in "the fishhouse." As it happened he was there on one of his inspection trips, and he insisted on showing them over "my experiment." It was a strange experience for the two young women, walking through the yard and then the "fishhouse" itself, feeling the concentrated gaze of the prisoners like a physical touch, and hearing their comment in mysterious whispers and chuckles. Chiefly the attention was on Joanna, in a fresh yellow dimity gown that was a miracle of compliment to her long and shapely figure. She walked amongst the Frenchmen with Rory at her side and Ellen a step or two behind, with all the dignity of a tall blonde queen passing some of her poorer subjects and aware of nothing but their misfortune.

But later in the carriage, when they had bade farewell to Rory and the officer of the guard and were out of earshot, Jo said in an annoyed voice, "Well! I feel as if I'd just walked naked through a barracks! Don't you?"

"I?" said Ellie, surprised. And then with a faint smile, "I felt quite invisible."

"You mean you didn't notice those Frenchmen grinning and nudging and whispering?"

"Oh yes. They seemed like a lot of mischievous monkeys. But I suppose men shut up like that would chatter about anything. They might seem very different outdoors."

"As far as I'm concerned I never want to see Frenchmen anywhere. Ugh!"

On the last day of August, as their holiday was drawing to its end, one of McNab's Army friends took the boys up the hill for an inspection of the Citadel. It was a warm day, and as usual the Ross household was up early, with the two merchants hurrying off to their affairs.

Sauntering down George Street with Ellen in the morning sunshine Jo said idly, "Tomorrow back we go to the island. Heigho! I suppose we've been everywhere and seen everything and done everything there is to do. Yet this seems too nice a day to waste just mooning about."

On a sudden impulse Ellie said, "Let's spend it on the water! Mr. Ross says there are wherrymen who take parties off to see the ships and the dockyard. And they're for hire at the Market Slip."

The slip lay at the foot of George Street, and when the two ladies came to the weedy wet steps they found several boats just pulling away, laden with sightseers of both sexes and all ages. The last was a small one, nearly full, and the wherryman, a gaunt fellow with a sunken dark eye gleaming like a candle in a pit, and a black patch over the other, called up to them, "Just in time, leddies, just in time. Hop in!"

"We'd like to see the ships and the dockyard," Joanna said primly.

"Yes, yes, o' course. We're going to see the whole business, ma'am, and the fare's a bargain—sixpence each. Ye won't see a show like this every day, not for a guinea you won't."

So they got in, and paid their sixpence, and sat close together on a thwart near the stern. The wherryman and a ragged boy of sixteen, who might have been his son, plied their oars and headed the boat upharbor towards the dockyard. There were six other passengers, three women, a stout man, and a shock-haired youth with dirty hands, badly bitten finger nails, and the beady questing eyes of a ferret. The stout man had quite a good top hat, but his broadcloth coat and trousers were on the shabby side, and so were his boots. A scarlet waistcoat lent him a dashing touch however, and before the boat had gone far he plucked a dark bottle from an inner pocket, tipped his head back and tasted its contents with the deliberation of a sea officer taking a noon observation of the sun.

This seemed to remind the other three women of something. Each had a basket, which she now picked over with satisfaction. Each basket held bread and cheese, a chunk of brown sugarcake, and two bottles of beer. Evidently they had come prepared for a long excursion. The ladies from McNab's island, who had come quite unprepared for anything, now began to inspect their feminine companions with curious side glances. At first, looking down the steps from the Market Wharf, Jo had taken them for gentlewomen, seeing their smart bonnets and silk gowns. But in closer view the ladies obviously were something less than genteel. As the boat moved away from the dock they pulled up their gowns to prevent them wrinkling on the hard thwarts, and in doing so gave to anybody's gaze a good deal of their legs, clad in wretched stockings and scrubby shoes, and of dirty and torn petticoats.

Their talk was even more revealing. They addressed each other as Kate, May, and Sal, and remarked that the long walk down from Barrack Street had put them all in a muck of sweat, that the footpaths weren't fit for an 'orse, and there was no place like the water on a bloody 'ot day like this. May and Sal were clearly in their twenties, and Kate perhaps ten years older. May had good teeth, but Sal showed black tombstones here and there in her smile. Kate was a large but well-shaped woman, quite handsome until she opened her wide mouth to laugh, showing no teeth at all in the front.

The stout man regarded them with large popped eyes the color of verdigris, like a pair of neglected military buttons sewn on his face a little too close to the nose. The unkempt youth in the bow ignored them all, staring eagerly ahead towards the dockyard, where all the boats seemed to be going. It was indeed a hot day. The sunshine smote the flat polished surface of the harbor and bounced up in the faces of the boats' passengers.

There was not a stir of air. In the burning silence the voices of the sightseers carried far. The sounds of the waterfront seemed hushed today, and as they drew near to the dockyard Joanna noted that even that noisy place was remarkably still.

The men-o'-war lay anchored in line at wide intervals, extending from George's Island to the dockyard, and the wherryman, with much rolling of his single eye, called off their names for the benefit of his fares.

"The furthest 'un, down by George's, that's the *Star*. Next is the *Squirrel*. Then ye see the *Ramillies, Melampus, Northumberland, Belleisle*—she's flagship—and the *Halifax* sloop-o'-war, just off the dockyard—she was built there last year, and got quite a few Nova Scotia men in her crew."

"*Belleisle!*" added the stout man. "She was one of Nelson's ships at Trafalgar."

"That she was," said the wherryman. "Barged right in to the French line and took on three or four of 'em. Had all her masts shot away, and lost heavy, but she stuck it out, she did, till the old *Swiftsure* got through to her."

"Don't tell me you was there, One-Eye," said Kate with one of her gaping laughs.

"I'll thank ye not to call me that, missus. The name is Nicholas —Nick for short. I wasn't at Trafalgar, no, but I've served me time in the Navy and yarned with enough Trafalgar men to know the story fore and aft."

Nick now turned his attention to the McNab ladies, jerking his bony chin towards the *Belleisle*. "That's where they had the court-martial, being she was the flagship. Had to be in a port some-where, d'ye see, for to get enough captains together. So the *Leopard* passed the four run coves over to the *Melampus,* which was com-ing north to Halifax."

Green Eyes put in affably, "One of the *Belleisle* marines that was on duty at the great cabin doorway told me all about the court-martial, over a mug or two of porter at the Anchor tavern. All four claimed they was Americans—all the run coves do that o' course—and two of 'em had papers to prove it, though they sounded no more Yankee than my foot. Howsomever they was let off pun-ishment. The court had better fish to fry—the other two. They hadn't a scratch o' pen to prove anything. They'd tried false names, but that was no-go 'cause there was old shipmates o' theirs to go davy they was men run from His Majesty's service. Fact is, them two coves knew they was dead men from the moment the *Leopard* nabbed 'em in the Yankee frigate. Tried to face it out, o' course. But when they saw the game was up they let their tongues run while they could—telling those captains round the board what they thought of 'em, and of His Majesty's service too, afore the marines hustled 'em away. So the sentence was for mutiny, deser-tion, and contempt. They been kept shut up a week to think on what was comin', and now they're a-goin' to catch it."

"What do you mean?" Joanna said uneasily.

"One's to dance the yardarm hornpipe, ma'am, aboard the *Halifax* sloop-o'-war—that's her lyin' off the dockyard, where we're headin'. So the shore maties may see what happens to coves that run, and talk mutinous, and give contempt to His Majesty's officers. Then, startin' from there, the other cove's to be flogged around the fleet, 'cause he's the one that give the captains the most contempt."

Joanna put out a hand and grasped Ellen's wrist. For several moments they felt stifled and sick, as if the man had flung a foul wet cloth over their faces. Jo spoke then, in a faltering voice gone thin as a child's. "You mean to say you're all going to watch a man hanged, and then follow the other poor wretch about the fleet?"

The answer was a chorus of "Ay!" "That we are!" in the pleased voices of Green Eyes, the ladies from Barrack Street, and the eager young ferret in the bow.

"Boatman," said Joanna in that faint voice, "put us ashore at once, please, this young lady and myself."

"What!" snapped Nick. "And fork back sixpence each?"

"You may keep our fares. All we want is to get back to town—now."

A roar of outrage from the other passengers. What! Turn back now, and miss the hanging and the best part of the flogging? That's what they'd paid their money for, and they'd have their money's worth. Kate added loudly, "Who the devil does she think she is?"

"I am the wife of Mr. Peter McNab," said Jo, addressing herself to the wherryman and hoping to impress him. "And this young lady is Mr. McNab's ward. We demand that you put us on shore at once—anywhere—over there." She pointed a trembling finger to the nearest land, a spot outside the town on the dockyard road.

Nick gave them a calculating look with his one terrific eye. A wherryman who plied for hire at the Market Slip knew the name and person of Mr. McNab well enough, and something of McNab's position, but he also knew that McNab had boats of his own and never hired wherrymen.

"Beg pardon, ma'am," he said with a leering politeness. "But I made a bargain with these 'ere ladies and gents and got to keep it. Stands to reason. And there ain't a minute to lose, no, not a second."

The stout man said amiably, "It's just a matter of coming along for the boat ride, ma'am."

Sal spoke up in a high mincing imitation of Joanna's voice, "Ho yes, my dear, it's just a nice day on the 'arbor arter all, and we don't 'ave to look at anythink narsty, do we—not even three sluts from up the 'ill."

Meanwhile the oars had lost not a stroke.

The wherry slid to a halt at last in a mass of small craft literally covering the water around the *Halifax* sloop-of-war. Every sort

of harbor wherry was there, and cod-hookers spangled with fish
scales and stinking of their trade, pleasure skiffs, small yachting
sloops, even some Indian canoes. They were filled with a chattering mob of all sorts, including some officers of the garrison and
other gentlemen and their ladies, but mostly men, women, and
children of the lower class. There seemed to be a large number
of females like May and Kate and Sal, tossing coarse chat back
and forth, and they all joined in the roar of laughter when a rough
fellow stood up in one of the boats, looked all about him, and
announced in a cheerful shout, "I vow there ain't a dolly-shop in
business right now anywheres in town!"

Joanna, filled with a shivering anger and contempt, sat like a
figure of stone regarding the hands clasped in her lap. Ellen did
the same for a time, in unconscious imitation; but the regal dignity that went with being Mrs. Peter McNab did not belong to his
ward, and Ellie was drawn by a dreadful curiosity to see and
hear what all this was about. She found herself ignoring the boat
mob, and gazing up at the black hull of the sloop-of-war, the open
gunports with one forward gun run out and gleaming in the sunshine, the occasional heads in round tarpaulin hats peering from
the ports at the crowd, the masts like great trees in winter with
branches set rigidly at right-angles, the standing rigging tarred and
stiff, the sun-faded hemp of the running rigging, and high aloft, at
the mizzen peak, the evil yellow flag stirring faintly with some
movement of the upper air that was not to be felt on the water.

The man with the podgy belly stood up again to peer. "The
boats from the other men-o'-war is there all right, and the launch
of the *Halifax*—I can see the marine drummer ready in her bow—
but I don't see no grating rigged, not yet anyhow."

Nick stood up for a look. "Right you are. They usually rig the
gratin' in the boat, an' flog the beggar there, alongside every ship;
and ye can see it all. But some flag officers don't approve a show
for people in the anchorage; and anyhow the boatswains' mates
can get better footin' on a deck and lay on sharper with the cat.
If you ask me, that's how it's to be done today."

A disappointed murmur from the Barrack Street ladies and
the ferret.

"Ye won't see a thing aboard the seventy-fours," Nick added.
"The upper deck's too high. It'll be better when they get along to

the *Star* and *Squirrel*. 'Course on a still mornin' like this ye can
hear the strokes plain, and hear the beggar yell like Billy-be-
damned."

"How many's he to git?" asked the ferret eagerly.

"Three hundred," said Green Eyes. "That's to be split atween
the men-o'-war in the anchorage, which is seven. 'Twon't come
out even, and I dunno how they'll manage that. We'll see, any
rate."

Kate pursed her mouth. "Three 'undred? I never 'eard o' such
a lot. Look 'ere, arf the men in the fleet's bin flogged, some time
or other. I seen many a one, ay, and felt the old scars on their
backs."

A scream of laughter from May and Sal.

"Bah! So've you two, many's the time. I always say ye can tell
an old fleet 'and by the Admiralty stamp on 'is back. I've often
arsked 'em, ''Ow many licks o' the cat was that, Jack?'—an' they'll
say one or two or three dozen. I once 'ad a main topman that'd
got six dozen in one go, a couple o' year afore. 'Is back still felt
like an old rope mat worn 'ard an' shiny by the scrape o' shoes.
Said 'e was a month in sick bay arterwards, an' six months afore
'e could use 'is back muscles good enough to go aloft. Now ye say
this beggar's to git three 'undred. 'Ow many dozen's that?"

"Five-and-twenty," said the stout man, with a smack of lips.

" 'E won't git arf way through it."

"What d'ye mean by that?"

"I mean the beggar'll faint—swound away—lose 'is senses."

"That may be," said Nick the wherryman. "But they'll lay it
on to him anyhow. Three hundred's what the court-martial said,
and three hundred's what he'll get, senses or no senses."

Now came a shrilling of boatswain's pipes, and bull voices
yelling down the hatches, "Hear there! All hands to witness punishment! D'ye hear there?" A great scurry of men on the sloop's
deck. Then, in a tense silence, a pair of marines appeared in their
red coats and gleaming black billycock hats, each with a bayonet
fixed and glittering on his musket. Between them walked a sailor
in shirt and trousers, with his hands lashed at his back. A rope
with a noose was slung from the fore yardarm on the starboard
side, with a pair of boatswain's mates waiting there. The marines
marched the man up to them, turned, and stepped smartly away.

The seaman stood with his face to the morning sun as the others slipped the noose about his neck.

A loud monotonous voice recited from the Articles of War, and read the man's crime and sentence.

"Now," said Nick in a hoarse whisper, "stop your ears, gals— the gun'll fire—and then look sharp. He'll be well on his way to the yardarm when the smoke clears."

Bang! A tremendous clap, a spout of flame, a cloud of dirty-white powder smoke with tinges of grey and even lavender, as it spread in the bright August sunshine. All the ladies jumped as if they were shot.

"There he goes!" cried the ferret.

"Lor, look at 'im kick!" said Sal.

A sudden buzz of comment all around the sightseeing flotilla, and some laughter, high-pitched and nervous, from the women. A group of seamen could be seen heaving on the hang-rope, pausing to take a fresh grip, and heaving again. The wooden block at the yardarm cheeped like a sparrow at every heave. It did not take long. The last wisp of gun smoke was still drifting away towards the Dartmouth shore when the limp figure of the run cove, all his running done forever, came to a halt below the yardarm.

"Now for t'other!" cried the ferret.

6

A sharp bark of command aboard the *Halifax* turned the faces of her crew from the object aloft to the deck. In the waist of the ship a long wooden grating had been placed on end against the gang-way entrance and fastened there; and on the inboard side of it with his face to the wood was a man, stripped to his trousers, his arms held up in the attitude of a Y and fastened with rovings of spun-yarn tied about his wrists.

The boatswain's mates, both burly men, one somewhat taller than the other, now stood at each side of the grating. The taller man held a red cloth bag, rather like the slim flannel powder bags

for cannon charges but much too long. It contained something
quite different but deadly enough. He drew out a handle of stiff
red rope as long as a man's arm, with nine cords dangling from the
end of it, each cord also the length of an arm, and half the thickness of a finger. He stepped aside, plying the rope handle, shaking out the cords to their full length, measuring the exact distance
of the naked back on the grating, placing his feet apart, springing
up and down on his toes, and glancing over his right shoulder to
make sure his swing was clear.

Again the loud voice intoned from the Articles of War, with a
slow emphasis on . . . "Every person in or belonging to the fleet,
who shall desert or entice others to do so, shall suffer death or such
other punishment as the circumstances of the offense shall deserve." Then the recital of the man's crime and the punishment
allotted by court-martial. The Captain, standing aft with his officers, all in full dress uniform, snapped out, "Very well men—do
your duty!"

The taller boatswain's mate had the stony face of a gladiator
under the life-and-death gaze of an emperor, taking no joy in his
task but aware that he must strike with all the force and cunning
that he had. He flicked back the cat with a long movement, and
then swiftly forward, with the strength of an iron arm and the skill
of a practiced angler making a cast. The cat's tails spread a little
as they fell, so that they left nine red welts on the prisoner's back
like the ribs of a partly opened fan. The people in the boats, seeing
the man only vaguely through the grating, heard a sound like that
of a carpet beaten and a hoarse voice shouting "One!" A pause,
then the swish and the vicious *flack* again, and a shout of "Two!"
At the count of twelve there was a brief pause while the cat passed
to the hand of the other boatswain's mate. Then the swish, the
flack, the shout of "Thirteen!" and again the swish of the cords in
air. At the count of twenty-four the cat changed hands again.
Again at thirty-six. At forty-eight there was a silence, and then the
Captain's voice, "Cut him down, and pass him to the boat."

"So!" said Nick the wherryman. "Four dozen."

"Leave us see now," said the stout man, closing his eyes for better calculation. "As I figure it, that works out at four dozen aboard
each o' the ships till he gets to the last 'un in the line, the little
Star. He'll get a dozen there, and that'll make the three hundred."

"Here he comes!" cried the ferret, and gnawed again at his finger nails.

The grating had been plucked away, and the culprit appeared in the gangway entrance, a well-built young man with brown hair drawn into a short pigtail. He shrugged off the hands that offered assistance and stepped down the accommodation ladder with fingers merely touching the man-ropes. Miss Dewar, looking up, saw that his face was high, with a glitter in the eyes that might have been tears, or a gleam of madness, or pride, or perhaps the "contempt" with which he had been charged. Whatever it was, he seemed a creature apart, as if he moved in a world far away from the ship, the waiting boats of the men-o'-war, and the staring crowd ashore and afloat.

He did not seem hurt at all, but when he turned and stepped into the boat there was a general "ah!" from the spectators. They could see his back now. Clearly one of the boatswain's mates had been right-handed and the other left-handed, for their strokes had bitten a crude diamond pattern of bright red stripes over his whole back from the lower ribs to the shoulders. The skin had broken under the lash, and each stripe was a shallow slanting gutter adding its trickle of blood to a stream down his backbone. Already the seat of his white cotton trousers was soaked red.

"A tough 'un, that," said Nick admiringly. "Never made a sound."

"Ah," said Kate, "but 'e'll 'oller at the next lot—mark my words."

"What makes you so sure?" asked Green Eyes.

"'Cause I know. I ain't missed a fleet floggin' in years—not if I knowed about it and could get a wherry. You wouldn't know why, not bein' in my trade. The way most of 'em treat you arter they've 'ad what they paid for; 'arf drunk, beatin' me an' the girls, tryin' to wreck the 'ouse. Ho yes! So I never miss one o' these. Pays it all back, some'ow—as if I swung the cat meself, at all the men that ever cheated me, or slapped me about, or broke me furniture."

"Looka the blood!" cried the ferret.

"Ay, look," said Kate. "Ye won't see so much of it from 'ere on. The cat don't just tear 'is skin off. It bruises the meat like a cudgel. By the time 'e comes down from the next ship 'is back'll be so swole up an' purple, you wouldn't believe. By the time they're through with 'im it'll be black—black as toast—black as a beef-steak charred on the coals, an' the raw meat red in the cracks."

The stout man glanced curiously at the McNab ladies. Joanna sat with her eyes shut, leaning forward, with her elbows on her knees, hands clasped over her ears. Ellen turned her pale face and black eyes from speaker to speaker, and to the prisoner in the boat, like a creature in a dream.

The boat from the *Halifax* had begun to move, and the mid-shipman in charge of it was yelling at the sightseers to get their damned boats aside and make way. The marine drummer in the bow of the boat struck up the slow rattle and thump of the "Rogue's March." The prisoner sat alone on an afterthwart. Each warship in the anchorage had sent a boat for the ritual procession, with oarsmen smart in round tarpaulin hats and clean duck frocks and trousers, a pair of armed marines sweating in red serge coats and choking in black leather stocks, and a midshipman at the tiller in short blue jacket, white duck trousers and glazed black billycock hat, very proud of this, his small temporary command.

For the dockyard workmen the play was over. They were clambering down from their high perches on the sheers and from the roofs of sheds. The sightseers in the boats followed the pro-cession toward H.M.S. *Belleisle,* the great three-decker next in line. They were all chattering now, and two of the wherries had brought along a musician to liven the passages from ship to ship, a man with a flageolet, another with a fiddle. Several passengers, mostly boys in their teens, had rattles of the kind used by night watchmen, and twirled them merrily from time to time. And now a man with the gaunt face of a Bible prophet in a halo of long white hair stood up and sang. He was in a smart varnished galley rowed by four pairs of oars, with a party of Army gentlemen and spritely females who might have been their wives or doxies—there was much ribald speculation in the other boats.

"That's Blind Jack," said Kate. "Sings very sweet, 'e does, for an old man. Comes in my place quite a lot, winter evenin's, just to sit in the warm, and warble a song now an' then for the cus-tomers waitin'. Picks up a good many shillin's in the summertime too, ballad singin' on water parties an' such. Some o' the swells like to spend a warm day rowin' or sailin' about the 'arbor and

the Basin, goin' ashore to eat an' drink in the shade o' the woods,
with a fiddler an' Blind Jack along for music."

"What's that he's singin' now?" said Green Eyes, putting a hand
to his ear.

"An old 'un," said the wherryman. "'I Sailed from the Downs
in the Nancy.'"

"Ye should 'ear 'im do 'The Death o' Nelson,'" Kate sighed.
"Bring tears to the eyes of a wooden figger-'ead, 'e could, that's
a fact."

"Or 'Tom Bowling,'" Sal put in. "'E does 'Tom Bowling'
lovely."

As the prisoner's boat reached the foot of *Belleisle's* gangway
ladder a gun spat noise and smoke from her top deck, and the clap
of it went echoing along the harbor hills. The man with the wet
red back went up the side unassisted by the marine before him or
the one behind. As they reached the deck the drummer in the
boat held his sticks silent, and the people in the watching craft
fell silent too. Above them the grating was tipped into place and
the man lashed to it by his wrists in that strange posture of a
Christ crucified backwards.

Again a harsh gabbling of the Articles of War, and the sentence
of the court-martial, every word clear in the hot still air. Again
the command "Do your duty!" to boatswains' mates. Again the
swish, the *flack,* the voice calling aloud the number of the strokes.
And again no cry from the figure on the grating. At the shout of
"Forty-eight!" the same pause, the curt command, "Cut him
down and pass him back to the boat," the removal of the grating,
the dramatic appearance of the prisoner in the gangway entrance.
This time the man came down the steps more slowly, grasping
hard on the man-ropes; but still his face was high. As he turned
to get in the boat, Kate cried, "See?" The man's back was now not
only torn, with strips of bloody skin hanging like rags, but it was
puffed and purplish, and the drain of blood had become a slow
ooze, as if it were choking at the source.

On the way to the *Northumberland,* with the hour getting on
towards noon, Green Eyes took a long pull at his bottle, and the
ladies from Barrack Street delved into their baskets. Kate produced a bottle screw for the beer corks, and they sucked and
munched hungrily. Most of the people in the other craft were

equally well provided, and some much better—the military gentlemen and their ladies had cold roast chicken and champagne.
The man with the flageolet played a jig with great spirit, and then
Blind Jack sang in his light sweet tenor several verses of "'Twas
in the Good Ship Rover."

Again the grim business on the deck of the *Northumberland,*
and again no cry from the man on the grating. But as he emerged
from the gangway entrance there was a murmur all through the
floating crowd. A stream of blood ran from his mouth, from the
whole length of it, covering his chin and splashing down on his
chest.

"He's bit his lip!" cried the ferret.

"Gammon!" Kate said. "I've see a lot o' lips cut, an' cut bad,
with a bash on the teeth; but I never see 'em run blood like that."

"Righto!" said Nick the wherryman. "It's his tongue. The beggar's bit his tongue to keep from yellin', that's what it is. Nothin'
bleeds so bad as a bit tongue—reely bit, I mean."

The man's head drooped now, and he came down the ladder
with several halts, gripping the man-ropes and feeling for the
next step with a foot, as if he were coming down a flight of stairs
in the dark. Once he stumbled and the marine behind caught him
by the pigtail and steadied him for a moment until he recovered
himself. He dropped into the boat at last and sat slumped on the
thwart, breathing in great gasps as if he had been running up a
mountainside, and with the red torrent gushing from his mouth.

Again the "Rogue's March," the procession of boats from the
men-o'-war with oars rising and falling in exact time, the oar
blades shining in the sun, and the disorderly swarm of harbor
craft moving on towards the *Melampus.*

Nick, the old fleet hand, remarked now the fresh black paint
on the frigate's sides, the glisten of white and of varnish about
her forecastle and the stern windows, the tautness of standing
rigging and ratlines freshly set up and tarred, the new canvas furled
on the yards. The *Melampus* was not alone in these matters, but
it was the first time that anyone had bothered to notice. As Nick
said, "'Struth! You'd think Old Cock expected a French fleet any
minute, the way he's drivin' to refit his ships. Cost a pretty penny,
too. 'Course, he stands well wi' the Lords of Admiralty, so I've
heard. Them that don't stand well there get their knuckles

cracked for every pint o' paint they use an' every new stitch o' canvas."

At the foot of the frigate's gangway ladder the prisoner raised himself upright in the boat, lurched toward it, and then as Green Eyes said, "fell in a heap like a string o' fish." The marines bent over him and said something to the midshipman, who cupped his hands and called something up to the deck. Promptly a voice there shouted, "Bosun! Bosun! Lower away a hammock and smart about it!" Down came a canvas hammock on lines from the ends. A brief delay in the boat, and a voice calling "Hoist away!" The laden hammock went up the side, and the watchers saw the man's figure writhing in it.

On deck the boatswain's mates removed the prisoner from the hammock, propped him upright, and lashed his wrists in place. Again the harsh voices and the desolate routine. Finally the man was lowered down the side to the boat in the same way he had gone up. The drum again. And so on to the *Ramillies,* which lay anchored in the harbor facing Citadel Hill. The prisoner was twitched aloft in the hammock like a batch of cabbages for the officers' mess, and again the staring people in the boats could see a confused movement in the canvas, as if the fellow, in some delirium of anguish, tried to struggle up a ladder.

The ritual again. But at the final order "Cut him down and pass him to the boat" there was a heavy thump. Silence for a time. Then an authoritative voice from the blue frocks and gold lace on the quarterdeck, "Surgeon! Examine that man!" A long silence. Then a voice from the gangway. "The man's dead, sir."

The captain again. "What! Are you sure, Mr. Hanaway?"

"Yes, sir. No breath, no pulse, no life in him at all."

Silence. Then the captain's voice, "Signal lieutenant! Signals! Ah, there you are, Mr. Pendlebury. Hoist the telegraph flag, if you please, and make to the flagship—um—" Evidently the signal lieutenant had come up on the run, for the rest was in a lower voice that conveyed nothing to the boats below. The spectators watched the telegraph flag go up the mast limp, and then fill out in the stir of loftier air. Then a succession of flag hoists arose, fluttered for a time, and came down again.

"Dead!" Kate said. "Arter what, twenty dozen?"

"'Twasn't the floggin' alone that done for him," said the

wherryman, "The beggar must ha' bit his tongue clean through. Deliberate. Like cuttin' his throat. Bled to death, inside an' out."

" 'E was still movin' in the 'ammick when they pulled 'im up the side," May said doubtfully.

"Ay," said the stout man. "But he wasn't when they cut him down, was he? I wonder how many strokes of that last lot was wasted, like. Floggin' a man dead as mutton."

A long wait in the afternoon heat, the boats weaving gently up and down, the ladies fanning themselves with handkerchiefs, the men sucking the last drops from their bottles. Somebody called across to the four-oared galley, asking Blind Jack for a song. The thin wispy man arose, and lifted his voice to the crowd.

> "Here a sheer hulk lies poor Tom Bowling,
>   The darling of our crew,
> No more he'll hear the tempest howling,
>   For death has broached him to.
> His form was of the manliest beauty . . ."

Above them a figure sprang to the hammock rail of the *Ramillies,* clapped a tin voice trumpet to its mouth, and bellowed down, "You there! Belay that caterwauling, or by God we'll have you up here and give you something to howl about."

A pause, and then the indignant bellow again. "All you people! Shove off! Shove off! Clear out the lot of you! This is no raree-show for a lot o' whores and idlers. Anyhow—it's over. Over and done with! D'ye hear there?"

Joanna McNab spoke then, for the first time since the show began. She did not lift her head nor open her eyes. She whispered, "Thank God," and shuddered. The military gentlemen in the galley were not disposed to move, bidding their oarsmen to linger, and staring up at the quarterdeck of the *Ramillies* with all the defiance they could muster. But the wherryman and fishermen lost no time in getting away. A captain in His Majesty's sea service was quite capable of seizing and flogging men like themselves, and there were the man-o'-war boats and crews ready for the fun.

Nick and his assistant plied their oars vigorously as the sight-seeing fleet scattered away from the *Ramillies* like a school of frightened fish. They headed for the Market Wharf. For a long time nobody spoke except the stout man, who asked Nick curiously, "What happens in a case like that?"

"Depends on the senior off'cer," Nick said rowing hard and beginning to puff. "I've heard tell o' men dyin' on the gratin'—usually coves that was a bit sick to start with, a bad heart, or too soon after other floggin's. And I've heard tell o' captains that ordered the full sentence carried out regardless—floggin' a corp to the last stroke. Well, this admiral's a tough 'un—oh yes, a tough 'un is Old Cock—but I daresay that there officer on the *Ramillies* was right. The beggar's dead, so the show's over an' done with. Arter all, ye got your money's worth. What d'ye expect for six-pence?"

He turned the deep glitter of his single eye upon them all.

Kate said, "Ah! What indeed! And 'ere's 'arf the arternoon left and many a sixpence goin' by the door. It's back to Barrack Street, girls, an' wash as fast as we can." They scrambled, tittering, out of the wherry and up the steps, with a show of plump thighs above their garters, and then they were gone, and so was the ferret. The podgy man with the green eyes lingered to help the McNab ladies out of the boat, and swept off his top hat with a gallant twirl of the wrist, "And now, ladies, is there anything more I can do for you?"

"Yes," Joanna said. "Please get us a cab—it doesn't matter what kind—anything." After that long rigid attitude on the hard thwart of the wherry she felt cramped all over, and her legs were trembling too much to take her far.

The stout man cast a sad look up George Street. It was a hot walk up the hill to Grand Parade, the nearest place where hackneys stood for hire. Ellen Dewar said, "Jo, it's only a little way to Mr. McNab's store, and he could . . ."

"Mr. McNab," said Joanna in a cold dead voice, "must never know a thing about this day's outing. We're going straight to the Ross house in Argyle Street, and once I get there I go straight to bed. I feel sick—sick! And surely you must, too. If Peter knew he'd be furious with us—especially me—for getting ourselves into such a horrible affair; and he'd want to thrash the wherryman."

"Then what shall we say? He's sure to ask where we've been and what made you ill."

At this point the podgy man noticed an empty hackney coach

turning the corner of Water Street. He whipped two fingers to his mouth corners and whistled like a boatswain's pipe. The coachman looked him up and down disdainfully. Then he noticed the ladies, and at once began to turn his nag.

"Thank you," said Jo in the cold voice. And to Ellen, "We shall say we went for a long walk about the town, and drank some milk at a stall, or ate something at a stall; and probably that and the hot sun upset us. It's a fib, but if you'd been married as long as I have, with a husband like Peter, you'd know that a wee fib now and then saves a mortal tirravee. And tomorrow, Ellie— tomorrow we'll go back to our island where we belong."

With that Jo stepped into the coach and Ellie followed her. Away they went without another word, leaving Green Eyes alone at the head of the Market Wharf. He stood there for a few moments, considering that last remark of the pretty blonde woman, and the tone of her voice as she said it; and for some odd reason he was reminded of another of Blind Jack's songs, "I'm a Long Time in This One Town."

Going down the harbor in the McNab sloop the following afternoon Joanna fixed her gaze ahead, as if she could put behind her not only Admiral Cochrane's ships but the town and everything there that had to do with ships, even Peter McNab. The two boys Peter and James on the other hand were still excited with all they had seen, and now, on the water, they gazed and chattered about the men-o'-war until the squadron was far astern and the island drawing near. Ellen Dewar, too, stared after the ships until they were shimmering dots in the haze of early autumn. McNab's island was now sharp and clear, and as he steered for the home cove Gahagan, casting an idle glance far to starboard, saw something that made his mouth gape. He all but shouted, then checked himself and sternly fixed his eyes on the cove and the friendly smoke of the "muckle hoose." Neither young Para nor Sheamus noticed the objects small in the distance at the beach end. Their faces and minds were still upon the town, now wrapped in a lavender veil like the smoke of a thousand incense pots, with just the top of Citadel Hill looming above, like a dream city vanished by magic.

The laird himself stayed on in town for three more days, driving himself, his clerks, his warehousemen and wagoners, finishing the last details of the fleet-victualling and other business in the town. From the Agent for Prisoners, just returned from Melville Island, he heard late news from home.

"D'ye ken, Mr. McNab, what's on your beach again?"

"What?" said Peter absently, running his eyes over an invoice.

"A new pair o' gibbets—those puir devils from the *Chesapeake*."

"Eh!" roared Peter, all fire and attention now.

"Ay, sir. On the orders of Admiral Cochrane, I'm told."

"Cochrane! Cochrane be . . ." But there Peter saved his breath. What was the use of damning admirals? They had the law on their side, and in Cochrane's case a good precedent only two years before. He could hear lawyer Cogswell saying so.

Nevertheless he came home in a boil, and every day went into a silent fury when his eyes wandered to the beach end. In cooler moments he thought on the effect of these executions upon the Americans. There was no further word from Malachi Sparling at New York, and as yet no interruption in direct American trade with Britain. A few days later a frigate came in past the gibbets, and McNab with his spyglass recognised her as H.M.S. *Jason*, which had sailed late in August to fetch despatches from the British envoy in New York.

On arriving at his town office next morning the laird learned more of the *Jason*. Five of her seamen had run off from a boat's crew at New York, and when a British officer tried to catch them he was stopped and hustled by a crowd of Americans. More than that, several other seamen of the *Jason* had uttered mutinous talk, and were under arrest. Soon after the frigate's return to Halifax, six men were tried at court-martial. Two were convicted and hanged at the *Jason's* yardarms in the harbor.

It was nearing the middle of October, with the first of the autumn rains beginning to beat the colored leaves of the maples off the trees. Boats' crews and carpenters from the *Jason* came out in the cold pelter to McNab's island, and when they left there were two more dead men dangling at the beach end.

That evening in the drawing room of the McNab house a watchful and apprehensive household waited for the laird. He had the air of a pregnant volcano, but he kept himself in hand and in his custom read aloud to the family and servants from London news-papers just arrived by the Falmouth packet.

"Parliament's passed Mr. Wilberforce's bill against the slave trade, and a good thing, too. But here's a bauchle of a clause—it gave the British slave merchants till next January to deliver their last cargoes in the West Indies. So there's been a great send-ing out of vessels all the past season, and fearful crowding in 'em, I'll warrant, and more than two months yet to go. Just the same, the damned trade's doomed, as far as British shipping goes, at any rate."

He paused, and shuffled the little pile of newspapers on the table.

"Well! That's dated away back last spring. Let's find the latest. Um. Um. Ah! September tenth. Summary of the war this year. Um! Another attack on Copenhagen and the Danish fleet. In and out again, like Nelson six years back. British troops landed in Egypt—road to India—important, that—but tcha! they had to get out again—driven back to their ships by a lot of Turks and Egyp-tians. Guid God! Fleet expedition to Constantinople—also driven back. And what's this? British Army in South America. South America! Captured Montevideo and Buenos Ayres. Then cut off and had to surrender. What the deuce! Is this the Cabinet's notion o' fighting the French? —wasting men and ships on popgun expedi-tions all over the globe, and not sae much as a French drummer boy engaged for a moment! Boney must be laughing his head off.

"Weel, let us see what else Boney's doing. Something tae the point, we may be sure. Ah! I thought so. He's beat the Prussians. The Russians, too. And what's this? Treaty at Tilsit. Where's that?"

A long silence while the laird read on in silence. Then he looked up and swept a fierce glance over the expectant faces of his household. He had forgotten the beach and the gibbets now. His mind was far across the sea.

"The clever scheming de'il! D'ye know what Boney's done noo? He's got the Emperor of Russia tae stop fighting and more or less go intae business with him. It says here they met on a raft, in a river between their armies, last June. They agreed on peace wi' each other, and divided up the rest o' Europe between 'em, from Copenhagen tae Constantinople, like a pair o' footpads plot-

ting the next night's work. Phew! D'ye realise what it means?
It means that Boney's pretty well master of Europe, bar the Russian interests. And Spain and Portugal, o' course. He'll make them
kiss the rod next, ye may depend. Then he'll have an empire
from the Baltic tae the Strait of Gibraltar and frae the Hook of
Holland tae the toe of Italy. Europe's not seen the like since the
Romans."

"Then we stand alone?" said old Miss McNab. "Britain against
all Europe?"

"Saving Spain and Portugal, as I say. And remember the Spaniards are old partners of the French against England. I don't doubt
they'll fall in line again when Boney gives the orders. Och, our
only comfort's the sea. Even a wizard like Boney canna cross
the Channel dryfoot wi'out first beating our fleet. And as ye've
heard me say many times, he can build ships well enough, but he
canna make seamen like ours."

Patriotic though they were, and impressed with the diabolical
fortunes of Napoleon, Joanna and Aunt McNab felt mostly relief at the turn of Peter's mind. Ever since Struachan the piper
had told them of more hanged men at the beach they had feared
an explosion when the laird came home. And now, without warning, an explosion came, and not from McNab at all.

Ellie Dewar cried out, "But how long can our nation go on like
this? I mean, most of the war's at sea, for our part. And how long
can our Lords of Admiralty go on forcing men into their ships,
and keeping them years aboard on a beggar's pay and worse food,
and hanging or flogging the life out of any who utter a word of protest, like the bonnie lad at the beach end?"

A small sharp cry from Joanna, with her eyes fixed on the girl's
own, eyes begging her to say no more. That frightful day on the
harbor water haunted her like a saint's vision of Hell. And if
Peter came to know about it Hell would be compounded tenfold.

McNab did not notice his wife's agitation. His attention was
all on Ellie Dewar, with her dark eyes afire.

"Bonnie?" he growled. "What makes ye think any puir de'il
at the beach end was a bonnie lad?"

"I mean the lad they whipped to death. I went to see him the
morning after they hung his body there."

The fear in Jo's eyes turned to shocked astonishment. With the subtle instinct of women she knew that Ellen was telling truth.

"Guid God! Were ye not afraid?" snapped McNab.

"Of a dead lad in chains? What harm could he do me?"

"D'ye mean to sit there and tell me ye went away oot there, over half a mile o' slippy stones, fra' sheer idle curiosity? Why, where was your . . . your sense o' decency, gel?"

The laird was working himself up to a fine fit of righteousness. At a wag of his finger the servants vanished, followed by young Jamie and Peter. Only Joanna, Aunt McNab, and the thin girl with the enormous eyes remained in the room with him. Ellen looked at Jo for a moment, and back to McNab.

"I heard Gahagan at gossip . . . so I went . . ."

"Ye went tae keek at a naked man!"

"He was naked, yes, but for the tar."

"Hoots, gel, wasna that a horrid sight?"

"Not as I saw him, no. He was young and well featured, and his body strong and beautiful. He was like that figurine, the black marble one of the Roman youth, on the window shelf in your library."

So she had examined the naked Roman too! In McNab's present mood there was not room for breadth of mind.

"I never thought tae hear a female of my household talk in such a fashion! Why, gel, it's . . ." He was going to say indecent, but that seemed too weak a word. "It's downright wicked!"

Ellie Dewar stood up then, with hands in small fists at her sides.

"The only wicked thing I saw was the wicked waste of a young man. A lad no doubt pressed away to sea, with never a word to his folk, caught in this everlasting war with no hope of discharge except the one they gave him at the last. That's true, isn't it? And you say the Parliament's done away with slave trade in British ships! Och, whenever town folk come to this house on their parties of pleasure, and cluster about the piano to sing, someone aye calls for Rule Britannia. And away they go with Britons Never Shall Be Slaves, when every day they see young men dragged away to His Majesty's ships, to be whipped out of their senses or hanged if they disobey—like any slaves from Africa. There's no escape but death, or maybe a crippled hand like poor Gahagan, or . . ."

McNab uttered the snort of a wounded bull. "So that's it! Gahagan! Gahagan talks too much."

"I've heard yourself in the same strain, Mr. McNab, about the Fleet. I've heard you say that admirals and captains get the good pay and food and the best share of prize money, while poor Jack gets little but the wounds and flogging."

Her eyes were like sea coals in the white face, framed by the black hair drawn in deep loops to her cheekbones and over her ears. McNab could find no ready answer. He could only sputter, "Ellie, that will be all!" She made a polite little bob, as old Aunt McNab had taught her long ago, and flitted away in a swift rustle of gown and petticoats.

The next morning McNab held a family council, Joanna and old Frances McNab and himself. They met like conspirators on a garden bench hidden from the house and out of earshot. It was in a rose arbor facing southward, the roses now withered to brown rags, and there was a view of the sea between the low grey stones of Devil's Island and the red bank of the Thrum Cap.

McNab opened the talk in the manner of a musket, *snap-flash-bang.*

"The gel's as mad's a hare in a March moon. Did ye see her eyes? A stark staring lunatic! Guid God! Who'd ha' thought it? Or have I been sae deep in business that I wasna paying heed enough tae what was going on at home? Eh? Did ye notice naething wrong wi' Ellie afore this?"

"I've seen nothing wrong with Ellie's mind, though something with her spirit maybe," Jo said. "Remember when she came to us, like the ghost of a small girl? The old laird was living then, and he summed up Ellie in a way I never forgot: 'Skin and bones, skin and bones, and a pair of eerie Hieland eyes as deep and dark's a loch.' Oh, she seemed ordinary much of the time, fussing over dolls and acting the Mama as little girls do. Sometimes I had to smile, seeing the way she'd mimic me with my own young ones. But otherwhiles I'd come upon her sitting by her lone, outdoors, and staring away over the sea, with such a desolation on her face that it was like to break my heart."

She sighed. "I'd tried to mother the girl like one of my own, but she wanted none of that. She'd turn those big black eyes and stare as if she could see through me to something or someone else. I'd a weird feeling sometimes that if I turned around I'd see whatever it was. It couldn't have been any memory of her mother. She, poor woman, died when her child was born. And I doubt she knew much of her father; for after his wife's death he took to the drink and died in a pothouse quarrel somewhere . . ."

"Stirling," murmured Aunt McNab.

"Well, wherever. To me the child seemed, well, fey. There's no other word for it. And now she's a woman grown and still she's fey."

McNab pushed out his lips. "Fey? Um. An orphan child sent away over the sea, a passage of sixty-nine days if I remember right, an awfu' stretch o' cauld grey water atween the puir bairn and all she'd ever known. A thing like that 'ud stick in a child's mind, and mebbe bring on melancholy long after. But let's look tae more recent times. Did ye notice naething odd-like aboot Ellie, say in her teens? Call it fey or daft or what ye will, ye must ha' seen some warnin' sign o' her present condeetion?"

Joanna shut her eyes, calling back Ellie Dewar in her teens. The girl was a slim flagon of moods. She would drift into a daydream and stay there long, with eyes open. By the expression in those eyes the dream was sometimes pleasant, often sad, but mostly just mysterious. Whenever the piper Struachan stirred the air with a reel she would leap up and dance like a pixie to the tune. Or again, at some reproof, for whatever reason, she would go into black sulks, not speaking, hardly moving, for hours at a stretch.

When Aunt McNab tinkled old Highland songs and ballads on the piano the girl would sing in a voice surprisingly rich and strong for a body so finespun. She seemed to like best the tunes on minor notes, but she could pass easily into the gay and lively kind and render them with the lilt of a gipsy in some wild bothy in the border glens. Whatever the mood and whatever the moment Ellie gave herself to it absolutely. She held nothing back. With Ellie it was all or nothing.

Jo murmured at last, "Now that I think of her going to see that poor fellow on the gibbet, I might remark that Ellen's maybe under a kind of fascination about death. The way, from a child, she was always at you or Gahagan to tell stories of wrecks, the ships that struck Devil's Island, or the Blind Sister, or Mars Rock, or the stony shoal by the Thrum Cap, and the dead sailors washed up on our island shore. Remember the day she coaxed you to take her for a walk to the Thrum Cap and show her the graves?"

"Ay. I mind that weel enough."

"Well, she's gone there ever since, by her lone. She goes quite often. In summertime she takes flowers to the graves—wild roses, blue flags, violets, goldenrod—whatever's in bloom at the moment."

McNab snapped his fingers. "Och! Sure! That's it! Daith! She's touched on daith! And wandering away oot tae the Cap! Guid God! She's apt tae throw herself in the water there, flowers and a', one o' these days, like the puir daft gel in the play. What's tae be done? Eh? We canna just sit by and let it happen. But how could we lock her up? I mean, apart from this queer spell that's on her she seems quite rational, does she not?"

"Lock up Ellen?" cried old Frances McNab. "Are you daft yourself? There's not a speck of harm in the girl, to herself or anyone."

"When I say fey, Peter," Jo added urgently, "I don't mean she's wishful to die or anything like that. I mean she's a visionary sort, that's all. At times she seems to see things not visible to eyes like yours or mine. Like seeing the strength and beauty of that dead man—as if she saw him alive and unharmed. What is it you Highlanders call second sight in the Gaelic?"

"*Da-shealladh,*" said McNab.

"Well, from what you've told me, and your father before you, the Highlands are full of folk with *da-shealladh*. And if they're all mad, who's left to lock them up?"

At this moment, by some common instinct, they both turned to Aunt McNab. The old gentlewoman was gazing towards the line of sea and sky. Her bony figure was sombre in black bombazine, with a touch of white lace at the wrists and throat. She made a remarkable presence, with her cloud of white hair that no pins or combs could quite hold in place, and the soft blue eyes that hid the steel in her.

"Are you both finished?" she asked in her mild thin tone, like a voice in a reed. She did not take her eyes from the sea.

"This chatter of madness and *da-shealladh* and the like? If you are, let us come to the truth about Ellen. As you say, she was sent here a child, lonely and sad and shy, with nothing but a pair of great black eyes to catch a body's notice. And from the time she came, what has she seen with those eyes? Not one thing but this house, this island, and a lot of books. Books! And she now two-and-twenty!"

"What's wrong with that?" demanded Joanna. "My parents brought me here a child too; and what have I seen since but this island and books, and a trip to the town now and again?"

"Ah, but you'd parents to care for you, and then a good husband, and bairns. That makes another world."

"What's in your mind, Auntie?" asked McNab.

"Ellen's a woman, Peter. To say it plain she's been a woman eight or maybe ten years now. And she's no more mad than I."

"Tach! Did she go tae peer at a dead man out o' pure sensibility?"

"She went not knowing why," said Aunt McNab to the sea. "Because she had to go. Because God made her a woman, with an instinct deeper than just the matters of eating and breathing, and gave her curiosity for a purpose. Don't cluck your tongues as if I'd said something not decent. God made Eve long before He made our Ellie—and would you say God makes mistakes? I may be just an old maid body, but Ellie's mind is as plain to me as yon telegraph flags on York Redoubt are plain to the signalmen in the Citadel.

"I was myself a girl of no great beauty, and my father a small lairdie who seldom had two guineas at a time to rub together. The McNab of Killen saw to it that I had a good education, God bless his soul, because I was of his ilk. But mark you that was all I had. A lass without *tocher,* as we say in the Gaelic. That's a girl with no dowry, Joanna. Well, a dowerless lass, and a pair of parents unco proud. Meaning, no matter how bonnie a lad offered, their girl could wed none but a gentleman. And mind, gentleman bachelors in the Highlands with money enough to keep a wife were scarce after the Forty-Five. So forbye I stayed a maid and watched bonnie lads go by, and the years of my young life go by too, till at last I was faded and dry, like a flower pressed in a book. Oh, I could play a love song fine at the piano, and a dance tune on the violin, but there was neither love nor dancing left in the world for

me. At last I came away here across the sea, to warm my heart at
the glow of other folks' bairns, as an old maid must."

"Why fash yourself wi' all that now, Auntie?" Peter said gently.

"Because I must. I say this for the sake of what I might have
been, and had, and loved long since. In Ellie I see myself—myself
at the age when a man's love is no longer a dream nor a wish, but
a want. And time fleeting."

"But what can we do about that?" cried Jo. "To be sure we have
young officers to visit us, in the parties from town; but you know
Ellie. She has no liking for crowds and jollity. She just slips away.
She'd rather be by her lone."

"Then what's to be done?" demanded McNab impatiently. His
mind was tuned to male affairs, in which everything went on plain
lines. Women were like the sea out there, smiling, murmuring,
gliding in pleasant undulations on the surface, but moved by deep
tides at the pull of mysterious moons. What were they really thinking behind all this talk, Aunt Frances and his Jo?

"We might go up to town more," said Jo. "You've only to drop
a word here and there, and we'd have invitations to dinners, balls,
parties of every kind. Ellie could meet all the eligible young men,
especially officers of the fleet and garrison—the kind every town
miss sets her cap for. And you could let it be known, delicately of
course, that Miss Dewar will have a handsome dowry when she
marries."

"Eh?" blurted McNab. And then, "Oh, ay!" with the surprised
note of a husband who had not thought of such a thing at all.

"I don't doubt," said Jo in the same musing voice, "we'd soon
find a young officer eager to wed a girl with dowry enough to buy
his next step in rank. We'd have our Ellie married off in no time
whatever. And what then? The way this war goes on, with fighting
wherever there's sea enough to float a ship, and places to attack or
defend all round the world, her man's bound to be ordered off in
a matter of weeks or months. And only rich officers can afford to
take wives and families wherever they go. So there's our Ellie by
her lone again, for years maybe, and dreading bad news at every
post."

"In time of war," McNab said, "a lot of wives put up wi' that."

"No doubt. But it's one lone wife we have to think about. And
Ellie's been lone too long."

"Whatna then?"

"If a husband's what our Ellie needs, we must take care who holds the man in arms—Ellie or His Majesty."

"Riddles! Riddles! Come to plain talk, Jo!"

"So we must find a man outside His Majesty's forces."

"Where, for instance?"

"In trade, where I found mine," said Jo with a lively glance. "A young merchant, or even a clerk of good habits and some promise. A steady lad and a canny goer, as you'd say yourself. A woman may well take a chance on such a one."

"And how," snorted McNab, "does our Ellie find this promising sprig, this bonnie clerk wi' a quill at his lug and a gold future under his nose?"

"That's for you to arrange," Jo said briskly. "The girl should have a choice, so you must bring a choice of men out to the island—one at a time, of course. And we'll ca' cannie, as you'd say. No pushing Ellie at a man, nor any man at Ellie. Just an easy family air, and maybe suggesting on a fine afternoon that Miss Dewar might take the visitor for a walk about the island, and tell him the story of this and that, to while the time."

"Ca' cannie indeed! Ellie's bound to jalouse what ye're at, wi' a' these clerks and factors coming tae look her over like farmers at a cattle fair. It's my opinion she'd be black affronted."

"Peter, dear, in this matter your opinion's not worth a snap. What do you know about women—even me, after all this time? Nothing! So pay attention to me now. We must go about this carefully. What was that drink your father mixed for special guests? I know *usquebaugh* was in it, but the whole was something else and I never knew the English of it."

"Athol brose. Old whiskey and new cream, wi' a judicious portion of strained honey well stirred in to blend 'em for the going down."

"Ah! And in a manner of speaking that's the very brew for Ellen and the young men. I mean our policy shall be subtle as the brose —they won't suspect what's in the matter till the spirit's at work inside."

"Tricks! Tricks! Ye know, Jo—and you too, Auntie—when women set themselves to catch a man they've no more moral conscience than a spider at her silks."

His wife and old Aunt McNab smiled at each other, and Jo held back the quip on her tongue. Whatever would the world become without women and their silks? As barren as The Beach—with a dead man at the end of it.

And so for the shy Miss Dewar came a strange experience, a succession of male visitors eager to tramp about the island and hear dire tales of shipwreck from her own mouth and no other. For the evenings there were long sessions in the candle-lit drawing room, enclosed by the handsome paneled walls, where the family conspirators insisted that Ellen play the piano while the current visitor sang. It was of no use for Ellie to protest that she couldn't play half as well as Aunt McNab; nor for a hapless man to confess that he hadn't much of a voice, or that he couldn't carry a tune at all.

Off came the cordovan leather cover that shielded from damp the precious Broadwood, purchased in London for forty guineas and shipped across the sea. The girl found herself blundering at the keys which gave such pleasant music to her touch when she was alone. The visitors bellowed or warbled as best they could, under the eyes of the whole McNab family, sitting polite and rapt on the mahogany chairs as if they heard the very music of the spheres.

During the long fine-weather season of the year 1808 more than a score of bachelor merchants and aspiring clerks came out to the island for a taste of this peculiar brose. They ranged from Ellen's own age to twice as much, and they came tall, short, lean, and round. All dressed in the town vogue, with trousers so tight to their legs that it was a great wonder to Ellen how they got into them; long-tailed coats cut away in front to display gorgeous flowered waistcoats; cravats fit to choke the life out of them if they dropped their chins an inch; beaver hats as round and tall and formidable as the Martello tower across the water in York Redoubt.

Some had long boots of soft leather with tops turned down from the knees to show the inner shade of brown. Most favored polished black hessians with pointed toes and a pair of gilt tassels dangling from the tops. None of this raiment was suited to rambles about

McNab's rugged island, where the gentlemen perspired and stifled and stumbled behind the light brogues of their guide. When at last they made their way down to the cove, uttering polite thanks and farewells to the laird and family, there was a somewhat bewildered air about them, and in some a positive air of thankfulness, as if at an escape. One young gentleman, comparing notes with others in town, declared that the real name of McNab's ward was Miss Deer.

Late in the autumn, at the close of what the laird's own humor called "this stalking season," his wife felt it time to question the object of all this concern. She decided to be blunt. She had come to realise that her stratagem had too much of the coy about it. There was too much sweet and cream in the brose, and too little honest Highland spirit. Moreover she had a poor opinion of the candidates for Ellie's hand. McNab had done his best, no doubt, but it was plain that unwary bachelors of the right kind were not to be found in every Halifax countinghouse.

Ellen had just returned from one of her lone walks, with a plaid shawl wrapped about her shoulders against the cool October air. To seaward the boats of the fishermen were busy netting the fall run of mackerel, the large fat fish that appeared now, just as the cod were leaving the coast for the deeper water of the Banks. On the island the laird and his boys, with their dogs and their light fowling guns, were having sport with the fall flight of wild ducks and geese and grouse and woodcock. Hardwood trees in autumn hues painted a band about the fir woods, and their leaves began to flutter away on the breeze. It was in many ways the best time of year, with bright busy days, and brisk starry nights to give pleasure at the fireplace, where dry birch and maple logs leaped in flames to the chimney.

At Joanna's question Ellen gave her a dark loch-deep look and a smile. It was not the usual faint smile of her lips but one that parted the full width of her mouth, and her teeth flashed like the white crest of a sea in a sudden ray of sunlight. Jo thought, *Why on earth doesn't she smile like that for young men? Is it because her mouth's a bit wide for the fashion nowadays?*

"Jo," said Ellen Dewar, "you'll think I'm stupid, and of course I am, for I didn't catch on to your matchmaking till about the fourth man—whatever his name was. The plump young man in blue, with the mop of curls—I'm sure he twisted his hair in papers every night. From then on I felt like Penelope in the Odyssey book. Only my suitors came one at a time."

"And you didn't find them interesting?"

"Oh, they were interesting enough, Jo. Especially when I knew what they were coming for. I was puzzled at first, mind, and then a bit frightened. But after that I just felt I was walking about on a stage in a playhouse, with a quaint comedy going on. Most of them were absurd—you must have seen that for yourself. For example that Hobbs man, the one who strutted so in his buckskin breeches and half-boots, trying to ape the military fops of Halifax, even to the forage cap and that frock coat with the enormous frogs and buttons! Or Mr. Goswell, the one who kept talking about his tallow chandlery, and saying his business was to lighten other people's darkness—just like that solemn owl of a New Light preacher that came out to see Mr. McNab last year.

"And then the polite widower, Mr. Pendleton, so nearsighted he all but doffed his hat to one of Auntie's nightgowns drying on the line. And the poetic young man from the Commissary Office, I forget his name too, though Heaven knows he was the only one that came to the proposing point. Begging me to be seated on a rock by the shore, and standing off a little way and leaning forward, with a face as pale as wax, and eyes turned up in his head —he looked exactly like the figurehead of the *Caesar*—and mumbling a lot of words he must have memorized out of a book. I slipped away through the trees with a hand on my mouth lest I laugh like a loon bird; and he was yet at his speech the last I heard of him."

At this point Jo's Irish blood flowed to her head and issued in laughter at the pitch of her voice, and Ellen joined in with her contralto tones. They sat leaning against each other, with the laughter running on and on, a quite musical duet. Their eyes glittered with tears, and at every fresh gust of hilarity their breasts leaped like wild creatures trapped in their bodices. They might have been sisters in their teens, delirious over some girlish nonsense. At last they fell silent, and Jo said in a shaky voice, "But surely, of them all, there must have been one you liked a bit?"

Ellen put up a slim finger and drew the last tears down to her mouth, first from the right eye, then the left. "Jo, the only one I liked even a bit was the lawyer's clerk, Thurston, the one with the sharp eyes and beak of a corbie crow. The moment we were alone he told me he'd no wish whatever to tramp miles of pastures and woods and beaches, and he guessed I hadn't either. At the law he said he'd learned to sniff intrigue at a mile, and here on Mr. McNab's domain he sniffed a romantic little plot, with me as chief victim. Did I wish to be a victim? I said No. And we returned to the house and that was the end of that."

Joanna was frowning, now that the merriment had gone out of her. "Ellie, when you say No like that you make it sound like the shut of a door. As if it wasn't in you to say Yes to any man, ever. Don't you want a husband and bairns, like me?"

Ellen herself was quiet again. After a time she murmured, "Like you, Jo? Oh dear, yes. But it was all so easy and so natural for you. I mean, you'd known Peter ever since you were boy and girl on the island, before he went away to Scotland for his learning. When he came back, how could either of you help being dipped in love? And from there to marriage was just going up a stair together without even thinking what was at the top. But me! If I'm to have a husband it seems I must make myself agreeable to a lot of strange men, and if one of them fancies me or my *tocher*—oh yes, Jo, I soon guessed about the *tocher*—he takes me to wife. Which means, after the parson's made it proper, I must go to bed with the man that very night and every night, and obey his every wish, as the wedding vow says I must." Ellie shivered. "Why, the mere notion of doffing my clothes to a man, and letting him . . ."

"Ellie!"

"Ah, you think I'm too kittle! The fearful innocent! Jo, whatever else I may be, I'm no innocent. Far from it. I've learned a lot of things on this island that had nothing to do with innocence. I don't mean gossip of the tacksmen and their wives and daughters, though heaven knows they're not o'ergiven to modesty in their lives or in talk amongst themselves. No, dear Jo, I mean visitors from town, and especially some of those fine ladies who come here on summer parties with their Army and Navy friends. Oh, they're gey polite, and circumspect when Mr. McNab's about, or you. But by themselves—Jo, you'd not believe what I've seen and heard in my quiet flitting along the wood paths, sometimes no more than a stone's cast away from the house, or from a chowder party on the shore—it's that bold. I'll tell you this much. I well understand what went on in Eden's garden—the part that's not explained in Scripture except some daft talk about a snake and fruit. And I'd have to know Adam long, and love him blind, to put myself in Eve's position or even face the thought of it."

Joanna's face went red, as if she herself were the timorous virgin, not this frank young creature beside her. Whatever would Peter say to such talk? The girl herself was quite serene, as if she had said nothing odd for a young lady brought up in the deep shelter of McNab's Presbyterian morality.

She went on calmly, "Tell me, Jo, whose notion was it, this parade of wife-hunters? Not yours, I'm sure. You've too much good sense."

"It was mine," said Jo firmly, "and Peter's and Auntie's—you may blame us all."

"But why did you do it?"

"We—we thought you'd be happier married."

"You want to be rid of me!"

McNab had foretold some such suspicion in the victim of their plot, and Joanna was quick to cry, "Oh, Ellie, no! Never! Married or no, you're one of us, part of the family, and a very precious part to us all. You must believe that, whatever else you think."

The blaze of anger and suspicion still flickered in those eerie Hieland eyes, but the voice was easier as Ellie said with dignity, "Jo, if sometimes I don't seem as blithe as you'd wish, it's my nature; I can't help that, and nor can anybody else."

7

That year 1808, which came to be known as "the time of Ellie's courtiers," was a time of much other concern to the laird. It began on a sour note. In the previous December an ill wind blew into port the *Acasta* frigate, with a hellfire captain charging mutiny against forty-five of his crew. Lawyer Cogswell, meeting the laird in the street, chortled with a breath like a kettle in the frost, "Well,

McNab, this'll make a pretty company on that beach of yours. One gibbet short of a round fifty, counting the four you've got already; and surely the Admiral can find another poor devil somewhere?" Then, seeing the laird's wrath, "Pish, man, calm yourself. The Navy's far too short of hands to hang seamen by the score. The court-martial's set for—what d'you Scotchmen call it—Hogmanay? —the day before New Year. They'll hang one or two for an example and give the rest a lick of the cat, depend on it."

McNab remained in gloomy doubt. He had a nightmare vision of his beach sprouting gibbets like the lantern posts of Barrington Street, and he went to the Hogmanay dinner in very dour trim. His father was one of the early members of the North British Society in the town, and Peter himself was now one of its most prominent members. The weather had to be very bad, or the wind wrong or the ice very dangerous, to keep him from the Hogmanay dinner after Christmas week with his family on the island.

He sat rather silent in that always jolly Scots company at the Fountain Inn, where the tables offered a feast of food and drink, the hearth fires and the candles blazed, a transparency lit with an Argand lamp showed forth the Scottish thistle in brightest green and purple, another glowed with golden letters *A Health to His Majesty,* and a pair of pipers took turns stalking up and down the room. Neither the pipes nor the whiskey could cheer McNab that night, and he was making a poor touch at the food when his friend Forsyth leaned across the table with magic words.

"Ha' ye heard the outcome of the *Acasta* court-martial? Only one man's tae be hanged. Nine get off wi' a flogging. And that's the absolute lot."

"Ah!" McNab turned and beckoned a passing steward to pour him wine. It was time for this relief.

"I've other news," Forsyth said, "though nae doot ye've heard it already from your New York friend, Mister . . ."

"Wheesht! No names!"

Forsyth looked about him. The big room was in a good-natured roar over the feast. "Och, man, we're a' friends here. But ye ken the man I mean."

"Ay, but I've no late word from him."

"Then ye will soon, Para. A wee bird says the Admiral's had a fast despatch from Chesapeake Bay—that Mister Jefferson's proclaimed his embargo on all foreign commerce. So it's come! And now the new trade can commence, eh? And ye'll take a strong hand in it?"

"Ay, but not at my island. I had some thought o' that but decided No. I've not met our new Admiral yet—what's his name, Warren?—but I jalouse he's nae different from the others when it comes to finding hands for his ships."

"Even if he gives his word?"

"Admirals have a habit of giving their word—and letting their press gangs take advantage o't. Imagine American ships wi' full crews, anchored in the lee o' my island hours on end, shifting cargo to Nova Scotia ships on my own charter, also wi' full crews. That's much too close to the admiral and his press—a temptation they couldn't put by. No, no, Forsyth. We'll do this business otherwheres, in bays and creeks well hidden to the west'ard, as far from Halifax as we can get—and as near to our Yankee friends. And now, not a word more!"

Sailing back to the island in the cold flat light of New Year's Day, when even at high noon the shadows fell short on the snowy slopes of the harbor, with the sun far to the south for winter and no warmth in its rays, McNab took note of a man-o'-war boat party busy at the beach point. All through the autumn and early winter he had hoped for a hurricane at the right time of moon to sweep the gibbets away, but the four posts remained with their shriveled horrors in rusty chains. Now there would be five.

"They'll not be tarrin' this 'un," Gahagan said.

"Why not?"

"The weather. He'll keep."

Early that spring, soon after the first of Ellie's hapless suitors came and went, two fishermen in a fast shallop from Cape Sable carried a mysterious note to McNab's office in Water Street. The laird showed it to his factor and growled, "Weel, I'm off!" and departed down the harbor in the smelly caboose of the shallop. The fishermen doused sail in the island cove and stopped at the little wharf long enough for McNab to pick up a boat cloak and a tarpaulin hat, and to inform Jo, "I'm awa' tae see off a new venture, my dear. Back in two or three days."

Eighteen hours later he was sitting in the comfortable cabin of the *Montauk,* of New York, with Captain Luke Phips and one Finley, the skipper of a Nova Scotia brig lying alongside. The hatches were off, and both crews were busy with booms and tackle, swinging cargo from one ship to the other. They lay anchored and moored together in one of the numerous harbors towards the western tip of the province, which ran into the land like the slots of a comb. There were no inhabitants but a few poor fishermen in scattered huts about the shores, and the view was enclosed by ridges of forest and screened by wooded islands from the sea.

In the cabin the three men lifted tumblers of punch mixed from best Jamaica rum, sugar, and the juice of limes brought north by the *Montauk*.

"The Planter's Ruin," said the Nova Scotia skipper whimsically, holding his glass up to the sunshine through the skylight and marking the rich amber tint.

"We should have a toast, eh?" He was a bald-headed man with a broad freckled face and humorous blue eyes.

"Confusion to the French," suggested McNab.

"Ah-ah!" Captain Phips wagged his head, and added, without cracking a smile. "Remember I'm neutral in this war of yours."

"Confusion to Long Tom Jefferson, then?"

"I can think of somethin' better."

"Whatna then?"

The American ran a shrewd glance from one to the other. "Why not Free Trade and Sailors' Rights? Arter all, that's why we're here. An' this is sure enough free trade."

"Free trade, then!" And they drank to that.

"What have ye below?" asked McNab.

"A thousand bar'ls o' prime wheat flour—add or bate a half dozen bar'ls in the count. All best Genesee. Mr. Sparlin' fetched it by wagon along the Mohawk Valley to Albany, an' then down to New York in sloops an' sailin' barges. I wish you could see them Hudson River craft. Up to sixty foot long, lots o' beam for cargo, an' painted rainbow fashion in stripes o' blue an' red an' green an' gold—a pictur' that's a fact. When I git too old for knockin' about salt water, that's what I'd like to be, owner-skipper o' one o' them river craft, movin' along in the breeze atween the high woods an' crags o' the Hudson like a child's toy in a horse

trough. Yes indeed. 'Course the Hudson ain't so calm an' quiet as
it used to be. Somethin' noo. Boat run by steam. I'm not bammin'.
It's a fact. Goes along spinnin' a pair o' water wheels like a grist
mill adrift in a flood. Contraption called the *Clermont* put together
by a feller name o' Fulton, that used to be a painter so I'm told.
She goes clear up to Albany an' back, chimbley smokin', b'iler
fizzin', an' paddles a-clappin' on the water like a hundred Pennsyl-
vany Dutch gals hacklin' flax. She beats the sailboats, but she don't
carry cargo enough to signify; an' she's too dam' dangerous fer
passengers, with that steam-b'iler ready to blow up any minute like
a bumshell with a short fuse. It's a caution what some fellers'll
waste their time an' money at, an' risk their skins to boot, now
ain't it?

"But to get to my cargo. Besides the flour I've got some casks
o' naval stores—Carolina pine tar. Need that bad, your Navy people, now the Rooshians have quit fightin' an' throwed in with
Napoleon an' shut off all the Baltic stuff. That's about all, I guess,
'cept a few small personal ventures o' my own an' the mate's—some
boxes o' good American cheese, an' several gross o' talla candles
an' the like. Here's a copy o' the manifest. As I understand the
deal, I'm to get your cap'n's receipt on this copy, soon's his mate
tallies everything into his own holds, an' the whole payment's to
be made to Mr. Sparlin' through Gustav Almquist & Company,
Saint Bartlemy, West Indies. All right?"

"Ay," said McNab.

"An' I'm to take on ballast here for the light run home. Where
do I pick up that?"

The Nova Scotia captain jerked his head toward the broad stern
window and the view of the harbor. Between the green forest and
the glittering blue water ran the line of stony shore.

"This place here," he grinned, "is where Noah threw out all
the ballast o' the Ark, jist afore the big squall blowed him clear
acrost the flood to Mount Rat-tat-tat."

"Ah!" Captain Phips threw his head back in laughter. This was
whimsy in a familiar vein. "Them Bible fellers never was to home
on water, that's a fact. Look at Jonah fetchin' up in a whale's belly,
on a simple coastin' v'yage that a drunken Injun could ha' made
in a canoe. Or Moses, say. You heard the one about Moses? The

Lord said unto Moses *Luff!* But not bein' a sea boy Moses put his
helm hard up an' run hisself plunk into the bullrushes."

"Tach!" This kind of sea humor always struck McNab as sacrile-
gious, a twiddle of fingers in the face of Providence; and now at
the start of this new venture he wanted all the omens to be pro-
pitious.

"Captain Finley, we'll get down to business, if you please. Here
is a pass, signed by Governor Wentworth, in case you're over-
hauled by any of His Majesty's ships. It confirms your manifest
in regard to the American origin of your cargo, and states you're
on a voyage of importance to His Majesty's government. And here,
too, are protection certificates, signed by the Governor, which you
and your men will show if there's any attempt to press them into
the Fleet. Each certificate states that so-and-so—you'll fill in the
names before you sail—is a member of His Majesty's Nova Scotia
Sea Fencibles, detached on special service, and exempt from im-
pressment while on such service."

"Will these things impress a short-handed frigate cap'n?" asked
Finley cynically.

"They're worth a try," McNab retorted. "Oh, to be sure, the Sea
Fencibles are only a fancy at the present time; but mind, there is
a plan of training our fishermen to serve in shore batteries in case
of war with—um! Well, in case of need, let's say."

They nodded, all three, in a peculiar silence. The notion of
American seamen at war with Nova Scotia seamen seemed pre-
posterous here, with the two crews working cheerfully together.
To Phips indeed the Nova Scotians looked and talked more like
Yankees than his own New Yorkers. McNab, not for the first time,
was impressed by the care and money the Americans spent on their
ships. They stinted nothing. Here in the captain's cabin was good
mahogany furniture, a carpet underfoot, and wall panels of polished yellow satinwood from Florida, separated by slim Grecian
pillars carved in American pine and painted a gleaming white.
The wood beading around the top of the panels and above the
cabin window was carved with great skill to resemble a ship's cable, with anchors at the corners; and on the bulkhead forward was
a magnificent carved and gilded American eagle holding an olive
branch in one claw and bolts of lightning in the other.

So, too, on deck he observed the taut spars, the quality of the rigging and canvas, the generous use of paint. And there were the *Montauk's* crew, obviously better paid and fed than any British seamen. To be sure some signs of their prosperity amused the frugal Nova Scotia men. It was odd to see American seamen with small cigars in their teeth as they worked about the deck, and wearing smart shoregoing top hats with their blue jean smocks and trousers, like town gentlemen in a volunteer fire company. But they went about their work with skill and energy, never wasting a movement or a moment, and they had about them an air of alertness, of interest in what they were doing, as if every man from cook to captain had a personal share in the enterprise.

McNab thought, As good as our best seamen, and better than most. And far better furnished in all ways. If the Yankees haven't got a fleet they've got the men and means of making war of a kind, and the chances are they'd give those gentlemen in London a jolt. But *tach!* Why speculate on *maybe* in America when there's fact to worry about across the sea? That damned Corsican standing taller every day, and throwing a shadow longer and darker. Guid God, how small the British islands look on the map of Europe now!

The fishermen brought him home quickly and safely in their shallop, skimming up the coast on a southerly wind like a gull swooping over the wave tops. Coming in from the seaward, as he had not done for years, the laird noted again how the pink heap of the Thrum Cap got its name. With distaste he noted something else. In going between his home cove and the town, the beach point was at a distance never less than half a mile. But coming in to the cove from the seaward meant rounding the point close-to, and the fishermen grinned and said something rude about the withered fruit of his "orchard." McNab was about to chide them angrily when they all noticed something else. Up the harbor beyond the small green dot of George's Island the anchorage was bristling with tall masts and yards.

"Hello, hello! There's a fleet in," said one of the fishermen. They had the bright unwinking eyes of sea hawks that can mark the smallest thing afar.

"Ay," said the other. "Them yards is much too square for merchantmen. But there's some don't seem to have the man-o'-war furl to their canvas—not tight enough by half. Must be transports.

They movin' sogers, d'ye s'pose? Mind your sheets now, here's where we haul wind for the cove."

Ashore on the island McNab invited them to the house, gave them drams of rum, paid a generous sum in Spanish silver dollars, and ordered the kitchen to provide them with provisions for their return voyage to Cape Sable.

The *Bonnie Jo* lay ready in the cove. In another hour, bathed, shaved, and dressed for a call on what Gahagan termed the Quality, the laird set off for town.

As the sloop passed George's Island he could see the ships closely. None were familiar. Boats packed with redcoats and muskets were putting off from the transports and rowing to the King's Wharf. The common routine of Halifax garrison reliefs was a matter of one regiment at a time. Usually a battalion reduced and sickly from West Indian duty came up to recuperate in the cool northern air, and the returning transport carried a healthy regiment from Halifax to the Caribbean and the deadly breath of yellow jack. But everything about these ships and men showed them to be fresh out from England, and there seemed to be an unusual lot of redcoats.

Walking towards Government House the laird had to pause while a battalion of infantry passed up Prince Street to the music of bugles and drums. Their youth surprised him, and so did their uniforms. Like everyone else in the town he was used to hard-bitten regulars tramping stiffly in pipe-clayed breeches, long black gaiters, red coats whose tails wagged to the knees, and cocked hats jammed hard over greased and powdered hair. These fresh-faced newcomers marched in plain grey trousers—trousers!—with red jackets that merely came to the waist in front, and just covered their behinds. Their hair was cut short, and free of pomade and flour. Their headgear was a black felt cap or shako that looked like a short piece of stovepipe with a leather peak at the lower end to shade the eyes. Altogether the deuce of a rig for a soldier! And even the officers wore it!

"Well, McNab, what are you thinking about?" said a voice in his ear. He turned and saw one of his officer friends in the garrison, dressed in mufti for a social call in the town.

"Ah, Major Corbett, I hardly know what to think. What's all this mean?"

"Well, for one thing it means there's been a healthy sneeze in the dust at the War Office. New dress, new hair, new everything—even a new way to fight. Fact! I'm told there's a general named Moore —Scotchman like yourself—served here as a subaltern during the old American war—John Moore—working out a remarkable new system of field training for officers and men—place called Shorncliffe, near Dover, where they expect Boney to land. You're looking at a new kind of British soldier."

"Ay, but what are they doing here, on the wrong side o' the water?"

"That's the question. It's all been done on the quiet. Nobody here, not even the Governor, received a scratch of pen about this movement till the ships were in the harbor. There's a deuce of a to-do. Fatigue parties pitching tents all over Camp Hill and half the Common. Commissary officers going mad. These new fellers have a general officer with 'em, senior to anybody here, and he gives all the orders now. Name of Prevost. Swiss feller I believe. Joined our Army long ago. Happened to be in command of a little garrison in the West Indies three years back—time of Villeneuve's raid. The French were dodging about to throw Nelson off their track, and they attacked a few of our West Indian posts to establish the scent so to speak.

"Landed a force on the island of Dominica, where Prevost was. Captured the main town and plundered it. Prevost and his fellers had to back away to the mountainside, although they kept shooting till the French went off again. And that was that. Well, the French were off to Europe as it turned out. And then of course Trafalgar. The Navy got a tremendous puff—rightly of course— honors and promotions right and left—but the Army felt a bit put out—'specially those gold-laced fellers at the Horse Guards. I mean, after all, they've made a botch of things and got the Army beat—whatever it tried to do—ever since this war started. Our Army's the best of Boney's jokes. So after Trafalgar the Horse Guards felt they had to puff a bit—honors and promotions wherever they could find an excuse. Amongst others this little cock robin Prevost suddenly found himself a hero—as if his sixpenny-ha'penny post on that dam' little sugar island was the Rock of Gibraltar! So today he's Sir George Prevost if you please, and a Lieutenant General to boot—though till now he'd never com-

manded more than a few companies of infantry in his life. And
now, begad, here he is, with a fleet and several thousand troops—
and nobody knows what for."

"Umf!" McNab watched the files of slanted muskets going by,
and the nimble grey legs swinging up the slope towards Camp
Hill. "Trousers! Tongs, as the slang goes. I can remember when
nobody but carters and sailors wore tongs. Even five years ago a
gentleman wouldn't be found dead in 'em, 'specially an Army or
Navy gentleman. And now they're all the rage. Mind, I can see a
point for soldiers. These lads can start fast and travel far, ay, and
fight well at the journey's end, something they never could do in
tight breeks and sixteen-button gaiters." He gave the major a
pawky look. "We Hielandmen found that out long ago, wi' the
kilt."

The last of the column went past, treading in the dust aroused
by foregoing legs. Already the sound of the bugles and drums was
dying away.

"Weel, I must get along to see the Governor," McNab said.

"You don't mean Wentworth?"

"Who else?"

"I've more news for you, my friend. Sir George isn't merely the
new C-in-C of His Majesty's forces in Nova Scotia—he's brought
his commission as Lieutenant Governor."

"What! D'ye mean Wentworth's out?"

"Of course! After all, Wentworth's had a long reign—he's an
old man—stiff in the neck as well as the joints. I don't imagine
many will shed tears for him or m'lady. Good afternoon, sir."

They tipped hats and parted, the laird in haste to Granville
Street and Government House. As he stepped through the tall
gateway into the walled garden a wide central path led the eye at
once to the handsome entrance; he noticed the main doors open,
a scurry of servants within, and a smart carriage-and-pair waiting
by the portico. Nobody answered his polite pull on the bell. Nobody noticed him at all. He entered the stately stone house, found
nobody in the drawing rooms, and walked through to the rear
door, where most of the voices seemed to be. It opened on the
quiet residential lane called Pleasant Street, and in the graveled
half circle of the tradesmen's entrance stood eight or ten wagons
and horses. The ground about them was stacked and littered with

trunks, portmanteaus, bandboxes, pictures, mirrors, and furniture, with more coming out of the door every minute.

Sir John stood in the midst of this confusion, a stooped pot-bellied figure with none of his customary dignity, barking orders to servants and wagoners. He noticed McNab at last, and drew him inside.

"This is a forced retreat, as the military say, and that's my baggage train. My library's evacuated already, so I'm afraid we must talk in here." He led the way into a small chamber furnished with a plain pine table and a pair of pine benches. There was a threadbare drugget on the floor, and the lone ornament on the walls was a cheap framed print of King George. Obviously a waiting room for tradesmen at the Governor's back door.

Sir John closed the chamber door, waved McNab to one of the benches, and sat down heavily on the other. "No doubt you've heard the news. I'm deposed—retired—turned out, with no more notice than I'd give a thieving footman. The new man, Prevost, came ashore and showed me his commissions as Commander-in-Chief and Lieutenant Governor, handed me a letter from Lord Castlereagh, and asked how soon I could move out. Castlereagh was cold and polite. Said that present conditions made it necessary to have a soldier in the Governor's seat. Thanked me for my long service to His Majesty's government. I'm to get a pension of £500 a year from London, and His Lordship trusts that the provincial assembly and council will provide a similar amount. He trusts! You know the assembly."

McNab felt embarrassed by these bitter disclosures. As a merchant he had been irked in the past by Lady Wentworth's lofty airs towards anyone "in trade," and while Sir John had more of the common touch he was inclined to be an autocrat, using his position and patronage to benefit himself, his friends and relatives. And despite all that he had never been able to keep up with his lady's extravagances. The man was notoriously deep in debt.

"Where are you going?" McNab asked, for want of anything else to say.

"To the Prince's Lodge at Bedford Basin. That's something they can't take away from me. His Highness"—Wentworth paused for a moment as if to doff an invisible hat in reverence—"presented me with the Lodge when he removed from here to

England. Of course the grounds were mine in any case, I bought them a good many years ago and had a little summer house on a knoll overlooking the water—the Prince made it into a bandstand after he built the Lodge on the slope behind. Well, as I say, we're removing there. It'll be rather inconvenient in the winter, six miles from town. His Highness used to turn out the garrison with shovels whenever a snowstorm blocked the road, but of course I can't do that, and I doubt if Prevost would turn out a drummer boy for any concern of mine. What was it you came to see me about?"

"The—um—American goods to Britain. We've made the first shipment, and I wanted to discuss future plans."

"Ah! Well, you'll have to take that up with my successor, although I daresay as a soldier his head will be too full of muskets and gunpowder to leave room for such things as corn-meal and cotton."

At this moment a servant rapped on the door and put his head inside.

"Beg pardon, sir, Her Ladyship's carriage is about to leave for the Lodge, and she wishes a word with you."

Wentworth jumped up, gave McNab's hand a brief shake, and hurried away towards the front of the house. And that, thought the laird, is the story of your life, my good sir, always on the busy foot at the beck of a shallow woman. He left by the tradesmen's entrance, with an ironic set of mouth, and walked by way of Barrington and George streets to the wharf and the *Bonnie Jo*.

Whatever filled the new viceroy's head kept him very busy. When McNab had an interview with him at last it was mid-summer—and not at Government House. One hot afternoon Ellen Dewar, sitting in the shade of the willows before the island house, watched a vessel enter the mouth of the cove. It was the slow black-hulled ketch that carried stores once a week to the forts at Point Pleasant and York Redoubt. A stop at McNab's island was very unusual, and so were the two passengers who came ashore in cocked hats and plumes, scarlet frock coats with much gold lace, white buckskin breeches and polished black riding boots. As they stepped up the path towards the house they flamed in the sunshine like a pair of scarlet macaws.

Ellie Dewar suspected more suitors, although she had not been

advised to prepare herself for visitors, the usual warning which
had the force of an order. So she was free to stay or flee. She did
not hesitate. With the flit of a squirrel her gown-tail vanished
around the house and along the wood path towards Back Cove.
In another moment McNab himself saw the officers approaching,
and hastened out of doors to meet them.

He knew the General at once. It was not merely the gold lace
and the finer cloth that marked him, it was the air of authority not
to be questioned, the air that generals and admirals gave off like
sparks wherever they went. Prevost was a man of ordinary height
with a neat figure and a very good leg for his tight white
breeches. A small Roman nose, sallow complexion, bright hazel
eyes—McNab was noting everything as they approached each other
—a mouth that could be severe but at the moment wore a pleasant
expression, age about forty. Um!

"Sir George Prevost, I'm sure!" he said, putting out his hand.
"An unexpected pleasure, sir."

"Mr. McNab?" Sir George shook hands. "May I introduce
Major Bowyer, my A.-D.-C.?" McNab shook hands with the major, a shorter man on the plump side, with a pair of cold grey eyes.

"I came out to inspect York Redoubt," said the General. His
English was fluent and crisp, but there was an accent here and
there of a man whose native tongue was French. "And while over
there I had a look at your island through the telescope. It seems
to me we should have a few guns on this side of the channel. The
redoubt is all very well as the outer defense against, say, ships-of-
the-line. Indeed it's impregnable, sir. No ship cannon could fire
at that elevation. But the strongest point about York is also the
weakest—the guns up so high. It's possible for some daring small
craft to slip into the anchorage under those guns, keeping close
to the western shore. I've seen it done, sir, in the West Indies,
so I speak from experience. There should be some sort of battery
—if only a light one—on this side of the channel, where the guns
could cover the water under York."

"The best spot for that," said the laird quickly and joyfully,
"would be the end of yon stony beach, where the gibbets are."
This was quite true, and it seemed to him at once that a squad of
gunners on the point would find the dead men ill company—and

the dead would have to go, Admiralty Court or no Admiralty Court.

"Exactly!" said the General. "And that's why I've called, Mr. McNab. I believe you are sole owner of this island, and naturally the Crown would purchase the battery site from you, or secure a waiver of your rights. I would like to be able to state in my report the owner's valuation. The sooner the report goes off to London the sooner we can expect action from the Board of Ordnance."

"Ah!" McNab's smile was a little rueful. "My father thought he owned yon beach when he bought the island, and so did I—till about three years ago. Then the Admiral decided to put a gibbet there, and I found that under the laws of Admiralty the beach is public domain. However," he went on eagerly, a little too eagerly, "that makes it all the simpler for you, sir, doesn't it? I mean to say, the Board of Ordnance has only to inform the Admiralty that you intend to fortify the beach point. After all, it's for the protection of the anchorage—the advantage of the Fleet. Personally I'm delighted."

Sir George regarded him carefully. The only Scotchmen in his experience had been Caribbean traders, gaunt and yellow, always trying to sell something. Nothing delighted them but money. The officers in York Redoubt had told him this one was a gentleman.

"Understand, Mr. McNab, this is merely a notion, one of several notions for improving the defenses of the port. And all must be approved in London—and Ordnance may think Halifax has guns enough. Well, we shall see." He gazed about him, noting the sheep in the fields, the shelter groves, the stone house on the knoll and its trees and garden. "And this is where you live, eh? A pretty spot, but somewhat out of the way I should think."

"It has its advantages, General. And of course friends come to visit me. Indeed here by chance I have the Governor himself— and may I ask him to do my house the honor of taking a glass of wine beneath my roof?"

Sir George was about to refuse politely. He had found out what he wanted to know, and with his experience of joint operations with the Navy in the Caribbean he was fussy about a boat kept waiting—even the garrison storeketch, which spent most of its time tied up at the King's Wharf in town. However it was a warm day

and the right time of afternoon for a cool sip of something, and
he was curious to see more of this merchant who, according
to the commander of York Redoubt, lived on his island like a
Highland chief.

"That's extremely genteel of you, Mr. McNab. I shall be happy
to take a glass with you, and so I'm sure will Major Bowyer."

Joanna was in the drawing room as the officers entered, and the
laird introduced them. A servant brought Madeira freshly decanted from the cask in the cool depths of the cellar, and drew
from a sideboard a silver tray and glasses. Sir George offered a
polite toast to the laird and his lady, and they chatted together
of small matters. After a time Jo withdrew. As soon as she was
gone McNab turned to the General with a keen look. "Sir George,
a question's buzzing in my bonnet. May I be so bold as to ask it?"

"Of course! What I answer depends on the question."

"I'm wondering what all this is about—all this defense business,
the new troops, and the ships?" He added with a frank Highland
grin, "I shan't be insulted if I'm told it's none of my affair."

The two officers glanced at each other, and Prevost said
suavely, "And I shan't be so rude, sir. I think it *is* your business.
I noticed your name in one or two of the secret service documents
that Sir J. Wentworth turned over to me. You are engaged in confidential relations with certain American merchants at the present time, I believe, with regard to supplies for Britain. You see,
I have been studying my new responsibilities on the civil side, as
well as the military! In view of those relations, Mr. McNab, you
know the present tensions between His Majesty's government and
that of the United States. Has it occurred to you that these tensions are leading straight to war? And that the war might come
very quickly?—like a thief in the night? If you have thought of
these things at all you can surely guess what all this is about."

"You mean you expect an American attack?" McNab said.
"Here? But that's impossible!"

"Ah! Exactly what the Admiral says—the Americans can't get
here by sea because they've no fleet—and they can't travel by land
because it's such a tremendous distance through the forest around
the Bay of Fundy. Aha! But who's to be sure they can't march
that tremendous distance? *Hein?* When the Americans fought us
before they had no navy and not much of an army—but they

marched all the way through the forest to Canada, captured Montreal, and came within a powder-pinch of taking Québec. Nobody thought they could get half the distance but they did. The truth is, distance means nothing to them, and they relish difficulties. When I was a subaltern I served with senior officers who'd fought the Americans in that war, everywhere from Carolina to Canada; and I learned from them never to underestimate the Yankees, and never to be surprised by anything they did."

The General sipped at his wine. "Wonderful Madeira, this. Nothing like a long sea voyage to mellow Madeira, *hein?* All that rocking, day and night, in the cask. I discovered that in the West Indies. Well! What was I talking about? Ah yes, the Yankees. Living in that enormous country of theirs, they think nothing of five hundred or a thousand miles. They are men with seven-league boots on their minds as well as their feet. For example! This is most confidential, Mr. McNab, you must not breathe a word of it. The other day a mysterious 'Mr. Edwards' arrived in Halifax from New York. He came to Government House and asked for a private conference with Admiral Warren and myself, on a matter of great importance."

He paused again, with a careful eye on the laird. "You have close dealings with certain gentlemen in New York. Do you know who this man was?"

"I couldn't even hazard a guess, sir."

"Then this will surprise you as much as it did me. He was Mr. Burr—the famous or infamous Aaron Burr. The former Vice-President of the United States, who might have been President. The man who killed Alexander Hamilton in a duel. In recent times he got into trouble with his government over a wild scheme for seizing Louisiana and Mexico and setting himself up as an emperor or something of the sort. He was tried for treason and acquitted, but the disgrace remains, and he's decided to go abroad. You are wondering what brought him here. Apparently he'd heard of a gathering of British troops and ships at Halifax. So he came to unfold another scheme. That we—Admiral Warren and I—sail down to Florida and seize the Spanish possessions there. After all we're at war with Spain, are we not? And—he didn't labor the point but it was there—with British forces well established in Florida, the American war party would have to pause and think a bit. They'd have the British on two sides of them instead of one."

Prevost sat back in the chair and enjoyed McNab's obvious astonishment.

"You see? This Burr. Typical American mind. A thousand miles—nothing!"

"How did you answer him?" blurted the laird.

A shrug. "The Admiral thought the man was mad. But of course Warren's a sailor with no sense of the land. I was inclined to agree with him at first, but then my sense as a soldier came back. After all, Burr as a young man was one of those very Americans in that amazing march to Canada, the men who nearly made it part of the United States. With such men what's impossible? You certainly can't put them down as mad. So we bundled him off to England, with a letter to Lord Castlereagh. I don't mind telling you, Mr. McNab, that the more I think of this Florida notion the more feasible it seems. The Spanish garrisons are small and lazy and scattered about a very long coast, open to any attack by sea. No doubt they have spies watching our forces in the West Indies. But we would come down from the far north with our troops and ships—out of nowhere so to speak. One rattle of gunfire, one sight of bayonets coming up the beaches, and all would be over."

"And what then?" said McNab.

"We'd summon an occupation force from the various British garrisons in the West Indies, a large number as no doubt you know. We'd then return to Nova Scotia with these ships and men. It's important, in the main, that I keep my force poised here. This province is a pistol pointed down the American east coast from Boston to Philadelphia. You have only to look at the map."

"And what about the Americans while all this is going on?"

"They wouldn't like it, naturally. Ever since Napoleon sold Louisiana to them for a few tons of silver dollars they've had an eye on Florida. But once we're there, and established, what can they do? There isn't a road in the whole of Florida. Most of the country's a swamp. You travel by sea or not at all. And that's the answer to your question. The Americans have no fleet worth mention. We have."

"You make it sound very simple, sir."

"Of course it's very simple! And once our forces are in Florida

the war party in the United States will have to change their plan
of seizing Canada. They'll have to look two ways at once. You
are a sportsman, I believe, Mr. McNab. You must know that a
fowler watching two birds at once will bring down neither. The
Americans know that, too. This could be the solution to the problem of His Majesty's government at the present time—how to
stave off a war with the Americans without giving up our blockade
of supplies to France."

McNab contemplated his glass with arched brows and a staring
eye, as if the fine Madeira had turned a little sour. According to
the news of the past few years, His Majesty's forces had been
chasing gaudy birds in all directions and bringing nothing down
—Denmark, Turkey, Egypt, South America, and a hundred smaller
ship-and-shore affairs—all adding up to the cost of a vast defeat
without a bullet's damage to Napoleon. He guessed shrewdly now
that Prevost's large reward for a petty West Indian affair was
leading the man to dream of further glories with another cheap
campaign to the south.

Some of these reflections must have shown in his face, for Sir
George leaped up suddenly and clicked his heels. The easy and
expansive man had vanished, and it was a curt soldier who said
with the French accent, "Thank you, sir, and *au revoir*. If London
approves the new battery you will be aware of it in due course,
when my sappers and gunners are at work on the beach point."
And off he went past the shady willows to the cove and the waiting ketch, with the A.-D.-C. trotting at his heels.

Joanna came into the room. "What was in the General's mind?
Not just a taste of your Madeira, I'll be bound."

McNab chuckled. She had been standing just beyond the door,
like any inquisitive wife. "He wants tae set some cannon and
gunners where the Admiral feeds the corbies."

"What does that mean?"

"The last o' the hangman here, I hope."

8

Ellen Dewar was happy when winter came. She always enjoyed
the sting of the cold, the skating on the lagoon behind the beach,
the tramping on snowshoes, and afterwards the warmth of the
house, the sheltered nest, the fortress besieged but valiant and
content. And now something else, more important than all that.
The cold weather meant that no more uneasy strangers would
come a-courting until another summer. After the hysterical conversation with Joanna the matter of marriage had not been mentioned by anyone in her presence, but she sensed it still in the
minds of the McNabs, and dreaded the coming of spring.

Early in December, just before the onset of the real cold and
the deep snows, Sir George Prevost had marched his troops from
their drafty tents on Camp Hill to the ships, and the fleet with
stiff and frosty sails had passed McNab's domain and vanished
over the edge of the cold pewter platter of the Atlantic. Where
were they going? The only hint was a number of large flat-bottomed boats for landing infantry on shallow beaches, made by
the dockyard carpenters. As the winter deepened, so did the mystery. There was no news.

March came at last, and the first soft winds and rains. When
the sky cleared, the snow decayed, and on the higher pastures the
brown sod began to show, and the first robins whistled about the
clearings. Suddenly McNab's ewes were in the throes of lambing.
This was the anxious time for the shepherds. A dangerous chill
lurked in the shadow of the woods where snow remained, and
over the pastures hovered the watchful eagles and ravens and
crows.

Many ewes ignored the shelter of McNab's lambing sheds, placed
with care about the island, and crept away to give birth in the
shoreside thickets of spruce and fir. Ellen Dewar joined in the daily
search for new-born lambs and exhausted ewes. Often there was
a black flurry of ravens tearing at the dead flesh of a ewe, and a

frightened lamb crouching in half darkness under the gnarled firs,
where snow survived like a stale grey breadcrust. Often Ellen
struggled back to the house carrying a motherless lamb in her
arms, just like McNab's tacksmen, who vowed she was the finest
shepherd of them all.

Then the lambing was past and so was the snow. A *pop-pop* of
fowling guns marked the laird and his sporting visitors and dogs
searching alder coverts for the spring flight of woodcock. One
afternoon, when the sun was warm in the Back Cove, Ellen sat
dreaming on the old grey wreck-mast by the shore, and Rory Mac-
Dougal came limping out of the woods by the path, and sat beside
her. These meetings were habit now. Rory's visits, regular as the
tides, had become part of his water journeys to the Northwest
Arm and Melville Island. The Agent for Prisoners was now a
vindicated prophet and he bore himself accordingly. The success
of his experiment with captives in the fish shed had impressed
Admiral Warren, the Admiral had written to London, and the
Transport Office had agreed to build a wooden prison, a little
Dartmoor, on the Melville Island site. Most of the old fishery
buildings had been torn down last autumn, and now that the snows
were gone the new prison was rising fast in a swarm of carpenters
and masons.

"By summer," Rory said proudly, "she'll be ready. No more
hulks. A decent place to keep my puir de'ils at last."

"Tell me about it," Ellen said dreamily. Her eyes were on the
surf at Devil's Island, fluttering like white fans in the sunshine.

"Oh, a barrack big enough to hold a thousand men easy—twice
that in a pinch—depends on what room ye allow to a hammock,
d'ye see, same as in a ship. Think of her as a man-o'-war the same
size as Lord Nelson's *Victory,* a hundred and fifty feet measured
at the keel, and fifty in the beam. Only two decks, o' course; but
wi' the whole space given over to the men—no cannon or store-
rooms or officers' cabins or anything o' that-like. She'll be a ship-o'-
the-line hard aground, wi' her masts and rigging gone and a roof
instead, and windows where her gunports used to be.

"And I'll run her like a man-o'-war. First thing in the morning
turn up all hands to lash hammocks and carry 'em out to sun and
air. Then make 'em swab down both decks, fore and aft—floors if
ye like. Once a week they'll go over 'em wi' holystones as well. All

doors and windows opened whiles the prisoners move about the yard. Except in winter, o' course. But ye've got to keep a ship clean and well ventilated if ye want a healthy crew. I'll divide the men into messes o' six or a dozen, each mess to choose its man each week to draw their rations. There'll be cookhouses in the prison yard. No fires in the prison itself except stoves to heat the place in winter.

"I'll grant parole by the day or the month to men I can trust, so they may find work outside and earn money for luxuries. Government work on the roads. All kinds o' jobs in the town, from cooks to dancing masters. Men must ha' something useful to pass the time or they drift into mischief or go melancholy-mad. I keep in mind the war's a long time going now, and may last Boney's lifetime. And they say he's just rising forty and sound as a brick. D'ye know, sometimes I wonder what the outcome of it all will be."

Ellen had heard all this before, and so had everyone in Halifax, and like everyone else she let MacDougal ramble on. At last he ran down, like a big mahogany clock whose weights have reached the bottom of the case. His gaze like the girl's was to the sea. The offshore wind furnished the waves with white crests that seemed to be hurrying off to a mysterious rendezvous under the horizon. The sky was the clear light blue of Rory's eyes except for a bunch of clouds like a swollen hand, with fingers frayed out to feathers by the wind.

"Mister MacDougal . . ."

"Na, lass, Rory!"

"Rory then. Rory, how old do you take me for?"

"Old?" he smiled. "That's a word ye needna think about; Ellie. You're only a gel yet, touching twenty. I weel mind ye as a bairn just out fra Scotland a few years back. I had employ at the dockyard then, and Mr. McNab brought me out here on a visit, the first time I ever set foot on the island."

"I am past four-and-twenty," Ellen said with impatience, "and the family think it's high time I was married."

The Agent for Prisoners gave her a side glance and fingered the old scar in his cheek, a habit when he was uneasy.

"You must have noticed all those young men coming here the past summer," she went on in a thin pitched voice, unlike her usual tones.

"Ay."

"Did you guess what they came for?"

"Ay, after a time I had suspicion."

Silence, except the west wind in the fir tops, and the swash of the tide at half ebb, tumbling yellow mops of bladder-wrack on the dark beach stones.

"Ye fancied one, no doubt," Rory said.

"I fancied none whatever."

"What was wrong?"

"Me. The family think so, anyhow."

"Weel, ye've a long whiles yet tae make up your mind on a husband."

"I'm afraid not, Rory. Not by all the talk I've heard among women since I was a child. A lass not married by twenty-five will get a poor chance after. She'll be an old maid to her death, as like as not. It's not the same with a man—a man can marry at any age. Can he not?"

"I suppose so, ay, in a general way, if he finds a woman willin'. But men get auld too, Ellie."

"What's your age, Rory?"

"Fifty-four."

"Is that old for a man?"

"Some say a man fifty's still in his prime."

"Does that mean he could marry a young wife and give her bairns?"

Her face was turned away now, but he could see a red rush under the light tan on her cheek. Suddenly he sensed a drift in this talk and there were two selves at strife in him, one a lad of Ellie's age, yearning and eager, the other a battered veteran of life and war muttering *This is none o' yours.*

Aloud he stammered, "Ay—ay, that could be."

She paused, with her face still turned away. Then in the small high voice: "Have you ever thought of taking another wife, Rory?"

"I suppose it crossed my mind a time or two."

"You've never felt lonely at all, at all?"

"Oh ay, I've felt that, many's the time."

Ellie turned her thin flushed face to him, and her black eyes gazed deep into his honest blue. "You need a wife then, Rory. Would I do?"

He heard himself muttering, "I'm an auld lame hulk of a man, lassie—and you a flower just out o' bud." And after a pause, in a sharp voice, "Besides, what the de'il would McNab say?"

Her eyes held his and would not let them go. There was a force in them that astonished him, and even made him afraid. She seemed no longer a slip of a girl but a woman with the knowledge of ages. The transformation was uncanny. His big hands opened and closed as if they longed for a rope to grasp, like a sailor caught in a boarding sea.

"But you're willing?" she insisted, not in the small voice any more but with the firm tone of a woman who has put all qualms aside, has weighed and figured everything, and is confident in her reckoning.

"Ay. But . . ."

"Then listen to me, Rory. The McNabs will be surprised, no doubt, but when they've got over it they'll approve. You're a good man—they know that—and a Scotsman—that's important. And it's their wish to see me married and settled." She paused and looked down, with half-closed eyes, at the hands clasped tight in her lap, so tight that the blood was hardly in them at all. "Of course, we'll not be over-hasty. The notion of marriage will take some getting used to, before and after. What I'd like now is to say we're be-trothed and have not quite decided when we'll wed. That will do to go on with."

His face was so amazed and troubled that she had a stab of conscience. *Using poor Rory for my own ends. Anything to stave off another summer like last.* But the stab was only momentary. *After all I'm not planning a deceit. I'll wed him when the time comes.* And when would that be? She could see the question in his eyes, wide and simple as a child's.

"Rory, I once heard something from McCallum's wife, a hu-morous woman and wise. She was talking of the coming of love. 'It's like cream in the churn. Ye may dash the churn as hard as ye like, but ye canna hurry the butter. That turns in its own way and finds its own moment.' That's how it must be with me—with us."

"How are we to tell this to McNab?" he said bluntly. For all the easy friendship of years he had a Highlander's awe of the laird.

She replied in that calm firm voice which had no doubts. "You'll go your ways now to Melville Island or wherever, and leave the telling to me. I'll first give the news to Mrs. McNab and Auntie. They will tell Mr. McNab. Then he'll demand to hear it from my own mouth, and I'll do that. On your next visit to the island, choose a time when the laird is sure to be here; and we'll stand together, you and I, and say it again before him. By that time he'll have got over the first surprise and he'll see it's for the best."

Rory nodded rather glumly for an affianced lover. "I'd rather face him first myself, Ellie. Why the de'il should I run off tiptoe as if I'd a bad conscience and let a lassie do my talking for me?"

"Because that's the only sensible way to go about it. I know the laird."

"Weel," he said heavily, "I'll be on my way then."

He shifted his footing for the effort to rise, favoring the game leg, and braced a hand on the log between himself and the girl. Suddenly Ellen put a hand on his. In all their acquaintance it was the first time one of them had touched the other. MacDougal paused for several moments as if wondering what to do. Her black gaze was on his face, unwavering, but whether in trust or challenge or what he did not know. At last he turned his hand and took the small one in his clasp, looking down at it almost with pity. Then he lifted it to his lips, with a quite natural gesture, as if he had been doing it all his life, like a—like a damned Frenchman. Then he was up and away without a backward glance.

The girl arose and smoothed her skirts. She sauntered slowly along the wood path. When at last she stepped into the house Rory and his sloop were a speck in the wind towards Point Pleasant.

To Jo and Aunt Frances she announced her betrothal with a careless ease, as if it were something of no great moment. Joanna was startled, not so much by Ellie's calm admission as by the revelation of MacDougal—Old Square-Foot—wanting such young flesh. With the quick imagination of the Irish she could fairly see the goat feet and the horns. And she foresaw the indignation of McNab.

As soon as Ellen left the room Jo uttered the question that somehow she could not ask the girl herself. "How long has this been going on?" Aunt McNab answered casually, "They've been meeting by the Back Cove, off and on, the past year—maybe more. Don't look so put about. MacDougal had a girl wife long syne. She died and he's been a lone man since. And can you not see the image that must have come to Ellie's mind, not all at once, and not yet clear, like something in a misty looking-glass? The father she never knew. The love and protection she wished for all her young days, a kind not even you or Peter could provide. Ah yes. And is it wrong? You know how kittle she was about the young men. She knows Rory to be kind and gentle. She could love him as she never could anyone else."

"Love him as a woman—as a wife?" cried Jo, still incredulous.

"Eventually, yes. They're man and woman, are they not? But that's a delicate subject, and we'll say no more of it."

The laird's reception of the news from Jo was not so much in anger as disbelief.

"Ellie and MacDougal? *MacDougal?*"

"Yes!"

"Are ye sure it's not a prank? A daft whimsy on her part?" McNab had never forgotten her visit to the hanged man, and he retained his suspicion that poor Ellie had a hidden disorder of the mind.

"I'm convinced of it. So is Auntie. The girl wants an older man. That's why she shied away from the others you brought out here."

The laird scowled. "And the aulder man wanted her, it seems. Was that honorable—courting my ward behind my back?"

"Now Peter, stop bristling. I doubt if Rory knew what was happening to a simple friendship till the girl made up her mind. Women do that, you know. Remember, I'd set my mind on you long before you knew what was afoot."

Jo was at her old game, teasing him out of his glooms and anger, and she won.

He put up a hand and stroked her hair. "My bonnie spider wi' the golden threads. And ye think it's all right—Ellie and Rory Mac?"

"I do."

"No matter what ails her mind?"

"Ellie's not daft, I've told you that. And once she's settled and happy that touch of the fey will take care of itself. It happens often with young women a bit on the sensitive. I confess I was astonished when she first told me about herself and Rory. Auntie wasn't. And now you see the light yourself. Say it!"

"Ay. Ay. I suppose so. And when's the wedding?"

"I don't know. The girl says nothing except they're betrothed. Knowing Ellie I'd say she wants time and acquaintance yet before she'll take Rory to the marriage bed. And she's other things to get used to. She'll hate the thought of leaving the island. We and our people are the only folk she knows, and she'd feel lost in the town. And for myself, I'd miss her company. So would you and all of us. I have an idea. Couldn't you build a cottage for her and Rory, here on the island, when the time comes? Now that Rory's prisoners are all to be housed up the Arm he might as well live here as in the town."

"True! True! And where should I build this love nest?"

Joanna thought a minute. "On the Back Cove. It's pretty there, just a short walk through the woods but well away from everyone."

"Ay, they seem to have discovered that," McNab said dourly. "And shall I build it now? Or in the summer? Or when?"

"Nothing now. Rory will be busy all this summer with finishing his precious prison, the cookhouses, the guardhouses and all the rest he's been havering about, the past year; and then the job of moving the prisoners out of the hulks and up the Arm. Besides I have a strong notion Ellie intends one more winter on her lone. You can build the cottage after that."

"And what about the *tocher?*"

"You'll build the cottage and furnish it well, that goes without saying; and I think a wedding gift of, say, a hundred guineas, would be very nice."

"Ye seem tae have it all worked out, woman. Does Rory Mac know aught of this—the cottage an' the *tocher?*"

"Nothing. And you mustn't breathe a word of it when he comes to face you with Ellie in a day or two. Let things be as they are. And for the love of all the saints be kind to them."

"Not even a bit of sarcasm for the relish of it?"

"Don't you dare!"

As it turned out McNab had no chance to dare anything when MacDougal came to the cove on the weekend. Ellen went to meet him, and drew him by the hand into the house. The laird awaited them in his library, puffing at a long clay and wrapped in smoke like Jehovah on the mountain. Rory barely had time to blurt out, "Muster McNab, sir, I have come to say . . ." when young Sheamus McNab burst into the room on the run. He pulled up sharply, kilt in a swirl, and cried "Father! Quick! The sea's alive wi' sails!"

The long pipestem snapped in three pieces as the laird sprang up. "Awa' wi' ye tae warn the tacksmen. You too, Rory." In a moment Ellie was alone in the room, down on her knees, not so much in thankfulness as to scrape up a scatter of hot tobacco before it burned the carpet. The laird had charged away up the stairs, two at a leap, to poke his spyglass from a window facing on the sea. Below he could hear the boy shouting, and then a confusion of women. Suddenly Struachan's bagpipes rent all other sounds apart with a pibroch wild enough to raise the dead. Across the harbor channel York Redoubt was alert, with flags flitting up and down the telegraph mast, and faint on the wind came a sound of bugles.

Young James had put it neatly. The sea was alive with canvas. Wherever treetops pricked the window view there was the mad illusion of ships sailing between them—sailing through the very woods. French? Had Boney slipped another fleet through the British squadrons in the thick weather of Biscay?

If so, was it a feint, like Villeneuve's in the Caribbean? Or a thrust to seize the lone British naval port at the mouth of Canada while Prevost's forces were off in the south? That seemed a likely move.

Now sweeping the glass he saw a backing of main topsails in many of the ships, while those in his right-hand view came on in single column. What were they up to now? The boy Peter was beside him now, fingering his *skean dhu* as if the French were about to storm the stairs.

"Para?"

"Sir!"

"Go down and fetch Gahagan. On the run!"

"Ay, sir!"

In a few minutes the old man-o'-war's-man came, breathing hard. McNab passed him the glass.

"Take a look yon. Some of 'em seem to be forming a column, the rest are hove-to."

Gahagan put up the glass and adjusted it swiftly to his eye. "Ah!

Ah! So they are. And the column comin' straight on for the harbor entrance. Begad, they're goin' to force the passage!"

"Tach! Nobody's as mad as that—least of all the French. Those long thirty-twos in York Redoubt would knock 'em to pieces one after another. Na, na! This is a trick. The column will round-to by Chebucto Head and keep the York gunners busy at long bowls. The rest'll land troops and guns here on the island, and more troops over there at Herring Cove, for a scramble through the high woods to the rear o' York."

"Wait a minute!"

"What now?"

Gahagan chuckled. "They're not French."

"What!"

"The leading ship in column's the *Thetis* frigate. And the one next is the *Penelope*—I'd know her fore tops'l anywhere. That's the frigate General Prevost sailed in, wasn't it, back afore Christmas?"

"But some o' those ships hove-to aren't English rigged—I could see that. Take a careful look, now!"

Gahagan swung the glass away from the oncoming column to the ships jogging beyond Devil's Island. "Sure! Sure, sor—a few are French. But they're not men-o'-war, nor transports by the size of 'em. Some merchantmen, I'd say, that our ships took prize down south."

"They're not Spanish? You're sure?"

"Sure, sor. Unless the Spaniards ha' changed their whole ship design from hull to canvas since we saw one last."

McNab took the spyglass and stared at them himself. True to the Governor's confidence he had not mentioned a descent on Spanish Florida in all the speculations of the town and of his own folk on the island. The breeze was freshening from the south and the ships in column came on rapidly, with others moving to join astern.

As the leading frigate drew abreast of the Thrum Cap there was a spurt of white smoke and the clap of a gun from her, sharp on the wind, and in answer the puff and dull boom of one of the great guns in York Redoubt. All the rest of the morning and far into the afternoon the ships came in, thundering their salutes, and receiving in turn the thunder of York, of the Point Pleasant batteries, of George's Island, Fort Clarence, and the Citadel. On the decks of the transports McNab's islanders could see red masses of troops and the glitter of band instruments, and between claps of gunfire they could hear the tunes of "Rule Britannia" and "Britons, Strike Home."

Evidently General Prevost had won a great victory somewhere. McNab's instinct was to flit up to town as fast as the *Bonnie Jo* could take him there; but he thought of the men-o'-war and transports jockeying for mooring places in the anchorage, every captain eager to drop his hooks as near to the town as the naval harbormaster would permit. A dangerous company for small civilian craft moving in the fairway. And Prevost would be too busy to spare a moment for any of "those fellows in trade." So the laird waited with impatience for three days, while the troops came ashore and once more spread their tent lines over Camp Hill.

When at last he got to Government House the laird passed a note to the officer of the guard and resigned himself to a long cooling of heels or an outright refusal. It was a pleasant surprise when the officer returned, snapped a brisk hand to his black shako, and said, "The General will see you at once, sir." McNab walked up to the portico with all the dignity of a Highland chief on royal business, acknowledged the salute and directions of an aide, and passed into what had been the south drawing room and was now the General's office. Four black-coated secretaries sat bent over a long table fair-copying orders and letters; red-jacketed orderlies came and went with papers in their hands; four or five officers in scarlet frock coats, with bullion epaulets twitching and twinkling like the curls of blonde coquettes, stood in conference with Prevost in the window bay.

When the aide announced "Mr. McNab, sir!" the General turned away from them at once and came forward, darting out a hand. His face was all good temper and self-importance.

"Ah! There you are, Mr. McNab!" A lively handshake. "Let us sit over there, away from this." They sat on a hard little sofa at the far end of the room. The laird began politely, "I trust you're as well as you look, sir, after the perils of the sea and—um—Florida?"

General Prevost laughed. His face and the faces of his officers had certainly been tanned in the vat of a southern climate. "Florida, my dear McNab? I have been much farther than that. I have been to the French West Indies. I have taken Martinique!" His eyes danced merrily. He was immensely pleased with himself. "If it hadn't been for my orders to return north, I'd have gone on to Guadeloupe and left the French no West Indies at all."

"I'm afraid I don't understand," McNab said. He was tempted to ask in what way a small French pimple in the Windward Islands could compare with the whole of Florida.

"I'll go back to the beginning," Sir George said amiably. "When our government got word of that *Chesapeake* affair and the war talk in the United States, they hurried me off to Halifax with ships and troops and somewhat vague orders. I was to put the Nova Scotia garrison and militia in readiness against a surprise attack. I was to encamp my troops at Halifax, but I was not to go to the expense of building winter quarters. And I was to send secret agents into the United States to see their preparations for war. Well, I did all that. By autumn, when Mr. Burr came to see me, it was clear that whatever the Americans thought of war they were making no preparations. Mr. Jefferson was still in office and his policy was firm. Now there was Burr's notion about Florida. I thought well of it, myself. A blow at the Spaniards, and a British footing on the south of the United States, all at small expense.

"However in September I had an urgent despatch from Lord Castlereagh. Spain had suddenly changed sides. As perhaps you know, the Spanish people are in revolt against the armies of Napoleon, and Portugal stands with them. British troops have landed in both Spain and Portugal, and the Cabinet intends a large effort there. They hope that with this example other captive nations will arise against the French. It may well be the turning point in the war. So henceforth no Spanish ships or possessions abroad must be touched. We must forget about Florida. Not to mention Cuba, Porto Rico, and all their colonies along the Spanish Main. Meanwhile, to save the cost of winter quarters for my ships and troops, I should move to the West Indies, make a demonstration there against the French, and return to Nova Scotia in the spring. *Voila!*" Prevost's slim agile hands flew out in gestures towards Camp Hill and the ships in the harbor.

"Now, my dear McNab, I will tell you more—in the strictest confidence, of course. I have a purpose in this, and later you will see why. I have received fresh despatches from London, and from the British envoy in Washington. Bonaparte was furious at the turn of affairs in Spain. He directed in person a great concentration of troops and forced our small army out of northern Spain like a pip squeezed out of a grape. But a British Army remains in Portugal, with reinforcements on the way. Now for the American news. Mr. Jefferson has retired, and the President now is a man named Madison. The embargo on all foreign trade had been rescinded, and in its place there is something called the Non-Intercourse act, which simply forbids all trade with England and France."

"Which leaves us where we were before," the laird murmured.

"Not quite. You will see in a minute. There is still a loud war party, mostly young politicians from the American south and west, but our envoy sees no chance of their getting power in the next year or two—maybe never. So our war scare here is over. I expect my regiments will be drawn away to Portugal and Spain as the fighting develops there."

"And you, sir?"

"I shall remain here as Lieutenant Governor," Prevost said blandly. "I confess my ambitions are now in a political as much as a military sphere. This is a small province you have here. Lower and Upper Canada are big ones. Most of the Canadians speak French, and so do I. Their present Governor General is an old British officer, a martinet and a boor, without a word of French. You see? A matter of waiting, and of course a word in the right quarter. But I am digressing, and you are wondering what anything of this has to do with you. The answer is Portugal, sir, Portugal! General Wellesley is to have large British forces there, and he is to train and arm a Portuguese army as well. All these must be supplied. Now, Portugal and Spain, I'm told, are very poor countries for supplies. The French will find that out. The British will bring in theirs by sea. Well! Castlereagh says we shall need all the American supplies we can get. That is where you and your merchant friends come in. From now on more and more of the cargoes must be directed straight to Lisbon."

"We can take care of that, sir."

General Prevost regarded him with eyes beaming good humor and something else, a little malice perhaps, the instinctive contempt of the soldier for the tradesman. "There is something else,

Mr. McNab. Something not so good for you and your Halifax friends. This transshipping of American cargoes is no doubt profitable for you trading gentlemen, but it means a great delay in delivery, *hein?* Before long, perhaps, the American gentlemen may be able to make delivery direct, in their own ships."

"How?" The laird's voice was interested but unconcerned.

"The new American law forbids traffic with England and France. Just those. If you look at a map of the Spanish peninsula you will find that the great Spanish port of Cádiz lies not much more than a fast day's sail from the Portuguese capital of Lisbon —General Wellesley's sea base. Now consider! The Spanish insurgents hold Cádiz. American ships and goods could be billed to Cádiz without breaking their country's new law; and if the goods found their way to Wellesley's army, that would be just an accident of fortune, *hein?*"

"General," said McNab, stern and sublime, "I think I can speak for my friends as well as myself. Anything that leads towards the end of this war is a good thing for us all. I would rather earn five shillings in peaceful trade than five guineas at the possible cost of some man's blood."

Sir George could only say one thing to that, and he said it handsomely.

"Your sentiments do you honor, sir, and I apologise if anything I have said left another impression. And now that we understand each other let us go about our business in our separate ways. Good day, sir."

He arose and put out his hand, and McNab shook it heartily. "There's one more thing, General. A small matter. What about that battery at the tip of my beach?"

For a moment Sir George looked bewildered. So much had happened since his brief inspection at the harbor mouth. Then his face put on the assured military cast. "Oh! That! I remember now. A small matter, as you say. The Board of Ordnance did not approve. And now of course the scare of an American war is past and the defense of Halifax is nothing to worry about. For you and me the only concern is the war with Napoleon."

He waved a hand towards the North Atlantic and shrugged.

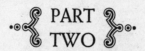

PART TWO

LA FURIEUSE

9

Cascamond lay on the main deck with a score of others wounded but fit to be carried up each day to lie in the sunshine and the clean Atlantic air. The others, with deep body wounds or shattered legs, had to remain in the gloom and fetor below. Down there in the crowded *poste des malades* lay the captain himself, brave old *Loup-de-mer,* smitten by a grapeshot in his belly. It was a marvel that he lived at all. Only a tough old Breton, pickled in salt water from his childhood, could have clung to breath and heartbeat for so long.

The English prize crew, busy with repairs to keep the ship afloat, would not permit a prisoner on the quarterdeck, not even one who was an officer like Cascamond, with a festering wound in the thigh, incapable of any hostility.

It had been like this ever since the fight in mid-ocean.

From the deck where Cascamond lay, near the jagged stump of the main mast, he could see the sail on the fore, the only mast of the frigate's three that the Englishmen had been able to keep standing. For weeks the battered hulk of *La Furieuse* had wallowed along at the end of a towline from the victorious English corvette. Although it had suffered a great spatter of shot-holes the prize crew had set the foresail, which made some difference in the tow, mostly because it steadied the hull a bit. *La Furieuse* still rolled badly, but it was not the former mad roll of an empty cask in a millrace, sickening even to the tough English seamen, agonizing for the Frenchmen down in the dismal *poste des malades*.

My poor *Furieuse,* thought Cascamond. She had lived up to her name in the fight but there was nothing of that about her now; only this hapless and dejected air of a wild beauty caught and whipped and bound, staggering along at the enemy's behind like a captive in a Roman triumph. The simile came to him from history lessons at the *lycée,* a vision of captives dragged behind the war chariots as part of a spectacle for the shouting Roman populace. Everything about ancient Rome seemed to have a significance nowadays —now that France was the new Rome, with her legions and eagles and her ever-victorious Emperor. Even the stubborn English had been saved only by their fleet and the wet width of La Manche.

The English were futile on land, of course. The sea was another matter. We French built better ships, and manned them with capable seamen, but we would not debase ourselves to produce sea-fighters as the English did. For all their talk of Freedom, as if they had invented it, the English notoriously made slaves of their poor to man their warships. They snatched up *canaille* from their streets and jails and forced them into their ships, as criminals in France were condemned to the galleys, keeping them aboard for years without a foot to shore, flogging them savagely for any slackness, hanging any man who uttered a word against his fate. Men kept at sea in such a manner had only one outlet in their hard and cruel lives, the chance of battle, in which they fought like wolves.

Eh bien. We in *La Furieuse* gave one lot of those wolves the fight of their lives—nearly seven hours of close action. Even the English seldom fought as long as that when they found themselves in a bad pinch. How astonished they had looked, the prize crew, when they came aboard and saw the frightful damage and the blood! It was incredible to them that Frenchmen could have fought so long, in such a state.

The prize-master, a gaunt and greying Scotch lieutenant named Sutherland, kept the unwounded prisoners at the pumps, while his carpenter and seamen patched the holes in the hull. There were some below the waterline, where shot had pierced her when she rolled, and for twenty-four hours after her surrender *La Furieuse* threatened to sink under them. Not until those hours of frantic labor were past, with the hull still leaking badly, did the Englishmen dare to turn a glance aloft. And in the meantime the main and aftermasts of *La Furieuse* had toppled overboard like rotten trees, leaving only the battered fore, with its topmast shorn away.

After three weeks of slow passage to the west the pumps were

still going day and night. Each morning Cascamond heard the
English carpenter reporting to the quarterdeck. "Sounded, sir,
and no change. Eight feet of water in the hold, with the pumps going full." Cascamond had guessed that for himself, feeling the
way the ship squatted in the sea and the ponderous roll, and seeing
the gush of the pumps, which hadn't the slightest look or reek of
bilge water; it was pure and bright, the Atlantic Ocean itself, flowing into the hull and up the pump wells and out again, like the
water of a fountain from the basin at its foot. All that additional
weight in the hold, sloshing amongst the casks of cargo, drew the
ship down and exposed the upper works to the waves, so that the
main deck gunports had to be kept closed and tightly caulked.
Thus, as Cascamond lay on his blanket there, he had a view of
the sky but not the sea. The sky was a blue rectangle framed by
the larboard and starboard gangways and the forecastle and quarterdeck, a North Atlantic summer sky, with clouds drifting on
the westerly wind like wisps of cotton blown off the far fields of
America. Ah, to be on one of those clouds, sailing high towards
France, instead of lurching and yawing slowly westward, always
westward, at the Englishman's tail!

A clatter of sabots. Goujon appeared, the boatswain's mate, a
wrinkled and bald Rochefort man in wooden shoes, patched blue
pantaloons, and a long blouse made of *toile à voile,* the thin canvas of an old topsail. Blouse and pantaloons were stained with
every kind of dirt to be found aboard a ship or ashore in Nantes
or Guadeloupe, a written list of everything Goujon had touched,
from tar to blood, in the whole of this last voyage. It was Goujon
and *Mousse,* the half-wit cabin boy, who attended to the wants of
the wounded men on deck.

"How goes it, Lieutenant?"

"*Ça va,*" grunted Cascamond. The bullet remained in his thigh,
which was swelling and burning more each day. The surgeon of
La Furieuse had been left ashore in Guadeloupe, dying of yellow
fever. The surgeon's mate, a bewildered young man, was certain
of one thing alone—that he could not probe a wound in a heavily
rolling ship.

Goujon gazed about him; at the splintered stumps of the aftermasts, like sheaves of wheat; at the lone forward mast, bereft of
its upper spars like a tall tree snapped off below the branches;

the patched-up bulwarks and port-lids; the grooves in the deck where English roundshot had played their deadly game of bowls; the wide bloodstains, gone black now and clearly visible despite the swabbing after the fight.

"Sacré nom d'un chien!" he growled. "How did all this come about? I still don't understand—none of us understand. We escape very neatly from the English fleet in the West Indies, we get good winds, we are halfway home. We sight an English merchantman and give chase. Suddenly appears, of all things, a French corvette flying the English flag. *Et voilà!"* Goujon threw out his gnarled brown claws in gestures that took in the state of *La Furieuse,* the English prize crew, and the "French" corvette towing ahead, invisible from where he stood.

"It's simple," Cascamond said, with his ironic smile. He lay on his back, a young man with dark blue eyes under bold arched eyebrows. His face had been tanned by the West Indian sun, but now after days of pain it had a yellow tinge. Ordinarily he kept his hair clipped short, with a single forelock drooping on his brow. A saucy little barmaid in Marseilles had told him once that he looked like Napoleon, "but longer, of course, and no belly." Now his head was a tangled black mop and his jaws a worn-out scrubbing brush. With the usual precaution the Englishmen had taken from the prisoners their knives, razors, scissors, every bit of sharp metal in their possession, even to sail needles.

"Simple comme bonjour," he said again. "You know, Goujon, that only a French-built ship could outsail *La Furieuse.* The corvette yonder is *La Bonne Citoyenne,* captured by the English earlier in this war, and now one of their fleet. They usually keep the French names on the ships they take; it gives them pleasure and impresses foreigners. But they don't use our term corvette. In their rating she is a sloop-of-war. His Majesty's *Bonne Citoyenne* —could anything be more ridiculous? Or does their king have an eye for a fine citizeness, even though he is fat and old, and some say mad? Maybe the English have a sense of laughter after all."

Goujon shrugged and waited patiently. Lieutenant Cascamond was given to these acid whimsies. The wounded officer closed his eyes and began to intone as if to a board of enquiry.

"Messieurs, if you please, I depose that the English sloop-of-war sailed from Portsmouth to escort some merchantmen over the sea to Québec. She lost them in thick weather well to the north-west of the Azores. A day or two later—such is the imbecility of fate—along came *La Furieuse* on her way from Guadeloupe to Brest. We sight an English lost sheep—in the English language that makes a *jeu de mots*—but never mind. She is a fine round-sterned barque, alone like a plump wench sauntering, and offering a soft pinch. So we tack and make after her. Suddenly out of a patch of mist pops a corvette flying the English flag, and in another moment running out her guns. So we turn and trot the other way—after all our business is not to pinch stray bottoms but to get a precious cargo home to France. The Emperor and all his officers and ladies must have their coffee and their sugar and their choco-late, *hein?* And besides we are armed only *en flute.* So away we run, all through the afternoon and night.

"In the night we hope to shake off this pugnacious Englishman in French clothes, but he seems to sniff our cargo in the dark. At morning light there he is, on our quarter, and reaching on us fast. So our old Sea Wolf—pardon, I should say *M. le Capitaine*—decides to halt and give the Englishman a fight. To put fire in our bellies he commands a big issue of wine well laced with gunpow-der, a mixture he declares more potent than the English rum. We are confident anyhow. Although we are *en flute* we yet have heavier guns than this corvette can carry, and our muster includes a party of soldiers returning to France from Guadeloupe. In all we have nearly two hundred men.

"But, ah, those damned English have something more than guns and men. They have the luck. The Devil himself is an Eng-lishman as all the world knows, and the Devil looks after his own. Early in the fight an English shot clips off our main topmast, so that it falls and dangles, with a raffle of ropes and torn sails drag-ging in the sea. We cannot maneuver our ship until that tangle is cut away—no short or easy job with English bullets whistling like snipe about our ears. Before we get done, *crac* goes another top-mast. Then the third.

"With all that top gear dragging alongside we are like a great Flanders mare hobbled and tied, while a savage dog runs in and out, snapping his teeth in her legs and belly. Mind you, the English don't know how to build a ship like *La Bonne Citoyenne,* but their patron the Devil shows them how to sail and fight her. She

dances back and forth across our bows, twirling to give us her
broadsides, first the larboard, then the starboard—*crac! crac!*—like
a malicious witch passing her whip from hand to hand. Now and
then we hit her, and she dances off to mend the damage. Then
she comes in again, *crac-crac,* slashing us with that whip of iron.

"In our crippled state we fight as best we can. And suffer,
pardieu! As time goes by there is a lot of blood mixed with the
wine and powder in our bellies! Six—nearly seven hours. The
wind falling, and the sun getting down the western sky. The Englishman comes in with the dying breeze, and this time we see the
flash of pikes and cutlasses. We know well what comes next. Another broadside as she closes in, and then those English wolves
will board us in the smoke."

Lieutenant Cascamond opened his eyes and regarded Goujon
for a moment. "I was at Trafalgar, you understand." Then with
eyes closed again, and resuming his tone of a report to a board
of enquiry, and with the same tinge of ironic amusement, "Our
old *Loup-de-mer—pardon, messieurs—M. le Capitaine* is down at
last with a shot in the body—what the English call grapeshot, although God knows they're big as plums. We have seventeen men
dead and thirty-two wounded. The hull is shot through, above and
below the waterline, with the ocean pouring in. The lower masts
are standing, but most of their stays are cut and they sway like
tipsy sailors trying to hold themselves upright while an officer goes
by. And night comes on with a rising of the sea, bound to pitch
those drunken masts overboard. So there's only one thing to do.
Yes, messieurs, we haul down our flag, which is holed and tattered
like a poor slut's petticoat.

"The English prize crew come aboard amid a silence like death
after the noise of the past seven hours, and their lieutenant has an
English flag bundled under his arm. They hoist it, with our poor
tricolore beneath. And there, messieurs, you have the whole dolor-
ous tale of *La Furieuse, frégate en flute.*"

Goujon looked down at him curiously. "Lieutenant, how do you
know so much about the English corvette, and her convoy to
Québec, and all that?"

"Bah! I have turned an ear to that *Ecossais* and his little gang
of sailors, knowing every word they said, all these days on the
deck. Listen, Goujon. After Cap Trafalgar I was a prisoner in

England. I was a senior *aspirant,* and due for my lieutenancy, but the English don't consider any midshipman of much account. I was allowed to live on parole in an English village, and to visit the homes of country gentlemen in a permitted area. So, because there was nothing else to do, I learned their language. I learned it so well that I can tell a Scotchman from a Devon man or a Londoner, just as we in France know a Picard from a Breton or a Provençal."

"Tell me something, then, Lieutenant, for the love of God. Why does this English corvette drag us away towards the west, towards America, when the best winds in this latitude blow the other way? Why hasn't he gone towards England?"

"Because in the English Navy one must obey orders or perish, no matter what's happened since the orders were made. The Englishman's orders were to take a merchant convoy to Canada. He dare not turn back, even with a prize of great value like *La Furieuse,* and admit that he had let his convoy go naked to the west. Everyone knows the English summer trade to Canada makes fat geese for our privateers, and the *corsaires* know exactly where to wait for them—on the Banks of Newfoundland."

Goujon glanced shrewdly at the straining foresail, and the lone mast like a stubby forefinger wagging slowly back and forth across the western sky as *La Furieuse* yawed at the cable's end.

"The damned Englishman will never overtake his convoy at this rate."

"True, but he follows his orders to the west, you see. And the English Admiral on the North American station will put in a good word for him."

"Why?"

"Because he brings a rich prize to that station. The Admiral will get a fat share of it."

"Ah! You know these English, Lieutenant." Goujon scratched his beard. "Long ago I was a fisher on those banks you mention— *un banquais,* as we say—and whenever a southeaster blew us leeward we had a glimpse of Newfoundland. But as I recall the fishers' talk, the country of Canada was four or five hundred leagues farther to the west, at the end of a great gulf, the Devil's home for mists and storms, and filled with ice in winter. Regard, monsieur, we have been towed three weeks now in this broad Atlantic, and

still no sight of shore, not even Newfoundland. If this cursed Englishman means to drag us all the way to Canada it will be winter
when we get there."

Cascamond closed his eyes again, shutting out the vision of
white clouds sailing home to France. "No fear of that, my old
banquais. The English have a naval arsenal below the mouth of
the gulf, a place called Halifax. And the Scotchman has said
that is where we go."

"And when we reach this Alfax—what then?"

"The English captain will repair his corvette at the naval dockyard, and go on to Québec in pursuit of his orders."

"And *La Furieuse?*"

"You can guess? Our frigate is only six years old, coppered
against the sea worms, and as swift as the wind with her full rig.
The English know a fine bit of shipbuilding when they see it. So
they will refit *La Furieuse* for the service of King George. It's well
accepted among the English that some of the best ships in their
Navy are those taken from the French. *Dieu!* How many have they
got from us, I wonder, since these eternal wars began? Has any of
those fat heads in the *conseil de l'amiraute* ever bothered to count
them up?"

Again it seemed to Goujon that Lieutenant Cascamond was
talking in a delirious dream to some invisible court of enquiry, and
saying things that would certainly cost him his commission at a
real one.

"With the exception of that little spell of peace they signed at
Amiens," the voice went on, "France has been fighting the English ever since I was a boy of nine; and all that time we have been
losing ships to them. It's no wonder the Emperor is impatient with
his admirals. He can ride his warhorse over all Europe, but he dare
not wet his boot toe in the sea."

At this point *Mousse* came with his battered pewter mug and
pail of foul West Indian water, six weeks in the cask, for the refreshment of the wounded lying on the deck. The cabin boy's real
name was Chardin, a youth from Bordeaux with washed-out
blue eyes and long yellow hair. His wits were dull even before the
battle. The first cannonade had sent him hiding in the darkness
of the *faux pont*, where the stinking mud of West Indian harbors

clung to the coiled cables and choked the little air. From there, after seven hours of terror, he had emerged a staring imbecile.

"Aha!" cried Goujon. *"Bon jour, Monsieur le capitaine du faux pont!* What news do you bring us today?"

"Land," stammered poor *Mousse.* "I smell it."

"Bah! You smell of the Guadeloupe muck in the cable tier."

"But no," said *Mousse.* "I smell trees, a forest of fir trees."

Goujon was about to make another and coarser quip about the scent of *Mousse,* but Lieutenant Cascamond cut him off. "No more of that! Perhaps the poor devil can smell trees. We must be drawing near to the Canadian forests, and any wind from north to south, round by the west, is blowing off the land." Goujon's merriment passed at once. He looked at Cascamond anxiously.

"What do you suppose the English will do with us at Alfax, monsieur?"

All the wounded men within hearing raised themselves on their elbows at this, and those who could walk crept closer. It was the question in all their minds. Cascamond was taciturn by nature, but the boredom of lying helpless all these weeks had loosened his tongue; and now the fact that he had been a prisoner of the English, and knew their language, made him an authority. He felt his new importance.

"I know nothing of Halifax," he said, giving the aspirate a pronounced *ha* to display his facility with the English tongue, "except it's the summer station of their North American squadron. When winter comes the warships flit away to the West Indies. The prisoners of war are probably kept in one or two *pontons* at Halifax —what they call hulks." Again the hard-breathed aspirate.

"Pontons!" The murmur went about the men. They had heard much of the hulks, those old warships anchored in backwaters of English naval harbors, with roofs instead of masts and yards, and damp and gloomy lower decks where French prisoners were crammed like barreled fish.

"I can only tell you how it was in England," Cascamond went on in a tone of boredom, as if all this was a tale not worth his breath. "You must understand that when the war flared up again six years ago all the English hulks were empty and abandoned, because their prisoners had been returned to France when the little peace was signed at Amiens. Well, they began to capture Frenchmen again, here and there at sea, and tucked them away in English common jails like thieves or vagabonds. But as more prisoners came, the old hulks had to be used again, at Plymouth and Portsmouth and Chatham, where the English have their chief dockyards.

"Then came the *grand débâcle*—Cap Trafalgar and all that. The English got a pretty haul. About twenty thousand of us altogether, French and Spanish. They had to put more hulks into use, and cram their jails all over the country."

"Including officers?" piped young Drouet, the wounded midshipman.

"No, the English placed all officers on parole, and paid us a small allowance, according to rank, for food and lodging. We were permitted to live in country towns, at a distance from the coast. I myself was with a considerable group in a little town called Wincanton, in the district of Somerset. We included sixteen midshipmen of all ages from twenty—like myself—down to a child of twelve. We *aspirants* rented a whole house together; it was the cheapest way, although mind you the English landlords charged a stiff rent even for a room. The money allowance to an *aspirant* was only a shilling or so a day, so we had little money left for food. We never saw meat, except when we were invited to dine with English gentry in the neighborhood. Mostly we lived on vegetables—potatoes, cabbage, onions, turnips, carrots, cucumbers—there were times, believe me, when we were glad to dig up dandelions for the pot.

"The parole limit was one mile exactly from the village. If you strayed beyond that, any peasant in the fields could knock you down with a hoe and claim the reward—a guinea—a little fortune in his life. So we had to be careful. Of course we broke the order here and there. The second autumn I remember finding a tree laden with apples, outside the parole limit. We midshipmen took turns at crawling through a field of grass, climbing the tree, and shaking down fruit to be stuffed under our jackets and carried off. The country gentleman who owned the tree soon knew what was going on, but he and his wife let us play our game. One day we painted a little sign, *Restaurant Pour Les Aspirants,* and hung it in the tree where they could see. We watched the woman peeping from a window, as she often did, and smiling and calling her husband to come and see. Oh, they are not all bad, those English!"

Midshipman Drouet heard this with interest, but the others were impatient. The treatment of French officers in English hands did not concern them.

"But, monsieur, the sailors . . . ?" Goujon said at last, seeing the lieutenant lost in this reverie of things past. "Twenty thousand prisoners," Cascamond said. "Mostly French, a veritable army landed in their midst. The English had a guard of soldiers on every hulk, but all these Frenchmen in their harbors worried the English government. Suppose they broke free, and took the weapons of the guards? So during that winter after Trafalgar they made plans for a tremendous prison away from the coast, and in the spring they began to build it. The place they chose was the midst of what they call Dartmoor, a desolation of rocks and bogs in the western foot of England. We Frenchmen on parole at Wincanton were in that region ourselves, and we heard the village people gossiping about this great work on Dartmoor, which would take four years to complete. The prison is planned like an enormous cart wheel of brick and stone; the spokes are the prison barracks, and the rim is a double wall with fortifications for the guards. It will hold at least ten thousand—some gossips said as many as twenty thousand. The work was still going on when I went back to France in an exchange, four *aspirants* for one English lieutenant. That was over two years ago, and nearly four since Trafalgar, so the prison must be occupied by now. I suppose they let their Spanish prisoners go home when that nation of mules rebelled against the Emperor last year; but certainly all the French must now be inside that miserable wheel at Dartmoor."

One of the walking wounded, a rough Norman with an arm in a sling, broke in loudly. *"Merde!* How does any of this affect us *matelots* at what you call Alfax?" For him all respect for officers had gone overboard at the surrender. Cascamond's air of indifference did not change. It was as if they were all imbeciles like *Mousse.*

"It concerns you very much, *matelot.* As I have said, I suspect the English have not much accommodation at Halifax for prisoners of war. A *ponton* or two perhaps. Since the war broke out again six years ago they must have picked up a lot of Frenchmen in the western Atlantic like ourselves. Where do they put them all? One can guess. Whenever a warship goes home from Halifax to England she takes some French prisoners, to ease the crowding of the Halifax *pontons*. That means all of you, sooner or later, will find yourselves in Dartmoor."

Again a murmuring. He could hear one voice saying, "But we shall be near France then, *hein?* That's better than a stinking *ponton* on the cold coast of Canada, the Devil knows how many thousand leagues from home."

Cascamond thought of winter on the high bleak moors of western England; the rains and fogs and snows; the great prison of brick and stone without warmth except in the cookhouses; and no hope of escape, no matter how near to France.

"You may be better off in a hulk at Halifax," he said.

10

The next morning all of them scented the land, English and French alike. The North Atlantic airs, cool, even cold in that latitude despite the mid-summer sun, turned miraculously into a wave of heat as if a vast oven door had opened in the mysterious west; and with nostrils starved and sharpened by many weeks on the sterile sea they sniffed a strong resinous odor that could come only from forests of pine and fir.

The next day, as Cascamond was borne up to the deck, he found a great buzz of talk, much waving of arms and pointing of fingers. Even the English sailors had forgotten their harsh discipline and talked aloud under the nose of Lieutenant Sutherland, instead of whispering at a distance among themselves. The land was in sight! Not only that but as Sutherland declared, the ships had made their landfall almost at the mouth of Halifax harbor, after all that long and awkward towing from mid-ocean. It was a feat of navigation and seamanship that even the glum Frenchmen could admire.

By late afternoon they were entering a gap in the stony face of the coast, with a vision of green hills and ridges in a low V that widened and shaded away to blue in the distance. The wind had veered, giving the laboring ships a fair thrust into the harbor.

Now that the sea was dangerous no more the English sailors opened all the gunports, and the warm scented air of the land passed over the wounded men on the main deck like a caress. Cascamond had his bearers put him down on the deck at a place where two empty gunports were open to his view, one on each side of the ship. Thus by turning his head he had a picture of the land in a square frame on either side, with no cannon squatting in the way. To larboard the shore seemed to be steep greyish-white rock, crowned by dark green woods, with a few huts of fishermen in the clefts at its foot. On one commanding height a battery with a round Martello tower was perched on the edge of the cliff. To starboard appeared a long island, partly wooded, with pastures rolling in low hillocks, and flocks of sheep like snow on the fresh green slopes.

Lieutenant Sutherland gazed ahead intently from his post on the quarterdeck. After a time there was a signal from the sloop-of-war, for he shouted and a party of his seamen scampered to the forecastle.

"What now?" muttered a badly wounded Frenchman at Cascamond's side.

"They go to shorten the towline for entering harbor."

"The entrance looks wide enough to go in as we are."

"It must have a narrow part somewhere."

Soon after, turning his restless head for the starboard view, Cascamond saw a low spit of beach stones jutting out from the island of the sheep. It was like a long grey finger pointing to the fort across the channel. In the frame of the gunport he could not quite see the finger's tip. When it came into view he was startled. First because it was so close, so dangerously close, a biscuit toss from the ship's side, although doubtless the Englishmen knew what they were doing. But something else startled him far more.

The point had gruesome sentinels. Six gibbets dangled skeletons with blackened shreds of skin and sinews clinging to the bones. Their wrists were chained, and so were their ankles, as if someone had feared they might get down and run away. Each hung by a rusty iron collar about the neck, and all of them turned slowly together in the sea breeze as if to watch *La Furieuse* go by.

"*Dieu!* What's this?" cried the man at Cascamond's side.

Cascamond had lost his first shock in a memory. At a farther distance he had seen such spectacles before, going into Portsmouth as a prisoner from Trafalgar, and two years later coming out of Plymouth in a cartel lugger bound for France.

"The English," he said contemptuously, "make a thing of hanging their *réfractaires* in such places. There is a *grève du bourreau* at the entrance of all their naval harbors, where everyone going in or out must see what hangs there."

"Why?"

Cascamond shrugged. "As our Voltaire once said, it's to encourage the others."

"You talk in riddles, monsieur."

"To frighten the others, then. They hang these poor bastards for mutiny—even for a few rash words spoken in the heat of rum. They are very ticklish about that, the English, because they have so many *canaille* in their lower decks. Early in these wars they had a great mutiny aboard their fleets at Portsmouth and the Nore, which is in the very mouth of London. It frightened those bold milords of the Admiralty, who fear nothing else on land or sea. So now they hang men or whip them to death at the least sign of rebellion, and exhibit their corpses in places like that."

A sharp crack of cannon now drew the prisoners' attention to the other side of the channel, where the fort sat on the cliff. A puff of powder-smoke arose from the rampart, and a line of bunting in various shapes and colors fluttered up the signal mast on the tower.

"They salute the corvette for our capture," said Cascamond. "The English telegraph to each other with *chiffonerie,* like a housewife's washing," he went on disdainfully. "Regard the twin-tailed pennant for example, like a pair of drawers. Our *sémaphore* is faster and more reliable, the wind can't flap it about like a lot of flags, but of course the English make fun of it; they say a Frenchman can't talk without waving his arms, even a pair of wooden ones on a pole."

They watched the tree-clad shores gliding slowly past. Here and there, mysteriously, cannon cracked and smoked from what appeared to be unbroken forest. Past these hidden batteries at last the town came into view. It was not large, this lone naval base of the English in North America. Streets of wooden buildings lay along the slope of a ridge on the west shore of the harbor, like the terraces of a vineyard on a French hillside. Some of the houses were painted in various colors; the wooden walls and roofs of the unpainted ones had weathered to a stony grey.

Above the town the ridge lifted to a squat green cone with its tip shorn off, and there sat another fort and signal mast, evidently the citadel. Turning his head for the opposite view Cascamond saw a small green island, a mere pimple, sliding past the starboard gunport quite close; and beyond it, at a distance across the harbor, a village set in rising fields and woods. The green pimple had a battery, from which came the familiar gun salute and hoist of flags.

And now *Bonne Citoyenne* and her prize began to creep past anchored warships, painted in the English fashion with bands of black and yellow—the yellow bands marking the gun decks, and checkered by square black gunports. Each ship had manned its decks and yards, and as *Bonne Citoyenne* drew abreast each crew cheered and waved hats three times, exactly together, as a commanding voice bellowed to them from the quarterdeck.

One would think it was another Trafalgar, thought Cascamond testily. Two of the English prize crew came to peer from the empty gunport at his left hand. In passing they ran a careless gaze over the Frenchmen sitting or lying on the deck, and one said cheerfully, "It's no wonder these Crappos can't handle a ship. They get everything arsy-versy. F'rinstance I asked one what he called the foremast there. I pointed my finger. *Nom? Nom?* I says—that means name in their lingo, see? And what d'ye think he said? Mizzen! So help me! Mizzen!"

Cascamond stirred. He could not resist calling out in his excellent English, "Sailor, a difference of language does not make us ignorant, like you. In our language the first mast is *mât de misaine*. And what you call the mizzen, we know as the *mât d'artimon*. Under those names we have handled them very well for a long time, I assure you. The French sailed across this ocean long before any Englishman put a foot on America."

The two sailors looked at him with astonished faces. It was as if the figurehead of *La Furieuse* herself—that painted virago with mouth agape—had uttered not merely English speech but the speech of a country gentleman from Somerset or maybe Devon.

"And now perhaps you will explain something that seems to me arsy-versy, as you say. We are going past the town. Can it be that your captain does not know where to stop?"

The seamen grinned sheepishly. One said, "The dockyard's further up the harbor. You'll see it by-and-by."

Gazing past them Cascamond could see a thin scatter of dwellings along the harbor shore, evidently on a road from the town to the dockyard. Behind them lay an easy slope of pastures and small crop fields. Each of the fields was enclosed by a low wall of piled grey stones. Like Brittany, he thought, and wondered how long it would be before he saw again the walled fields of St. Malo.

At last the dockyard began to appear in his view, and the more talkative English sailor pointed out its features, standing at the side of the gunport so that he could get a good view.

"That there house, the white 'un on the point—that's the Commissioner's. You can see a bit of the big masthouse behind it, though you can't see the mast pond and spar canal. Now there— see—there's the boat sheds and slips. And there's the anchor store. Now wait a bit—ah—here's the sheer wharf. Them sheers stick up in the air so high ye can see 'em for miles up an' down the anchorage. And there's the careening dock, just past the sheers. Behind 'em's the sail lofts and riggers' store and hawser store. Now you'll have to wait a bit, to see where you go next. It's past the telegraph mast there on the knoll. Now! See? That there's the hospital wharf, and the hospital up the slope a bit."

The man said "ouse" and "awser" and "tellygraft" and "orspittle," but Cascamond understood him easily. The naval arsenal of Halifax was nothing to compare with those of Portsmouth or Plymouth, or Brest or Toulon; but evidently enough for the purposes of the English in these waters. Most of the buildings seemed to be of dark stone, and arranged in a grim order like those of a prison; but the hospital, a small wooden affair, was painted a flaming red. It looked no bigger than a dwelling house.

Sutherland's voice again. "Hands forward to the anchors, there!" And again a scramble of seamen to the forecastle, including the chatty one by the gunport. Cascamond could see nothing of their work but he followed it by ear. The splash of anchors; first what the English called the best bower, and then what they called the little bower, although both weighed much the same. With these on the harbor floor the ship would ride in a secure arc, whatever breezes blew. Then a shout to furl the foresail, followed by a long business at the capstan, hauling and stowing the great hemp towing cable. To spare his own weary sailors Lieutenant Sutherland ordered the able-bodied prisoners to work at the capstan bars and in the stifling dark of the cable tier. It was one of the sharpest ironies of the whole affair that the towing had been done with the great cable of *La Furieuse* herself, new from the naval rope-walk at Brest and sent aboard for the special voyage to Guadeloupe; and now that it had served the English purpose her own men had to haul it back and stow it in the prize.

The frigate swung slowly and obediently to her anchors, giving Cascamond a shift of view, the dockyard, the shipping in the harbor, the village on the other side and the surrounding woods from which, on knolls here and there, a pleasant-looking villa peered at the water from a bower of trees.

The English seamen were coming aft again, laughing and playing pranks with each other, as if the magical air of the shore had done away with all discipline as well as the pains and toils of the weeks at sea. One said gleefully, "We'll get a bit o' liberty here, lads, depend on't. And money to spend. The Old Man'll be in an easy mood, what with a pat on the back from the Admiral, and the prize money, and all."

Amid the patter of naked feet a young seaman asked eagerly, "What sort o' place is it? For a bit o' fun, I mean?"

An older voice chuckled, "Like Gib. Not much of a town, but any amount o' fun. None o' the cheap Spanish wine ye get at Gib, mind; but the merchants here do a great trade wi' the West Indies, so rum's nigh cheap as water. In Allyfax ye can get merry for thrippence an' dead drunk for a shillin'."

"And what about women?"

"Aaaaah! Better than Gib, even. More sluts to the acre than anywheres I ever see—outside o' Portsmouth Hard, o' course."

The unwounded prisoners went ashore first, in boats from the dockyard. Then the walking wounded. Finally those like Cascamond, who had to be lowered down the frigate's side in hammocks. The English seamen went about it with surprising gentleness; but

Cascamond found it agonizing for all that, the lift into the hammock, the bent posture in the thing which set the swollen leg throbbing as the hammock dangled down the side, the movement into the boat, and then being lifted up to the hospital wharf, and finally carried by litter up to the prim red building on the slope. Cascamond found himself at last on a hard little cot in the lower story. The windows were wide open to the summer breeze, and outside he could see the lightly wounded and the unhurt prisoners shuffling into a column, with a squad of redcoated soldiers at its head and another bringing up the rear. At a series of barked commands the soldiers fixed bayonets and shouldered arms with stiff precise movements. The sharp steel of the bayonets flashed in the sun. A drum began to patter. At another sharp English bark the whole column moved its legs like a caterpillar and soon vanished from Cascamond's sight towards the afternoon sun.

He was astonished and disturbed. Why were the Frenchmen being marched away towards the west, towards the woods outside the town, like cattle for slaughter? He called out to one of the hospital attendants, "You there! Why are the prisoners not going to the hulks?"

As usual the fellow was taken aback by a Frenchman speaking English in the voice of a west-country squire. After a pause he said, "The hulks? The hulks is anchored in Bedford Basin, up that way." He jerked his head to the north. "They don't use the hulks no more. The prisoners go to Melville Island."

"Then why do they march away from the harbor?"

"Melville Island's in the nor'-west arm o' the harbor, that runs back into the woods behind the town. The island's nigh at the end of it, in a little cove, with a footbridge to the shore. So they march by the road around the Arm—that's what we call it. It's on'y three miles or so, a brisk hour's march."

Cascamond raised his brows and sucked his lips. It did not seem like the seafaring English to march anywhere if it was possible to go by boat.

Darkness came, and the long night, in which there was no gift of sleep. Now that the world was strangely firm, after the long tossing of the ship, he had that sensation of something wrong which wakens every seaman in the first few nights in harbor or ashore. The room was a bare chamber facing on the harbor. It contained a dozen cots, on which badly wounded Frenchmen grunted and groaned, drifted into brief naps, snoring heavily, and awoke with sharp yelps of pain, like sleeping dogs whose paws are trodden by a blundering boot. A lone lantern hung on the doorpost, and in the shadow beneath it the night attendant, an old English seaman, sat in a chair and snored.

In the morning another grey pigtail took his place, and after a time brought bowls of soup to the prisoners. To Cascamond he said, "The sawbones will be in, by-and-by. So will old Rory Square-Foot."

"Who is that?"

"Cap'n Rory MacDougal, Agent for Prisoners here. In the hulks Rory was forever counting heads and measuring deck space, and now he does the same at Melville Island. So many square feet per man, see? The number of prisoners he can squeeze into the space depends on the length and width allowed for the hammocks. He'll want to question you for his first report on the new lot. So will one or two other gentlemen from the town, it's likely."

"Why?"

"Because you speak English good, the only one in your lot that does. They'll want to know about your ship, and what's in the cargo, and such."

"Ha! You can tell Mr. Square-Foot that I'll speak to nobody but the surgeon—not until I've had my hair cut, my beard shaved off, and myself washed. I am a French officer and they shall not see me looking like an animal."

The attendant stared at this shaggy animal for a moment, shrugged, and went on with his round, delivering iron spoons and bowls of soup. Cascamond forced himself up on an elbow and swallowed the soup, a good thick *ragoût* of fresh mutton and vegetables that even an English cook could not spoil. After the long diet of salt meat and biscuit it was like a fresh taste of life itself.

Soon afterwards the surgeon arrived, a lean sharp-featured man with sandy side-whiskers, wearing green coat and trousers and a brown top hat. With him was a pallid young man in a smock of worn but clean duck, evidently the surgeon's mate. When they came to examine Cascamond he lay back and shut his eyes, trying to harden himself for the inevitable sentence on his leg. He knew the exact words—*This will have to come off.* He was clad only

in the shirt, torn and filthy now, to which the sick-bay attendants
of *La Furieuse* had stripped him when he was carried down to the
poste des malades a lifetime ago. His leg felt hot and enormous,
and the pain had sent exploring fingers through the hip to his middle parts. Already it was touching the very source of his manhood.
Even if the leg were cut off, that evil intrusion would remain, and
it seemed to him that it was better to die, and as quickly as possible. He felt the surgeon's fingers on his thigh, pressing lightly here
and there in the puffed flesh about the bandage. Then, opening
his eyes, he saw the man put his nose down to the wound and sniff
like a questing hound.

"Um-hmmm!" The Englishman straightened himself with no
more facial expression than the Sphinx of Egypt. "You're an officer and you speak English, is that true?"

"Yes."

"Then tell me what's in there—a shot or a splinter?"

"A musket bullet, I think; we were fighting at close quarters and
it knocked me down. But all sorts of things were flying then, and
it might be anything from a splinter to a grapeshot."

"Um! Swelling and fever. Putrefaction. Characteristic ooze. Tomorrow I'll probe for whatever it is, and get it out of you."

"And my leg?"

"I'll tell you about that when I see what follows the extraction."

The surgeon and his mate passed along to other patients. The
hospital attendant had told the doctor or someone else in authority
about Cascamond's demand, for soon came a barber with scissors, razor, brush, soap and bowl. The tangled mop of black hair
fell away under the scissors as the man obeyed Cascamond's directions, giving him the short trim favored in the French service,
and leaving the usual forelock. And now came the grey attendant,
with wash-ball and towel, and a small wooden tub of steaming
water. He rolled up his shirt sleeves, exposing a pair of strong
forearms tattooed with anchors and mermaids. He drew a sheath
knife from his belt and cut away the bandage and the shirt, which
he cast to the floor with the flick of someone throwing aside an
unspeakable nastiness. Quite skillfully he went on to wash the
French officer from head to feet, turning him this way and that as
gently as possible. Cascamond could not help gasping at the pain
of these movements; but even so he found a dour humor in the

spectacle of himself being swabbed like a soiled baby in the hands of this whiskered and tattooed nurse.

When this was done, and a new pad and bandage applied to the wound, he lay on his back staring at the ceiling, where flies crawled and buzzed in the still air above the breeze from the windows. It was worth the added pain to feel clean again. He felt refreshed; it was almost pleasant to lie there, not moving a finger, giving himself up to this luxury of cleanliness, and resolutely keeping all thought from his leg. For a time he dozed. Then a bustle in the room brought him back to wakefulness. An attendant pointed a finger. "That's the one."

Two men came to the cot. The first wore a blue frock coat with brass buttons, and trousers of white duck. His hair was a grizzled brown, receding from the forehead, and his eyes had the bright blue of a summer sea. The short whiskers hid part of a great scar on the left side of his face. He limped, and Cascamond suspected a wooden leg at first, and then decided on a stiff knee. Clearly a battered sea dog posted ashore in his middle age. He carried sheets of paper attached to a wooden back, and fumbled for a pencil in a waistcoat pocket as he came up to Cascamond.

He wrote carefully, reciting aloud as the pencil moved. *"Halifax, N. S. August Five, Year Eighteen Nought Nine."* Then, "You are the prisoner who speaks English?"

"Yes."

"I am Captain MacDougal, Agent for Prisoners of War."

"Well?" Cascamond made his voice brusque. This relic of the wars must learn from the start that he was dealing with an officer.

"I represent the Transport Office in London, which is under the authority of the Board of Admiralty and has full charge of prisoners of war."

"I know all that."

"Then you have been a prisoner before?"

"Yes, in England." He saw the Agent's blue eyes glint with suspicion.

"Oh no, I didn't break parole. I was exchanged by cartel with some others in the spring of 1808. Your Transport Office will have a record of that, I'm sure—you English make a record of everything."

Captain MacDougal scribbled a note on the sheet.

"Now! Your name, please?"

"Cascamond, Michel Cascamond. Would you like me to spell it for you?" He went on to spell it, pronouncing the letters in the English fashion, with easy fluency.

"Your present rank?"

"Lieutenant."

"Age?"

"Twenty-five."

"Your home?"

"Saint-Servan, a village of Brittany. Near Saint-Malo, which is more important. Put down Saint-Malo."

"Very well. And your ship?"

"*La Furieuse, frégate en flute*—you don't understand that, of course." And as if speaking to a child, "Our frigate had forty-four guns. But we were to fetch a heavy cargo from the West Indies so half the cannon were taken off. To reduce the weight, you see. And with half her gunports empty she was, as we say, like a flute."

MacDougal smiled dourly. "I know what *en flute* means, m'soo, even though I don't speak French. Yours isn't the first flute we've taken to play our own tunes on. But let's go on. The name of your captain?"

"Lamarant Daniel. A *Malouin* like myself. How is his wound?"

"He's dead. Died as they lowered him down the side. Um! Let's see, now. What was the nature of your voyage, exactly?"

Cascamond hesitated. From the moment of capture he had determined to give no information of naval value to the English. Yet now that he thought on the question he realised that he had nothing of naval value to betray. That last voyage of *La Furieuse* had been ordered merely to provide luxuries for the tables of the Emperor's new aristocracy.

"We sailed from Lorient last spring, to pick up a cargo of sugar, cacao, and coffee in Guadeloupe. We were there some weeks. Finally we joined four other ships at anchor inside the islands which we call the Saints. English warships were cruising outside, and we were all *en flute*, so we had to make a run for it at night. The English overtook and captured two the next day, but we others got away free."

"Until your frigate ran afoul of Mounsey."

"I do not understand."

"Commander Mounsey of the *Bonne Citoyenne*. He captured you."

"Ah! Well, we gave Mr. Mounsey a long fight for it—one that he will remember all his life. What was his butcher's bill, do you know?"

"Yes. One man killed and four wounded."

There was no trace of a sneer in MacDougal's words nor in his face. His eyes remained as tranquil as a summer sea.

"It was a very unequal battle, of course," Cascamond found himself mumbling. "As I say, we were only armed *en flute*."

"As you say. But of course even *en flute* you had twenty cannon at least. And the sloop had eighteen, of smaller weight."

Still that calm look on MacDougal's face. Cascamond hated it, and hated him. "You seem to know a lot about the ship, monsieur. Why bother me?"

"You've told me enough for the present, Lieutenant. Now permit me to introduce Mr. McNab, a merchant of Halifax."

The second figure now came forward, a stocky man in the forties, with a ruddy face, pleasant dark eyes, black hair beginning to show grey, and clipped loosely in the fashion of English civilians with a straggle of locks about the ears. He wore a plain brown suit, and was old-fashioned enough to wear knee breeches and stockings in this new age when Englishmen of fashion were copying the trousers of the French.

"Peter McNab, at your service," he announced, in an educated voice that Cascamond could only define as part English and part Scotch. "Perhaps you noticed my home as you entered the harbor, the long island on your starboard side."

Cascamond's lips twisted in a malicious grin. "You mean to say you live at the hangman's beach?"

McNab frowned. "I own the island and live there with my family and tenants. I regret to say I cannot choose the tenants of the beach. That's entirely a matter for Admirals on the station." Something in McNab's tone implied that he had no high opinion of admirals on the station.

"Why are you here?" snapped Cascamond.

McNab answered mildly. "I come here often, sir, to visit the sick —British or French—and bring some little comforts that are not on the ration list. But as it happens this time I have a question to ask.

I intend to bid at the public vendue when your ship's cargo is sold by the order of the Prize Court. Nobody seems to know much about the cargo or its present condition—nobody speaking English anyhow. Unless it is, perhaps, yourself."

"Ha! I can tell you that the ship has eight feet of salt water in the hold, and salt water does a cargo no good, as you must know."

"Then the cargo is not worth considering?"

Cascamond relented. "Of course it is. The cargo is all in large casks of strong West Indian oak, which should be tight. Except those hit by shot, you understand—we got more than a dozen shot below the waterline."

"And what is the cargo?"

"Thirteen hundred barrels of coffee, and I forget how many of sugar and cacao—a good lot anyhow. In France it would have been like gold."

"I assure you it's more than a pennyworth here, sir. Thank you for your courtesy. I'll not weary you more at the present time, but I'll be calling again once or twice a week, and I hope to see you back to health."

As McNab turned away Cascamond called out, "A moment, monsieur. You may tell me something in return. If I recover as you hope, where shall I go when I leave the hospital?"

"You'll be sent to Dart . . ."

"Dartmoor! Infamous! I am a French officer and entitled to parole!"

"The place is Dart*mouth,* monsieur—the village across the harbor. French officers are sent over there on parole, and given a money allowance for board and lodging. You'll find a number of your compatriots living quite happily there and in Preston, which is a pretty little hamlet in the woods behind Dartmouth. I should add, of course, that a prisoner of war who breaks parole may be knocked down by anybody for the regular cash reward. And he loses his officer's privilege. That means confinement with the common sailors on Melville Island, and if he ever tries to run from there, the punishment of the Black Hole for several days and nights, on sea biscuit and water."

Cascamond made a sour smile. "It seems that your Transport Office *does* have a little Dartmoor here."

"I don't know about Dartmoor, sir, but the rules are the same

here as in England. Formerly prisoners of war were stowed aboard
hulks anchored in Bedford Basin." McNab pointed. "Up there at
the head of the harbor. The sick and death rate was bad in the
hulks, though. Four years ago the naval authorities took over a
fishery station on Melville Island, and housed some prisoners there
as an experiment."

"In old fish stores?"

"Yes, and for all that more healthy than the hulks. So this year
the Transport Office, under the direction of the Admiral, has built
a new prison on the island. A wooden building suitable to this
climate; well lighted and aired with windows, and fitted with stoves
for cold weather."

"It sounds like a veritable hotel. How many guests have you
there?"

"At the moment about six hundred. The number varies. The
prison can hold many more."

"You seem well acquainted with all this, monsieur. Do you visit
Melville Island also?"

McNab smiled. "Of course! So do a lot of other people. In Halifax it's all the rage, as we say. Ladies and gentlemen, old, young
—even children. The prisoners make little things for sale, and on
Sundays they're allowed to hold a sort of public bazaar. It gives
them some money."

The merchant gave him a nod and moved off. *Run,* thought
Cascamond morosely, going over the whole conversation. What a
word to mention to a man with a leg like mine!

The operation was a nightmare, the dream of a maniac. It began in the morning, when the other prisoners were fed and he was
not. Instead the surgeon's mate came with a square case-bottle and
a tumbler.

"What's that?" demanded Cascamond suspiciously.

"Rum—smell!" He held the bottle to Cascamond's nose, and
then poured the glass half full. "Drink that down, if you please."

"I can't drink it like that—neat, as you say. Fill up the glass with
water."

"All right, sir. I'll be back soon with another. You'll have to
swaller a lot o' rum before Mr. Haddox operates."

Cascamond took a drink of the grog and made a wry face. In Guadeloupe he had learned, amongst other things, the difference between good rum and bad. The French in the West Indies made an art of distilling liquor from sugar cane, and in the homes of well-to-do planters he had sipped rum as bland and tasty as good cognac. This stuff in the glass was a harsh black rum from Jamaica or Demarara, the kind produced in vast quantities for the ships and dockside taverns of the English.

When the surgeon's mate came back again Cascamond protested. He would not swallow another drop of that black lye. Even mixed with water it was terrible.

"You must! You'll need a lot of it inside you when Mr. Haddox begins to probe that leg—you'll even pray for more. Here now, drink this down."

"What I shall need is opium."

"You'll get opium later on. But first you'll swaller at least half this bottle o' rum. It's surgeon's orders."

"What if I refuse?"

The surgeon's mate gave the prisoner look for look. "Then you'll be treated like any loony that won't take his medicine. You'll be strapped down, and you'll get all the pain with nought to ease it. You won't like that, Frenchie, I know. I seen it done."

Cascamond searched his mind desperately for argument. "This rum is bad. Together with opium it would make poison. I am no doctor but I'm sure of that. Go to your Mr. Haddock—is that his name? Haddox, then. Go to your Mr. Haddox and tell him Lieutenant Cascamond demands opium alone."

The Englishman smirked at this, and then howled with laughter. He turned to the grey pigtail by the door. "D'ye hear? He wants me to tell Haddox that rum and opium's poison. Haddox!"

The attendant joined in this burst of merriment and Cascamond thought, What animals! They have no heart, even with each other, and to a wounded Frenchman—pfui! Aloud he said, "This is nothing to laugh about! I am a French officer and I demand to speak to Mr. Haddox himself."

The surgeon's mate put up a hand and made a comical business of wiping the smile from his face and rolling his eyes at the attendant.

"I beg pardon, sir," he murmured. "You must forgive me, sir.

But it's like this, sir. Mr. Haddox don't find rum and opium a bad mixture—not a bit of it. Fact is, Mr. Haddox drinks down one o' these case-bottles every day. Not all at once, o' course; but a nip here and a nip there—rum's meat an' drink to Mr. Haddox, I can tell you. And opium, he takes opium every day, too—'specially when he operates. Steadies his nerves and keeps him sharp for the work. Sharp for the work, see? That's a joke, Frenchie. Laugh, man, laugh!"

Cascamond threw himself back on the cot. These English! He could now feel the effect of the grog in his empty stomach. A warm and reckless sensation rose through him to the brain.

"Very well," he said thickly, "if I am to be the victim of a drunken opium-eater there is only one thing to do. Give me the rum."

Within another hour he was so drunk that he could hear himself laughing foolishly, in the very tones of poor *Mousse,* and attempting to sing a sailor's snatch about the *putains* of Bordeaux. In this state he was carried to a small lime-washed room which the attendants called "the shambles," and laid upon a large table grooved down the middle and at the sides like the gravy gutters of a dish for roast meat. There he was given opium at last, and more rum to wash it down. For a time the surgeon's mate and two attendants, both powerfully built old seamen, watched him carefully. He tried to fight back swooning waves that surged through his head. At last the surgeon's mate turned to knock at a door, and Mr. Haddox came forth.

In a last flash of clarity Cascamond saw the surgeon encased in a canvas apron from neck to toes, but still wearing the top hat. The face approached and bent over him. It seemed enormous. The long Roman nose, the foxy eyebrows and side whiskers, the small pursed mouth of a cuttlefish, the long jaw, the deep lines that ran from a point above each nostril to a point between the mouth corner and the fuzz of the whiskers, the wide-set eyes of a bloodshot grey, with their pupils shrunk to a pair of printer's dots. The staring eyeballs seemed to swallow him. He felt himself drowning in some frightful maw beyond, in which loathsome creatures, half human and half beast, writhed about him.

Then miraculously he was in a well remembered garden in Guadeloupe, in a night of stars, with an air of the trade wind faintly stirring leaves overhead. A pretty woman panted softly in his arms, and his nostrils were filled with a fragrance of warm flesh and verbena. Then the scene changed abruptly like the painted glass slides of a *lanterne magique.* He was on the deck of *La Furieuse,* in the choking fog of powder smoke, with the guns uttering thunder cracks and leaping back against the breechings, with the shouts of gun crews reloading and prying them up to the ports again, and the crash and jar of English shot, and himself running up and down the gun deck with commands and encouraging yells, slipping in the blood underfoot and recovering himself again and again; and then at last slipping and not recovering, and falling down, down, down, as if the deck had vanished and left a pit as deep as hell. And beyond all these fantasies, in another existence far away, someone or something screaming endlessly, like a pig fastened, neatly stabbed in the throat vein and left to bleed to death slowly in the slaughter vat.

Then he was retching, in spasms that seemed to tear his insides from their fastenings. He felt his eyes bulging, and seeing nothing but sparks in a darkness. And between the spasms he could hear his own voice crying murder, *"A l'assassin! A l'assassin!"* At last he fell back into the pit again, and it swallowed him whole.

He came back to life in the room where the other French wounded groaned on their cots. There was sunlight at the windows, and the warm breeze from the invisible pine forest blowing through the room. His head ached madly and his mouth was like an old dry shoe. He was exhausted, lying on his back and barely able to turn his head. There was a great pain in his leg, but there seemed to be a trifle less of the old burning in his hip and privates. A feeling of pincers twisting in the wound; as if Mr. Haddox were still trying to "get it out of you," whatever *it* was. After an age of torture the pale visage of the surgeon's mate bent over him, saying in a flat voice, "So you've come to at last. How d'ye feel?"

Cascamond tried to speak, to say how he felt, in the most violent words he knew; but the parched leather of mouth and tongue refused to make a sound. The Englishman's voice said, "I'll tell Mr. Haddox you're out of the opium. He'll be making his round by-and-by."

11

An eternity, sometimes dark, sometimes in a glare like the sun at noon, mostly in dim twilight. In the glare he lay fully conscious, given up to pain. Then opium and a mouthful of grog, and the drift back to fantasy again. As before the dreams or illusions followed one another in a mad procession that had no relation and meaning. One recurred several times. It was not that pleasant memory of the love affair in the garden. In this he walked with steps that made no sound whatever, beneath palms, beneath great flowering trees that filled the night air with their scent. Between the tree boles there was a distant glimmer of moonlight on a sea. And there were huts, small and dark and silent, where people cringed as he passed. Because he was one of the living dead, the bodies without souls, the *zombies* who walked in the nights of Haiti and Guadeloupe and Martinique.

But at last he awoke in the hospital, body and soul together, and with a mind sharply aware of everything about him. In English sea slang the sick-bay attendants were "loblollies" or "loblolly boys," although most of them here were seamen old enough to be grandfathers, too old for ship duty. They took good care of him in a stolid way, as if they were still aboard ship under a petty officer's eye, cleaning a gun fouled by firing, or swabbing a bloodstain off the deck.

Each morning and afternoon Mr. Haddox came slowly through the rooms, wearing his top hat (Cascamond wondered if he slept in it) and smelling of rum, although he never seemed the least bit tipsy. He gave exactly the same attention to the French as to his English patients, and in the irrational way of sick men Cascamond resented that as much as anything else about him. One day he snarled, "Tell me, how does one become a surgeon in His Majesty's Navy?"

Mr. Haddox gave him a stare with those large pale eyes and their strange pupils. In his deep voice, which seemed to come from the very caverns of the sea, he answered, "You're wondering what sort of ignorant fraud has got you in his clutches, Mr. Cascamond. Well, I'll tell you. Every surgeon in His Majesty's sea service has to pass an examination at Surgeons' Hall, in London. That doesn't mean anything to you, of course. It doesn't mean much to me, either. Any fool in England can spend seven years grinding pills for a physician, or acting as dresser for a hospital surgeon, and then he's qualified to set up on his own account. If he's got a bit of sense he goes into private practice with his feet safe on the ground. But if he has a notion to see the world he can memorize a little book-stuff about gunshot wounds, yellow jack, and scurvy, enough to pass at Surgeons' Hall; and then he can go to sea and kill more British sailors than any gun crew of Napoleon."

He paused. "However, sir, there are some odd fellows like myself that have a curious interest in the mysteries of medicine and surgery, and go to considerable lengths to penetrate 'em. I myself spent three years in the study of medicine at the University of Edinborough, the finest medical school in Europe or the world—don't mention Leyden to me, if you please—and as for Paris, bah! After that I was four years a dresser for surgeons in Guy's Hospital, London, where you get everything from falling of the foot to tumor of the brain; not to mention such workaday matters as the bloody flux, consumption of the lungs, or cutting the bladder for the stone. I don't mind telling you there are men making their fortune at fashionable practice in London that haven't a farthing's worth of knowledge compared to mine."

"Then why are you here?" sneered the yellow face on the cot.

"Ah! The inevitable question. I could give you a thousand answers, my sarcastic friend, but why should I quibble with a French prisoner of no importance, who may be dead tomorrow or next week? Two reasons will do. One's rum, the finest product of the West Indies. The other's the poppy of the East, a coarse flower that stinks but has a miraculous juice—in a word, opium. You see, I'm frank with you. I have an addiction to R and O, and a man in that case must place himself where he'll find R and O always in good supply. Hence His Majesty's sea service. For an example of my professional knowledge and capacity take your case. I drew out of your leg a musket ball, flattened one side. Must have bounced off something—deck probably—and I'm told you French don't wash your decks or anything else as often as you might. So you were all that time with an ounce of lead in your thigh plus the taint of your own ship, some West Indian filth undoubtedly, left by someone's shoe. And not one damned thing done about it till you got to Halifax—to me—with a leg like an elephant's and the inflammation creeping to your private parts. You looked like one of those poor devils of lepers I used to see in the East, in my first days at sea, when I became familiar with so many things undreamt of at home. And for all that, I've kept you alive, Cascamond . . . I really have. Not that I care a damn for you. Simply as a matter of professional interest."

"*Baste!* What does your professional interest think of my leg this morning?"

Mr. Haddox motioned to the loblolly beside him, and the blanket was swept back for the surgeon's gaze. Cascamond fixed his own gaze on the ceiling, as if he had never seen flies and flaking limewash before. It was enough to imagine his leg, from the misery in the thigh, from the dead sensation below the knee right down to the toes, and the stench that arose and fouled the air about his bed.

In a few more moments he was gasping with pain and crying out, "Why the devil don't you give the wound a chance to heal? Prying it open every day! Do you think that because I'm a Frenchman I have no more feeling than a lump of salt pork?"

"I'm merely keeping the wound open to let the corruption drain out of you, Cascamond. All Frenchmen have a certain amount of corruption by nature, born in 'em. That's why they worship Napoleon, the master of corruption, body and soul. But you, Cascamond, have more than usual, due to the combination of an English bullet and French dirt. So you have a large wet wound to be drained. My object is a small dry one, of course, but there are many possibilities, many indeed. I won't deceive you. You may yet lose that leg. And if things should go from bad to worse, you, yourself, the entire Lieutenant Cascamond, could drop off the hooks like a rotten carcass in a meathouse. Others have, with less to account for it."

Mr. Haddox waved a casual hand towards the grassy slope at the rear, where the hospital's dead, English and French, were buried without ceremony by grumbling workmen from the dockyard. The burial ground could not be seen from the room where Cascamond lay, but he knew about it from remarks of the attendants, overheard in his lucid hours. Few of the English graves, and none of the French, were marked by stick or stone. A Halifax butcher, a contractor to the Navy, fattened cattle in the pastures above the hospital, and his wandering animals munched the grass on the old graves, snuffed curiously at the bare earth of the new ones, and dropped their *merde* impartially on both.

The surgeon passed on, and Cascamond heard his deep cold voice in the adjoining room. From a little distance came the sounds of the dockyard; the clamor of hammer and adze and saw and plane; the *click-clack* of huge capstan pawls on the sheer-wharf; a clanging of anvils; a musical *tink-tink-tink* of caulking irons; and a variety of thumps and claps and knocks that he could not identify. In a small wooden tower a brass bell was struck every half hour, marking the time in the sea fashion of the English, in paired or single strokes that counted up to eight, and then went back to one again.

Drouet the young *aspirant,* recovering quickly from a shoulder wound and free to move about the hospital floors, reported to his fellow Frenchmen the result of quick peeps from an upper window. *Bonne Citoyenne* had gone, after a week's repair carried on not only by day but by lantern light at night. *La Furieuse* had taken her place at the sheer-wharf, and the immense arms of the sheers had drawn out of her, like bad teeth, the battered foremast and the stumps of the other two. Now they were swinging into her, one after another, new masts from the spar canal. The English were wasting no time in fitting her for their service. In a few more weeks she would be cruising the Atlantic as H.M.S. *La Furieuse,* a contradiction to suit the peculiar English humor.

Cascamond had expected further calls from Captain Mac-Dougal, but apparently "Old Square-Foot" was too busy with his arithmetic at Melville Island, stowing the latest batch of prisoners. Mr. McNab came to the hospital regularly, bringing a hamper of boiled chickens, pork jelly and such-like delicacies for the inmates, English or French, who seemed most in need of nourishment beyond the common fare. The hamper always included a bottle of rich port wine for Cascamond, to be sipped a little at a time "to build up the blood." Cascamond did not like to tell him that the loblolly boys sipped most of it, without regard to blood, his or theirs. He asked how the sale of the frigate's cargo had gone.

"Quite well," said McNab. "I was successful in bidding for the cocoa and most of the coffee. I was outbid on the sugar, but then sugar's not so hard to come by as the other things."

Cascamond put on an air of surprise. "Do you mean to say that you have difficulty in your West Indian trade? Because of the French? Doesn't Britannia rule the waves down there, as she does everywhere else? That's what you sing, is it not?"

McNab laughed. The young Frenchman's glibness with the English tongue was familiar by now, but he was always coming out with unexpected quips like this. "Britannia rules the most important waves—the ones that beat on Europe, Lieutenant Cascamond. Elsewhere, in the West Indies for example, it's always easy for French privateers to snatch up lone British merchantmen and take them in to Guadeloupe. However that game's about up. Our forces will seize the last French ports in the West Indies by next year."

"*Chansons!*—as we say in France, monsieur. Now tell me news of Europe."

"You mean of Napoleon, who makes all the news in Europe nowadays. He seems to be doing remarkably well, I must confess. This side of the Russian forests only the British seem to be able to call their souls their own. Your emperor has beaten the Austrians again—he must find that a bit monotonous—and just now his troops are swarming over Spain." McNab gave Cascamond a humorous and shrewd glance. "Napoleon may be in some trouble there before the year is out."

"Why?"

"The Spaniards are up in arms."

"*Baste!* Spaniards! They won't fight worth a damn. I can tell you that. I saw them at Trafalgar."

"Um! Well, a British army has gone to help the Spaniards. That may make a difference."

Cascamond laughed. "Monsieur, you are far behind the news! Why, before our ship left France last spring we read in the *Moniteur* about that army of yours. When the French soldiers attacked your redcoats they ran like sheep all the way from Madrid to Corunna. What's more they scrambled aboard their ships and left their general dying on the shore."

"You shouldn't believe everything you read in the *Moniteur*, my friend," McNab observed amiably. "I grant you Sir John Moore's expedition was forced out of Spain. But our men gave you French a bloody nose and a pause at Corunna before they buried their general on the ramparts and went aboard their ships. However, that's past and done. What I speak of now is another British army now in Portugal, under a general named Wellesley."

Cascamond frowned. "One has not heard that name."

"He has served mostly in India, I believe."

"India? You mean he has fought naked Hindus, who barely know which end of a musket hurts the most? Come! Do you really think a man with no more experience than that can stand against Napoleon?"

"That we shall see, Cascamond, that we shall see. I understand this general's family have pretty strong influence in London. An officer with influence there can get pretty well anything he wants —ships, troops, money, supplies—and with all those, my friend, even a very bad general might go a long way."

Cascamond closed his eyes, the usual signal that he was weary of talk and wished to be alone. As a parting shot he remarked, "You know, there's one thing I will admit about you English. You never give up. You fight well on the sea, and so you never despair of doing the same on land. It is simply beyond your comprehension that a frigate is not a regiment, and that a fleet cannot march to Paris."

McNab chuckled. "You may yet see a march of redcoats in the streets of Paris, Cascamond. All things considered, I hope you do."

"You wish me a very long life, monsieur. I thank you very much."

The crisis came and passed ten days after the operation, when Mr. Haddox took his morning sniff at the wound and arose with a rare smile as if Cascamond's leg were a bed of roses, although to the patient the stench was just the same. "It's on the mend. Definitely. Mind, it'll take time yet. If you were a praying man I'd say keep on praying. But of course you Frenchmen nowadays don't put your faith in anything but women and Napoleon."

"How long before I can leave this pesthouse of yours?" Cascamond grinned.

"If all goes well we shall be rid of you before the leaves are off the trees. About mid-October, say. By then you'll be in the ferry-boat to Dartmouth, ay, and scheming how to break your parole and run away, like all those honest Frenchmen over there."

"Will you warrant me a leg fit to run on?"

"It's your head that'll need a warrant, not your leg, monsieur. Where do you plan to run? France is, what, three thousand damned wet miles away."

"There is the United States. How far is that?"

"The nearest part is—say—three hundred miles. A hundred leagues along a rough coast in cold latitudes, where the prevailing winds blow off the land and often blow men in small boats to the Devil—a very clammy Devil, too."

"Are there no roads?"

"None worth a tinker's curse outside the towns. Anyhow, Nova Scotia's all but an island." Mr. Haddox uttered one of his sepulchral chuckles. "Those French fools over in Dartmouth have stolen the ferryboat so many times it's the joke of the town. A mere harbor shallop, moved by oars, with a rag of canvas to help the ferryman when the wind is fair. I'd as soon put to sea in my grandmother's old straw hat. Yet every month or two some of your bold Frenchmen creep down to the shore and steal off with the thing. Usually they're hailed by the harbor guard-ship before they get far past George's Island, and they're caught this side of McNab's. If they do get away they spend two or three days and nights in the North Atlantic, cold and hungry, rattling on hard wooden thwarts, and soused with brine like herrings in a fishwife's tub. At last they make for the shore and give themselves up. After that it's Melville Island, and no more jiggery-pokery about parole."

"Why do you tell me this?"

"Because you seem to me the cocksure sort who'd think he could beat a game that all the others lost."

With that the surgeon moved on, chuckling in that cadaverous voice of his. He enjoyed these little duels and so did Cascamond. It was one of the things that lightened the dullness of the days.

By this time most of the wounded from *La Furieuse* were well

on the way to recovery, for the hopeless cases had vanished into
the ground where the cattle browsed. The spirits of the convales-
cents rose with the mending of their flesh and bones, and each
day they amused themselves with impudent French comment on
their wardens and everything about them, especially the English
mania for cleanliness. The grey loblolly boys, swabbing the floor
with mops and buckets every day, and twice a week scouring it
with holystones, worked under a rain of cheerful insult that was
literally over their heads. On their part the Englishmen had genial
but obscene terms for the "Crappos" who caused them all this
trouble; but the presence of the remarkable *Crapaud* lieutenant
who spoke fluent English put a stopper on their tongues. Respect
for an officer was ingrained in them like the salt in ship's beef after
years in the cask.

The day came when Cascamond was able to leave his cot and
totter once up and down the room, leaning on one of the faithful
loblollies. The effort exhausted him; but the next day he was up
again, and made the length of the room three times, amid encouraging chatter from his fellows. After that Mr. Haddox brought
him a walking stick, so that he could exercise as he chose. It was
like a magic wand. The mere ability to go to a window and look
forth, instead of peering awkwardly from the cot, on a cramped
elbow, gave him an intoxicating taste of freedom.

This advance in his recovery was reported, for it brought a visit
from Captain MacDougal. "Mr. Cascamond," said Old Square-
Foot bluntly. "Ye'll be out of here soon, I gather. So far ye've been
a charge of the Office for Sick and Hurt Seamen. As soon as ye
leave hospital, however, ye come under the Transport Office.
Which is me. I take it ye'll give your parole as an officer and a
gentleman?"

"Of course." As he said this Cascamond watched the bright
blue eyes carefully, but they gave no sign of what MacDougal
really thought. The word of a French officer and gentleman had
lost its substance in the flames of the Revolution.

"Um! Well, to begin with ye'll need an outfit of clothing, shoes
and so forth. Got any money?"

"I had a good sum in my cabin aboard *La Furieuse*—eleven
gold napoleons, thirty or forty Spanish silver dollars. For that matter I had plenty of clothing. All stolen by your English crew."

"Or some of your own, after ye were struck down. Sailors are sailors, eh?"

"The point is, I haven't a thread or a sou."

"Ah! As it happens, Mr. Cascamond, ye're fortunate in the acquaintance of Peter McNab. He mentioned to me that he'd advance whatever ye needed to clothe yourself when ye left the hospital."

"Why?"

"I gather ye'd been courteous to him. Something about your ship's cargo. But McNab—McNab does things like this anyhow. The Scots are a soft race, really, and we're greatly misunderstood. Well, anyhow! As an officer on parole ye'll get a money allowance from the Transport Office, not much, but enough to pay your board and lodging, and a bit over for washing and sundries of that kind. If ye stint yourself a bit ye can pay back McNab's money over a period of time. That's a matter for you and McNab, of course. And by the look of the war ye'll have lots of time."

"The other French officer-prisoners, what do they wear?"

"Well, Lieutenant, in this country a man must dress for the climate, which isn't the climate of Paris or even Brest, say. But naturally they keep at hand a smart uniform in the French naval mode, for visiting the gentry who have villas on the Dartmouth side, and such-like occasions. Ye can have a new uniform made by a verra good French tailor at Melville Island, a prisoner there. Ye'll have to supply the cloth and buttons and so forth—and pay the man for his labor of course. McNab and I can arrange all that."

"Even to the measurements?"

"I'll see the tailor calls on ye tomorrow."

And on the next afternoon the tailor came, a merry little man from Le Havre, with tape measure, pencil and paper. As he busied himself, Cascamond asked, "You came under guard?"

"No, monsieur. A number of us are permitted to go each day to the town, where we make ourselves useful as cooks, tailors, valets, hairdressers—*que-voulez-vous?* It's only an hour's walk by a road through the woods and fields, very pleasant in summer weather."

"And in winter?"

The man rolled his eyes and shuddered dramatically.

This remarkable fellow arranged not only for the uniform, but for shirts, drawers, hat, hose, and shoes, all to be made by skilled hands in the prison, with materials from the store of Peter McNab & Sons. There was an air of magic about it. Within a week a lean limping *protégé* of the Office for Sick and Hurt Seamen was able to appear in the full dress of an officer in the navy of Napoleon, blue and white and gilt, a somewhat startling spectacle for passing dockyard hands as he hobbled about in the sunshine of the hospital grounds.

He was thus arrayed, and improving his walk with the aid of the stick one afternoon, when he noticed a smart carriage and pair trotting along the dusty road from the town. The carriage turned in to the hospital yard. The coachman pulled up, and Mr. McNab descended and helped a lady down. As they walked towards him Cascamond had no attention for the merchant. His eyes and mind were entirely on the person in lavender bonnet and gown beside him, with a hand inside his arm. A slender woman of, say, between twenty-five and thirty, it was difficult to tell with blondes and this one was very blonde indeed, with hair the color of a new hemp cable and eyes of sparkling blue. But his main impression as she came up to him was that of a flower, slim and cool and beautiful, as in Brittany a boyish Cascamond had sometimes found violets at the edge of a wood. A daughter of McNab? She did not seem quite young enough for that.

The merchant said, "Monsieur, I should like to introduce to you my wife. My dear, this is Lieutenant Cascamond of the French naval service." The lady inclined her head, smiling, and Cascamond ventured a deep bow, which proved unfortunate. He nearly fell on his face, and only saved himself by a wild thrust of the stick at the last moment. He recovered his balance in a fury of impatience and embarrassment.

He had not seen a woman in months. He was inclined to be cynical about women, as he was about everything; but as a Frenchman he knew they were like food and wine, something a man might get along without but not for very long. Women knew this, of course, and made the most of it for their own ends, as they had from the beginning of time. Wherever a man went, whatever befell him, Eve was there with her tempting fruit, like those apples on the tree at Wincanton—*restaurant pour les aspirants*.

Since the age of seventeen when, nervous and blundering and desperate, he had proved his manhood with a woman for the first time, Cascamond had tasted the fruit of Eve in ports from Rouen around to Marseilles. His Eves therefore had been French and Spanish for the most part, and a few Portuguese; and of course there had been some furtive encounters with farm girls and maid-servants during his two years on parole in England.

Yet he was not given to loose-fishing. As a commissioned officer, even as an *aspirant,* he had chosen to take his amours among women more fastidious or at any rate more difficult than the sluts who sprawled with common sailors for a sou.

In Guadeloupe on this last voyage the wife of a rich planter had given him the most gratifying sensation of his life, his first con-quest of *une femme très comme il faut.* She was a pale and hand-some creole of pure French blood going back for generations in the West Indies, a *grande dame* in that little aristocracy of the islands which had managed to survive the Revolution and was now quite in fashion. Was not Josephine, first lady of the Empire, a creole from Martinique? His success with such a prize intoxicated Cascamond. Even in the most intense moments of their amour he was conscious of a refrain in his mind like that of a catchy song . . . *the Emperor . . . chose . . . one . . . like . . . this . . . like this . . . like this.*

The lady had a complaisant husband, a man with an air of ele-gant exhaustion and a habit of spending days and nights away, on mysterious business that was never explained. In truth Lieuten-ant Cascamond was no conqueror at all. A woman slowly dying of ennui and petulance had caught fire at the sight of this young man in the glamour of naval uniform, moving with the vigorous step of one who is fresh to the languid airs of the tropics, and she had drawn him into her pretty arms with such skill that he was sure she had fallen into his.

They enjoyed each other thoroughly; and when Cascamond left, after some last delirious hours on the eve of sailing for France, he felt a quite poetic pang. The ship and his duty were tearing him away from the great love of his life, a romance that would stay in his heart and mind for ever. But sad to say, in his harsh experiences later the lady faded in heart and mind, like a portrait hung too long in the reflected sunlight of a West Indian salon. He had seen such

wraiths in elaborate gilded frames on the walls of mansions at
Basse-Terre and Pointe-à-Pitre, like reflections in old mirrors, or
faces glimpsed behind frosty panes from a winter street in Brest.

All that seemed years ago and of no moment now.

Before Cascamond stood a woman in the flesh and in the present; and with the intuition of a Frenchman, sharpened by experience, he saw that flesh as if she wore nothing but her bonnet and
shoes. Long legs moulded beautifully from the ankle to the thigh;
a rich curve of hips melting away into the slender stem of the
waist; and then the breasts—*ouf!*

And in the presence of this image of beauty he, Michel Cascamond, had just made himself ridiculous!

True, there was nothing amused about her gaze, but that made
the matter worse. The light blue eyes regarded him with pity, as if
he were a lame beggar on the road or a sick dog in a ditch. The
fine new uniform did not impress her a bit. She seemed to see only
what he saw himself in the shaving mirror every morning, a gaunt
young man with eyes made of hard blue chinaware and sunk in a
face of lemon peel. Or did she see only a foreigner bobbing up and
down on a stick, like one of those jerking wooden monkey toys the
sailors made? She murmured some little politeness about his health,
and her accent puzzled him. Scotch? English? Welsh? Welsh perhaps, but he had heard that all the Welsh were short and dark.
Irish? Again he had only hearsay, which avowed the Irish a
freckled folk with hair like shredded carrots. With the bland arrogance of servants of the well-to-do the coachman had whistled up
some of the hospital attendants, and they were carrying from the
carriage several baskets of apples, pears, and plums.

"Picked in our orchard on the island," McNab said with pride.
They watched men and baskets disappear inside the red walls of
the house of pain. The merchant went on, "Mrs. McNab would
have come before this—she often visits the hospital with me—but
Dr. Haddox didn't think it advisable too soon after your wounded
were landed here."

Because we howled and stank, thought Cascamond. Aloud he
said, "Madame is very kind to come at all; and speaking for every
Frenchman here, I am glad that madame was not permitted to see
us at our worst. Even now"—he shrugged and drew attention to his

lameness by tapping his leg with the stick—"we are far from our best."

"You look very well, Mr. Cascamond," the lady said, with the ease of a woman of manners and in that elusive accent which intrigued him more and more. "And let me compliment you on your English. One would never know that you were French. You speak like an Englishman. Mr. McNab tells me you learned the language as a prisoner in Somerset."

"Yes, madame. And after two years there I was freed in a small exchange of prisoners. Now as you see I am a prisoner again, on the far side of the Atlantic, and this time a bit the worse for war." He slipped the pun out glibly, and was pleased with this further display of his English.

Under the brim of the bonnet the blue eyes looked into his with the gaze of a perceptive child, and he felt a flush of blood in his thin face, as if she read something in his mind.

"By any chance, Mr. Cascamond, do you read and write in English as well as you speak?"

"Not so well—I should say, not so *easily* as I speak it, madame. When I read or write in English I have to think of each word, how it is spelled, and how the words are put together. When I speak English I don't have to think at all. It's just as if I were talking in French. But to answer your question—I can read and write English, yes."

He saw her eyes turn quickly to McNab and back to himself again, and in that moment he sensed the passing of a message. In another moment she was giving a smiling nod and saying, "Well, Mr. McNab and I must go along to the poor fellows still in their beds. Goodbye, Mr. Cascamond, and I hope your leg keeps mending well. We shall see you again, my husband and I, before you go to Dartmouth."

Cascamond did not risk a bow this time, but took his hat in his free hand and gave it a graceful and profound sweep that conveyed all the politeness of a bow, indeed all the homage of a genuflexion. The merchant touched his black top hat, the lady took his arm, and they walked away to the open door of the hospital.

Cascamond resumed his awkward exercise. He wore a hat cocked in the fashion of the Emperor—"athwartships" as the English sailors said. So set it caught the breeze along the harbor slope and he was obliged to jam it down firmly, almost to his eyebrows. He thought whimsically, I'm like *La Furieuse* after the fight, limping along with my *misaine* set in a head wind.

When he returned the carriage was gone. The senior hospital attendant, Adams, an Englishman with long white hair and a face pitted blue by sparks of gunpowder as if by a tattoo needle, sat ruminating on the hospital steps with a lump of tobacco in his cheek.

"The McNabs have gone, I see," Cascamond said.

"Ay, sir."

"Mr. McNab is a merchant I believe. Would you call him a rich one?"

"All merchants is rich, sir, far as I can see. Some's just richer than others. I'd say Mr. McNab's not as rich as some, but well enough off. A good big shop, goes in for ship-chandlery too, and some commissary contracts with the army and navy. That includes supplies to the French at Melville Island. You take the prisoners alone—up to a thousand at times—as good as a contract to victual a regiment. Besides which he raises tons of wool—worth gold nowadays—on that island of his at the harbor mouth. Ye must ha' seen it, comin' in."

"Yes, of course. Where they hang the dead sailors. Why does a rich merchant live in a place like that?"

Adams turned his head and squirted a brown stream into the grass. " 'Cause he was born out there, and mostly brought up there, I s'pose. His father—that was old Peter—this un's young Peter, though he's in his forties now and got a boy Peter of his own—old Peter McNab bought that there island for a hatful o' gold guineas, so I've heard, back when this town was started fifty or sixty year ago by the Lords o' Trade and Plantations. Built a stone house on it and cleared most o' the woods for sheep pasture. Wanted to live like a Highland lord; and so he did, with bagpipers and all the rest of it. And so does young Peter now, him and his wife. . . ."

"Ah! Madame McNab! She is not Scotch like him—or am I wrong?"

"She's Irish."

Up went the Frenchman's black eyebrows. "Irish! Then she is Catholic?"

"That's what I hear."

"And he—McNab?"

"Presbyterian."

"That sounds to me like—how do you say it?—oil and water. Does it go well, this marriage?"

Adams gave him a glance in which he detected reproof, as if he had asked an indecent question. "If you mean, do they get along well, the answer is Yes, they do. They've got two fine boys, and on their island they entertain the best people o' Halifax, includin' the English an' the Cath'lic clergy."

Cascamond sensed the bristle of the man and asked no more. But this was interesting. How piquant that the first woman he should meet in this dreary English outpost halfway to the Pole should be a beauty of the cool fair sort, so rare, and such a challenge to a man of warm blood! Moreover a woman with a husband years older than herself, of another race and religion, and absorbed in his shopkeeping like so many of the English.

The fact that she was Catholic did not mean she was pious. He himself was nominally Catholic; but his father had perished in the Revolution, and he had been brought up from the age of five in the schooling of the republic, which made a mockery of all the old sacred notions of people like his mother. It was true that the Emperor had restored the Church, but everyone knew that Napoleon was no pietist, that in fact he had a contempt for religion. And Napoleon was everybody's idol, even Cascamond's, who had no respect for gods or idols otherwise.

Well, a man needed to be well and strong, with two good legs under him, whether he wished to march or make love. That applied to lieutenants as much as emperors. Time, my friend. Time! Meanwhile he could think about the look Mrs. McNab had flashed when she was making polite talk about the excellence of his English. What did it mean? There was a whole language in the expression of a woman's eyes. Even a glance had a message for a man sufficiently alert, like the flicker of a semaphore to a skilled *télégraphiste*.

Perhaps he had missed something; but there would be other chances for signals. Now that she had resumed her visits to the naval hospital he would see her once or twice a week until he was discharged. After that he would be shoved away on parole in that *trou perdu* across the harbor. Dismal thought! Of course one could do many things in a lost hole, as he had found in England.

He lay long awake that night, thinking of the McNabs and pondering on the life they lived. He pictured the Atlantic beating on their island shore, and sea birds crying, and sea winds rumpling the fir woods, and sheep flocks nibbling over the pastures, and wild Scotch shepherds blowing bagpipes—whatever bagpipes were. (He remembered verses at school about shepherds and pipes, and apparently they went together.)

And there she was, in the midst of all that, the cool fair flower with the dew still on her, quite untouched—never mind that maladroit English word Missus. There she spent most of her days and nights, while her merchant tested dollars on the counter of a shop in Halifax. And she with those hanged men in her view whenever she looked from her windows—*macabre!*—yet strangely stimulating when he thought of it. Love and death plain. Like some of the fantasies that came from Dr. Haddox's R and O!

Yet they were real. He, Michel Cascamond, had seen the island, the merchant, the flower, and those dead fruit of the sea, the symbol of Britannia's rule. By what strange twist of time and circumstance they had been brought together it was impossible to guess. He wondered deeply, and fell asleep at last.

12

On a bright autumn day Cascamond left the naval hospital in a chorus of cheerful English farewells. He was the last of the wounded Frenchmen under treatment and his tart humor had enlivened the weeks of his convalescence for everyone. Even Dr. Haddox stood on the hospital steps and waved his hat, the only time Cascamond ever saw him with it off.

He had signed his parole, the Agent for Prisoners had paid him the accumulated prisoner-of-war allowance for a lieutenant, and he had it in his pocket, a sum of five pounds and some shillings. He wore his uniform, and in addition to the things made for him at

Melville Island he had obtained through Peter McNab a portmanteau, a suit of plain broadcloth, a pair of stout shoes for everyday wear, a small mirror, and a new English razor in a shagreen case. He rode to the town in a hackney cab and with a feeling of grandeur passed through the lower streets to the Market Wharf. He was in good time to catch the ferry to Dartmouth. Four other passengers waited at the dock, a farmer and his wife, a workman with the smell of the soap-boiler's trade about him, and a mulatto woman in the rags of an Army greatcoat, cut in two to make jacket and skirt, and without shoes or stockings.

At the last moment a short round-faced fellow of about twenty came hurrying around the corner to the dock, swinging in one hand something done up in a large knotted handkerchief. He wore the cocked hat, blue jacket, and white pantaloons of an *aspirant* in the Navy of France, and Cascamond recognised him at once. It was Drouet, the senior midshipman of *La Furieuse*. In the frigate they had been acquaintances in the way of duty, nothing more; but now they fell upon each other like brothers long parted, laughing, kissing cheeks, and crying out in French, to the amusement of the other passengers. The ferryman grumbled, "Aboard, *if* you please!" and they ran down the steps and sat on a thwart together, with the happy chatter of boys out of school. The ferryman collected threepence from each of his white passengers and accepted from the mulatto a penny, which was all she had. He sculled his boat clear of the dock and hoisted a patched brown lug-sail to the harbor breeze.

The Frenchmen compared notes, going over the names of the dead and wounded. Drouet said at last, "You then, and I, and *aspirant* Sebastien, are the only surviving officers of *La Furieuse*. We shall see Sebastien with the other *paroles* over there." He waved a hand. The ferryman was steering for a cove in the farther shore. A small village stood on the slopes about it, with fields and gardens marked off by low walls of roughly piled stones, and beyond them a forest rolling away in dark green waves until it vanished in the purple haze of autumn.

"How many French officers are there?" Cascamond asked.

"About fifty or sixty, it's difficult to say exactly. We live in a scattered way. Some are naval officers, some officers of privateers, some Army officers captured in Haiti and Martinique. The Agent for Prisoners, Capitaine Macdoo-*gal,* makes no distinction."

As the ferry approached the cove Cascamond gazed at the village of Dartmouth. A straggle of houses and stores about the waterside with their unpainted wooden clapboards and shingles gone grey with time and weather; the somewhat better but neglected homes and warehouses of a bygone whaling industry, established by Quaker exiles from Nantucket years ago and since abandoned; a few smart country houses of Halifax merchants who liked to spend the summer months within ferry-reach of their business but away from the noise and hot stench of a naval town.

In clearing the woods the first inhabitants had spared some trees about their houses, mostly big maples and birches, whose leaves were now in autumn color, such color as Cascamond had never seen in France, blood-red, pink, yellow, gold and brown, and enchanting blends of one and another. The dark spruce and pine on the ridges behind made a contrast for all this, as if the whole scene had been contrived by a painter exuberant with wine.

"But this is a pretty place!" Cascamond exclaimed. "How could one mind a stay there?"

Drouet gave him a pitying look and pushed out his small mouth like the delicate snout of a chinaware pig on a mantelpiece. "You will not be staying there, *mon lieutenant.*"

"*Comment?* I was told Dartmouth."

"A general direction. French officers formerly stayed in this village on the harbor, yes. Early in the war the English built a house here for the first dozen or so, and when there were too many for that the others took lodgings with people of the village. Unfortunately some restless devils were always stealing a boat and trying to slip off to the United States. About five years ago the English got bored with all that, and ordered the French officers on parole to move two leagues back into the forest behind Dartmouth to a small settlement called Preston. A few Halifax merchants and officials have summer villas there, but mostly it is just a collection of small farms. That's where we find our lodgings, on the farms. We Frenchmen visit each other as we please, we join in parties of the country folk, sometimes in summer we are invited to dine with a merchant in his villa. And that is our little world. We are forbidden to go more than a mile from it. Anyone who sees a French-

man beyond that may crack his coconut and claim a gold piece
from the Agent for Prisoners."

"*Baste!* The same rule they had in England when I was a prisoner, Drouet. We found ways to stretch it. So do you, apparently.
What are you doing now, so far from Preston? And what have you
there in the handkerchief?"

Drouet grinned. "One finds ways, as you say, though it wouldn't
do to play the game too often. Me, I obtain a written permission
from Capitaine Macdoo-*gal* to visit doctors in Halifax. I complain
of a weakness of the lungs." Drouet coughed theatrically and hung
out his tongue like a tired hound. He held up the knotted kerchief.

"And I bring back medicinal powders for my ailment."

"And what sort of doctors must you go so far to see?"

The *aspirant* winked a merry brown eye. "A house of very
pretty physicians—one consults them separately each time of course
—who are happy to take care of my well-being for a small con-
sideration—sixpence as a rule."

"Are there no women in this place in the woods?"

"Certainly. Countrywomen with no more shape than their own
cows, and stinking like them too. And if you don't mind a taste of
dark meat in the *ragoût* there are some people called Maroons,
brought to these desolate northern woods from Jamaica years ago;
they look like the *sacatras* of Martinique and Guadeloupe; some
of the women are quite well made, but I do not fancy them myself.
So you see, Lieutenant, in Preston there are perhaps fifteen women
of tolerable looks and age and possible inclination. What makes
it worse, some of our Frenchmen are serious. I mean they and
some farmer's daughter are in love, and would marry if they could.
That cuts down the supply, you comprehend. It's all very difficult.
So from time to time I have my lungs."

"And what is the medicine in the handkerchief?"

"Just a supply of snuff, for myself and some French friends, one
of our little luxuries. When the English went from here to capture
Martinique last spring they brought back a lot of booty, including
the good *macouba* snuff that is made there. One can buy it in the
tobacco shops of Alfax."

During the whole of this conversation the ferryman and his
other passengers regarded the Frenchmen with curious but un-
comprehending faces, as they might have contemplated a pair of

twittering sparrows. The boat came at last to a small wooden wharf in Dartmouth Cove. Grey wooden houses and stores drowsed about it. At the head of the inlet a stream fell down the slope and frothed into the tide. In a stony lane above the landing place a stubby farm horse stood with a dusty high-wheeled gig, attended by a youth of about seventeen in linsey shirt and grey homespun trousers. His feet were bare, and his long yellow hair was like a haystack in a gale.

"This," Drouet said, "is the son of the farmer with whom I stay. He is stupid but amiable like his parents. Come with me—they will be glad of another lodger I assure you, and we can share what they please to call a bedchamber. It's no hotel, *bien entendu,* but it costs only a half-crown a week, so one does not complain. The food comes from the farm and the forest and streams. In a rude way it is good, although the woman's cooking is vile. Sometimes she permits me to cook a dish myself—a fresh salmon, a pie of wild pigeons or partridge—you will see the kind of thing."

With his own easy command of English it amused Cascamond to hear Drouet stumbling over an introduction to their youthful driver, using jerky and strongly accented phrases that he had picked up in the past two or three months. Cascamond nodded, smiled, threw his portmanteau into the back of the gig, and climbed in with the boy and Drouet. The gig lurched up the ridge past the houses and huts, past steep rocky fields where cattle grazed, and after a jolting struggle reached the first crest and the edge of the forest.

As the trees closed overhead and behind, shutting off the last view of the harbor and the ships, it was like the silent closing of a dungeon door. The rich smell of pine and fir, which had seemed the very breath of Paradise when *La Furieuse* entered the harbor, was now stifling. In this gloomy green shade, the hot still air, the surrounding silence, Cascamond had a sensation of being slowly smothered in the folds of a giant blanket. He had lived by the sea or on the sea since he was born, except for his years as a prisoner in England. Even there the Somerset countryside was open, the only woods were shady patches on the face of the land, and at Wincanton on stormy days and nights the sea winds blew over the hills and moors from La Manche or in the other direction from the Bristol Channel.

As the gig dragged Cascamond farther and farther into the depths of this enormous green prison his hope of escape someday withered, and so did his spirits. Drouet sensed this, and kept up a lively chatter about the sport to be had in these woods and streams.

"We Frenchmen are not permitted to have a gun in our hands —that is the regulation of the Agent for Prisoners. But our farmer is *complaisant,* a German named Kolp, and he encourages this young oaf and me to hunt for food with his rusty old musket. We get all sorts of wild fowl from pigeons to ducks and geese, and there are tasty animals from hares to a monstrous deer that stands higher than a man, with horns like the spread hands of a giant, which they call *mousse,* as we call a cabin boy. I have mentioned the fishing, it is really good; fat trout swarming in the brooks and ponds, and salmon that swim up the larger streams from the sea. In these forests there is always something to fish or shoot or snare, from the time the snow melts until it comes again."

"And what about the time of the snows?"

Drouet closed his eyes and shook his head. "The other Frenchmen tell me it is hell turned inside out—a torture of cold instead of heat. An eternity of short days and long black nights, with snow to the hips, and an air cold enough to freeze a brass monkey's double-shot. Why France ever owned or fought for this country I shall never know. It is not for Frenchmen, this, unless one could arrive in April and depart by November. For the rest of the year the Devil can have it—he's an Englishman, of course."

Here and there the forest opened in a small wayside clearing with a wooden farmhouse or cabin, usually of logs, and the October sunshine filled this hole in the woods like a bright pool in a desert. In one place there was a surprise, a substantial villa of white-painted clapboards and green shutters, with a garden before it, and birch and beech trees thinned to a sort of park behind, with all the undergrowth cleared away. A brook ran through the grounds, and paths wound among the trees, passing rustic benches and an oval pool in the shade, lined with stones and obviously made for a fishpond.

"But who dwells here?" said Cascamond astonished.

Drouet chuckled. "A Frenchman! Yes! A *ci-devant* named d'Anseville, formerly governor of the colony at St. Pierre, an island off the coast of Newfoundland. The people there were mostly codfishers but d'Anseville lived in the style of the old regime, a governor's mansion, a military aide and secretary, a dozen servants, the best of food and wine—you can guess the sort of thing. He remained in charge there for a time after the Revolution, simply because the committees in Paris were too busy killing *aristos* at home to bother about one in a small colony in North America. Then, just in time, an English expedition captured St. Pierre and carried off d'Anseville and his staff as prisoners to Alfax. The English with their weakness for aristocracy considered d'Anseville a prize, allowed him a fat pension, and sent him over to Dartmouth to live on parole. You may be sure he didn't take long to find excellent lodging—with a lady younger than himself, the daughter of an English officer. Her father had died and left *Mees* Floyer sufficient money to live quietly and comfortably with a servant or two. *Voilà!* A natural *liaison*. After a few years they built this pretty retreat on the road to Preston, where in summer they entertain parties of English officers and merchants and their ladies, like a pair married and of the best position. Do you wonder that when Napoleon signed the little peace at Amiens this *ci-devant* made no attempt to go home to France, where he is said to have a wife? Or that, when the war resumed, he again placed himself as a prisoner on parole so that the English would continue his pension? He is always polite to us other Frenchmen when we meet, even though we are of the new France which despises all his kind. We could knock on that door now, you and I, and be invited in for a glass of wine. We might even see *Mees* Floyer."

"Good! Let us do that!"

"*Baste!* She's no beauty and no longer young. Besides, he's a spy for the English, we all know that. Why would they pay him all that money, year after year, if they did not look to him for information and advice? Including advice about French officers who come and go along this road! It is the only route from Preston to the port of Alfax, you comprehend. Everything must pass this way."

The forest closed in again. The gig bounced and rattled along the road, at a pace no faster than a man could walk.

"How do you manage for drink?" Cascamond said. He had a dismal impression of leaving behind every civilized comfort known to man.

"Ah, those damned English capture a lot of good French brandy and wines in one way or another. Think what there was in *La Furieuse,* for example. Well, it's all to be had at prize sales in Halifax. Old d'Anseville does himself well. We other Frenchmen aren't so well off, and we have to buy it through the farmers, who get it from the merchants—a double profit to be paid. We manage a few bottles of brandy now and then, and there's always rum of course, but mostly we must content ourselves with *vin ordinaire.* Fortunately the English don't care for that and sell it off cheap. Ha! Do you remember old Loup-de-Mer lacing our *ordinaire* with gunpowder to make us powerful? He really believed it. What an affair!"

They came at last to a low hill cleared of timber and the larger boulders. At the top sat a small wooden dwelling, with a log barn, a pigsty, and an enclosure of sticks for fowls. A pair of cows stared at the approaching gig, and as it reached the crest the Kolps came out of the house, a stolid man and woman in grey homespuns, and stared with eyes exactly like the cows'. Again Drouet made introductions, and this time Cascamond broke in with his precise English and asked if he could lodge with his friend. He proffered a week's lodging in advance and got their consent at once.

He paused then with Drouet while the midshipman pointed out the features of Preston with the familiarity of an old inhabitant. Nearly all of the farms had been cleared on low hills, for the convenience of rolling boulders away to the bottom, and as a result there was a view of many, sitting on bumps in the landscape like islands in a deep ocean of trees. In the wrinkles of the land Cascamond could see streams like threads of silver lace, and here and there the blue mirror of a lake.

Drouet talked on, with careless gestures. "Most of the Preston habitations are like this although some are better. There are a few summer villas of Halifax gentry, a fad of some years ago started by the former English governor Wentworth. He built one—you can see it, that white speck on the hill far over there. He engaged some of the black people from Jamaica for his servants and farm laborers, and built cabins for them at the back. They say M. Wentworth enjoyed a handsome Maroon girl whenever his lady wasn't looking, and left a *café-au-lait* memento toddling about the servants' quarters. A pretty scandal, eh? And consider our *ci-devant*

governor of St. Pierre, old d'Anseville and his English *Mees*. You
see the effect of this air even in high circles. There is fun sometimes, *enfin,* in these scenes of solitude." He said this with a wry
grin and they both burst out laughing as they turned away to the
house.

They entered the kitchen, the heart of the *ménage,* with furniture entirely home-made; a long table, benches, a tall-backed settle by the fireplace, three or four odd-looking chairs sawn out of
barrels and set on rockers, with seats of cord padded with sheep
fleece. The middle of the floor was covered by an oval carpet
made from rags of various colors, first plaited into a sort of rope,
and then sewn in coils like a tremendous flat snake. The bare parts
of the pine-board floor were much worn by the passage of feet,
especially by the clogs of Mrs. Kolp. A thick reek of bygone cook-
ery, of human sweat, of tobacco, and of the barnyard, saturated
every part of the hovel.

The parents slept in a bedchamber off the kitchen. The stairs to
the upper story were steep and narrow like a ship's companion-
way, and up there Drouet showed Cascamond two meagre chambers, without doors, but each with a small window in the gable
end. Each room had a chest-of-drawers rudely fashioned from pine
boards, a couple of stools, a straw pallet lying on the floor, and a
chamberpot. The slope of the roof obliged the two men to stoop
except in the middle of the floor.

"The boy George sleeps in that hole there," Drouet said. "This
is ours," and he swept the barren little garret with one of his magnificent gestures. "What do you think of it?"

"I've seen better quarters in a codfish lugger," Cascamond said.

"No doubt. Our *matelots* in the prison at Melville Island live
much better than our officers out here."

"How do you know that?"

"Many of them are allowed to work in the town. Some of our
officers get to town also. A few words, sometimes a scrap of paper
with information, pass between us and them. Nothing of great importance, except to spoil the English game of separating our officers from any contact with their men. To beat the English at
anything, that is always of importance, *hein?*"

Cascamond gazed about the poor little chamber again. "Appar-

ently the English wish to degrade French officers—to make us live
like pigs."

"Not at all. They don't care a damn how we live. The Agent
pays us the allowance, and we can do what we like with it. We can
spend it mostly for lodging—some of our more fastidious Frenchmen live quite elegantly here—or we can spend it for clothes, for
gambling, for a woman. Ha! We can chuck it down the *poulaine*
if we like." He jerked a thumb at the window and the view of a
little cabin like a sentry box at the back of the house. "Most of us
choose the cheapest lodgings we can find, and spend the rest for
fun. As an *aspirant* I get little enough for fun. You of course,
Lieutenant, are in a better position."

Cascamond did not miss the gibe in that. He had made it himself
many times when he was a midshipman among the French officers
at Wincanton.

"We are all in a bad position," he said sourly. "And we must
blame those futile idiots who stole the boats at Dartmouth. An
officer could live agreeably there. Now, instead, we have this." His
hands expressed his contempt for every sorry detail of the Kolp
ménage.

In this mood he settled himself into the life of the paroles at
Preston. As Drouet had observed, there was much visiting back
and forth. There were card games of *Boston,* of *Napoleon,* and
interminable games of *tric-trac* huddled over a board and pieces.
Bottles of brandy and rum, and kegs of *vin rouge,* appeared mysteriously in farm carts returning from Dartmouth. When the supply
was good there were parties, with food cooked by some gourmet
among them, and they wore their uniforms or the rags of uniforms,
and there were speeches, and shouts of "Vive la France! Vive
l'Empereur!" The villagers of Preston were accustomed to these
sprees and looked upon them with indulgence. After all, the cash
allowances of the Frenchmen found their way largely to Preston
pockets, and coin was coveted by the farm folk, who had to barter
their products for merchandise in the stores of Dartmouth and
Halifax.

Already the winds were turning chill, and the gaudy leaves lost
their hold on the hardwood trees and blew about the roads and
fields. On calm nights came frost, glistening and then melting in
the next morning's sun. Then came heavy rains, which set the

dense forest sopping and dripping and turned roads to wallows of mud. Then appeared snow, and ice on the lakes, and after that the streams. Drouet and Cascamond followed the practice of old hands, the officers who had been years in the backwoods, and bought coats and trousers of thick homespun, mittens, caps, and long stockings knitted on the farms, and moccasins made from the skin of moose shanks with the hair inside.

They joined in the chase for moose, tramping on snowshoes (very awkwardly at first and at the cost of chafed feet), searching for tracks of the great beasts in their winter grounds about the swamps. Sometimes the chase went on for two or three days, the hunters each night making a bivouac of fir branches in a hollow in the snow, and curling up like dogs about a fire, freezing one side, roasting the other, turning over from time to time, and napping uneasily, with their breath freezing on the hairs of an old bearskin drawn about head and upper body in the fashion of the Indians.

Much of this effort and endurance went for nothing. Too often Kolp's old musket, their only weapon, snapped without fire at the opportune moment. When they were successful there was a long and desperate labor, making a crude *tabagan* of poles lashed together with strips of raw hide, cutting the carcass into quarters, plucking from the steaming mass of guts the heart and liver, part of which they roasted on sticks and ate like wolves, and then the long drag through the woods, avoiding thickets and using the open ice of lakes and streams wherever possible. The worst labor came at the last, when they were exhausted, climbing the Kolp hill, which seemed to have grown to a mountain. For Drouet one exhausting hunt was enough. Cascamond prided himself on being a Breton and therefore tougher than anyone else in the world, and he found a grim satisfaction in proof. Yet it was a brutish business, all of it, a descent to the level of the Indians in their savage climate and their savage land.

At night when Cascamond retired with Drouet in the garret, each wrapped in a quilt stuffed with wild goose feathers, they talked until it was warm enough for sleep. By the light of their coarse brown candle, of the kind made in Preston kitchens from the tallow of wild game, Cascamond could see frost sparkling on the points of shingle nails protruding through the roof. The featherbeds made the body comfortable and sleep possible, but otherwise one might as well be lying outdoors. Even the contents of the humble earthernware *pot* at the foot of the bed would be frozen long before morning.

How many winters like this? He wondered. *How many years?* Some of the officers had been taken prisoner as far back as 1803 —six years—and the war was no nearer an end than when it began in '93. He saw men long in this kind of captivity who had slipped year by year into a squalid way of life, dressed in greasy country homespuns, gulping whatever food was put before them, drinking themselves to a stupor whenever they could get stuff to drink, easing their male hunger in the flesh of some unwashed slut among the farms or in the *cabanes* of the Maroons.

Now that snowdrifts blocked the road, so that even an ox-sled could not wallow through to Dartmouth, there was an end of Drouet's visits to his pretty little doctors. Of all the hardships of the winter this was the most cruel. He lamented it aloud at night in the garret, when he lay in the featherbed awaiting sleep, and while the frost outside cracked trees or started house-nails with the bang of a musket.

Cascamond sometimes cut him off impatiently, but his usual view was one of amused tolerance. With only six years' difference in their ages he was vastly more experienced in life and war than this talkative youngster, who went over his adventures one by one as a monk told the beads of a rosary. To Cascamond the casual amours of the past were not worth remembrance any more than a meal he had enjoyed when he was hungry, except that passion in Guadeloupe. They were like old tales of war, too much alike, and *chansons en tout cas*.

When it came to war young Drouet was fond of giving a full account of the only battle he had ever seen, the last fight of *La Furieuse*. Among the French at Preston such yarns were told and embroidered and retold, as children pass a rainy day with fairy tales. Cascamond found himself held in a peculiar respect because he was a survivor of the most frightful disaster of the war and would not talk about it. Often he was pressed to tell the tale of Trafalgar. Always he refused with contempt. "Bah! The mess was bad enough. One does not wish to go back and eat it again, like a dog at his vomit." This gave him the repute of modesty, and

Drouet often explained to others that Lieutenant Cascamond put on this surly front as a shield for the bitter remembrances and emotions of a patriot.

The winter crept on. In the bright keen weather of February some of the more energetic officers visited back and forth on snow-shoes. They scraped aside the snow on the nearest pond in the woods and amused themselves with make-shift skates carved from wood and fitted with bits of old iron. They learned how to chop a hole in the ice and dabble a hook and line for trout. A bit of fat salt pork on the hook was sufficient bait, and when they yanked a fish into the air it flapped a few times and then froze stiff.

But there were storms for days and nights on end, when they could do nothing but huddle with the farm folk by the hearth, hearing the boom of the wind in the chimney and the slash of snow on the panes. The frugal candles gave their only light in these evenings. The only book in the house was an old German Bible which the Kolps, being unlettered folk, could not read. From time to time the woman would fetch it from the cupboard and turn the leaves slowly with great reverence, as if some ineffable bless-ing was to be drawn from it merely by the touch. They spoke Eng-lish with a German accent which Drouet found doubly hard to understand and sometimes baffled even Cascamond. Thus without reading, with only worn and threadbare small talk, the strangely mixed household crouched away from the storms as if in a cave, and wishing they could hibernate like bears until the spring.

Early in March the farmers of Preston took their oxen and horses, their sleds and shovels, and broke a road through the drifts to Dartmouth. The vagrant snowstorms of spring, wandering in from the sea, would block the road again, but from this time on the people would keep it open. Traffic with Dartmouth and Halifax was now regular and profitable. Town folk were short of supplies after the long winter, and the merchants offered high barter values for vegetables stored in farm cellars and for fresh beef and pork. The farmers on their return from market brought among other things rum and red wine, which they sold at a good cash profit to the Frenchmen.

Towards the end of April the last snow melted away and the road began to dry. Drouet, armed with a pass from the Agent for Prisoners, took his delicate health to Halifax for two or three days

and returned with a long ecstatic account of the treatment. By
May some carriages of Halifax gentry appeared, bringing servants
to prepare their villas for another summer. And one day a mes-
senger delivered at the Kolp farm a neatly cocked note on fine
paper, addressed to Lieutenant Michel Cascamond.

At the moment the lieutenant and Drouet were fishing for trout
in a stream beyond the farm hill, and when young George Kolp
came running and panting with the note in his fingers Cascamond
was mystified. Like all the Frenchmen at Preston he was expecting
the man they called Capitaine Macdoo-*gal* any day now with the
quarterly payment of their parole allowance. Other than that he
had not the least expectation of notice from the outside world. He
opened the note with hands still soiled from his fishing, and read:

> *Brook House, Sunday, May 20, 1810*
>
> *His Excellency M. Nicolas d'Anseville requests the
> pleasure of the company of M. Michel Cascamond for
> wine and conversation, at four hours in the afternoon of
> Saturday, May 26.*

It was written with a fine hand, and in French except for the
words Brook House.

He showed the note to Drouet with a brusque, "What the devil
does this mean?"

The midshipman read it and smirked. "That old goat d'Anseville
cannot satisfy his wild *Mees* any more. The long nights of winter
have exhausted him. And who is better to relieve him at the bedpost than a man who could handle *La Furieuse?*" He was delighted
with his pun and shouted, "Long live the nights of spring!"

"Imbecile! It can only mean one thing. This *ci-devant,* this spy
for the English, wants me to tell him something. What can it be?"

Drouet shrugged and threw out his hands. "Who knows? Perhaps the story of Cap Trafalgar." He glanced up, smiling, and was
appalled by the look he got.

"What do you say?" snapped Cascamond.

"A jest—yes—only a jest," stammered the *aspirant*. "A stupid
joke like the one about *Mees,* who is a cold fish, one hears. Why
are you angry?"

The fire went out of Cascamond's eyes—the fire which had

burned for a few moments like the blue flames of brandy—and the
scowl departed, leaving only the wary cynical look which was his
daily wear. He turned without another word and strode away towards the farm, leaving Drouet and young George to pick up his
fish pole and the string of trout he had caught. At three o'clock on
the Saturday afternoon the Kolp gig, with George as coachman,
set off with Lieutenant Michel Cascamond. The prisoner had
bathed and shaved with care, and Drouet with the household scissors had trimmed his head to a round black bullet with the usual
drooping forelock. Aware that the *ci-devant* was inviting him to
go beyond the prisoner's mile, in effect to enter a trap, Cascamond
determined to enter it wearing his full naval uniform as if it were
the flag of France, a flourish of defiance. His only embarrassment
was the ridiculous horse and gig. Just before reaching Brook House
he bade young Kolp stop and let him out, adding that George was
to await his return there, in the woods up the road out of sight.

Cascamond walked into the open, entered the gateway in the
neat white fence and strutted up the garden path like a cock approaching another's dunghill, ready for the fray. A Maroon was
at work with a hoe at the back of the garden under the direction
of a slender woman in grey silk. She had a gentle face, but she
was not beautiful in any way, and Cascamond guessed her age at
something close to forty. She looked up as he approached, met
his bold stare with one of cool indifference, the *sang-froid* of the
English, and turned her attention back to the gardener as if Cascamond in full fig were nothing more than a butterfly flashing a moment in the sun.

He stepped on to the house porch, and before he could sound a
defiant thunder on the great brass knocker the door opened. He
expected a lackey of some sort but perceived at once that he was
in the presence of M. d'Anseville himself. It was a quaint encounter, the young officer of Napoleon and the old officer of Louis
the Sixteenth. D'Anseville might have been an engraving in one of
the few books Cascamond had ever seen depicting the life of the
ci-devant aristocracy. A lean figure in the sixties with a face drawn
tight over the bones, a sharp Roman nose, a pair of faded grey
eyes that obviously needed the aid of the quizzing glass suspended
by a ribbon from his coat lapel. The hair powdered like snow,
drawn into a queue, and tied with a silk ribbon. The exquisitely

ruffled cravat, the fine white coat and waistcoat embroidered with
silver lace, the china buttons, the deep cuffs, the tight white
breeches and stockings on legs like sticks, the narrow high-heeled
shoes with arched golden buckles.

Cascamond, determined not to be at a loss, whatever happened,
said the first thing that came into his head. "Monsieur, one would
think we have both dressed for a part in a play. What a pity it has
no title!"

D'Anseville put up the quizzing glass to his right eye and regarded his visitor pleasantly. "What a pity that there should be a
play at all, monsieur, when there is so much reality about us. Enter,
if you please." He led the way into a small but beautifully furnished drawing room. Several of the pieces were French and of
such elegance that Cascamond guessed they must have come from
the official mansion of the governor at St. Pierre. According to the
Preston gossip M. d'Anseville was really one of the petty aristocracy, not important enough for a fat sinecure in France, nor a post
in the East or West Indies where a governor could grow rich in
five or ten years. It was said that d'Anseville's wife had refused to
face life amongst the codfishers and stayed in France, and as he
was a devout Catholic he could not marry this cherished English
companion in Nova Scotia. At all events here he was, a figure of
chiseled ivory dropped from the chessboard of the old regime; one
of the lesser figures, a pawn which had lain unnoticed when the
Revolution destroyed the others along with the king and queen,
the castles, the bishops, and the knights.

The pictures on the walls included one or two landscapes haunt-
ingly French. From a corner a staff protruded at an angle, with an
ornamental brass lance-point at the tip, and from it hung in folds
the white banner and golden lilies of *ci-devant* France. A violon-
cello and bow lay on a table nearby. Cascamond had a ludicrous
vision of the old exile sitting before that emblem of the Bourbons
and drawing deep groaning tunes from the 'cello.

M. d'Anseville took the visitor's hat and motioned him to a
chair. He sat himself at a distance, as if to dispel any suspicion of
intimacy, and leaned back, resting his forearms on the arms of the
chair, and dangling his lean hands. There were rings on three fingers of each hand, and one on the left thumb. The ex-governor of
St. Pierre was a walking jewel case.

"Alors, what shall we talk about?" he said, and answered his own question with, "Let us talk about France, our native land. I do not speak of kings or emperors, so you may put away your distrust, Lieutenant. Where is your home?"

"I am a Breton. Saint-Malo. And you?"

"I was educated in Paris, but my home was a small estate by the Garonne, at La Réole. I lived at La Réole for many years. Then I was given a post in North America, as perhaps you have heard."

"Yes."

"A beautiful country, our France. I have not seen it in twenty years. Now that I am getting old I find myself dreaming in my bed of the Garonne Valley. Even napping in a chair in the afternoon, as an old man does. You know the Garonne, perhaps?"

"Only the mouth of it. I have been to Bordeaux often enough. I seldom had an inclination to travel inland. A few kilometres perhaps, here and there."

M. d'Anseville seemed a bit puzzled at the word kilometres, but he made no comment. In his conversation with the new breed of French officers he found them speaking what was in many ways a new French language, and he was never sure whether the words and phrases he could not understand were born in the mouth of the Republic, or of the new Empire, or were merely an unfamiliar naval slang.

He closed his eyes as if he were slipping into one of his afternoon naps, and then said suddenly in English, "You speak this language also, I believe?"

Cautiously, Cascamond snapped, *"Comment?"*

The ivory pawn in the chair went on in English, "One knows many of the Preston people. Do you think it is a secret that Lieutenant Cascamond speaks English like an Englishman? I should think you would be proud of such an accomplishment. A difficult language. I was here a long time before I could speak it with any ease." He opened his eyes with their vague gaze and smiled. "I have been here amongst the English seventeen years, and still, as you notice, I speak the language with a French tone unmistakable. Now let me hear you speak it like an Englishman."

Cascamond shrugged. "Very well, I speak English like this. I learned as you did—as a prisoner"—he could not keep the contempt from his voice—"although I was not a prisoner quite so long as you."

"Ah! You speak English very well indeed. Bravo! And how did you escape?"

Cascamond thought, Does this relic think he's being subtle, or does he take me for a fool? He favored the relic with a broad smile.

"I didn't escape, as you put it. I was released by cartel. The English exchanged me, and some others they considered of no account, for one of their naval lieutenants who happened to be the son of a milord. I've often wondered which side got the best of it. For France I was, myself, an unfortunate exchange."

"Why?"

"Because I was soon captured again."

"Capture is not always a misfortune, Lieutenant Cascamond. No doubt you have heard all about me. If the English had not captured me in the early summer of '93 I should have been recalled to France when the guillotine became so busy—I'd have made my last sneeze in the basket, as they say. But that is not a pleasant subject. Let us have wine. What is your preference?"

Cascamond answered with a lift of shoulder and a grimace, the expressions of a man who does not care a damn for his host or for his wine.

"Ah! You leave it to me! I thank you for the compliment. As a man from the Garonne naturally I think of what my English friends in their vague way call simply 'claret.' To be more particular, I have some excellent Château Haut-Brion, taken from a French merchantman en route to the West Indies. The man in charge of the sale of prize goods at Halifax called it 'O'Brien,' and of course so does my butler, a manservant from Dartmouth."

D'Anseville turned to the sideboard for a small silver hand bell, which he rang in his languid way, and at once a maid popped into the room as if shot from a gun. She must have been poised outside the door waiting for just that sound. A big red-haired wench, probably a clodhopper from a Dartmouth farm, trained by Miss Floyer, and dressed in a black gown with a white apron and mobcap.

"Susan," said the old French dandy, "ask James to open a bottle of wine, a particular wine called O'Brien—he will understand —and bring it with a tray and glasses."

In a few minutes Cascamond was sipping and nodding approval, not as an expert but simply as a Frenchman enjoying the taste of something French and good.

"I know nothing of your part of the country," d'Anseville said. "What is the wine there?"

"We don't grow grapes in Brittany, sir, except in the south, on the Loire about Nantes, where they make good white wine and brandy. In the north and west we are mostly fishermen and sailors, and our climate has much wind and rain. The West Indies trade brings us rum, and as we say 'rum combats rheum.' In that way we Malouins are like the English, whose sailors drink rum as a ration every day."

"They also drink lime juice as a ration," observed d'Anseville wryly.

The talk went on in this way, Cascamond wary and the other apparently half-asleep. At times M. d'Anseville opened his eyes to make a remark and put up the quizzing glass as well, as if he were curious to see the effect of what he said. But what he said was never of much point, and Cascamond noticed that the glass seemed to be aimed over his shoulder. He could not decide whether its object was the case clock by the window behind him or the window itself, which faced over the flowerbeds to the road. Or was it sometimes the clock and sometimes the window?

Eventually there were voices from the road. Somehow, without the *gaucherie* of turning his back on his host, he managed to veer his head and shoulders enough for a side glance at the window. A smart carriage-and-pair stood at the gate with a Negro coachman, and Miss Floyer was putting out her hands in welcome to a lady coming through the gateway. He could not see the visitor's face, for it was hidden in a large yellow poke bonnet. And now M. d'Anseville was speaking again and Cascamond turned his attention politely to the old beau in the chair.

". . . the month of May in this country . . . delightful . . . brings the flowers and the visitors . . . just as March brings the warm winds and the birds."

The door opened and the two men came to their feet, Cascamond making a smart *volte-face* that would have done him credit at a drill or a captain's inspection.

"Lieutenant Cascamond, allow me to present you to Miss Floyer and . . ."

Cascamond did not catch the name of the other, partly because d'Anseville's thin diffident voice was now coming from behind him, and partly because Miss Floyer entered first and drew his immediate attention. He bowed stiffly, and on looking up received the same cold acknowledgment of that first moment in the garden. He understood it now. She really loved this old aristocrat of hers, and as a woman of refinement she loathed the Frenchmen up the road, who despised him and leered at her. He admired her loyalty—even her *sang-froid*. After all, who had more *sang-froid* than a Breton, and especially a Malouin like himself? He turned his hard blue gaze from *Mees* to the visitor, and lost all his calm in a flash.

La Fleur! He had called her that in his mind ever since their first meeting, because she had the look and the cool freshness of a flower in the morning dew. Now, tall in a green gown and pelisse, and with that big yellow scoop of the bonnet, she looked like . . . what the deuce did the English call it . . . diff . . . daff . . . daff . . . daffodil! And this daffodil was smiling and raising an arm to him as if putting forth a leaf.

"How nice to see you again, Lieutenant Cascamond, and to find you looking so well!"

He bowed over her hand, and looking up exclaimed, "Madame! What a surprise! During the past seven months I became certain that I had passed out of the world, with nothing but a memory of people like you—you were so kind—and Mr. McNab of course."

She moved away to a chair and sat, and Miss Floyer did the same but at some distance, leaving the two Frenchmen together with the beautiful blonde visitor.

"Tell me about life in Preston," said Joanna McNab to Cascamond. The yellow scoop caused her face to appear in a tinted shadow where the eyes shone like gems of amethyst, strange and enchanting. She gave her whole attention to Cascamond as if whatever he had to say was of great importance, and he found himself stammering vaguely, lost in the charming vision under the bonnet. Then, pulling his senses together, he began a light description of life among the French paroles, the easy things, the droll things, the surface things; nothing of the deprivation of healthy men cast away like shipwrecked sailors in the midst of nowhere, nothing of the monotony, the squalor, the sense of a living death.

While she listened to this, the maidservant came in with a tray of china and silverware, and Miss Floyer poured cups of tea for Mrs. McNab and herself. As Cascamond described his hunting and fishing, jumping up to demonstrate with lively gestures and postures, he paused frequently to sip his wine, and whenever the glass was low, M. d'Anseville was at his elbow to fill it.

In one of these pauses for refreshment Mrs. McNab said, "I can see you've been outdoors a lot, without your telling me. You look so fine and brown. In February and March the sun on the snow burns the face as if it were midsummer—I've noticed that on our island. And your leg's well healed, too. You haven't the slightest limp."

Cascamond was flattered by this notice. With the warmth of the wine in his veins he felt self-assured in a way that he had not felt since that conquest in Guadeloupe. When the clock struck the hour of five it seemed absurd. It was impossible that he could have talked for an hour—he, the taciturn Cascamond.

"I must be leaving soon," observed Mrs. McNab. "Our sloop is to pick me up at Dartmouth about six, and I must stop there long enough to thank Mrs. Tremain for the lend of her carriage."

"Before you go," d'Anseville said quickly, "I must show you the new hedge, to screen Margaret's rosebeds from the north winds. And of course the extension of the fishpond—you must see that too."

The lady came to her feet saying, "Do you mind?" with a smile at Miss Floyer and Cascamond. "I'll be back in a minute." They departed, and Cascamond was alone with d'Anseville's mistress. He found the situation droll. He could not imagine anyone less like a concubine. She was such a plain creature with her greying brown hair, her quiet movements, her air of a nun on a visiting day. In the silence he plucked his brains for something to say and found nothing. It was Miss Floyer who spoke.

"Where did you first meet Mrs. McNab?"

"At the naval hospital. She was a visitor and a very charming one."

"She's also a good wife and mother, happy with her family. Please understand that, Lieutenant Cascamond."

He was startled not so much by the words as the piercing grey look aimed straight into his head like a rapier point. These English! You never knew what was behind their cold masks until the thrust came, or the blow.

"Why do you say that?" he answered after a silence.

"Because I know what's in your mind when you look at M. d'Anseville and me—and Mrs. McNab. What you think of Nicolas and me is not important—we are accustomed to that. But you must be careful of what you think of Mrs. McNab. She is, I repeat, a good woman. A saint. And you aren't worth the leather of her shoe."

Cascamond's astonishment was giving way now to a wicked amusement. Did she think he might attempt a rape of the saint? Here and now, in the presence of herself and d'Anseville? What made her so suspicious? He could almost hear the voice of her shriveled protector, warning her year after year against the prisoners-of-war up the road, all ravenous for woman-flesh. He was tempted to laugh, but the look of the grey eyes chilled him.

Joanna and d'Anseville were standing by the fishpond, among birch trees with buds just breaking into leaf.

"As you see," the old gentleman said, "he must have learned his English from people of a good class. I am informed that he was captured at Trafalgar and spent some years as a prisoner on parole in England, which seems a sufficient explanation. As an officer he would have entry into the homes of people of some position. In your letter you asked me to determine if he spoke a good sort of French. By then it was winter and I had no opportunity. I can tell you now. What he speaks is not the French of Paris, of course. But I used to hear it said in my Paris days that the best French was spoken in Touraine and particularly in the town of Tours. Myself, I came from the region of Bordeaux, and I speak what I hope is an educated tongue with the natural accent of a Bordelais. Now, the officer inside there is a Breton. The Breton people I believe have a language of their own like the Welsh and Scotch, and when they speak French it is sometimes difficult to understand them.

"However this officer happens to be a native of Saint-Malo,

where most of the men go to sea and mingle with other Frenchmen and with foreigners, so that one might call them citizens of the world. Also this young man belongs to a new generation educated by the state, with a view to future officers for the Army and Fleet. You cannot have an engineer, an artilleryman, or a navigator without a good knowledge of mathematics. And for a clear understanding of orders, given or received, an officer must know the best use of the language, written or spoken. This officer is, I should say, an example of the training under the republic and the empire, with all its faults and omissions—religion for example—but also the special advantages."

He saw that Mrs. McNab showed some impatience.

"You must pardon an old man's wandering. I felt that you should know all about this man first. Now to the point. I think he is qualified to teach the language as it is spoken in official circles in France today. Of course the gentlemen of France today are the *parvenus* of Napoleon, but that cannot be helped."

"And how much pay should I offer him?"

M. d'Anseville considered a moment or two. "He receives from the Transport Office, through Captain MacDougal, the allowance of a lieutenant on parole, about two guineas a month. I think if you offered him an extra two guineas, with board and lodging, he would consider himself fortunate."

"Very well! Thank you so much, my dear friend. You have solved a problem that has troubled me for some time. Shall we return inside?"

The long hostile silence in the drawing room was broken by the reappearance of Mrs. McNab and d'Anseville. Cascamond opened his half-closed eyes with the relief of a man who has been locked in a cage with a touchy leopardess. Mrs. McNab came towards him and he stood up at once.

"I must be leaving soon for Dartmouth," she exclaimed, "so I won't beat about the bush. Lieutenant Cascamond, I have two sons in their teens, educated at home, on our island. My husband considers it important that they study the French language—would you consider coming to teach them? For a year, say? We would provide excellent board and lodging, and pay you two guineas each month."

Cascamond was completely taken aback. What a brisk and businesslike daffodil it was after all—and with two sons in the teens! She must be considerably older than himself! Yet she did not look it. Indeed how lovely she was in that green silk sheath, like a tall stem, and with the animated face and eyes looking out from that huge yellow flower!

His *sang-froid* was returning now. Apart from amorous possibilities there was a very practical side to this offer. Release from that existence in the Preston woods. Life by the sea again. Decent food and lodging. And money into the bargain! With a total income of four guineas a month he could pay off his debt to the merchant McNab and save at least thirty guineas in a year. And then? A man who found himself at the mouth of a busy harbor, who spoke English well, and had a purse of gold, could surely find a way to the United States, and thence back to France! The possibilities ran ahead in his mind like the links of a golden chain. But one was missing. It was the first.

"Madame, I am a prisoner-of-war, forbidden to go more than a mile from Preston. Merely for being here, in this house, I could be deprived of all my rights as an officer and thrown into the *cachot*—the Black Hole under the prison at Melville Island!" He folded his arms dramatically and stared hard at d'Anseville.

"That," said the clear voice under the bonnet, "is no matter at all. The Agent for Prisoners can grant any permission he wishes— and he happens to be an old friend, a frequent visitor to our island, indeed promised in marriage to my husband's ward."

"Captain MacDougal?"

"Of course. So you may consider the matter settled. I'll have to explain everything to my husband first, and then to the Agent for Prisoners. You'll receive a letter and a pass in due course, and Captain MacDougal will see that you get to our island."

Cascamond stammered, "Do you mean to say that Mr. McNab did not . . ."

A peal of laughter from the depths of the bonnet. "Of course not! This has been entirely a venture of my own. In a way I'm playing a little game for my own ends. It's part of the pleasure of being a wife. And mother, of course. We women are all schemers, Lieu-

tenant Cascamond, and our best effort is to make men do what we
wish without suspecting it for a moment."

Again the laughter, and a roguish look from the bonnet. She
turned the laughter and the look to d'Anseville and Miss Floyer,
called out thanks to them, and ran to the carriage. In a few moments she was gone, waving an absurd little handkerchief.

Cascamond faced about, and found the *ci-devant* and his lady
with the fixed stare of people who have performed a distasteful
office and now consider it finished. He offered his thanks for their
hospitality, with a click of heels and a bow that was little more
than a jerk of his head and shoulders, and took his departure. He
could feel those disapproving stares on his back until he turned
the bend of the road into the woods, where the gig was waiting.

So it was all a planned affair! Planned by the pretty flower of
McNab's island with the connivance, however reluctant, of d'Anseville, and the frank disapproval of *Mees*. What did it matter if Mrs.
McNab was thirty or thirty-five, with looks like that? And a lady!
He was to be a lady's lover again, this time in that strange scene
of the island of the sheep and the hanged men, with the arrogant
British captains sailing past! He remembered a time in England
when General Rochambeau was on parole at Wincanton with his
aide Chalot; and Chalot's famous love affair with Letitia Barrett,
and Rochambeau's quip, *"Alors,* that is the best way to invade
the English. On the couch!"

He could see and hear Rochambeau now, that fat jolly figure
of Bacchus, with his red boots, his brilliant hussar uniform, and
his merry tales of war with the blacks in Haiti and then skipping
off to safety as a prisoner of the British fleet.

13

The Agent for Prisoners steered the *Rob Roy* into Dartmouth
Cove and tied up at the ferry wharf. The sky was grey and dripping, and he and his one-boy crew waited in the little cabin, raising
the scuttle now and then for a glance up the lane which led to the

Preston road. At last a gig clattered down to the wharf, and the
French parole Cascamond jumped to the ground. Over his uniform was a sodden homespun blanket belonging to the Kolps. He
whipped it off and tossed it into the back of the gig, and came
down the wharf with a step that was almost a dance. Young Kolp
followed with his portmanteau. At the sloop's side Cascamond
thanked the youth, shook his hand, and contrived to leave a shilling in it, all with a *grand seigneur* air.

He stepped aboard, leaving the portmanteau to be carried to
the cabin by the *Rob Roy's* crew. With a careless salute he announced, "Captain MacDougal, I received your letter with the
permission, and I'm sorry to be late. As you see, the hackneys of
Preston are not all that one might wish."

Rory grunted, and went about the business of getting the sloop
out of the cove and headed down the harbor. He had never quite
liked this prisoner, from the time of that first interview in the hospital, and only at the urgent request of Mrs. McNab had he agreed
to these arrangements. The fellow was too cockahoop altogether.
And why should a pair of good Scots lads, young Sheamus and
Para, be taught the language of Napoleon?

Several merchantmen lay at the Halifax wharves, and a small
man-o'-war was careened at the dockyard, but the North American squadron was still on its winter station in the West Indies, and
the fishing schooners were all off to the Banks. Dartmouth Cove
was soon astern, and after passing the peering guns of George's
Island the town of Halifax became a mere blur in the drizzle. Then
the sloop was running down the fairway between Point Pleasant
and the north tip of McNab's island, and the rain ceased. Rory
poked a thick finger to starboard.

"Point Pleasant. The garrison has batteries in those woods—ye
can see a Martello tower covering the land approach. And down
by the shore—difficult to the eye at this distance—there's a gibbet
wi' the pirate Jordan on it."

"Oh? I thought the beach of Mr. McNab was the place for
gibbets."

"McNab's beach is for naval bodies only. A pirate's another
kind o' cattle."

"I see. Those naval bodies on McNab's beach when my ship
came in here—I suppose they've gone to pieces since?"

"Pieces or whatever, the Admiral replaced 'em September last. Some mutineers from H.M.S. *Columbine,* a boatswain, three seamen and two marines, a bonnie company."

As the tip of Point Pleasant slid past Rory stabbed his finger again. "There's the nor'west arm of the harbor. The first English expedition here thought it the mouth of a big river, and marked it so on their map. The Indians knew better. They gave it a crack-jaw name that means It-runs-down-to-an-end, for so it does. And near the end is Melville Island, where we keep most of our French prisoners. I suppose you know that?"

"One has heard of it. The Black Hole, eh?"

"Our prison's light and airy," Rory said testily. "The so-called Black Hole's a cell underground for punishment. When a prisoner breaks the rules we shove him in there to contemplate his sin a few days on sea biscuit and water."

"No flogging?"

"None. That's a rule also. The Admiral complained to me once, half in joke, that we treat the French much better than ourselves. Take you, for instance. Ye can't go home till the war's end, but otherwise you're free as a bird. At McNab's ye'll live as a gentleman, with money in your pocket, and never an hour to sea. What lieutenant in the British service can say half as much?"

The *Rob Roy* began to draw in toward McNab's Cove, and Cascamond could see the slate-roofed main house, the cluster of barns and tenant cottages, the undulating woods and pastures, and stretching far to the right the long grey finger of McNab's beach, with its grisly company on the nail.

"I understand that one of the McNab family is your *fiancée,* Captain."

"If ye mean Miss Dewar's to wed me, ay. She's McNab's ward."

"And when is the happy day?"

"That's not decided yet."

"You will live in Halifax after the marriage?"

"No. McNab wants to build a cottage for us on the Back Cove —the east side o' the island. I'll keep my sloop in the west cove, though. From there it's an easy run up the Arm, or to Dartmouth for a visit to the Preston officers. Now that the prison hulks in Bedford Basin are empty there's no point in living in the town."

Cascamond smiled. "You'll be able to keep an eye on me at McNab's, eh?"

"If ye need it, ay," said Rory dourly.

As Cascamond stepped ashore on the McNab wharf, Mac-Dougal passed him the portmanteau. "This isn't a regular trip, ye ken, and I must be on my way to Melville Island. Yon's the house, and ye've met the mistress, so there's no need of introduction. Go on up, then, and meet your pupils." Rory's tone and manner implied "and carry your own damned baggage!"

Eyes had been watching from the house, for when Cascamond was part way up the slope with the portmanteau the door flew open, and out came a pair of youths in kilts and clean white shirts, running to meet him. Cascamond had heard that Scotchmen wore something like the short *jupons* of girls in French officers' brothels —it was an old joke of the war—but he was amazed to see these flying kilts and the unmistakable male legs bare down to the short stockings. The youths greeted him politely by rank and name and introduced themselves. The older boy James, who was seventeen perhaps, resembled his mother, fair-haired and tall. Peter was a black McNab, about fifteen.

And now their mother was coming down the house steps. The sun was out of the clouds and her bound hair gleamed like a sheaf of barley. She was wearing another of those long straight gowns in the latest mode, not green this time but a thing of patterned blue. He kissed the hand she put out to him and let it go after just the exact moment of politeness and just the exact pressure to convey the warmth of his regard.

She was saying vivaciously, "This is an event for all of us, Lieutenant, and we do hope you'll be happy here with us. Your duties won't be long or hard, because of course the boys have other studies with Aunt McNab—you'll meet her later on—and Mr. McNab usually reviews their arithmetic in the evenings. A French lesson for an hour in the morning, an hour's French conversation or vocabulary in the afternoon, and the rest of the time is yours to spend as you wish."

In the sunlight without a bonnet her eyes seemed a lighter blue than before, with almost a violet tint, which reflected itself somehow on her lower eyelids, a faint shadow on the white skin, like the violet shadows on snow about sundown. And her skin was that

of a young girl. It was impossible to see her as the dam of these
brawny cubs. It was meaningless to reckon up her age. A woman of
this rare sort had no years.

"First you must see the house," she said, and the little troop of
McNabs conducted him through the rooms of the lower floor. In
the drawing room he was introduced to the old gentlewoman they
called Auntie, and he made a very deep bow, seeing the respect
in which they held her.

In the library Mrs. McNab said, "This will be your schoolroom."
Cascamond made a circuit, glancing over the books on the shelves,
and taking some down to see the title pages, partly out of curiosity,
partly to impress the McNabs. Some of the books were familiar,
he had seen them in the homes of gentlemen in Somerset, indeed
pored over them in his ardent study of English during those years
at Wincanton.

He flicked open Chesterfield's *Letters to His Son, Goldsmith's
Poems, Robinson Crusoe, Plays of Shakespeare,* Campbell's *Pleasures of Hope, Guthrie's Geography,* Johnson's *Rasselas, Hoyle's
Games, Joseph Andrews, Roderick Random, Pindar's Works,* Dib-
din's *Mirth and Metre,* Tate and Brady's *Psalms,* Watts' *Psalms
and Hymns,* Munchausen's *Travels.*

Apparently Mr. McNab had a thirst for universal knowledge.
Cascamond noticed *Walker's Gazeteer, Every Man His Own Lawyer, Entick's Dictionary, Laybourne's Ready Reckoner, Long-
mate's Peerage, The Seaman's Assistant,* and various nautical
almanacs.

Some of these books were merely names. Their contents he
could only guess. But then he was surprised and delighted to find
a shelf of Diderot, Beaumarchais, Rousseau, Montesquieu, Voltaire, all with the air of a bygone age, and not at all the sort of
thing to expect in the home of a staid Scotch merchant.

"But these!" he exclaimed, running a finger along the books.
"What are these doing here?"

"Oh, those!" said Mrs. McNab. "As a boy my husband studied
French at school, and for some years he kept up his French reading. It's still a polite accomplishment among British gentlefolk,
even though the French are their deadly enemies." She smiled at
one of the deadly enemies. "Mr. McNab has forgotten most of his
French, though, now. Lack of practice. Still, he wants the boys to

have the accomplishment, in fact he's determined on it. And he agrees with me that I was very lucky to find a teacher so excellent in both languages." She was so delighted with her success that she radiated light and warmth as a lamp does.

The McNabs now trooped upstairs to show him his chamber, Sheamus again carrying the portmanteau. "We do hope you'll be comfortable," Mrs. McNab was saying with an apologetic note, "though the room's very small. You see, we're rather crowded upstairs, what with my husband and me, and the boys, and Auntie, and Miss Dewar, and of course the cook and maid. Our Scotsmen call it 'the muckle hoose' but it's no great mansion as you see."

The chamber was small indeed, without room for much more than a narrow bed, a small commode with a bowl and pitcher, and a chair. There was a piece of red carpet, and the wallpaper had a pattern of roses. He guessed that a maid had been obliged to give it up for the new French teacher.

"My dear lady," he said honestly. "Compared with my lodging at Preston, this is magnificent! Magnificent!"

"Ah! Then that's off my mind. Now we'll leave you to unpack your things and wash, after your journey. We have a light dinner at noon, and tea and scones about four; but our chief meal's at evening when Mr. McNab gets back from town. That's usually about seven."

"And when shall I start my lessons, madame?"

"Not today. You'll want to get settled in, as we say, and later the boys can take you for a walk and show you something of the island. Now, my lads, let's be off."

And so Cascamond settled in. At the noon meal Miss Dewar appeared and he was introduced to her, a thin creature with round black eyes, black hair, and a withdrawn, almost sullen manner. And this *femme farouche* was the affianced of Captain Mac-Dougal! He had pictured somehow a broad hearty Scotch creature like the man himself. It was the belief of the French officers at Preston that the Agent for Prisoners enjoyed a full captain's pay and also had a sticky hand in the funds sent from London for their maintenance. Cascamond had found the same belief among his fellow paroles in England. The Agent was always a cheat, the prisoners his victims. So old MacDougal was quite a catch for this meagre female subsisting on the charity of McNab! After marriage they would become a *bourgeois* caricature of old d'Anseville and his miss.

In the afternoon the youths took him for a walk, at least he walked and they sprang about like restive dogs. The woods were still wet from the morning's rain and Cascamond stepped carefully, not to spoil his shoes. At four o'clock, exactly as madame had said, the family gathered for tea and buttered scones. At six the laird arrived. He had left town early. He wished to meet Cascamond again and to spend a long evening in talk with him. His wife had given him M. d'Anseville's word that Lieutenant Cascamond spoke a good French tongue, and now he wanted to measure the whole man—in English.

To Cascamond the evening meal was fantastic. He had never imagined anything like it. The long table; the cloth of Irish linen white as snow; the silver candelabra whose candles burned the clear flame of pure spermaceti; the fine porcelain and china and silverware, the variety and quantity of the food, the excellence of the wines and brandy. A French cook would have done far better with the food of course, but it was nothing to quarrel about. And there was the procedure, beginning with a long address to God recited by the master of the house, and ending with the after-dinner brandy, when a piper in Highland costume filled the air with an eruption of wild music and swaggered up and down the room for half an hour.

He supposed that the meal and the performance had been staged for his first evening with the clan; but as the days went by he found it a regular thing. With the arrival of the fine weather season there were frequent guests at the board, naval and military officers, and Halifax merchants and officials, usually accompanied by their ladies. And afterwards, when the bagpipes had subsided in dying groans and the piper disappeared, there was another kind of music in the drawing room, where the old white-haired aunt sat at the piano, or stroked a violin while Miss Dewar tinkled the piano keys. Usually someone sang a solo or two. At intervals they all sang old Scotch and English ballads, with good enough tunes but with words that to Cascamond seemed foolishly sentimental or utterly incomprehensible. On occasion the bagpiper was called back again, and then the McNab boys danced, uttering sharp hoots and cries, with enthusiastic applause from the guests.

Cascamond wore his uniform for these affairs, partly because it was the only really good suit he had, and partly for *panache*. The British Army officers and their ladies were pleasant to the young Frenchman, and so were the civilians. The naval officers were inclined to be cool. They had no high opinion of Napoleon's sea personnel whether officers or not. Some asked him where he learned English so well, and when he said that he had been a prisoner before, in England, their obvious conclusion was that here was another *crapaud* who surrendered at the first broadside.

Civilians asked him how he happened to be in Halifax, and he entertained them with a witty account of the last voyage of *La Furieuse*. On these occasions McNab always warmed his heart by telling his guests of the fight that *La Furieuse* had really made, the heavy loss in her crew, the death of her captain, and the severe wound of Lieutenant Cascamond himself. This brought a look of new respect from naval officers if any were present, and in the succeeding silence he could toss off gaily his story of the English seaman and "those Crappos" who couldn't tell a foremast from a mizzen.

Sometimes he was asked if he knew Captain or Lieutenant This or That—French officers on parole, all teachers of French or dancing or fencing, having permissions to live in the town. Thus he found that a surprising number of French officers like himself had obtained a special liberty through the influence of someone like Mr. McNab. More than that when McNab's visitors, especially the ladies, talked of wartime life in Halifax the conversation usually came around to the scarcity of capable servants and tradesmen, and out popped French names again. Drouet had told him something of this, but it surprised him to learn that almost one in ten of the people living about Halifax harbor was a French prisoner-of-war from the West Indies or taken at sea, and that scores of them moved freely about the town itself.

During one of MacDougal's visits to McNab's island, Cascamond quizzed him about this system or lack of system. *"Tach!"* said Rory, "they're well guarded. Climate and geography—the best wardens in the world. Think, man, where we stand! There's one prison wall," throwing out his left hand to the sea, "and there's the other," pointing his right hand to the hard rock face of the coast and the forest that came to its edge. "Oh, ay, some rash fools try it. Most of 'em fetch up in the Black Hole at Melville Island. The rest perish on the sea or in some wild thicket by the shore. The Transport Office in London knows a' that, o' course, and leaves me a free hand. Any man of position in the town can hire a French servant or tradesman on a pass from me, provided he warrants the fella's return whenever I demand. Every quarter-day I put a bit in the *Gazette,* notifying all employers that French prisoners-of-war on parole or permission must report at Melville Island for a muster. They come, they're counted, and that's that."

There was a suggestion of contempt in this easy attitude, and Cascamond burned to prove MacDougal wrong. The chance would surely come. A matter of patience, watchfulness and audacity. So it was, too, with La Fleur. She had been attracted to him he was sure, from that first meeting in the grounds of the hospital. During the winter she had hit upon the way to get him to her island, and with the coming of spring she had contrived it with great skill. The difficulty now was that they were never alone. The house swarmed with people day and night. Even in the garden or the orchard there were always servants about, or she was accompanied by her boys or by McNab or the old aunt, or else she walked to her knees in a froth of dogs.

He could only express his ardor with deep looks, which would have conveyed everything to a Frenchwoman. Unfortunately La Fleur did not seem to understand French in any sense. There was no response but that of a good-natured housewife to a guest. Of course she had to be careful under so many eyes. Was that it? Was she waiting her moment and refusing to betray her emotions until the moment came? Patience—patience, my boy!

The French lessons went on well. His pupils were bright lads, and they had been well acquainted with the discipline of study by that quiet old gentlewoman whom Cascamond called, in his mind, La Duchesse. McNab himself seemed absorbed in business and his mind ranged far. This Scotch merchant, like all the people of Halifax, had absolute faith in a satisfactory end to the war, probably some sort of compromise, leaving Napoleon his gains in Europe and the British their gains abroad.

He entered into long evening discussions with Cascamond about Martinique and Guadeloupe, and the Frenchman thanked his

stars that he had been observant about the plantations there, and
could talk with professional authority about wharves and lighters,
and the fine points of navigation amongst the islands and the
reefs.

One summer evening when Cascamond was in his chamber
reading *Rêveries du Promeneur Solitaire* there was a light tap
at the door. He tossed Rousseau aside and went on tiptoe to open
it, full of romantic expectation, and was confounded to find
McNab himself standing there. The laird looked about the room
with his shrewd black eyes.

"This is pretty much of a hen-coop, isn't it? Used to be Mairi's
room—the chambermaid. I've noticed ye like to get off by yourself like this. Oh, I quite understand. After all things are much of
a sameness here of an evening, and a man wants a chance to do
some quiet reading or maybe just have the pleasure of being by
himself. Something occurs to me. Would ye like a dwelling of
your own, maybe? Or do ye prefer it here?"

Cascamond was still shaken by the appearance of the husband
when he had hoped it might be La Fleur herself, taking a wild
risk after all the disappointments and delays.

"I . . . I don't mind it here," he said stupidly. And then, rally-
ing himself, "Dwelling? I don't understand."

"Just a wee cot of two rooms, not far away in the trees towards
what we call Strawberry Hill. I built it for a man o' mine, an old
soldier of a solitary sort who wanted to live in the wood. He died
of a seizure last year. The cottage is in good repair, and furnished.
Nothing fancy, mind, but a comfortable bed and chairs and so
forth, a stove in the bedroom for winter nights, and a Franklin
fireplace in the outer room. Ye'd continue to have your meals
with us, of course, and as much of our company as ye choose;
but ye'd have always a shell o' your own to withdraw to when ye
want." The laird ran another glance about the little bedchamber.
"That's what I came to tell ye, Cascamond. Take a stroll by the
path to Strawberry Hill tomorrow if ye like, and see the place.
The hut's off the path a few steps, near the end o' the wood, about
three hundred yards from here. I'd as soon have ye in the house,
myself, but if ye want the cottage it's yours."

"Thank you. Your thought is very kind," Cascamond said.

"Oh, it's my wife's really—women have an instinct about these things."

"Yes? Ah yes, of course. They have, haven't they?"

He moved his small baggage to the hut in the wood on a bright August morning with a westerly wind flicking white mare's-tails across the sky.

He was pleased with his new abode. It was no bigger than a Preston log cabin, but neatly built of sawn timber, boards, and shingles, with a window of eight small panes in each of the two rooms. At some time, probably when it was built, the shingles had a coat of limewash; but only a few specks of that remained, and the naked wood had weathered to a grey so dark, and so tinged with lichens, that the cottage merged with the shadows of the trees and was almost invisible until one came upon it. After years of living side-by-side with other men, in ships, in seaport lodginghouses, in the frugal prisoner-of-war quarters at Wincanton and Preston, the prospect of this solitude was enchanting.

McNab had sent servants to put the rooms in order, and to place fresh bedding and a warm quilt. There were candles and a tinderbox. There was a good Argand lamp from the "muckle hoose." There was dry fuel in the woodbox and a gallon jar of whale oil for the lamp. On a corner shelf in the outer room was a neat stack of French books from McNab's library, and even some copies of the *Moniteur,* taken lately in a prize. In all this evidence of care for him he seemed to detect, like a fragrance, the person of La Fleur.

She had planned this, then, as the final solution. It was here that she would come to him, on stormy evenings when McNab had to remain in town and the household had gone early to bed; in a stolen hour of an afternoon, somewhere between the noon meal and the French conversation and the scones. He sank on the bed and closed his eyes, giving himself up to daydreams that like wine on an empty belly were all the more intoxicating for long abstinence. He had not touched a woman in how long? Well over a year. He counted up the months since that last embrace in the Guadeloupe garden. An eternity! But, ah, the reward! The blue eyes alight with invitation, the white flesh eager for his caresses.

How much better it was to hunger and thirst, and finally sit
down to a feast, than to fritter the appetite with nibblings all along
the way. Drouet and his sixpenny bits!

Well, enough of that. Too much dreaming could drive one up
the mast. He resumed his exploration, following the path past
the hut and through the firs and birches until he emerged on an
open knoll, cleared for pasture long ago, and in early summer
dotted with wild strawberries. It jutted like a tongue into the
lagoon behind the stone beach, and the tip of the beach was near
enough that he could see distinctly the sinister figures on the gibbets. Across the channel rose the rugged height with the fort on
top, and at its foot the fishermen's nook called Sleepy Cove. At
last he turned his face seaward, with his back to the hangman's
beach, looking past the Thrum Cap to the waves of the Atlantic,
white-tipped by the offshore wind.

Out there, if one steered carefully true east and sailed a thousand leagues or so, he would come to the coast of France. To be
exact—Cascamond had traced it on the maps in McNab's library
—he would come to a certain spot on *les landes,* the sands and
sea-ponds and salt marshes and moors which line that coast from
the mouth of the Gironde almost to the Spanish border. And if
he tramped from that spot over the sands and moors, still going
true east, he would come at last to the rich green bank of the
Garonne, not far above Bordeaux.

He wondered if old d'Anseville ever thought of that, or if he
knew. Perhaps that was why the *ci-devant* had chosen his abode
at Brook House, hidden in the woods, where he would never see
that glittering reminder of the long way home.

"Well," Joanna said, "thank heaven that's settled. Bridget didn't
like sharing her bed with Mairi, Mairi complained that Bridget
snored, and both of them vowed they were frightened by the
presence of a Frenchman just a step or two away. They expected
him to get up any night and cut every throat in the house. Of
course they'd never seen a Frenchman before, nothing but the
lampoons in the English newspapers and the shop-prints, which
always show the French as something between a monkey and a

wolf. I tried to reason with them, but it was no use. 'It's his eyes, the way he looks at us,' they said."

"And what way's that?" McNab asked.

"Oh, he has a very straight way of looking in your eyes, you must have noticed, almost as if he could see the inside of your head. 'Bold'—that's what Bridget and Mairi called it, silly creatures. Better a bold eye than a shifty one, I say. Of course sometimes . . ."

"Sometimes what?"

"I don't know. Sometimes I've noticed him gazing at me. Nothing offensive. Not even strange really. I mean it's so like the look the dogs give when they think you'll take them for a run. You know, grateful and adoring. And after all, when you stop to think of this young man—of any young man—and all he's gone through, that frightful wound, and suffering for months, and then a whole winter shut away in some hovel at Preston—and now we've rescued him, and found him employment, and made him one of the family—why shouldn't he feel grateful and anxious to show it? The most natural thing in the world. Think of one of our own lads in such a case!"

McNab chucked her under the chin. "That's my lass—all heart and imagination and never a doubt of anyone. Well, we shall see how this Frenchman likes our company for a year. I daresay at the end of it he'll be glad to get back to his friends at Preston, or maybe after this experience he'll apply for a pass to teach French in Halifax. Most of the prisoners are lively young fellas, eager for the amusements of the town. Some of 'em are putting on pantomimes now in the theatre, as part of the garrison entertainments. What we used to call dumb-shows in Scotland. I'm told they're very good. Tell a whole story without a word—just the eyes, the hands, the shoulders, the postures, and the twist of mouth. They can set you laughing or crying or make your skin creep. What are you smiling about?"

"Those two silly females cowering in their beds, just because of a look from Cascamond. Like your pantomimes. A good thing Napoleon hasn't the gift. We'd have been conquered long ago, and not a shot fired in defense."

14

The day was gone again, and dusk began to fill the path through the trees like the waters of a dark spring flowing up from the ground. He had watched the path so often and so long without reward that he had given up watching, as with his stern Breton will he had shut away those tantalizing daydreams. It was only an accidental glance at the pane, as he was about to light the lamp, that showed a mysterious figure in a dark gown. At once every nerve in his body was alert and tingling. The pine splinter he had ignited at the fire went back into the fire with a quick toss. He stared eagerly. The shadows and bends of the path gave only vague glimpses as the figure approached. He opened the door and heard a swish of skirts.

"Hola!" called a voice. His heart fell into his shoes. It was a male voice, the voice of the Irish priest. He had met him on occasions in the McNab house when others were present and there was no private conversation. Among the French officers at Preston Father Burke was known as *cet irlandais*. He was not French, he was on friendly terms with the English, and he was a priest— three good reasons for contempt. The fact that he could speak French added suspicion.

Always observant, Cascamond had discovered that La Fleur gave money to the priest, but never in the presence of her husband. All priests preyed on the religious weakness of women, of course; and it was interesting to see money of the hard-headed Protestant merchant going to the Pope. It was even more interesting to see that La Fleur had at least one definite weakness, and that she indulged it with insouciance behind her husband's back. If she gave his money in secret to a wheedling Irish priest, why not a secret gift of something else to a young and ardent Frenchman? *Cela revient au même!*

"Good evening," Cascamond said coldly in English. "Will you come in?" He turned once more to light the Argand lamp, first rubbing the charred edge of the wick to a neat round trim. They regarded each other in its yellow glow, sitting on the rush-bottomed chairs with which the room was furnished, one at each side of the fireplace.

Cascamond had on the plain broadcloth trousers and coat he had bought for ordinary wear on leaving the hospital. After nearly a year at Preston and on McNab's island it showed the signs of daily use. Although the stuff was stout enough it had a certain wrinkled shapelessness, with a polished gleam on the trouser seat and the shoulders of the coat.

"The nights are getting cool now," the priest said.

"Yes."

"How are you getting along with your teaching?"

"Very well. The boys are intelligent. They're very interested in ships and the sea, and naturally so am I, so our French conversation tends to run that way. They pick it up rapidly."

"You are staying the winter?"

"Yes, of course. I engaged for one year."

Father Burke put up a finger and stirred the thin hairs on his chin. In a tall and rather gaunt way he looked somewhat like old pictures of Cardinal Richelieu.

"I hope you don't mind my calling on you like this, Lieutenant. In the house I never get a chance to talk to you alone. Are you a Catholic?"

"I was born a Catholic, yes."

"Um! I find that many of the French prisoners answer my question in just that way—as if they'd grown into something else. But your Emperor has restored the Church, has he not? And he is the man you serve."

"So. But that does not restore me, myself, to the Church."

"Surely, my son, you don't still believe in a supreme Goddess of Reason and all that bygone rubbish of the Revolution? You were just a child then!"

Cascamond stirred and frowned. He answered in a voice as bleak as a February night. "My father was one of the *chouans,* the Breton partisans who fought against the Revolution. He was killed in battle with soldiers of the Revolution. And because he had been the leader of a band of *chouans* my mother was shut in

prison and I was taken away and brought up as a foster-child of
the state. You know what that meant in the matter of religion."

"And have you no resentment against the state which did such
things to you and your parents and your Church?"

"None!" said Cascamond in the cold voice. "My father's band
were salt smugglers and he'd been their leader for years, the cunning and daring one who arranged everything, including the sale
of the stuff to people dodging the salt tax. Like all ignorant peas-
ants they were suspicious of people in towns, and when the town
people of Brittany came out for the Revolution the *chouans* rose
against them. They told themselves that they were fighting for
the Holy Church, and like all fanatics they were cruel—cruel as
wolves. But they weren't really fighting for anything except their
own ends, especially the smuggling which was their trade; and
they hated the Revolution and the new laws, including the law
of conscription. The troops of the Revolution overcame them at
last, and paid cruelty for cruelty. What else could one expect?
France was assailed from outside by emigrant nobles and priests
with foreign armies, and by murderers inside like the *chouans*.
My father was lucky to die as he did, and not on a lamppost."

"How old were you then?"

"About ten or eleven years."

"And your mother—what about her?"

"She was good to me and I loved her, as I hated my father. But
she was a dupe of the priests. She had no love really for anything
but the Church. She should have been a nun. She is dead now
and I presume safe in the arms of Jesus and the Virgin."

He said this with a scornful smile, watching the priest's face
for an expression of anger or distaste.

"I can see that your foster parent taught you thoroughly," Father Burke said.

"If you mean I was given a sound education, yes, and finally
an appointment as midshipman in the Navy. If I'd remained the
mere brat of a wild Breton smuggler what would I have got?
Pfitt! So you see, all that I am belongs to France. France is my
father and mother, and my religion also. I believe in nothing else."

"That, too, has a familiar sound, Cascamond. Well, I came
here in my duty to seek souls in need of religion, and I find that

Lieutenant Cascamond needs nothing whatever. So I'll get along back to the house."

Father Burke arose and offered his hand for a polite farewell. A glitter of malice came to Cascamond's blue eyes. He did not get up from the chair. He made no attempt to shake the hand. Instead he plucked a shilling from his pantaloons and dropped it in that outstretched palm.

"For the poor," he said, dipping his head in mock reverence.

The Irishman paused. "Are you a sporting man, Lieutenant? Will you play toss for this coin, double or nothing?"

"Of course!"

"Heads or tails?"

"Tails."

The priest spun the coin. It fell to the little carpet and they bent over to see it in the yellow pool cast by the lamp.

"Tails!" cried Cascamond, and picked it up in triumph. The priest drew a shilling from his robe and dropped it into Cascamond's hand beside the other.

"For the lost," he said, and walked away into the darkness with a faint swish of his robe among the ferns.

At the end of August, sitting late by the drawing-room fire with Joanna and Aunt McNab, and after long communion with his pipe, Peter announced, "In less than four months our Frenchman's brought the lads along well, verra well indeed. Already they can chatter French better than I ever could, after years of schoolmasters. They read and write it wi' more difficulty, to be sure, but that's natural."

The servants had gone to bed. It was the time for intimate family talk, and Joanna waited apprehensively. Was Peter about to bring up that notion of "polish" across the sea, as he had brought it up, like a gun to her head, every year for the past three? Always with his nonsense about French. She thought she had spiked that gun with Cascamond.

McNab puffed slowly at the long clay, staring into the fire. "I'm glad I insisted on a knowledge of French," he said blandly, as if he saw her mind. "A polite accomplishment every young gentleman should have."

"Yes, you've said that a good many times."

"Weel, as it turns out, there's something further, my dear. In the past year or so I've thought more and more o' trade wi' the French West Indies, or the ones that used to be French. Our forces have taken Martinique and we'll have Guadeloupe next year; and there's a black king ruling Haiti, which used to be the richest French colony in the world. In all those places there's opportunity begging in the way o' trade, and nobody taking advantage. Why? Because none of our merchants have the French lingo, and anyhow we're all too busy wi' war. But, look you, the war won't absorb us forever. You take this business of getting American cargoes to British hands. All verra well but how long will it last? General Prevost put a flea in my ear. The time will come maybe soon, when our American friends can ship direct to Spain for the British Army, without breaking their government's law of Non-Intercourse. So it's wise to look about for other business. I've been talking to Army and Navy gentlemen here who were in the expedition to Martinique; I've talked to Cascamond, who knows Guadeloupe; and I've talked wi' other prisoners, including a French brigadier from Haiti, a verra intelligent man, as black as the ace o' spades.

"I think next year I'll send a trade venture to Martinique for a start. I'll have to use an agent there, o' course, the only way to do business wi' foreign people. But it means I must have at my own end o' things in Halifax one or two reliable clerks who have a working knowledge of French, and something of ships and cargoes and so forth."

"Cascamond!" Jo said at once.

"Na, na. I've nae reason to distrust the fella, mind, and nae doot MacDougal would grant the permission. But in the pit o' their hearts all these prisoners are fanatical about France—France and Napoleon—and I had dealings wi' His Majesty's forces, land and sea, that any French spy could make use of. Also there's the American business. Any betrayal o' names—owners or ships— would ruin our friends down there and the business besides. I canna take any risk o' that."

He puffed at the pipe again, with the deliberation of a man about to announce a great decision. Aunt Frances was gazing in silence into the fire, absorbed in old dreams of faces in the coals,

her customary attitude at this time of night. Jo was watching him
with the searching stare of a wife who suspects a husband up to
something.

"So next spring I'm taking young Sheamus intae the business,
and the year after that I'll take Para. I painted '& Sons' on my
sign a long while ago; it lends any business a note of pairmanence,
and now's the time tae make it true. They'll lairn the business
as I did from my own father. And I don't know a better way."

He leaned forward and tapped the pipe bowl delicately on the
hearth to empty it. "Weel, I'm off tae bed." And away he went up
the stairs, leaving the women to cover the wood coals with ash to
keep fire for the morning, and to make all safe for the night.

As his heavy footsteps died away the two women turned to
each other. Aunt McNab wore a smile of amused indulgence. Jo
laughed in utter triumph.

"So you've won!" Auntie said. "It's been a long battle, eh?—
off and on."

"Hasn't it!" flashed Jo delightedly. "Every time he brought up
that notion of sending the boys to Scotland or England, I . . .
I . . ."

"You glared at him the way a lioness must, when she suspects
her mate of a notion to eat the cubs."

"Oh come!" laughed Jo.

"You did! Ferocious! Ferocious! And having brought him up
short with that, as sailors would say, you'd put on your beguiling
look and talk his notion away. Between fear and fascination
he'd not bring up the matter again for a twelve-month. For an
old spinster it was an education in the wiles of a wife and the
chinks in a father."

"You flatter me, Auntie! Fortunately he's been so driven with
business these past few years that he'd no time to delve into the
boys' education but once in a long while. And how I dreaded
those moments! Every time I succeeded in putting him off I'd
offer a special prayer of thankfulness to the Virgin—she knew so
well a mother's fears and trials. And now it's all settled!"

"Of course," said Miss McNab with a shrewd look, "it means
the boys will be away in town with Peter all day long, and often
night-long when the weather's bad. I'll be frank with you. It's a
good thing. Apron strings—apron strings! You can't keep lads

from growing up and wanting to step into the world. You've lived and thought so much for the boys that you'll find their absence hard, I'm afraid, my dear."

"And won't you?"

"Of course. I'm as bad as you. Life just won't be the same. Tut! A moment ago we were laughing. Now we're on the edge of tears, the pair of us. It's still only the end of summer, and we'll have the boys to ourselves a whole fall and winter yet. Let's get these coals covered for the night and away to bed ourselves."

Cascamond sauntered along a path towards the south tip of the island. It led through pastures, cultivated fields, patches of spruce and fir woods, and then became a faint track through a wilderness of scrubby birches and alders. The island narrowed gradually until he could see a glint of water through the trees on either hand. It was a warm October day, a Sunday, with the ghost of a sea breeze, just enough to carry the McNabs up to town for their religious services. They had set off soon after dawn, when the sea breeze began to blow, taking with them many of the servants and tenants and children. The *Bonnie Jo* was crammed.

All this fuss over religion was ridiculous, but what made it fantastic to Cascamond was that these Sunday expeditions gathered together Protestants and Catholics, in the greatest amity. He knew from conversations in the household how they proceeded after they got to town—McNab and his boys and the other Presbyterians marching up to St. Matthew's for morning service, Mrs. McNab and the Catholics walking together to St. Peter's. They dined with various town friends afterwards, and returned to the island late in the afternoon or in the evening according to the winds. Usually in the evenings Aunt McNab sat at the piano and there was singing of Presbyterian hymns, in which any servant or tenant or wife or child could join. Usually the drawing room was standing full, and although the Catholics with one exception did not join in the singing they obviously enjoyed the music and the atmosphere of holiness that it seemed to bring down as if from Heaven.

The exception was La Fleur. Mrs. McNab was puzzle enough to the Frenchman, but this somehow outraged him. How could a wife who professed herself a devout Catholic, who frequently

gave sums of her husband's money to the Irish priest, sit down
and sing the songs of heretics? There was one of these Scotch
hymns in particular, with the most doleful tune and words, which
she sang together with her husband as the others listened. It was
a favorite performance. And simply by the repetition of it, Sunday
after Sunday, before he was granted the seclusion of the hut in the
wood, Cascamond had come to know every note of the tune and
every one of those words.

*The hour of my departure's come, I hear the voice that calls me
    home;*
At last O Lord let trouble cease, and let thy servant die in peace.
The race appointed I have run, the combat's o'er, the prize is won;
And now my witness is on high, and now my record's in the sky.

Protestant, Catholic—or Hindoo for that matter—how could a
young and beautiful woman lift her voice in anything so like the
last lament of the dying? She had a sweet voice, too. And when
he went over the words, translating them into French for a perfect
understanding, the phrases did not make sense, one with another.

Did she never wonder what it meant when she sang:

Not in mine innocence I trust; I bow before Thee in the dust?

God knew she was innocent, didn't he? If not, he—Michel
Cascamond—could testify. And didn't all the McNab tenants
know her as the Saint?

With these ruminations he plunged through a dense fringe of
twisted and salt-bitten spruce trees and saw before him the ocean,
with a short beach curving out into the water like a fishhook, on
the tip of which, like a fat lump of bait, sat the knoll called the
Thrum Cap. The beach made a natural causeway, about a cable's
length or a bit more, two hundred metres, say. He made his way
out over the stones. On reaching the Cap he found it to be a hillock of red clay and gravel, exposed on the sides, especially to
seaward, but topped with green turf.

He scrambled up for the view and came upon someone else.
Miss Dewar sat there in the grass. He was astonished but she was
not. She had been watching him on his way along the beach. She
was in a plain grey gown, gathered under her breasts with a ribbon or band of some sort, otherwise it would have hung straight

from her thin shoulders to the ankles. Although she had tucked her feet under this dull garment he could see the toes of a pair of old brogues. Her black head was bare. A bonnet lay on the ground with the fingers of one hand in the strings, as if she had begun to catch it up when he appeared.

Her eyes regarded him watchfully but quite unafraid, indeed her air was one of seeing a trespasser on property not only private but in some way sacred.

"Good afternoon," he said; and it was then that he saw the graves and the withered bunches of the past summer's flowers.

"What are you doing here, Mr. Cascamond?" she said quietly.

He thought for some moments. Then he said, "I suppose I wanted to stand on the one part of this island which is nearest to France, and to look out over the sea and wish myself there. Silly, eh?"

She considered. "I don't think it's silly, no."

"This is a long walk from the house. Do you come here much?"

"Quite often."

"May I sit down?" he asked, as if he recognised her ownership. She nodded indifferently and glanced away to the sea as he squatted on one of the graves.

For expeditions with the McNab boys, walking or gunning or gathering lobsters at low tide, and for rambles of his own, he had obtained a pair of stout sea boots, brown duck trousers, a check-ered black-and-white shirt, and a short blue pea jacket, all of the sort that Peter McNab & Sons sold to fishermen. He was wearing the shirt and boots and trousers now, with the jacket slung over his shoulder.

"Who are these buried here?" he asked, with a gesture at the graves.

"Sailors who were shipwrecked and washed ashore on the Cap or the shore hereabouts. Mr. McNab's father buried the first ones here many years ago."

"I see no new graves."

"There hasn't been a body on this side of the island for some years, thank goodness, though there were wrecks on the outer ledges, and even on the Thrum Cap shoal."

"And you bring flowers, I see. But why? I mean—these men

were strangers. Perhaps some were even Frenchmen, who knows?"
This with a quizzical grin.

"It doesn't matter who they were—or why I bring flowers. I like
to come here. When I was younger I thought something like you.
I mean I thought this was as far as I could get away from the
island—and the nearest to Scotland, where I came from."

Cascamond nodded. He had heard the story of the orphan girl
from various members of the McNab *ménage,* as if she were an
oddity that needed explanation. She was still looking seaward
and he was able to study her. About the house, where the golden
beauty of the Saint illumined everything, the Dewar girl was
only a shadow flitting in the background. Her figure, so far as he
had been able to observe it, was best described with a French
word, *maigre.* Her face was thin, too, with a certain jut of the
cheekbones, and although the skin was clear it had the same
brown as the faces of the tenants' wives and girls who worked in
the fields. Her nose and chin were small and finely made, but
the lips between them belonged to a wider face. In certain lights
she seemed all black eyes and long straight mouth, with a ridiculous pair of dots in place of a nose. He had never really examined
her before, and now in close detail his first judgment was confirmed. She was of no allurement. And a woman *sans attraits*
did not count as a woman at all, except in that faceless multitude
of the old, the decrepit, or deformed.

Miss Dewar seemed well aware of that, submitting to his male
scrutiny with the indifference of one who has nothing to hide, indeed as if she were used to such examinations and knew the
verdict by heart. Yet her attitude had not the cold English hostility of d'Anseville's mistress, another woman *sans attraits.*
Cascamond had never known much about the Scotch, thinking
like most Frenchmen that the word *anglais* covered everyone
north of La Manche, and that the only difference of Scotchmen
was that for some mad reason they wore a petticoat instead
of trousers. After several months' study of McNab and the old
aunt—La Duchesse—and after various conversations with Captain MacDougal, he had come to realise that the Scotch were to
the English what the Bretons were to the French. He even felt
an odd affinity. And as Miss Dewar was as Scotch as the laird's

own whiskey the affinity extended even to her. The thought amused him.

"Tell me," he said to break the silence. "Why is this called the Thrum Cap? I know your language fairly well, but what is a thrum?"

"Thrum's a coarse kind of wool. In cold weather British sailors used to wear knitted caps of red thrum—most of our fishermen still do. This knoll is one of the harbor marks. Captain Mac-Dougal tells me that when you sail in from the seaward you notice the red bank of the knoll standing up like a thrum cap."

"I see. And that small island over there to the east, at the mouth of this bay, what is that called?"

"Devil's Island."

"Why?"

"Because of so many wrecks there. It's all stones, and low and hard to make out in bad weather, and many sailors have perished there. God made the world, but the Devil came along and interfered with the arrangements. That's what Rory says, anyway."

"Rory?"

"Captain MacDougal, the Agent for Prisoners."

"Ah! To be sure! The man you are to marry."

She turned and gave him a deep black gaze.

"Who told you?"

"He did—Captain MacDougal. He said that you and he will live in a cottage at the Back Cove. I've noticed you walk that way a lot."

"For that matter I walk all over the island. And there is no cottage yet. Mr. McNab will build that when the time comes."

"And may one ask when that will be?"

She shook her head and turned her eyes to the sea again.

This was droll. She did not wish to talk about the greatest event of a woman's life. It seemed a passionless affair. A marriage of convenience by every sign. The notion of Old Square-Foot engaged in lovemaking with this dark unsmiling virgin defied his imagination. How old was she? She looked like a lean ship-boy in skirts for a lark but she must be a woman of twenty-five; maybe his own age, twenty-six; maybe more, it was hard to tell. And Old Square-Foot at least twice that!

As if to forestall any further questions Ellen Dewar said, "Do you like the sea?"

"The sea? The sea itself? No. I think no one but a fish likes that. In the life of a sailor the sea is just a way of getting from one port to another. It's often a hard way but usually the ports make it worth the trouble. When you hear a man say he likes a sailor's life he's thinking of the ports or he's a liar."

"But in or out of port, the life on board, how do you find that? For example, in French ships, do they flog men or hang them, as they do in ours?"

"We whip a man sometimes, but rarely hang one. In the English fleet of course it is different. We—how shall I say—in France we get our men from another sort of humanity. Many of our seamen are volunteers from the ports, who do not wish to serve in the Army; the rest come from the national conscription, which, let us say, gives a better representation than the scrapings of your English press gangs. In consequence we don't have such great need of punishments. But this is an unfortunate subject. Let us say it's a part of war, which is not a jolly business. Men get hurt, and many die. Others are shut up as prisoners, like thieves and robbers, not for a week or a month but for as long as the war lasts, which may be as long as they live."

"But you can hope for exchange, can't you?"

"I was exchanged before, in England, but that was just a piece of luck. Unfortunately the war has been a sea war for your people, and so you English have captured a lot of us, and we have taken few of you. Naturally the English government doesn't want to release trained seamen, especially officers, who would rejoin the French fleet."

"Even if they gave their word not to fight again?"

A caustic laugh. "Parole? France doesn't recognise parole."

"But aren't you on parole? You gave your word not to escape, didn't you?"

"I am still a prisoner."

"It seems to me you have quite a bit of freedom. At least you're not shut up in a hulk or a jail. You can walk about in the sun, like this."

"Ah! But this is a prison after all. Your Captain MacDougal pointed out to me the width of the ocean, and the length of this wild coast, and of course the storms and the cold. So one is securely fastened here. The state of being a prisoner is to be held away from home, away from one's friends, away from everything that makes life pleasant or even endurable. Do I sound very sorry for myself? I am!" And he laughed, not in his usual way, with the unmistakable note of contempt, but as if he enjoyed a joke on himself.

Miss Dewar said, "Joanna—Mrs. McNab—told me that you fought bravely in your ship and got a terrible wound, and suffered a long time before you got well. That's something to feel sorry about. But I understand how you feel about freedom. Sometimes I feel a prisoner myself."

"What!" He looked his astonishment. "Who holds you here?"

"Never mind."

"Then how are you a prisoner?"

She sprang up and brushed the grass from her skirts. "I must be getting back. The afternoon's far gone, and it's quite a walk to the house."

"Do you mind if I walk back with you?"

"As you wish."

In the scramble down the Cap he put out a hand to assist her, but Miss Dewar evaded it and went on with success and even grace. She was as supple as a boy. On the awkward footing of the causeway's round and sea-smoothed stones, with frequent leaps from stone to stone, she moved like a dancer where he slipped and stumbled. He said something to that effect, and she paused and turned her head, balancing herself on a large stone with her arms thrown out exactly like a *danseuse* poised.

"That's because I've had practice."

"At the—what do you call it—Highland Fling? Or on these stones?"

"Both!" She was smiling. The smile ran the full length of her mouth, and it was not grotesque after all, there was an odd charm about it—her teeth perhaps—one did not often see teeth as fine as that in a woman so far past sixteen—or perhaps it was the tilt of her head. Then she was away again, skimming over the stones like a blown feather. She was so used to this solitary game of hers that she forgot his presence or ignored it, plucking up her gown and petticoats for easy movement.

It was impossible to keep up with her, and Cascamond paused in his floundering to observe this airy phenomenon. In flashes he could see black cotton stockings to the knees and sometimes above the knee a glimpse of knitted red garters. The legs in the stockings were slender but well made, not the broomsticks he had suspected. He began to wonder, with some amusement at his own curiosity, if the rest of Captain MacDougal's *fiancée* were quite as meagre as he had supposed. In this mood she seemed another creature altogether, nothing like the furtive mouse who moved about the McNab house without sound and almost without a body. How to describe it? Something sprightly and a bit impish, a bit of the wanton. He had once seen a little sloop dancing over the waves outside Brest, just like the girl on the stones, and he recalled the sloop's name, *Lutine*. The very word!

Already she was at the end of the beach, setting foot on the main island, and in a stroke of sorcery *Lutine* vanished and quiet Miss Dewar took her place. She led the way along the track through the birch woods and the fields, walking briskly. There was little conversation. Once she pointed aside to a small farm and said, "The Culliton place—Joanna's home."

"*Comment?* I mean, what did you say?"

"Mrs. McNab was born there."

"Do you mean Mr. McNab married the daughter of a tenant?"

"One of his father's tenants."

"But I thought Mrs. McNab was a lady!"

Miss Dewar stopped and looked back at him. "Of course she is! What's her home got to do with it? None of those fine ladies in Halifax can hold a candle to Jo in looks or manners or anything else." She added severely, "I thought anyone could see that, Mr. Cascamond."

"I was thinking of what one saw in England," he said slowly. "I mean, over there, as far as one could understand, a squire did not marry a girl from one of his farms. If he did, he was no longer recognised by the gentry. In England you must be a gentleman, or have the influence of gentlemen, if you wish to have anything or be anything—for example an officer in the Army or the Fleet. In France it is different, of course. We are not—what is the word, snob?—snob!—we are not a nation of snobs. I myself was the son of a Breton smuggler, and left an orphan without a *sou*. Yet my

country gave me an education and made me an Officer of the Fleet.
That could not happen here."

"Well," she exclaimed, "this isn't England either. In Scotland
the poorest man of the clan can hold his head up with the laird.
And this is New Scotland."

He could only mutter "So?" and follow at her heels, thinking
of the Preston farmers and their deference to the ladies and gentlemen of the summer villas.

When Miss Dewar came to the place in the woods where the
path forked, one branch leading to the McNab house and the
other to Cascamond's hut, she walked on a pace or two and then
turned. He had stopped in the hut path.

"This has been very nice," he said politely. "Would you mind
if I went again to the Thrum Cap?"

"You may go anywhere you wish," she answered, and with a
swift smile and a flash of dark eyes, a glimpse of *Lutine* for a moment, "After all, you're on parole, aren't you?" She turned to go,
and for some vague reason he tried to prolong the talk, calling
out the first things that came to his tongue.

"Do you go always to the Cap on Sundays? Why do you never
go to town with the McNabs? Are you not religious?"

"You ask too many questions, Mr. Cascamond. As for the
town—I hate the town and most of the people in it. I'll never set
foot in the town again. Mr. McNab finds that hard to understand,
but his wife knows. Mr. McNab thinks I'm a little touched."

"Touched?" He wrinkled his brow over the meaning of that.

"A bit daft. I suppose you don't know the meaning of that either.
Well, it's no matter. Goodbye!" She whirled about and was out
of his sight in half a minute.

PART THREE

AFFAIRS AND CONSEQUENCES

15

On the next Sunday afternoon, moved by the prod of boredom more than anything else, Cascamond journeyed again to the Thrum Cap. It was not a good day. The air off the sea brought a fog soon after the departure of the churchgoers, and it hung about the island all day. The Cap was an eerie place, with nothing to be seen except the green mounds of the old graves on its top, and nothing to be heard but the doleful crying of gulls and the swish of the tide along the shingle beach. Cascamond had a weird feeling that he was marooned on a lump of red clay in the midst of an ocean rising stealthily to drown him.

After two hours, still undrowned, but wet and chilled in spite of the pea jacket, he stumbled away over the stony hook to the main island and returned glumly to his hut, where he made a fire in the Franklin stove and stripped off his wet clothes and hung them to dry.

At evening he donned his carefully brushed broadcloth and walked to the McNab house. The fog remained about the island and the harbor mouth, as it often did when the harbor itself was clear, and the vague breeze baffled back and forth, now from the east, now the west, now falling dead calm. With these conditions the Sunday pilgrimage would be late returning, and Cascamond sat down to dine with old Miss McNab, who went up to town only when the weather was fair, and young Miss Dewar, who never went at all. Most of the servants had sailed to town in the *Bonnie Jo* in the morning, and a tacksman's daughter waited on the table.

The three sat in their accustomed chairs about the board, the two women facing each other near the middle, and the Frenchman in solitude near the foot, where on ordinary days he had the pleasure of sitting close to La Fleur. There was small conversation. Old Aunt McNab had spells of loquacity when talk was buzzing about the board and everyone took part, but at times like this she drew a personal silence about her like a shawl. Cascamond asked quietly, "Did you go out for a walk today, Miss Dewar?"

"Yes."

"In this cold mist! You didn't go far?"

"I walked all the way to Ives Point, the north tip of the island. The fog wasn't so thick there. I could almost see the town."

So she had gone in the other direction a distance as far as his own tramp to the Thrum Cap. But of course, as she had told him before, she rambled all over the island. Some other things she had told him were still a mystery. Why did she feel herself a prisoner? Surely she could go anywhere she wished? Why did she so loath the town and everybody in it? And what had she meant by "a little touched?" The word "daft" was clearer to him—McNab used it a lot—but Miss Ellen Dewar did not seem anything like a lunatic. She was *une originale* certainly. He searched his mind for an English word for that, and failed.

The McNab sloop did not get into the cove until ten o'clock that night, and whatever spiritual comfort they had found in town the churchgoers were hungry and cold. Customarily in the evening before Cascamond retired to his hut the laird invited him to join the family in a "nightcap," another odd use of a familiar word. The old aunt McNab always sipped a small glass of whiskey before she went to bed, the only time she ever touched strong drink of any kind; and Joanna and Ellen usually took a glass of port wine on summer nights. McNab himself liked strong drams of whiskey cooled by hanging a bottle in the depths of the well all day, but when the chilly evenings set in he preferred to mix a hot rum punch, in which the Frenchman joined him. And so tonight, after the family churchgoers had dined late and the boys had gone to bed he poured whiskey for Aunt Frances, wine for the two younger women, and made punch for himself and Cascamond. Peering at the Frenchman over a steaming mug he asked, "What the de'il d'ye find to do wi' yourself on days like this, eh? No lessons to teach, and ye say ye've no religion to observe. Nothing!"

"At Preston one learned the art of doing nothing," smiled Cascamond, and sipped his punch. "It is an accomplishment of prisoners."

"Och, ye need something on your mind. Look here, man, would ye like to write a letter to France—your parents, say? I can't warrant it'd reach 'em, or that ye'd ever get a reply, but I'm told there are ways and means of communication in spite o' the war."

"Unfortunately my parents died long ago."

"A wife then?"

"No." Cascamond looked past the laird to Mrs. Jo, dreamily turning a delicate wine glass in her fingers. Ellen Dewar as usual was almost invisible, a shadowy figure in the alcove beyond the fire.

"Not even a sweetheart, sir. A ridiculous confession for a young man, I admit. But truly there is nobody to care that much"—he snapped the second finger of his left hand against the base of the thumb—"whether I am dead or a prisoner or anything else."

"How sad!" cried Jo, with the swift warmth of her Irish heart. "To have no one—no one at all! I've thought of that so much since Father Burke told me how your parents died, and how you were brought up as an orphan from eleven or so."

"So was Ellie," murmured old Frances McNab absently, as if Ellie were not there, and as if she needed a defensive word.

"Well," said McNab with a cough, "I just thought to mention the chance of a letter in case ye'd some private worry on your mind. It's a dour companion, that, for a man long from home."

Cascamond tipped the mug and drank down the last of his punch. He arose and bowed. With the punch singing in his head he intoned, "A man in war comes to know pain in many forms, including loneliness, for which the doctors have no medicine. Good night, *mesdames*. Good night, *monsieur*."

He went out into the foggy dark with the step of an actor who has brought off a small role well. "And it's all true!" he exclaimed to the dripping trees. "Every word!" He exulted in that emotional response from the pretty blonde woman who obsessed his mind. This, then, must be the way. Sympathy. She must feel drawn to him, to his loneliness, his *délaissement*—to Michel Cascamond the friendless and forlorn.

The prescribed afternoon hour of French conversation was not confined to the house. Cascamond preferred to spend it outdoors with the boys, and so did they. Wandering with them along the shore he would point to an old boat hauled up and turned on its side for repairs. "*Alors!* Tell me, to careen a real ship, how does one say it in French?" And when James and Peter uttered the phrase he would repeat each word, to assure the pronunciation. "*Abbatre . . . un . . . vaisseau . . . pour . . . le caréner. Bon!* This seaweed washed up on the shore here? *Balayures de mer. Balayures . . . de . . . mer.* Correct! It really means 'the sweepings of the sea' . . . a good term also for me and other Frenchmen washed up on these shores, eh? *Balayures de mer!* Swept up high and dry, the lot of us. But seriously now, let us consider something still afloat. What your father calls flotsam. There is a lot of it about this island in a time of shipwreck I am told. So—flotsam! *Débris flottants . . . encore . . . débris flottants.* But when it is cargo afloat from a wreck? Your father tells me these distinctions have importance in English sea law. Tell me then? *Marchandise jetée à la mer.* That is correct. Now see there, a schooner coming out of the harbor. How do you call a schooner? *Goelette . . . goelette . . . Bon!* And now tell me, please, on what tack is she sailing at this moment? . . . *point d'amure . . . point d'amure . . . Bon!* As you see she is what your father calls a coaster. Tell me in French, please, a coaster . . . *vaisseau de cabotage . . . oui.* Now regard that ship coming in. If you were on look-out you would cry Sail Ho! What do you cry in French? *Navire en vue! Navire en vue!* Correct. And now here is an old one. We've had it a hundred times, so I wish to hear it correctly on the first try. What name has that?" And Cascamond darted a finger at the far tip of McNab's beach.

"*La grève du bourreau.* The hangman's beach. Correct!"

They were on one of these rambling discourses along the eastern side of the island one day, following the foot track through the shore woods in a file, like Indians on the war path, with the teacher in the lead. Suddenly Cascamond pulled up short, and the boys with him. Just in front of them the shady wood path opened into the sunshine of the Back Cove, and framed by the fir trunks and

branches as if in a picture sat Ellen Dewar and her husband-to-be.
Their seat was the old mast lying at the beach head, and Mac-
Dougal had an arm about her shoulders.

Para Dhu—dark Peter as his father called him in the Gaelic—
hissed, "What a lark! Here's old Rory spooning with Miss Ellie!"

"It's the only chance they get!" laughed James. With his blue
eyes and blond hair he was like his mother, and now especially
like La Fleur in one of her livelier moods. "You know how in
the house they sit apart, as if they hardly knew each other. But
there comes a time when Rory's sure to give a great harrumph
and say, 'Weel, lassie, what d'ye say we go to look about the spot
to build the cottage?' And off they go to the Back Cove."

The boys were leaning out to see past Cascamond, and nudging
one another. A lark indeed! Cascamond smiled himself. But
spooning? The word was unfamiliar in this sense. He could only
suppose it meant making love. The couple on the log did not appear to be making anything. The young woman sat with her eyes
closed, as if asleep, and the grizzled Agent for Prisoners seemed
to be talking very gravely to himself. And this went on and on.
If they were making love it was a very strange way of doing it,
even for the cold-blooded British. At last the boys became restless, and Peter whispered, "Och, let's away back along the path
a bit and strike off through the woods to the house." The others
agreed with nods, but first James said with a mischievous grin,
"Monsieur, you told us once that the French word for a lady's
courtier is the same as for a midshipman."

"Correct! The word is *aspirant*."

"Then hark at this, if you please. *Il est un bien triste aspirant,
le capitaine MacDougal!*"

Chuckling, they turned and headed away through the trees. On
the way back to the house, and often thereafter as a private joke,
they repeated together in a chant, "*Il est un bien triste aspirant,
le capitaine MacDougal.*"

It never failed to send them into fits of laughter.

There was a new stir in Halifax. On orders from London, Governor Prevost's troops had begun to move away across the sea.
The 7th Fusiliers, Prince Edward's old regiment, had already

sailed for Portugal in June, and at the beginning of October the
Welsh Fusiliers got their orders for Lisbon. That young British
general from India—Wesley or Wellesley, nobody yet seemed quite
sure which it was—had now got still another name. In Portugal he
had beaten large French forces and one or two of Boney's pet generals, something so unusual in this war that a grateful government
promptly made him Lord Wellington. The new name was in all
the newspapers, even in captured copies of the *Moniteur,* which
contemptuously spelled it *Vilain-ton.*

Peter McNab had friends among the officers of the Welsh Fusiliers, and he took his wife and boys and Aunt McNab up to town
for the farewell festivities. There were to be dinners and dances,
as well as public marches and reviews, and the McNabs were gone
from the island for three days. On the second day of their absence
Ellen Dewar made a journey to Strawberry Hill. The path through
the wood took her past Cascamond's hut, which was closed and
silent, and eventually she came out on the long grassy knoll, almost surrounded by the lagoon, where in July the island wives
and children picked baskets full of wild fruit. It was what fishermen called an open-and-shut day, with patches of black cloud,
patches of sunshine, and occasional showers of rain. Ellen had
brought a cloak against the showers, with a hood to slip over her
head. She laid it on the ground and sat.

In the years of her teens, this had been one of her favorite
places, with its wide view over the lagoon and the stone beach to
the waters of the harbor and the distant town. After the age of
twenty, when the first gibbet appeared like an evil tree at the beach
end, so much closer than at the McNab house, she had shunned
the spot. Indeed like Joanna she refused to eat strawberries gathered here by the servants, as if that figure on the gibbet had pol-
luted everything in sight. At twenty-two she had gone with Joanna
for a few days in town, and spent that horrible afternoon in the
wherry on the harbor. Early in the morning after she got home
from that experience she had ventured to Strawberry Hill again,
by what impulse she did not know, and gazed from that distance
at the new bodies dangling on the point; and then came that compelling urge, at once pitiful and sickening, which drew her trembling along the beach to gaze once more at the young man who had
suffered like a Christ and died without a cry.

All around the little peninsula of Strawberry Hill the water of the lagoon lay calm, with the white wings of sea-swallows flitting over it. When the sun was out, the water sparkled with the exact light blue of Jo McNab's eyes; but when cloud passed overhead it had the color of Cascamond's, and something of their hard cold quality. The lagoon was formed by McNab's beach, which ran like an untidy wall between it and the open cove and went on to poke a stony finger into the harbor channel. From the west shore of Strawberry Hill a branch of grey shingle crept out to join the main one, so that together they formed a crooked Y, with the lagoon in the upper gap and the dead men swinging at its foot.

Far up the harbor smoked the chimneys of Halifax, and at anchor off the town lay His Majesty's ships *Diadem* and *Regulus,* waiting to embark the troops and their wives and families. Sitting with eyes half-closed Ellen Dewar tried to picture those women and children, on foot and in the baggage carts, following Wellington's drums through Portugal and Spain. It would be hard but rather wonderful to be a soldier's wife, keeping close to her man in his hardships if not his dangers, and following behind every fight, seeking him out, ready to bind his wounds or at the worst to see him into a decent grave.

Here, she thought, we see the ships pass, we watch brave people going by, year in, year out. We never offer ourselves to pain or mischance or adventure. I dress and undress, eat and sleep, and that's all. Each day a blank page in a book without a story. Why? Must I have a man to write upon me like a pen if I'm to have some meaning in my life? Rory? As Rory's wife I'll have more to do, no doubt. Bairns. I'll pray for bairns. But even then, is that all? Shouldn't a woman have something else, the thing that sets Jo's eyes alight when she sees her laird at the day's end? Love's the word. The love of a woman and a man. Try as I may, I can't see that with Rory.

A mass of black cloud had climbed up the sky, and suddenly the view of the town and the ships vanished behind a grey wall of rain. She could see it advancing down the harbor towards the island, a really heavy downpour, and she snatched up the cloak and fled. Even so, by the time she reached the edge of the woods the rain had crossed over the stone beach, ruined the mirror of the lagoon, and rushed up Strawberry Hill. It overtook her in the path through the trees and she put the cloak about her and plucked the hood into place. The noise of drops pelting on the birch leaves was tremendous, and in the open path the water seemed to rush as the rain rushes from a roof into an eaves trough.

She was running, with the hood shutting off all view except the path before her, when she was startled by the voice of Cascamond. She turned her head and saw the hut, and the Frenchman in the doorway calling to her.

"Come in here!" he said sternly, as if this were some moment of emergency aboard a ship, and she a seaman passing. And like a seaman she obeyed instinctively. He moved aside as she stepped into the outer room, where the Franklin fire was blazing cheerfully. The rain made an uproar on the roof and flooded down the panes. He closed the door. He was dressed in his coarse seaman's boots and shirt and trousers.

"Permit me!" he said in the same brusque tone, removing her wet cloak and hanging it on a peg by the fire. He drew up one of the rush-bottomed chairs, placed it before the fire, and made a gesture that drew her into it, sitting as meek and abashed as a child caught wading in a forbidden pond.

"Your feet are soaked. Take off those shoes."

"Oh, no," she said, hurriedly tucking them under her skirts.

"Don't be a little fool!" He knelt before her, pulled one foot into sight, and drew off the shoe. Then the other. Unlike her usual footgear for her walks these were dainty things of fine cloth, with thin leather soles and no heels, and fastened by black tapes cross-laced up the ankle. He placed them carefully on the iron shelf at the front of the fire, and propped them so that the warmth would reach inside and dry them. Her feet fled back under the gown. Her stockings were of good white silk but she behaved as if they were the poorest cotton and full of holes. Ruthlessly he reached under the wet hem and drew one of those timid feet into the firelight and began to chafe it slowly, first from the ankle to the toes, and then along the sole. At his first touch the foot went rigid, with the toes curled, like a small animal cringing in fear. Gradually it relaxed.

"They don't matter," she protested. "Really!"

"In October wet feet always matter."

After a time he put the foot down and commanded, "Now give me the other." It came forth and lay submissive in his hands. He went on like this, stroking and gently kneading one foot and then the other, with his shoulder against her knees, and his gaze on the fire.

A strange and marvelous feeling crept through Ellie Dewar from her toes to her thin flushed face. If I were a cat I'd purr, she thought. How gentle he is after all. In spite of that outward manner. He's suffered too much himself ever to be cruel. Still, I can't let this go on—what would Joanna think—I *know* what the laird would think.

"It seems to me the rain's letting up," she said in a small voice.

"Bah! The sky's as black as night and raining halberds."

"Halberds?"

"A French expression. You'd say cats-and-dogs. Tell me, what were you doing over this way? There are no strawberries in October."

"I . . . well . . . I wanted to see the view from Strawberry Hill. I haven't been there in a very long time."

"And what did you see there except the town, which you detest?"

"Oh, various things."

"For example?"

"Well, for example, the ships that are to take the Fusiliers to Portugal."

"You will see them much better when they sail past the hangman's beach. A bad omen for them, I'm afraid. Within six months most of those redcoats will be as dead as the poor devils on the gibbets. You English may have the best admirals but we Frenchmen have the generals."

Ellen tossed her head. "In Portugal our Lord Wellington is doing very well with your wonderful generals. He's beaten two or three of them already. You should read English newspapers instead of those old *Moniteurs*."

"I'd rather have an old truth than a new lie. But let us not quarrel about that. The generals and the admirals can do all the quarreling in—I pray your pardon—this damned war. Can you guess where I went today? To the Thrum Cap. I've been out there several times since I found you sitting on the top in that ugly grey gown, like a monument to all the widows of the sea. I like what you wear today much better. The pink silk and lace dress, the silk stockings and shoes. I've never seen you wearing silk except at evening when visitors are in the house."

"That means you haven't looked at me very much. I don't blame you. I'm not beautiful like Jo, nor distinguished-looking as Aunt McNab is."

"And would you like to be beautiful and distinguished?"

"I don't think so, I'm much too shy. Think of all the stares!"

"Pretty women enjoy stares."

"Jo's so blithe and innocent she wouldn't notice. Indeed I doubt if she knows how beautiful she is. If I could be anyone else I'd like to be Jo. Not just for looks. For happiness. She loves her husband like a bride, after all the years married. She loves her children. And husband and children adore her. What more could a woman ask?"

"And you really believe no other man could give her pleasure in love?"

"I can think of nobody boor enough to believe that, let alone fool enough to try. And I've seen a much of boors and fools here on this island—visitors from the town."

This came so tartly that he was shocked. For a few moments his hands were still, as if they forgot what they were about. At any moment he expected her to snatch her feet away and tell him to stop this foolishness. But she did not. He resumed the stroking. The rain drummed on, and now a strong wind began to thrash the wet trees. He thought of a catch he had heard weather-wise English seamen chanting.

If the wind's afore the rain, set your tops'ls back again:
But if the rain's afore the wind, then your tops'l halliards mind.

Under the black sky the wood was all shadow, and the hut was dark. They had not spoken in a long time, sitting as if in a trance, watching the fire dying into ashes. A picture came into Cascamond's mind, that vision of Ellen and MacDougal sitting woodenly just like this, and young James chuckling, *"Il est un bien triste aspirant."*

He arose and turned, putting out his hands to hers and lifting her to her feet. She met his gaze with a long look of black eyes luminous in the small glow of the fire. She freed her hands and with an air of resolution walked into the inner room. He waited a minute, hearing within the room a rustle of garments and then the faint creak of the wooden bed. When he came to her she did not say a word, she made no sound but her tremulous breathing and a single gasp as he closed into the slim white flesh she offered to him. After his long hunger here was milk and honey. Like the food in miracles it could be devoured again and again. With the gentle force of a lover he devoured her, and lay quiet and content for a time, and then found her again, passing his hands over her flesh as if to make sure that she was real and not something dreamed; and then again the hunger and the feast.

A long time later, asleep at her side, he awakened with the sudden instinct of a seaman whose senses warn him of change in the weather or the ship. The wind was still blowing but the rain had ceased, and outside the bedroom pane the yellow gleam of a stormy sunset told him the hour. Ellen had risen from the bed and dressed. She stood now in the half-dusk with the back to him, arranging her hair with that blind skill which all women have in their fingertips. He wondered what she would say. The old cries, the worn banalities that women have flung at men at such times ever since the world began? "I'm so ashamed!"—"How you will despise me!"—"Why did it happen!"—"I wish I could die!"—"It's all your fault!"

She remained silent, moving into the outer room, putting on her shoes, catching the cloak about herself, and drawing the hood over her head. She went to the door and opened it, and stood there as if in a profound contemplation of the dripping trees. Or was it of the past two hours? Cascamond paused in the bedroom doorway, resigned to a storm of reproaches. At last she spoke. "Michel?"

"Yes?"

"I didn't come this way for the view from Strawberry Hill. I came to see you here, in the cottage. You were out when I first came by, so I walked past and waited on the hill."

"Yes, I guessed that—finally."

"What else did you discover finally? Did you find that I—that we made love well together?"

"Yes." It seemed stupid to utter just that hissing English word when there was so such more to say, but nothing else came to his tongue.

She remained mute again for a long time, with her back to him. Then, quietly, "Michel, do you want me to come to you again?"

In his relief he gasped a muddle of words, not at all the skilled and practised jack of hearts but stammering like the boy he had been at his first affair.

"What? . . . Ah! . . . but yes . . . of course . . . do I want . . . what a question!"

16

Now was the time of the autumn wild-fowling, with flocks of geese and ducks alighting from the north to rest and feed in the lagoon and the coves, and at McNab's invitation there were parties of eager sportsmen, dining at his board and sleeping on makeshift beds all over the house and in the cottages of the tenants. In the presence of the family and these lively guests Ellen was her old self, the girl who sat remote from the talk and almost had to be dragged to the piano when the laird commanded evening music from Aunt Frances and herself.

It was strange, living two lives, together and apart. Cascamond dutifully pursued his lessons with the McNab youths and made polite conversation with the guests, most of whom were young officers of the garrison. Now and then Ellen's eyes met his, and for a moment those dark pools came alight in a way that must have betrayed her to any sharp observer; but it was only for a moment, and the Frenchman himself kept his gaze impersonal, as it had been with McNab's ward from the first. In him the only noticeable change was that his eyes now went seldom to the blonde mistress of the house, and when they did something was missing, as if Jo herself had been transformed into a person of no more than a polite interest.

Autumn passed slowly into winter, stripping the leaves from the birches, the maples and alders, leaving untouched the green bristle of spruce and fir, so that in the mixed woods between the McNab demesne and Strawberry Hill the little hut kept its concealment. Ellen made her journeys there with a daring that sometimes appalled Cascamond, and with an ingenuity that amused him after the first snows whitened the ground. She then avoided the path and its telltale tracks. Instead she walked in the other direction from the house to the lagoon shore, where the tides kept bare a fringe of sand and pebbles, and sauntered slowly along this frozen strand until the house was out of sight. The long south inlet of the lagoon, which made Strawberry Hill almost an island, reached into the wood within a short distance of Cascamond's abode. It might have been created for this secret visiting, for later on, when the cold weather put a hard floor of ice on the lagoon, it made an easy approach. It was concealed from the McNab house by the curve of the wooded shore, and it betrayed no footsteps because the northwest gales of winter swept away the snow like chaff from a threshing floor.

Ellen had a dilemma on fine afternoons when young James and Peter, and sometimes Joanna herself, decided to enjoy skating on the lagoon. Then she could only join them and keep her eyes away from the place where her feet longed to go. Fortunately the others liked the broad sweep of the ice, turning back before Strawberry Hill, where the slender inlet pointed like a betraying finger into the woods. Often enough she had the lagoon to herself, especially on days when wandering squalls of snow filled the air, and blew along the ice like a cold white smoke. When Cascamond had finished his afternoon lesson and returned to the hut, she put on her warm Canadian blanket cloth coat with the monk's hood, walked to the lagoon shore, strapped on her boat-shaped wooden skates with their iron keels, glided about the main sheet of the lagoon for a time and then vanished.

On evenings when the laird was busy teaching his boys the art of double-entry bookkeeping, the conversion of doubloons and dollars into pounds, shillings and pence, and the mysteries of invoices, manifests, and bills of lading, Ellen went outdoors to skate in the light of the stars. This had been a peculiar pleasure of hers for years. Like all her lone wanderings it was accepted by the McNabs as a natural phenomenon; and if she returned from these

nocturnal excursions with a flushed face and shining eyes it was
not unusual, and nobody thought a thing about it.

Snowstorms blew in from the cold reaches of the North Atlantic
and howled about the dwellings for days and nights on end, heap-
ing drifts to the windowsills. For sieges like this the laird provided
Cascamond with an emergency store of food and drink, so that
he need not flounder through a blizzard to eat at the family board.
He rather enjoyed being "snowed in," as they said, even though
it meant that Lutine could not come to him. There were other
times when afternoon or evening social affairs at the house kept
her dutifully at home and made the longed-for journey to the
wood impossible. Often a week went by without a rendezvous,
and when they came together at last they clung to each other as if
they had been parted for a twelve-month.

He called her Lutine now, always Lutine. She made a *moue*
when he first tried to explain the word.

"You think I'm some sort of naughty spirit—a female imp?"

He laughed. "You're not a sort of anything, Lutine. You're what
we French call an *originale*—you're just not like anybody else. And
before I met you the only Lutine I ever saw wasn't an imp or even
a woman—she was a little sloop under sail. She danced over the
waves as I saw you dancing over the stones at the Thrum Cap,
with her sails catching the breeze like your own gown and petticoats. Yes, and she tossed her head and wagged her pretty little
stern, just as you did. Her lines were drawn like yours, with what
the English call a fine sheer forward . . ."

"That will be quite enough. You almost make me seasick. Anyhow my lines are too narrow for any sort of beauty. You've said
yourself that when you saw me first you considered me a meagre
thing."

They lay together on the bed, in the snug warmth of the bedroom stove, seeing themselves, now clearly, now dimly, in the
flicker of the fire in the other room. They had made love and were
pleasantly languid.

"That was at first," he said. His fingers played gently with her
breast.

"No one could say this is *maigre*. You are thin, yes, but for a
thin girl you have some unusual details. Altogether your lines are
very interesting. You are well designed like the other *Lutine*."

"Now I'm a ship again!"

"And a very charming one."

"Pooh! I'm all eyes and mouth, and with my clothes off I'm like a winter rabbit, snared in the woods and skinned for the pot— barely enough meat to cover the bones."

"I could eat this rabbit, bones and all."

"Well, leave my eyes, please, so I may look at you. I couldn't liken Michel Cascamond to a little ship dancing anywhere; but you have a handsome body. A young man well made in all his strength is really more beautiful than any woman."

He chuckled. "That's a matter of opinion. I have a handsome face of course."

"Not at all! I'll take you down a peg, sir. I like your face but it's not a bit handsome any way I look at it. Quite the contrary."

"But I think it's very good. I admire it every morning when I shave."

"Pooh! That round black head of yours, like a bullet. You get old Mrs. Struachan to clip your hair, apparently with her sheep-shears, leaving that lock on the forehead, like Napoleon in all the prints. You have that tight little pout of his, too—like an angry Cupid. But you haven't Boney's nose, and without that you can't resemble him, no matter how you try. Your nose is really quite nice. The rest of your face isn't much. That olive complexion, with a shade of blue about the jaws, even when you've just shaved, and two or three pits from smallpox. And finally those dark blue eyes, which you aim at everyone—even me—like a double-barreled gun."

"But the rest of me is beautiful, you say!"

"Yes, and that's enough of that. Let's be serious for a change. There's something I wish to know."

"Yes?"

"You've had girls before, that's obvious even to simple me. Did you love them?"

"At the time, yes."

"And with me—is this just another time?"

He frowned and was silent for a minute. Then, "What shall I say, Lutine? You are honest in everything you say and do, and I must be the same with you. I had no intention of making love to you, as I did with girls at other times. So it's not the same as the other times. This thing of you and me came out of the blue, and I

don't know what to make of it except that you are a darling who
makes me content to be her prisoner. I don't try to think beyond
that. In war one learns to pass the time from day to day. What happened yesterday is gone and can't be changed for better or worse.
What will happen tomorrow cannot be seen and only a fool would
worry about it. This day, this hour, you, me—this is all that matters. Love, you say? Ah! Women put a great importance on that
word. And they insist on their own interpretation. For them everything between a man and a woman must be forever or they
cannot enjoy it. It may be only a delusion of the moment but they
insist on the delusion. A man believes only what he can see from
the masthead. He knows there is a horizon. Women don't. They're
always gazing to the far side of the world and seeing the things they
wish to see, which probably are not there at all. I come back,
then, to what I said before. Here, now, you are my love. Yes. If
we were in France, or anywhere in time of peace, I would marry
you and make you a fat *maman* with a dozen children. But as it
is I am a prisoner of war, a war without end, so that I must escape
when I get a chance."

"But why, Michel, why? Why go back to the war, to suffer mis-
eries again, perhaps to die? You said I made you content."

He lay back with a long sigh. "You don't understand. I couldn't
expect you to. I said I was content to be your prisoner, yes. I
never said I was content to be Captain MacDougal's prisoner. I
never could be content to live as a tame monkey of the English like
old d'Anseville, or like so many of the paroled officers at Preston
who have abandoned hope. My duty is to escape, to return to the
service of France. But there's something else. Something more
powerful than duty, and worse than—what do you say—the sick-
ness for home? I confess to you it is fear. I am afraid."

"You? I don't believe it! Afraid of what?"

"Of death, *ma chérie*. Not death itself, but a death degrading
and miserable, like the end of those poor English devils at the
grève du bourreau."

She sat up and bent over to kiss his taut mouth, and her hair fell
about his face like an intimate curtain to shut off the world.

"Tell me, Michel darling, whatever it is."

Without opening his eyes he said in a low voice, "Very well,
Lutine. Since it's you and only you. What I have to say will seem to

you mad but it is true. You must think back five or six years, to the
battle off Cap Trafalgar, which is still the greatest battle of the war
to you English. I was there. And I was the man who killed Lord
Nelson."

Her mouth fell open like an astonished child's, as if he had announced that he was Judas Iscariot. "What on earth do you
mean?"

"What I said. Listen, Lutine. I was a midshipman in a seventy-
four, the *Redoutable,* when the English fleet attacked. Our ships
were drawn up together, French and Spanish, to receive them,
and I was in charge of five or six men in what your English sailors
call the mizzentop. That is a platform on the top of the lower mast
aft. The lower mast, you comprehend. Not a great distance above
the deck. We were armed with muskets and a few hand grenades
for close action. The English never did this. I learned afterwards
that Lord Nelson always forbade shooting from the English tops,
because it could not accomplish much and the powder flash might
set the sails afire. This had become an order in the English fleet;
and in their talk and in their newspapers after Trafalgar the English people made a great virtue of it, as if it were a sin and a crime
to fire a shot anywhere above the deck.

"An English ship bore down on the *Redoutable,* and at the same
time engaged a big Spaniard, the *Santissima Trinidad,* and our
own flagship, the *Bucentaure.* You can't imagine the noise and
confusion of big ships firing every gun at close range. Even in the
mizzentop we were made deaf and choking for breath, and blind,
for at every broadside, English or French, the hot powder smoke
came up in a cloud about us, biting our eyes and throats. There
were times when we couldn't see more than our fingertips.

"At first we didn't know the English ship except that she was
one of their biggest—she loomed up higher than our *Redoutable.*
Someone shouted that it was the English flagship *Victory,* but in
all that thunder and smoke my ears were singing and my eyes
weeping and I didn't give it a thought. Our ship and this big Englishman were roughly alongside each other, with yardarms and
rigging tangled, and the hulls grinding up and down in the swell.

"Suddenly in a clearing of the smoke I found myself looking
down on the Englishman's quarterdeck. As I have said, ours was
a smaller ship than the *Victory,* and so our mizzentop was less

than fifteen metres from her deck. I saw there two officers walking together. One had some stars or other decorations on his breast and was evidently an officer of importance. All this at a glance of the eye, you understand.

"Now, I was not a good shot, as you say in English. I had fired a musket perhaps twenty times in my life. In fact none of us in that top were experts. A seaman with a musket is as clumsy as a cow. But there was the decorated English officer directly below, so close that I could have thrown down the musket itself and hit the man. And just at that moment came a pause in the rolling of the ships. I simply pointed the gun at him and pulled the trigger. It was impossible to miss. He fell to the deck, and I noticed then that he had only one arm, which he put out to break his fall. I knew who he was then, of course, and so did every man in our mizzen-top. I heard a shout of triumph. Maybe one of the voices was mine. I do not know.

"After that, a great confusion of firing and smoke. The English marines were shooting at our tops, and most of my men were killed or wounded. I myself had my hat shot off—I remember it sailing away into the smoke to leeward—and a bullet struck one of the rigging blocks and dropped into a pocket of my jacket. I could do nothing more there. I made my way down the rigging to the deck. The *Redoutable* had been smashed terribly by the Englishman's starboard guns. Our lower gunports were closed after the first broadside, to shut out boarding parties. We had been warned that the English would attempt this if they got alongside. But it meant that we could only fire our upper deck guns. By this time the ship was a wreck, choked with dead and wounded men. And by the time a heavy swell of the sea tore the two ships apart we in the *Redoutable* had ceased fire. We could do no more.

"The sun went down and we drifted through the night, a floating hell full of corpses and wounded men screaming in the dark. Many English ships were as badly damaged as ourselves, and there was a storm coming up from the southwest, with the Spanish shore close on the lee. The English made great efforts to save their prizes. Soon after daylight an English ship, the *Swiftsure,* took our ship in tow. The storm fell on us all, blowing like the Devil, with rain in a flood as if we must drown one way or the other. Some of the captured ships were blown ashore on the Spanish coast. The English themselves finally destroyed most of the prizes because there was no hope of getting them to England or Gibraltar. Our own *Redoutable* broke her towline during the gale and sank with most of her crew. We had thrown some of the dead overboard but the wounded remained and went down with the rest. I myself floated clear, grasping a rope on a piece of spar broken in the fight. After many hours in the water a boat from an English ship picked me up. And so I was taken to England, a prisoner for the first time. As a midshipman I was sent with some other officers on parole to the village of Wincanton in Somerset.

"When I reached Wincanton I learned that the English people were in a rage of grief for their famous Admiral. It was said that Napoleon had gathered expert riflemen from the mountains of Tyrol to post themselves in the tops of the French ships, and to aim for the great Nelson, who was sure to expose himself on his quarterdeck. And I heard it said over and over again that if the English ever found the man who did kill Nelson they would hang him as an assassin.

"So, even among the French prisoners, I kept my mouth shut about the affair. They knew I had been taken at Cap Trafalgar, there was no denying that, but of the rest I said nothing. I determined to escape, and I worked like a madman to learn the English language and speak like an Englishman. Whenever prisoners were moved, and strangers came to join us on parole at Wincanton, my heart was in my mouth until I knew there were none from the *Redoutable*. When at last I got an exchange back to France you cannot imagine my relief. I rejoined the Navy of course. It was my trade. For a time all went well.

"Then I was captured again. So here I am again in the hands of the English, with the ghost of that old affair at my heels."

"But," she cried, "all that was five years ago—more! What does it matter now?"

"It matters to the English, I assure you!"

"Oh, don't be ridiculous!" Ellen said, in a voice of Scotch common sense that might have been McNab's. "They can't hang a man for doing his duty!"

Cascamond sat up beside her and jerked a thumb in the direction of the hangman's beach. "They can put a man out there on any charge they like, Lutine, no matter what you say about your famous English justice. After all what kind of justice did they get, any of those poor devils on the gibbets? They were forced into the English naval service, and when they took an opportunity to run off, or to say what they felt about their treatment, they were killed and strung up as a warning to others, like dead crows in a corn-field."

"True, but they weren't French prisoners. A prisoner-of-war can't be flogged or hanged—I've heard Rory MacDougal say it a thousand times."

"Ah! Listen, Lutine! Some time ago—during this war, mind you —a court in Halifax gave a French prisoner-of-war what we call the hemp cravat. The charge was murder—killing a fellow pris-oner—and perhaps he was guilty. But perhaps he was not. Perhaps they hanged him on that charge for something else. So it has been done here. And what's been done once can be done again. No, no, it's not ridiculous."

Ellen made a little cluck of vexation. "Michel, you're living in a nightmare made entirely by yourself. Look! That mast-top you were in. You say you had five or six men with you. Only those men knew who fired the shot at Nelson, and you say most of them were killed in the fight."

"Ah, but three at least were living when the fight was over, and they could have told others who survived when the ship went down."

"Oh come, dear Michel, do put all that nonsense out of your mind! I'll have no more of these phantoms of yours. Here! Put your arms around a living woman who wants you to make love to her."

She slipped her arms about his neck and put her warm mouth on his. But the kiss was brief. His lips were cold and set hard. With an impatient gesture he freed himself and sat with his knees drawn up, leaning forward, chin on knees, hands clasped about his ankles.

"You had better go away, Lutine. I cannot make love now. I am haunted, yes. Go and leave me to my phantoms."

"But Michel . . ."

"Go! Get out!"

In a storm of emotion, half anger, half anguish, she dressed with hurried movements and fled. Through the tears she had one parting glance at the brooding figure on the bed, in the flicker of light and shadow from the fire. And that night in her own bed, dreaming uneasily after long lying awake, she saw that naked figure with a terrible familiarity. It was the figure of the flogged man in the boat, and later on the gibbet. They were one and the same, except that the face was Cascamond's. She wakened with a cry and lay trembling. Was this the fearful gift of which she had heard? *Da-shealladh?* What had drawn her to that silent figure on the gibbet more than three years ago, the body that turned out to be exactly Michel Cascamond's?

She came downstairs the next morning with shadowed eyes and a drawn look, and when Cascamond came into the house for breakfast she gave him a mournful look as if he were already dead. But he had got over his own mopes, that was evident. He was well and cheerful, even happy. And he did not give Ellen a glance. He ignored her. Gradually the haunting grief left her, hearing his lively talk at the board and seeing his appetite for the food. But with the grief gone, her anger came back. She hated him.

Three weeks crawled by, five hundred slow and miserable hours. The anger, the Scotch pride stung by that shouted "Get out!" as if she were some town draggletail paid and dismissed, kept a stiff command over the longing to be in his arms again. When they met at meals or in the drawing room her eyes were sullen. The worst part was lying sleepless in the dark, remembering his every touch and kiss and those murmured words of tenderness which, however often repeated, always came to her ears as fresh and wonderful as when she heard them first. Then the pride and anger telling her that all of it was a game with him, one that he had played many times with many women. He had learned it with skill, just as he had learned the English language, and with the perfection that could only come from practice.

He had tired of her, as men do—wasn't that the burden of all the old wives' tales? All he wanted now was escape. That absurd story about Lord Nelson! And he thought she would believe it! That alone was proof of his contempt for the credulous fool he called Lutine. She wondered how many other women had come and gone in his glib life, and what other tales he told. With bitter humor she recalled one of those moon-calf courtiers of hers, warbling over her at the piano:

> Sigh no more, ladies, sigh no more,
> Men were deceivers ever;
> One foot in sea and one on shore;
> To one thing constant never.
> Men were deceivers eeeeeee-ver!

After three weeks of this she put away her pride firmly and walked to the hut by the roundabout way of the lagoon ice. At the tip of the inlet she found a beaten path in the snow leading through the trees to the hut. He had tramped there every day by the look of it. Why? There could be only one reason. He had come to the ice edge to watch for her, day after day, in those free hours of the afternoon when she usually appeared, and perhaps also in the evenings. In this little path pressed hard by his repeated journeys she saw the proof of his longing for her.

Blue woodsmoke pouring from the chimney told her that Cascamond was at home, and when she opened the door there he was, sitting before the fire, working on something which he tried to put aside, to hide, as he turned to see who it was. He stood up then, and she saw that he had made a little flagstaff, fastened in a flat wooden base, a toy no more than eighteen inches high, with all the correct stays and halyards, and at the masthead a flag, the tricolor of France.

All the way there she had wondered what to say. *You see I've come back.* No! That was obvious. *I couldn't stay away any longer, Michel.* So was that. *Have you missed me?* That might do for the beginning. But now she found an easy opening in the toy on the floor.

"What a beautiful little thing, Michel! Do show me!" And when, rather sheepishly, he picked it up and offered it for inspection, "Where did you get the pieces of silk for the flag? And the needle and threads?"

"From La Duchesse—the aunt McNab. So that she might not suspect what I was making I said I was amusing myself with what you call patchwork, and I wanted small pieces of all colors. I think she guessed, though. She is a wise woman, that. When she gave me the pieces, the blue, white, and red were on top, in that

order. Now let me show you something. These little rigging-blocks
are real. They cost me a lot of trouble, but they work."

He took the halyards off the tiny cleat and lowered the flag to
the foot of the mast. "See? You came, Lutine, and conquered. To
you I strike my flag!" He placed the toy on the table and turned to
her with a whimsical smile. She was in his arms in a moment.

As always the winter mails from England came after long delays by the Bermuda route. On a day in March, with the snow
melting fast, McNab read in old London newspapers that Boney
had divorced his Josephine. King George was a confirmed lunatic
at last, at the very time when England was celebrating his jubilee,
the fiftieth year of his reign. The Prince of Wales, that fat volup-
tuary, would now be Regent. Even so loyal a subject as the laird
could not forbear a notion that His Majesty mad was better than
"Prinny" sane. As for Napoleon, there was a rumor that he in-
tended marriage with a daughter of the Austrian emperor. Mc-
Nab mentioned this to Cascamond. "A long leap that, eh, from
a creole of Martinique to an archduchess of Austria?" Even
Lieutenant Cascamond had to admit that it was. Otherwise the
news did not amount to much. After last year's marches into Spain,
Lord Wellington was in his winter lines again, and that was all.

At intervals McNab sailed on his mysterious errands down the
coast, sometimes in fishing sloops, sometimes in the *Bonnie Jo.*
On one of these expeditions Malachi Sparling turned up in one
of his ships from New York, and as they lay in a barren little harbor transferring goods from the American to a Nova Scotian ship
the laird brought up tentatively the matter of shipment direct to
Cádiz.

"The port's firm in the hands of the Spanish patriots, Sparling,
in fact it's now the center of their government in free Spain. The
French troops hover outside the town, but they daren't do a thing
while Wellington's to the north of 'em. Every time he pokes his
bayonets towards Madrid the whole of those ragtag French troops
in the south of Spain have to come pelting back for their own
safety. Meanwhile the British fleet controls the sea, and it's an
easy sail to Lisbon from Cádiz."

"Um, yes. But I don't think it wise yet to send our ships di-

rect to Cádiz. The present system's awkward and expensive, but"
—with a faint smile on the lean face—"the British government's
paying all the costs, including a profit to people like you and me.
As far as my own government's concerned, this method remains
unknown or merely suspected and ignored. An open move to send
the supplies to Cádiz might upset everything. Sleeping dogs, my
dear McNab, sleeping dogs!"

"What about the war talk in your country, Sparling? I hear it
still goes on, although our government in London seems to think
there's nothing to worry about."

The New Yorker passed a thin hand over his lips. "I wish I could
be half as sure of anything as your gentlemen in London are of
everything," he grumbled. "Their men-o'-war keep on with the
search at sea, and they're still grabbing every foreign seaman they
can lay hands on. Which means our war preachers can keep on
with the same text. So far, I know of no active plans for war.
Certainly no effort to raise troops or build a fleet. But don't let
that fool you. Every fresh-water American knows how to use a
rifle, and a powerful lot can shoot the eye out of a squirrel. In the
salt-water states another lot of Americans know how to build
smart ships and how to handle 'em. Add up all that, and subtract
what England can do, land or sea, this side of the ocean, while
she's got Napoleon just across the Channel and her army's in-
volved in Spain. What's the answer? You know as well as I do.
My country's got nothing to lose and a lot to gain by a pounce on
Canada. The whole continent north of Mexico under the stars
and stripes. I touch wood, sir, I touch wood!"

"But," McNab persisted, "surely the situation's better than it
was just after that *Chesapeake* affair?"

"I wouldn't say so. Not a bit. Oh, there's not so much hot talk
now as then, but there's something worse. A kind of cold making-
up-the-mind. A growing feeling that war's the only solution and
it's got to come. However, that's not what we're here for, is it?
Let's get back to our business. Here's the manifest. We've been
over the rice and Indian meal, and the salt pork and beef. There's
five thousand sides of leather. That'll keep Wellington's men in
shoes a week or two, eh? And what's left? Sixty kegs prime beef
tongues corned. That's the lot for this one."

17

Rory MacDougal limped ashore in the familiar cove sniffing the
April air and feeling thirty years younger than he was. Ah, the
spring o' the year, the spring o' the year! Soft air in the sunshine
after rain. Robins and sparrows home from the south and lilting
all over the place. Mayflowers already in bloom at the edge of the
woods. Frogs piping away at evening like a chorus of drunken
boatswains. Even the sea alive again, with the codfish back on the
coast after wintering somewhere in the ocean deeps, and the first
run of salmon turning up in fishermen's nets off the Thrum Cap
and inside Chebucto Head. More important than all, the sap in his
heart again as he thought of Ellie Dewar.

The winter had been more than usually long and dull. Gales and
snow and ice had kept the *Rob Roy* tied to a frosty wharf much
of the time, and when he did get out to McNab's island for a brief
call it was a case of sitting in the house, for his game leg and the
depth of snow made a walk with Ellie impossible. Never a moment alone with the girl who was to be his bride, he hoped, in the
coming summer; and as they sat side by side in the family presence Rory even had to do the talking. The girl seemed to close
herself at his approach, like one of those flowers that fold their
petals at a touch. She was hidden inside this tight mask, all but the
black eyes, as mysterious as ever and lately some way haunted.

Despite his hearty manner in public and his warm interest in
the prisoners, he was a solitary man. In his drab Halifax lodging
he had passed the winter as usual with the aid of rum, especially
the long evenings when he sat in his room drinking the stuff in
Cape Horn drams to dull his mind for sleep. To friends who rallied
him about this solitary drinking he coughed and humphed and
mumbled about a tropical fever suffered in his naval days in the
Far East, which had a habit of recurring in winter with agues
and shivers in the night. Sometimes these winter spells lasted days
as well as nights, and his friends enquired with concern. They got

nothing out of the tight-mouthed woman who kept the lodging-house except that Captain MacDougal had a touch of his old ailment, nothing serious; and they passed word about the town in a jocular way that Old Square-Foot was under the weather again. Then Captain MacDougal would be seen once more, limping along the snowy street to his office, muffled in his old blue fearnaught sea-coat, with a Scotch bonnet pulled over his ears, his face purple in the cold, his eyes bloodshot, but in all respects a man in firm command of himself and his affairs.

Well, all that was past for the season, another of the many he had passed in this cold town, and now the northward march of the sun had banished ice and snow again. He was free to sail about the long harbor and its nor'west arm, and to resume his regular calls at McNab's island. Now he and Ellie could saunter away to that precious spot on the Back Cove where she had made known her wish to marry him. Only there, it seemed, could her spirit find that same miraculous mood.

He came to the McNab house in the latter part of the afternoon. The laird was still at business in the town, and he found nobody about the place except McNab's wife and old Miss Frances, out in the garden, looking over last year's posy beds and planning a new summer's planting. They greeted him, and when he asked for Ellen, Jo said, "Oh, she's away on one of her rambles—you know Ellie! As soon as the boys got through their French after dinner they were off with their guns, and Ellie took the other direction." Joanna waved a hand to the track going through the McNab fields and the tenant farms towards the south.

"She's off to the Thrum Cap, as like as not. It's a favorite place for her when she's by her lone."

"Weel," he said, "I'll dawdle that way and maybe meet her coming back."

He stumped away blithely. At the edge of the wood he noticed the path branching off to Strawberry Hill but he kept on to the southward for more than half a mile. The track was rough with stones and old stumps, and after the winter's lack of exercise he found the going wearisome and hot. He paused at one of the tenant cottages and sat on the doorstep while the goodwife fetched buttermilk and a mug. He made no mention of his errand, merely that he was out for a bit of a walk; but after an hour, with the sun getting low on the western treetops, he asked, "Ha' ye seen Miss Ellen go by since noon? She was maybe on one o' her jaunts to the Cap."

"No," said the woman. "She didna come this way at all."

"Ye're sure?"

She laughed. "Naething bigger than a sparrow goes by that I dinna see."

He arose and thanked her, and limped back the way he had come. When he came to the fork at the edge of the wood he stopped and looked at the bypath. He had not walked that way for years, not since one July when the McNab lads were small and eager for a feast of the sweet little strawberries on the hill at the other side. He remembered the hut in the wood, and the dour old soldier who lived there like a hermit on the charity of the laird. It was now the dwelling place of Cascamond, he knew, and it struck him that he had not seen the Frenchman for some time. The year of permission to live on the island would expire next month along with Cascamond's teaching engagement, and then the former lieutenant of *La Furieuse* must go back to Preston. Did he understand that? Rory turned off to remind him.

The path wriggled around boulders and clumps of spruce and fir, and maple and birch trees with their summer dress tight in the bud. He remembered that the hut was near the back of the wood, where in a few more steps a glitter from the lagoon showed through the trees. He was stepping around a fir thicket when he heard Ellen's voice and the Frenchman's, and he pulled back his forward foot and peered. Cascamond stood in the open doorway of the hut, Ellen outside, at the foot of the small doorstep, with a shawl about her head and shoulders—Ellie on tiptoes, with her face upturned in Cascamond's hands, and her mouth to his. The kiss was long, with pause and renewal, a leave-taking of lovers.

MacDougal stood agape in the shadow of the firs. What he was seeing was no more credible than a vision of Joanna McNab, say, arm in arm with Napoleon and humming the Marseillaise. He turned away, shaking his head to clear it of this chimera. And he retreated a few steps on the path with the stealth of an Indian, as if those absorbed creatures at the hut could have noticed anything short of Gabriel's trump.

He leaned against a maple trunk to recover himself, with arms folded on his breast. For this visit he had put on his best blue coat, polished every one of the brass buttons, rubbed his shoes with grease and blacking, got himself into a tight new pair of yellow nankeen trousers, and crowned his grizzled head with a splendid black top hat, straight from London with the first spring merchandise and purchased only yesterday. In his hand was a stout ash walking stick with a gunmetal knob like a small cannon ball, a gift from the dockyard staff when he left to take up his post as Agent for Prisoners.

His mind cleared. And hardened. What he had seen explained the change in Ellie since her surprising proposal to him last year by the shore. The girl was young and impulsive. After that succession of dull fellows who came from town to look her over and went away, and after her own resolve to marry him, Rory Mac, then appeared the young French officer wounded in the wars, with his appealing captive air, his glib English, and that subtle knack with women which all Frenchmen seemed to carry in their pockets like a key to every lock.

In these times, with so many Halifax men at sea in men-o'-war and merchant ships and the fishing fleet, there was constant gossip of town girls and wives philandering with French prisoners. In his office he was assailed with complaints from indignant papas and mamas and the rages of cuckolded husbands. He writhed now when he thought of his invariable replies. "A prisoner on parole is a man like any other, isn't he? If temptation came his way what could ye expect? If it hadna been a Frenchman 'twould ha' been someone else and probably worse. Get along wi' ye now and leave me to my work! I canna keep seven hundred to a thousand men shut up like dangerous lunatics just because some silly females canna keep their knees together when a man's about!"

This rueful revery was broken by the sight of Ellie coming around the bend of the path. She saw him at the same time, a new Rory with a strange smile on his scarred face and a glint of murder in his eyes. She stopped with a gasp and looked back. Cascamond and the hut were out of MacDougal's view behind the firs.

"Weel, Ellie?" Rory said, with that grin and glint.

"What are you doing here?" she demanded, as if he had no right.

"I came to see my prisoner Cascamond, and I saw him weel

enough—and you too, my gel, bussing him farewell at the door. A pretty peecture to be sure. How long's it been making?"

"I don't know what you mean." She caught at that futile straw knowing Cascamond must be hearing every word, and hoping to gain a few moments while he slipped away into the hiding of the trees.

"Ellie! Ellie!" Rory said in a deep voice. "Ye canna lie to me. Not you! How long?"

She pressed her lips together and shook her head. Rory took a firm grip on his stick and stepped into the path. In desperation she cried, "Very well! Since last September. And you mustn't blame Michel. I'm the wicked one. I went to his hut one day and . . . and invited him to make love to me."

"Just as ye invited me to be your husband someday?"

She looked away miserably. "That was before I knew Michel. I didn't have any notion about him until we met on the Thrum Cap by chance one afternoon. We sat and talked. It was no more than that. But then I knew. I could love him as I couldn't love you or anybody else. Michel didn't know. Not till the day I first came here to the hut. And I came of my own accord. You must believe that, Roderick. And try to understand . . . please!"

MacDougal's terrible little smile had gone, but his blue eyes blazed like a pair of Bengal fires. She turned her head and saw Cascamond walking towards them. The sun was below the tree-tops, leaving the western sky all red and gold, with black stripes of cloud across it like a grate of coals. She caught Rory's arm and cried, "Michel, go back!"

"Lutine," Cascamond said calmly, "leave us, please, and go on to McNab's. This is entirely a matter between the Captain and me." He was in his fisherman's clothing, brown duck trousers, checkered shirt, coarse leather sea boots. His face was pale but his eyes were steady. He added, "I knew this must happen, *chérie*. It's only luck that it didn't long before."

Rory put the girl aside with a sweep of his arm and rushed for-ward, limping and roaring "Ah, ye blaggard! It's nae daft female ye've got tae deal wi' noo!" He swung the stick's heavy metal knob at Cascamond's head. The Frenchman just had time to twist away, and suffered the full blow on his shoulder. It staggered him, and the agony of bruised nerves sent a tingle of pins-and-needles through the left arm and made it half useless. Nevertheless he caught at the stick with both hands, and clung to prevent another blow. MacDougal had no choice but to put his own free hand to the stick as well, and try to wrench it from the Frenchman's grasp.

The tussle became a grotesque bear dance, both of them stamping about, now in the path, now in the bushes, and tugging the stick this way and that. A tree branch soon knocked off Mac-Dougal's hat, and the grey-and-tawny hair flew about his head in damp wisps and locks. He was strong but so was the prisoner. Rory knew well that defeat was certain in the difference of their ages and their legs, unless he could get the stick free quickly and crack the fellow's head in one or two blows with all his strength. To save his breath after that first savage outcry he did not utter another word, although his head seethed with bitter sea oaths.

To the watching girl the struggle of the two men, silent except for gasps and grunts and the crackle of trampled bushes, was more terrible than anything she had imagined of battle with sharp weapons and cries of war. A frightful strain showed in their clamped jaws, the breath hissing through teeth, the swollen veins at throat and temple, the trickle of sweat that made their faces shine. MacDougal's eyes bulged with effort and the rage of murder. Cascamond's were simply desperate. He knew but one thing, that he must cling to the stick or perish.

At last with a violent effort MacDougal wrenched it away and struck at the Frenchman. Ellen screamed. Cascamond bobbed swiftly and heard the stick whistle above his head. Rory drew it back for another blow, and the stooping man did the only thing he could. He dived forward, head down, hard at MacDougal's belly. The result was quick and calamitous. MacDougal uttered an anguished "Ha!" and fell backward with the Frenchman tumbling on top of him, and MacDougal's bare head smote a boulder among the bushes with the dull crack of a fence post under the mallet.

Cascamond got to his feet, a little dazed himself, and Ellen came in a rush crying, "O Michel, Michel!" and slipping an arm about his waist. Together they looked down upon the Agent for Prisoners. Blood ran from beneath his head and quickly formed a puddle on the brown carpet of last year's leaves. His face changed from scarlet to purple, and from his nose and mouth came a medley of sounds, snoring, gargling, rattling. Then his eyes rolled up into his head, showing only the bloodshot whites, and the noises stopped. He lay horribly still. Cascamond and the girl stared at him as if turned to stone themselves.

Then Ellen gasped, "O God! He's not . . . Michel, he can't be . . ."

Cascamond nodded, with an air of profound melancholy. He had seen too many men die not to recognise another.

"Lutine, you must get back to the McNab house as fast as you can. Go and say nothing of this affair."

"But they'll miss Rory when he doesn't come back by dark!"

"Yes. And sooner or later they and the dogs will find him. Then they'll come to the hut."

"And you, Michel?"

"I shall be there. I shall say that Captain MacDougal met me in the path, that we had a quarrel over my money allowance. The rest will be the truth. He struck me with the stick, we struggled for it and fell, and his head . . ."

"Ah, no! No, Michel. They'll never believe that. They'll take you to the jail at Halifax and they'll see you hanged at the beach end. You must tell everything, and I shall bear you witness."

Cascamond shook her roughly. "You will say nothing—do you hear? Not one word. You would only ruin yourself and you can not save me. Nothing could save me. The English were bound to kill me sooner or later."

Ellen was silent but her mind was running furiously. She gripped Cascamond's arm with surprising strength for a slight woman and dragged him away from the sight of that accusing figure on the ground. "Michel," she exclaimed, "you must run away. It will be dark soon."

"Run where?" he said bitterly. "McNab's men and dogs will find me, anywhere on the island, as soon as morning comes."

"I know! The Thrum Cap!"

"You think they won't find me there?" he said in the same voice.

"Listen to me, Michel. This time of year some fishermen from up-the-harbor set nets just outside of Thrum Cap shoal. In case they get a big haul they have an empty boat or two pulled up on the shore inside the hook of the Cap. They come out to look at the nets every morning and evening, and by now they're away up the harbor for the night. The empty boats they leave at the Cap have oars, and maybe a sail, I don't know. But you can take one of those boats and get off to the westward—make your way down the coast. With luck you'd be picked up by a Yankee fishing schooner. At this time of year they're swarming out of Marblehead and places like that, on their way to the Banks of Newfoundland."

"And if I don't meet an American?"

"Then you must keep on along the coast. You'll have to go ashore sometime for shelter and food and water. Have you any money?"

"Yes, quite a lot—about thirty-five pounds."

"Ah! Then you'll be able to make your way as far as Cape Sable —that's the end of the land—the end of Nova Scotia, anyhow. You can't go over the sea from there to the States—not in a small boat. I've heard Mr. McNab say it's two or three hundred miles and rough with the great tides running in and out of Fundy Bay."

"Then what do I do?"

"Go around the cape and follow the shore towards Fundy. There are little fishing settlements, and after a time you'll come to fishermen who speak French. Their ancestors came to this country before the English, long ago, and they're called Acadians. They suffered cruelly in the old wars. They're poor but very good people, and they'll shelter you."

"How do you know all this, Lutine?"

"I've heard Mr. McNab at talk with coasting skippers and fishermen. He has some mysterious kind of business—I don't know what—that takes him down Cape Sable way every month or so. It's not the fish business, though he's often bought dried and salted codfish from Acadians and he knows them well. I've heard him laugh to Joanna that some of Rory's escaped prisoners reach those villages and remain there, working as Acadian fishermen, while Rory marks them off his muster roll with R for 'Run,' and finally D for 'Dead.' "

"You make it sound almost possible, Lutine," he said vaguely.

"Almost? For a seaman like you? Of course it's possible! So get away! Get away now! Sometime, somewhere, we'll find each other, Michel. Write to me when you're safe, if you can, and let me know where you are. And now kiss me quick and go—and God keep you!"

He reached the Thrum Cap in the black heart of night, having avoided the easy track past the tenant farms until he reached the uninhabited end of the island. Besides the clothes he wore, he had tied up in a blanket his pea jacket, a canvas draw-purse holding his carefully saved money, the hut tinderbox, a clasp knife, a corked jug of water, five sea biscuits and a small chunk of salt pork—the last of his winter emergency store—and in a pocket of the jacket a small pencil map of the coast, scribbled from one of McNab's charts last summer in the library.

A single boat was drawn up on the cobblestones of the beach behind the Cap. He found it by smell, really, for it stank of fish. He passed a hand along the gunwales, feeling for thole pins. There were two sets of the pins, crudely whittled from birch sticks with the bark still on the upper part. In the boat's bottom lay a pair of oars and—marvelous!—a small sail with a pole that fitted into the forward thwart. The boat was what the fishermen called a dory, and what McNab's Scotch sheep-men called a coble—almost the same as the Breton *caubal*. It had a flat narrow bottom and flaring sides, with a small square stern and a high pointed bow. Cascamond had seen them in quite heavy seas, and knew how well they rode in any weather, properly handled.

He launched it quite easily, and thanked Lutine's intuition that it was this craft and not one of the heavier fishing boats, which a lone man could not move. The night was cloudy and dark, but holes opened and closed in the black ceiling through which he could glimpse momentary stars. A light breeze blew out of the east, good for sailing but razor sharp, as if it came off the ice fields up by Cape Breton. He set the little mast in the forward thwart and got the sail up, steering with an oar laid in a slot at the stern. The sea moved with a long swell as black as the night itself, and he had an anxious hour or more before he got used to the feel of it, and of the sail and oar. By then he was nearly frozen, and he had to drop the sail and take in the oar while he put on his pea jacket and wrapped the blanket about his legs.

Not a gleam of any sort showed from McNab's island, but on the farther side of the harbor mouth he could see the lights of York Redoubt and of fishermen's cottages at the sea edge between

there and the harbor head. With these over his right shoulder he
steered for the harbor mouth until he found the gleam of a lighthouse to the west. This, he knew, was one of the few on the coast,
warning mariners off the Sambro reefs. It gave him a good position mark for many miles on his course towards the west, and
he went on with a growing confidence.

This was a wild and rough coast with an outlying tatter of islands and reefs, all perilous to the mariner, as he knew from talk
of McNab and MacDougal as well as his study of the chart. Yet
it was no worse than the coast of Brittany where he had sailed as
a boy, often at night on smuggling expeditions with his father.
Above all he had faith in that strange insight of Lutine. He had
called her an elf out of pleasantry, a nickname to tease her; but
now he began to feel a superstitious belief that his sprite had a
gift or an instinct beyond the common intuition of women. Lutine
could see through darkness and through time. She could even
see him now, with those deep black eyes which glowed when they
made love. And the thought of that warmed his heart.

When the sun came out of the sea like a huge fire balloon, it
brought light and a touch of warmth, and provided him with a sky
compass. He could see the coast low and far to starboard. During
the day, as he held to his westerly course, the land disappeared.
A study of his precious little map showed that the coast receded
in two deep bays, as if some enormous sea beast had taken two
bites out of it. By keeping on his course he would fall in with the
land again tomorrow if the weather held; and here in the open
sea was his best chance of being picked up by a Yankee fisherman.
At various times through the day he caught a glimpse of sails on
the horizon, but it was impossible to guess what they were.

He resolved to make his food and water last through this day
and the next. When he saw the coast again he would go ashore
and get more. And after long thought he compiled his story. It
was useless to pose as a fisherman, although he had the right
clothes and the right kind of boat. The dwellers on the coast would
be fishermen themselves. They would ask what he was doing, alone
in a dory, without a fishline or a scrap of net. They would ask
where he was from, and where he was going. They would ask
questions about the fishery which he could not answer. They would
suspect at once that he had stolen the boat and was on the run

from Halifax. And if they suspected him a French prisoner he was worth a guinea to them, payable at Halifax.

So there was only one tale possible. He was on the run, yes, but from one of His Majesty's ships. A son of respectable English parents in Somersetshire, he had been carried off by a press gang. He had served five years in the war, and now he was tired of it all and determined to get to the United States. This ought to gain their sympathy, for all these people suffered from press gangs sent along the shore from Halifax, and many a man had been snatched out of his boat or cottage, carried off to the wars, and never heard of again. He spoke with an unmistakable English accent, and he had heard so much English naval talk from McNab's guests that if need be he could repeat it by the hour. And, finally, he had money to pay for everything he wanted—food, water, a little rum, a boat compass, and so on.

During the second night the wind and sea increased, and it occurred to him that if the boat shipped water he had nothing, not even a cup, to bail it out. Also he was desperately tired. It was impossible to sleep, for the sail and steering oar required constant vigilance. At times in the night he dozed away, only to be wakened in minutes by a dangerous yaw and a heave as the boat fell broadside on to the sea. The night was clear. He looked first for the Great Bear, with its pointers to the polar star, and then the other constellations came into place and he could pick a star to steer by. Again the night was cold, and he longed in all ways for the sun.

Daylight came as an angry yellow band along the east, with a sky clouding fast, and the wind changing to the south. A bleak rain began to patter on the sea and into the boat. The shifting of the wind made his westerly course more difficult, especially as it baffled and sometimes came almost directly ahead. He ate his last biscuit and washed it down with the last of the water. From time to time he stood up, to ease the cramp of his legs and to get a view. The trend of the land was to the southwest according to the map, and if his navigation had been reasonably good he should be coming into sight of it again.

Late in the afternoon he made out a round lump rising out of the sea on his starboard bow, like an island at first, and then other lumps that merged until a stretch of coastline lay before him. He steered for it, and plied both oars for more speed. In the open sea, with nothing to measure by, the dory seemed to surge along at a great rate. But here, with the land in sight, it crawled. The showers had ceased, and the sun bored a hole in the dark ceiling and put down a single ray like a glittering sword. It caught the edge of the coast and lighted up a few small white triangles which could only be the gable ends of whitewashed cottages, a settlement of some sort. Again Cascamond called up the image of Lutine and looked in her eyes and thanked her.

By sundown he was entering a gap in the shore, on the sloped sides of which small cottages faced each other across a cove; and there were fields and tilled ground studded with rocks, and behind them the dark green forest of spruce and fir, typical of this coast, which he had first noticed on the journey to Preston. The land was not high, and what had seemed bold hills when he first sighted them sticking out of the sea were now merely knolls and ridges with a stony face on the shore. Inside the cove were stagings and small wharves made of poles cut from the forest above, stout enough for the boats tied up to them, and elsewhere about the cove shore were platforms of poles and brushwood where the fishermen dried their catch in the sun.

A stream rattled out of the woods to a small dam and sawmill. The houses of frame and shingles, all neatly limewashed, the sawmill, the good condition of the boats and stagings and sheds, the chorus of cow bells jangling, the grunting of pigs and the clucking of poultry, all spoke of a thrifty and handy people. Blue smoke pouring from every chimney showed that the evening meal was cooking. A few men moved about the stagings, putting last touches on a day's work. They looked up and saw the dory approaching, and one called out, "Hullo dere, who's dat?"

It might have been the voice of Cascamond's host at Preston, the German settler Kolp. He answered wearily, "Just a sailor moving down the shore, and nearly dead for something to eat and a night's sleep."

He tossed them the boat's painter and in a stiff and awkward fashion climbed up to them. They all began to speak at once, and in the same guttural English. He remembered something said in the McNab house about German settlers, excellent fishermen, on this part of the coast. Their questions were what he had expected, and so was their attitude, darting suspicious glances into the boat, and over himself from the sea boots to the black stubble on his jaws.

"Who are you?" "Where you from?" "Where you goin'?" "That your dory?"

"My name's Harry Martock," he began. "From Halifax, bound to the westward—the States if I can find a passage over. I can pay for food and a night's lodging." Most of his money was in guineas, just as it had been paid to him. These gold pieces were tied in the canvas purse and stowed away in a deep pocket of his pea jacket. For simple purchases he had put in a trousers pocket a few shillings and half a dozen Spanish dollars, the chief currency of the coast. His fingers felt for three of the dollars and drew them forth.

"See!"

They looked at the big silver coins and nodded to each other as if to say, "The fellow's no beggar, anyhow." For his part Cascamond looked from one to another, meeting their stares with his own keen gaze. They were sturdy men with shaggy brown or blond hair and weathered faces, dressed in trousers and smocks of grey homespun. He was looking for the leader. In any village, any group of men, there was bound to be one. His inspection came to a stocky old man with sharp blue eyes and greying blond hair and whiskers. Ha!

At that moment the old man spoke. "You're on the run from Hal'fax, mister, ain't you?"

Cascamond laughed. He had rehearsed the laugh for this question and this moment. "Yes, sir. I won't deny it. I've run from a frigate there. I was pressed from a good home in Somerset—that's in England—and spent five years in His Majesty's service, with His Majesty's pay and vittles, and sometimes a touch of His Majesty's cat. Some of you know what *that* is, I lay! Well, I had enough, and I'm off. D'ye blame me?"

"No," said the old man. "You come with me. My name is Caspar Tiel, and I lost a son to the press three years ago. You can have supper and a bed with us, but you must get out again first thing in the morning. It's against the law—harboring deserters. So it'll cost you a shilling for board and bed, and a dollar for the risk."

Without a further word Cascamond handed over a dollar and a shilling, and before long he was seated at the board in one of the

neat white cottages above the cove. Supper appeared in a huge
bowl heaped with steaming *sauer kraut,* and "Harry Martock"
was urged to help himself. The old wife's English was much more
guttural than her husband's, and when Cascamond had taken a
good helping of the *kraut* she cried something that sounded like
"Tig Teepuh! Tig Teepuh!" She made scooping gestures. It came
to him that he should dig deeper with the great wooden spoon.
Down it went into the bowl, under the *kraut,* and brought up fat
sections of stewed eel, the *pièce de résistance.*

The pale green shreds of pickled cabbage were new to Cascamond, they looked like chopped seaweed, but he was so ravenous
that boiled seaweed would have tasted well enough, and the
stewed eels were delicious. After a tremendous quantity of this,
washed down with tea, he sat in a torpid state by the stove while
Tiel talked. Soon he was asleep. He must have been there an hour
or more, dead to the world, when the old man shook him into
wakefulness and suggested a proper bed. When he got to that, a
cot under the rafters with the usual quilt and featherbed, he simply
threw off his clothes, crawled in, and died again.

He came to life at cockcrow, with a faint stain of light on the
windowpanes and a sound of men busy at boats and fishing gear
down by the water. Breakfast was a bowl of warm corn meal and
milk, sweetened with molasses, and over the table Tiel gave him
parting advice.

"You'll find no more German people past here, Martock. The
settlers on the coast from here around to Yarmouth was mostly
Yankees from New England. Small fishing villages like this, but
two fair-sized towns, Liverpool and Shelburne, afore you get to
Cape Sable. I wouldn't go in either of them ports if I was you.
They have a lot of shipping business with the West Indies, and
the Admiral sends an armed schooner there to press men from
time to time. You get caught, they hang you, eh?"

"Or flog my hide off."

"I told my woman to fill your water jug. It's there. And here's
food, the best we could do. Corn bread, some butter, cold roast
moose meat—you like moose meat?—no biscuit, we're out of biscuit. Could give you salt fish but you'd have to go ashore and make
a fire to cook it, and anyhow it's thirsty stuff. I'll put the food and
jug in this little keg, in case you ship sea water. Oh yes, and here's

a wooden bailing scoop. Can't spare a compass. And no rum. Not a drop in the place. So there you have all you can get. And it'll cost you . . . ah . . . two dollars."

I shouldn't have shown him more than one, thought Cascamond, but he paid over the money with good grace.

"As I said, it's a bad risk, helping a sailor on the run," the old man said smugly, and popped the dollars into his pocket. He had the look of pleased cunning which comes to the face of a peasant who has fleeced another in a bargain.

Cascamond walked down to the boat with the keg on his shoulder. The fishermen at the waterside gave him brief nods or ignored him altogether. Clearly they wanted nothing to do with him in case he was caught and made to talk. He rowed the boat out of the sheltered cove into the sea wind, which was now from the northwest, and stepped his little mast and sail. Now for Cape Sable, he thought. Keep your eyes on me, Lutine. I need you.

As the little dory crept on towards the southwest he thought deeply of Lutine, wondering what had followed the discovery of MacDougal's body and the disappearance of the prisoner. It would take a couple of days for the men and dogs to search the island thoroughly, but before that the net fishermen would have raised hue and cry about the theft of their boat. He hoped with all his heart that Lutine was safe in her own silence. There was still one danger to her, the one that had haunted his mind ever since their first lovemaking, that she might find herself with child. He pictured the family inquisition. Who was the man? What could she say? Her betrothed? The only time she and MacDougal had been out of the family's sight since last year was the afternoon of his death.

One thing was certain. As matters stood, the obvious killer of MacDougal was the Frenchman who had run away; but so long as Lutine managed to keep her secret there was no apparent reason for the killing. They would never know—McNab and his islanders, and the officials at Halifax. Oh, they would hang him if they caught him, reason or none. His flight was as good as a confession. But they would never know. There was a melancholy satisfaction in that.

Sometimes in the long and dreary hours at the steering oar his mind lapsed into a delirium in which his old sardonic demon arose and capered, thumb-to-nose. What an affair! He, the man who

killed Lord Nelson, unknown in English hands all this time! And
under their noses making love with the affianced of the Agent.
And finally cracking the head of the Agent and getting away. As
good as a playhouse comedy. And the title was Rochambeau's
old quip, "This is the way to invade the English." He gave a
shout of savage laughter to the empty sea. Then the demon was
gone. Instead came the face of Lutine, sad and reproachful, and
he responded at once. Ah, forgive me, *chérie*. Remember only the
good half of me, please. It was no comedy, our love, believe me.
Of all the strange things in my life this was good and true. God—
if there is a God—keep you safe and bring us together again!

He passed fishing shallops, some on the move, some anchored,
with their crews of three or four men busy jigging for cod with
handlines over the side. They paused long enough to look at the
dory with the brown lug sail, to wave at the lone voyager, and
that was all. These dwellers of the coast were used to going from
place to place in such small craft and obviously thought nothing
of it. Then he began to see larger craft—schooners, a brig or two,
and a full rigged ship coming out from the land. Evidently a port
of some size lay there, screened by an island. He consulted his
map and found that it must be the town called Liverpool, with
"Coffin Island" marked outside. He recalled the German's warning and decided that in all ways he should avoid a place so
ominous.

The other port he must avoid, Shelburne, lay about forty miles
ahead. There, too, ships would be going in and out, with the
strong chance of a man-o'-war amongst them. The sea remained
moderate and the wind steady, and he dined in good cheer on cold
meat and corn bread-and-butter, washed down with sips from the
water jug. He had planned to steer inshore at the end of each afternoon, to seek some uninhabited cove where he could tie up the
boat and get a night's rest and sleep. But now he decided that
his best course was to stay well to seaward and pass Shelburne in
the dark. When morning came he could put in to shore and rest
a few hours. The map showed that Cape Sable was a dangerous
place, beset with reefs and strong tidal currents. It was, as Lutine
had said, the end of the land. Like Ouessant, he thought, the rocky

tip of Brittany, the devil's own meeting place of tides and winds, a sailor's nightmare. He would have to choose his weather to get around Cape Sable, and he would need full daylight for the venture. He sailed on through the night, tired and chilled, with one great ache from his haunches to his knees. Human flesh was not made for the sharp angles and hard surfaces of a dory—certainly not for twenty-four hours a day. Two or three lights bobbed along the black horizon and disappeared, the masthead lanterns of ships hull-down. Then to the west appeared a strong lantern light which grew taller every minute. With a cold shiver of dismay he realised that only a big ship could have a masthead light as high as that, and no merchant ship would be coming out of Shelburne in the middle of the night. He shifted his course, a futile gesture, for if this was a man-o'-war coming straight towards him no mere dory with a scrap of sail could run away from it. Then, with a sigh of relief, he guessed the truth. He had heard McNab deplore the lack of lighthouses and say that only two existed on the whole coast, one outside Halifax, and the other on an island off the port of Shelburne.

A lighthouse! Pouf! What a difference! And as this steady gleam went slowly past he felt again that watchful presence of Ellen Dewar. If I were religious, he mused, I would believe in my *ange gardien*. As it is I have my Lutine, who is a woman besides, spirit and flesh in one. I kiss your feet, Lutine, because you save me from harm; and I kiss your lips because I love you.

Towards the end of the night the stars were covered by a low scud of clouds coming up rapidly from the southeast, the breeze became uneasy, puffing this way and that, and the sea began to rise in a lumpy way. It's going to blow, he thought. Damned hard, too. A wild southeaster, with spray to blind you—and a bad lee shore. Get in, then. Find shelter while there's a chance. He steered for the black loom of the coast, visible only as something darker than the night itself. He had taken so many risks that the hazard of running in blind upon this dangerous coast meant nothing more to him.

The sea was still rising, a forerunner of the storm, and as he drew in to the land he began to hear a distant rumble of surf. Then he was amongst small islands and reefs, where the surf was visible in patches of white. He steered between them as best he could.

The wind was now so light that the dory was barely more than drifting. Rain fell, a few drops and then a deluge. A stretch of open sea now—no white patches on the dark—but the surf still booming farther in. And now no stir of air at all, only that sick breathlessness which comes before the first hard gust of a storm. He took down his sail, slid both oars between the thole pins, and began to row, face to seaward, back to the rising grumble of the unseen shore.

He was so weary that his mind was stupid, and it was only in a dull way, as a matter of little interest, that he noticed a sort of bleaching of the night in the east. And so, with the day and the storm coming fast together, he turned and saw that he was heading into trouble. An unbroken stretch of surf exploded on rocky shore. Pulling hard, he got the boat's bow turned to the northward just as the first hard squall struck him like a slap in the face. There was a pause in the wind, then another squall, then another, and after that a ceaseless blast that grew stronger every minute.

The little dory seemed to fly, even without the sail. Water slopped over the stern, and it was desperate work to keep the boat before the wind and at the same time use one hand to ply the bailing scoop. He had no notion of the time as it passed. His whole concern was that continuous dance of surf along the shore. There must be a break in it somewhere. The map had shown much of this coast as a succession of ragged headlands and inlets of the sea, like the edge of a giant saw.

He noticed a break at last and steered for it. On either side of that break the sea smashed and thundered. After a time through the spray he saw land—land rising on both hands, shaggy with dark woods. He had entered the gap, whatever it was. Twenty minutes of this—half an hour perhaps. Then the miracle he had looked for. The dory turned a bend of the inlet and passed into shelter like a traveler stepping out of a storm into a cave. Not quite a cave, though. This one lacked a roof. High overhead the storm thrashed the forest on the ridge crests, while down by the harbor shore there were only eddies and occasional puffs; but the rain fell hard, in fat drops that pocked the water of the cove like a continual volley of pistol balls.

A pair of tottering log huts, the remains of a pole wharf, and of old drying-flakes made of brushwood, showed that the place had been used for the fishery at some time in the past. Cascamond tied the boat to one of the few sound piles of the wharf, carried his sodden blanket up to the huts, and found a corner of one still covered by part of the old roof, an affair of poles and sheets of bark. The floor was of hewn logs. He scraped away a litter of dry porcupine dung, spread the blanket and attempted to sit down. Instead he sprawled on his back as if shot. He was asleep almost as soon as his head touched the blanket, wet as it was, and all the noises of Trafalgar could not have wakened him.

18

The storm roared on through the day, the night, and all of the next day. The sea leaped upon the shore outside the cove with the thunder of ships-of-the-line at broadsides, and he could feel an almost continual faint tremor in the ground beneath his feet. He ventured from his shelter long enough to fetch the keg with what was left of his food, and the water jug. It was fortunate that the food had been stowed in the keg, for the boat was half full of water, much of it rain.

On the afternoon of the second day, as he huddled in the dry corner of the hut, a visitor came out of the rain and paused in the doorway. It was a porcupine, probably a former tenant, and at sight of the man the visitor's tail came up and so did a thicket of sharp quills. For a minute or two neither of them moved. Then the eyes of the porcupine, like bright jet beads, began to turn, and suddenly the fat little monster waddled away. Cascamond sprang out, picked up a stick, and killed the beast with a few blows on the head. In his hunting adventures in the woods at Preston an Indian had shown him how to kill and skin a porcupine and roast it on a stick, and he remembered that the meat was good and tasted like a strange sort of mutton.

So now with his clasp knife he slitted the unprotected belly, scooped out the guts, and with care skinned off the bristling pelt.

The rain had ceased at last. With the knife he dug some dry splinters from the cabin floor, and after some patient work with the tinderbox he lighted a small fire on the ground outside. To this he added dry or nearly dry sticks from the woods, seeking them under the overhang of boulders and beneath old wind-fallen trees, as the Indian had done. The roasted carcass provided meat for two meals.

By the fire he dried his clothes and warmed himself, the first time he had felt really warm since leaving McNab's island. When the last breath of the storm had died away he bailed out the boat and made ready to sail at morning light. Studying his map he reckoned the cove not more than twenty miles from Cape Sable, and with a fair breeze he could make the hazardous voyage around it while the daylight held. Everything would depend on wind and weather, of course. Apart from the reefs, and the powerful tidal currents he had heard about, there was the supreme danger of a new gale blowing from any northerly point between east and west. Cape Sable was truly the end of the land. The boat would be blown far to sea, with a poor chance of getting back or even surviving in the waves that were bound to rise under the combined forces of wind and tide.

With all this in mind, and with the wisdom of old experiences off stormy Brittany, he was able to curb his impatience through two further days and nights in which there was calm air and fog, and then another gale, this time from the northwest. He explored the woods about the cove. The bygone fishermen had made a path up the slope where they cut and dragged down the logs for their huts and stagings, and there were other tracks where they had cut firewood. None of these went far. Wild hares scuttled from the bushes and Cascamond wished for a gun. He found some old fishing line in one of the huts and used it to rig snares in some of the hare paths, but he caught nothing. Even the porcupines, slow on the ground, usually managed to elude him by a surprising speed up the trees, although he killed two more.

Their meat, which tasted so well before, now seemed like boot leather flavored with fir gum. The nights were cold, and he had a poor choice of lying by the fire in chill drafts from every side, or in the bleak shelter of the hut. If only those fishermen had built chimneys and hearths in their damned huts! But floor

marks and a round hole in each tumbled roof showed that they
had used stoves, and even carried off the smoke pipes when they
left. There were fish in the cove; he could look down from the old
wharf and see them as dark shapes flitting about the piles. He
searched every inch of ground between the huts and the shore,
looking for at least one lost or discarded fishhook, but found none.
When he recalled the tale of that fellow Crusoe, in the leather-
bound book in McNab's library, he thought glumly *I'd like to see
what you'd do here, my fine fellow, with nothing more than I've
got.*

The yearning for movement, for action of any sort, turned his
mind to the chances of reaching the Acadian villages by land.
Walking around by the coast meant a tremendous journey, skirt-
ing each of those innumerable coves and harbors, many of them
inhabited by English—or New English—settlers with awkward
questions to ask. No, the only possible way was to strike overland
through the woods. His map showed Cape Sable as the beckoning
forefinger of a half-closed hand. A straight compass line across
the wrist from his present assumed position would be no more than
fifty kilometres. But compass or none, he knew from his winter in
the Preston forest that a man could not walk a straight line anywhere through trees, and that in any case he was bound to come
upon impassable swamps and lakes, and streams too deep to
wade.

A journey of fifty kilometres on the map might be twice or three
times that on the ground if he had to walk around many such ob-
stacles, and all he had heard and seen of the Nova Scotia landscape told him that lakes and bogs and streams were everywhere.
As an experiment, with the sun as his compass, he walked into
the woods from the head of the cove, heading west. The going was
rough from the start. The woods were dense, there were many
boulders, and even the small open patches had a tangle of bushes
as high as his shoulders. The shadows, the still air, the thick smell
of spruce and fir, the deathly silence, all brought back that old
sensation of a green dungeon which first oppressed him on the
way to Preston.

After perhaps an hour of this he saw open sunlight through the
trees ahead and plunged forward eagerly, only to find himself on
the edge of a long swamp extending right and left as far as he could

see, with a natural canal wandering down the middle, wide and sluggish and black as ink. He turned back to the cove in disgust.

At last he set off by sea. The wind was east and moderate, with low cloud covering the sky and an occasional drizzle closing the view. As he saw the jumble of small islands and rocks through which he had passed in the storm he marveled—and thanked Lutine. He steered outside them now for plain sailing towards the cape. He could see blue hills far inland, but the coast was nowhere high, and it squatted lower and lower as the day went on. By afternoon he was passing a shore as flat as a bench and partly wooded. There was still no sign of the sandy cape which the French name implied. Evidently his guess had been bad. Finally the bench came to an end. There was a narrow water gap, and then a small islet with a jumble of sand dunes. Beyond these pale heaps, none more than thirty metres high, lay nothing but open sea. So this must be Cape Sable. How insignificant-looking after all!

And now what of that famous tide, which flowed past Cape Sable on the west and ran more than two hundred miles into the land—the great Bay of Fundy? According to Mr. McNab it rose and fell more than forty feet at the head of the bay, with six-or-six-or-seven-knot currents along the bay itself as the tide ebbed and flowed.

Cascamond was not in doubt long. After turning that innocent corner past the sand dunes he saw a multitude of reefs and islands, marked with white surf, straggling to the northward as far as his eye could reach. The wind was still moderate and so was the sea. What made the water froth like a mill race about those ledges and islands? The tide of course, the famous Fundy tide. And it was on the flow, sweeping through that ragged maze like a broad and mighty river. Already his boat was caught in it with no escape. The small flat-bottomed thing could make no headway against tide and wind if he turned about. Indeed he had no wish to go about. This tide-stream would take him up the great bay to where the Acadians lived. There might be some danger in that rush among the ledges but when he thought of that night of storm when he found the cove of the porcupines he felt assured. Somewhere in the maze ahead he could surely find a nook before dark, a place to shelter for the night and await the next day's flow.

After a league or so however he was not sure of anything. He had taken down his sail but the boat went along as if towed by an invisible whale. He was in the maze now, with a curious illusion of reefs and islands sailing towards him and past him in an eager procession going to the south. Some islands were low and barren, others fairly high, with steep banks or cliffs crowned with woods. In places there were wide eddies, in others strangely heaped waves, as if the tide were tumbling over itself in its haste to get up the bay. Cascamond crouched at the steering oar, edging the boat away from the worst hazards, but feeling as helpless as if the dory were one of the paper boats he had made as a schoolboy and tossed into the Rance.

There seemed to be no friendly coves in these islands, and in less than two hours night would fall. He tried to call up the comforting image of Lutine, but she would not come. Something's happened, he thought gloomily. In another moment he found himself in one of the places where waves shaped like pyramids jumped up and down as if poked by some monster below. The boat rose and fell crazily for several wild minutes. Then it filled over the stern and went away from under him. It simply vanished. He had one glimpse of the empty keg dancing off, and that was all. He was in the sea, in the great salt stream, swimming desperately but without hope.

The cold water seemed to squeeze his body like a giant hand. He could hardly breathe. The leaps of this tidal overfall tossed him back and forth as if in sport for a time, and then threw him aside. He could see a wooded island going past. No use trying to swim for it. All he could manage was to keep afloat. But now the island lost that illusion of moving against the tide. It seemed to be standing still. And as the minutes went by it grew higher and clearer. He could make out individual trees. So he was in one of the eddies formed in the lee of these obstructions by the split rush of the tide. He had an instant terror of being sucked into the maw of some enormous whirlpool, but nothing of that sort appeared. He was floating on the edge of the eddy and it carried him towards the island's lee shore.

Hope came again to his indomitable mind, although he saw danger, too. The island seemed fairly large, about the size of Mc-Nab's, and so the eddy must be wide. It would sweep him along

the northern shore and then out to sea again in the course of its
great wheel. The chances of getting ashore seemed thin. As he
drifted closer he saw that the violence of storms and tides had cut
a sheer face on the island, apparently of brown rock fifty to a hundred metres high. Not even a monkey could get up there, let alone
a man starved and exhausted and wet. There was nothing to do
but drift.

At last he could see a point covered with gnarled spruce trees.
On the other side of it the main tide rushed and foamed in the fading daylight. This, then, was the place where the great eddy would
swing away from the shore and carry him off to the north. With
the strength of desperation he swam hard for the shore. The point
was quite near. Something slippery brushed against his knees.
And another. A fish? *Dieu!* Sharks? Were there sharks in these
cold waters? And now again, and this time he felt something slither
along his leg. It was kelp, the kind that grew in deep water, with
stems like greased rope.

Now the shore towered above his head, and he could hear the
loud wash of the eddy along the foot of it. What seemed a sheer
rock face before appeared now as a naked bank of hard clay
mixed with stones; and here, in this one place, the constant
scour of the tides had cut under the bank and caused a recent
landslide. To his disordered mind it seemed to say, as clearly as a
printed sign, *At your service, monsieur.*

As he thrashed with arms and legs towards the slide his knees
bumped painfully on a sunken rock. Then in his swimming strokes
he touched one with his hand. The bottom of the bank was a
litter of rocks that had tumbled from the tide-bitten face. He
scrambled over them somehow and dragged himself clear of
the sea. For the moment he was content to rest, to gather strength
and breath, but he dared not stay there long. With the tide in full
flow the sea was rising fast, and the watermarks on the bank overhead showed how high it could come.

The struggle to the top was terrible. Several times a loose rub-
ble of clay and stones gave way and carried him down a precious
distance that he had gained at the cost of his finger nails. When
at last he hauled himself over the edge he lay face down on the
turf, surrounded by a litter of old sea-urchin shells flown up there
and cracked and picked clean by foraging gulls. It was nearly dark.

His fingers were raw and bleeding. So were his knees, protruding
through the torn trousers. He had lost a boot, and the toes of the
bare foot were in the same state as his fingers. And now the cold
night fell on his sodden and weary body. He had no strength to
crawl away into the shelter of the scrawny trees. He heard himself
whispering hoarsely, "Lutine, I am dying." And then the night
triumphed. All was black.

His eyes opened to a dazzle of sun high overhead, and he felt a
dreamy warmth that reminded him of Dr. Haddox's rum and
opium. He was lying on thin mossy turf, a narrow shelf between
the trees and the sea bank. The trees had strange shapes. Apparently on these islands, exposed to the blast of every wind and to
salt spray flung up in the storms, the trees nearest to the weather
could grow no higher than a man's knees. Their lean trunks
writhed away from the bank, bending and twisting close to the
ground, and from their branches dripped long straggles of the
moss called old-man's-beard.

In the meagre shelter of this outer fringe the next rank of trees
gained a little height, and the next rank more. Some distance back
from the bank were trees maybe three fathoms tall. All were ever-
greens of a dense bluish-green sort which the Nova Scotians called
"cat spruce," and in this desolate place they grew in a tortured
huddle that a man would have to fight his way through.

Cascamond did not move. He felt in no way capable of fighting
anything. Even the urge of hunger was gone. It was enough to lie
in the sun. He watched it pass the zenith and go some way down
towards the west. There was hardly a breath of wind. In the sky a
few skeins of white wool drifted across the blue.

He became aware of something moving in the tops of those
grotesque trees. Turning his head he saw three ravens. Their black
sheen in the afternoon sun was like the gloss of Lutine's hair. That
was his first thought. Something beautiful. Then something very
ugly. He cleared his throat and declared, "So, messieurs, you think
I'm here for you, eh?" The ravens watched him with bright eyes.
One opened its wings and closed them again. Into his mind came
one of those ridiculous ballads which the McNabs and their visitors were so fond of singing to the old aunt's accompaniment on

the piano. In a croaking voice not much better than the ravens' own he quavered aloud what he could remember: *There were three ravens sat on a tree, Down-a-down, hey down, hey down.* Then something-something-something that he couldn't recall. And, *Where shall we our breakfast take? With a down-derry-derry, derry-down-down.*

Imbecile, he thought, control yourself. Besides, there are more than three. Six—seven. There will soon be a dozen. He had seen them gathering like this when he and his hunting companions at Preston cast aside the entrails of a moose, and he could hear young Kolp saying, "They never touch anything alive. They wait till they're sure it's dead. Days sometimes. They have patience."

Nevertheless the gathering of this ominous company on the tops of the weird trees forced him to his feet. After all, they might not always wait. He looked about for a stone to throw, and found nothing but the bleached round shells of the sea urchins, too light to hurt anything. He picked one up and threw it at the black watchers, shouting, *"Hors d'ici, canailles!"* and waved his arms. He was stiff in every muscle and the movements hurt damnably, but the ravens opened their big wings and sprang from the tree-tops into the air, moving off with hoarse cries and rising until they were circling far overhead.

Marchons! said Cascamond, and began to thrust his way into the wood, moving for the sake of movement, with no idea of where he was going. After he scrambled through the outer tangle and got amongst taller trees the going was less difficult. The dense crown of the trees admitted little sunlight and permitted no undergrowth. Even the lower branches had perished and rotted off long ago. By occasional glints of the sun he steered instinctively towards the south, as if he were on McNab's island, heading for a rendezvous with Lutine on the Thrum Cap. His right foot, bootless and with only the rags of a cotton stocking, hurt at every step; but he was indifferent to pain as he was to hunger, walking in a kind of half-sleep, with a sensation in his skull as if his brains had liquefied and someone stirred them with a spoon.

At intervals he found a convenient boulder and sat to rest. After many such rests he came into a wide space where the trees were all naked and dead and the sun was strong. The tree skeletons were charred black. His brain ceased to whirl for a time while he

considered this phenomenon. There had been a fire in this desolate forest. How? Lightning? Or had men been here? He kept on
towards the south, and after a time crossed a strip of swamp which
must have been wet enough to halt the fire, because there were
green trees beyond. It was almost dry now, parched by the sun on
the burned land all down one side. The fire must have happened
several years ago.

Then, in the shadow of green woods again, he came upon a small
round pool. He dropped to the ground and drank like a thirsty
animal. The water was brown but it was cold, and it flowed from
the pool in a slow trickle to a patch of swamp a little way to the
right. Now he noticed something else. The spring hole was lined
with carefully placed stones. Some human hand must have put
them there, and where there were hands there must have been
feet. And now he saw a path, a narrow track among the trees,
and the scuffle of fallen spruce needles showed that feet of some
kind had passed there recently.

He tottered off along the path. The trees began to shrink in
height, and assumed more and more the groveling shape of the
ones he had first seen, where the ravens perched. So he had
crossed the island and again the shore was near. Already he saw
through the trees a twinkle of the sea. He came out of the wood
on a small bay with a half-moon beach of shingle at the head of it.
The beach shelved steeply like the inside of a washbowl, and the
woods at the back of it were littered and festooned with driftwood
flung in there by storms at high tide. Some of this weathered grey
stuff consisted of drift trees and logs from other islands or perhaps
the mainland, but there was a lot of ship wreckage, and in one
place an entire deckhouse sat among the trees as if it had been
planted there for castaways like himself. What was more, it had a
galley-pipe and a wisp of blue smoke. All impossible, of course.
I'm dead, he thought, and this is some mad dream on the edge of
hell.

He made towards it along the crest of the beach, with the cob-
bles rattling at every step. As he approached, the cabin door opened
and out came two men, one with a musket which he cocked and
held ready to fire. The unarmed man was young, about nineteen,
with a mop of red hair and a red fuzz on his jaws. The man with
the musket was about thirty-five, a heavy fellow with a belly. His

hair was in a pigtail and he had black-stubbled jaws like Cascamond's.

"*Hola!*" said Cascamond in his raven voice.

"Stop where y'are!" said the man with the musket.

Cascamond halted. If this was the anteroom to hell the inhabitants had very earthly clothes. These wore dirty duck frocks and trousers, and shoes badly worn and scraped as if they had traveled the beach a great deal. Seamen of some kind, but whether fishermen or merchantmen or runaway naval men he could not guess.

"Who are you?" demanded Red Hair.

"My name is Harry Martock. I'm on the run from a frigate at Halifax. My boat sank off the north side of this island. I managed to get ashore, as you see." He said this very carefully and slowly in the rasping voice, like a schoolboy reciting a lesson in spite of a bad cold. And then, "Who are you, and what are you doing here?"

Black Jaws lowered the musket, but held it ready at his waist. "That's a fair question. A fair question, eh, Jackie boy? Well, Mister Harry What's-name, we ain't on the run from anywheres, and our boat didn't sink. We come here a-purpose. Ain't that right, Jackie boy?"

"Right," said Jackie boy.

"There's some as would call us wreckers, and some as would call us beach rats and shore-pickers and such; but let's say we're in the salvage business and let it go at that."

While he said this, Jackie boy sidled out of Cascamond's view, came up behind him and suddenly ran his hands over the castaway's trouser pockets.

"If you're looking for a weapon, I have only an old clasp knife," Cascamond said, without moving.

"Hand it to me," said Jackie boy. Cascamond drew forth the knife and passed it behind him to the waiting hand.

"What about money?" called Black Jaws.

"I have three dollars and four shillings."

"Hand 'em over to Jackie boy—for safe keeping, like."

Cascamond did so. It gave him a sour satisfaction to think of his pea jacket somewhere on the bottom of the sea with nearly thirty guineas in the pocket.

Black Jaws lowered the musket. "By the look of you, I guess you're what you say y'are, What's-name. Hammick?"

"Martock, Harry Martock."

"Martock, then. My name's Joshua." He pronounced it "Josh-ooway." "And that there shipmate o' mine is Jackie boy. Which is all you need to know, far's names is concerned. And now let's see about you. You're in a hard case. Them hands and knees, eh? And hungry, I lay."

"Yes."

"Well, I guess we can fix that. Like a swig o' rum?"

"Yes, please."

"Jackie boy, lend Harry a hand and take him inside."

Now that they had robbed him of the knife and coins these gentlemen of the salvage business accepted him as a lodger. Inside the deckhouse he was seated on a bench and given a tin mug with a generous splash of rum from a small keg in a corner. They poured similar drams for themselves.

"We ought to have a toast," said Joshooway. He lifted his mug. "May he who made the devil take us all."

They drank, and Joshooway burst out laughing. "That's a good 'un, ain't it? Tickled me, that, from the first time I ever heard it. 'Twouldn't suit a parson, though. Eh? Now about vittles. How long since you et a square meal, Harry?"

Cascamond shrugged. "Some days."

"Ah! Now what would ye say to some good pickled beef tongue, a hunk o' the best English cheese, and fresh pilot biscuit fit for a captain's table?"

The rum was stirring life into Cascamond's corpse. He laughed. "What would I say? I'd say the salvage business must have found a damned good shop hereabouts. Or should I say a ship?"

His hosts burst into guffaws and slapped their knees. Jackie boy went to a chest and brought forth exactly what Joshooway had described. Cascamond put his whole attention on the food. Even the sight and pain of his torn fingers failed to spoil his appetite. He ate and ate. When he had finished, he murmured politely, "Do you mind?" and flopped down full length on the floor.

Jackie boy went outside and came back with some fine linen handkerchiefs. These he tore into strips, and he proceeded to bandage Cascamond's fingers, knees, and toes, a long and com-

plicated task which he performed very neatly. Meanwhile Joshooway was busy with the rum, and after a time he began to talk
about the salvage business.

Cascamond could not understand it all. There were words and
phrases he had never heard before. But in substance Joshooway's
tale was that he and Jackie boy were part of a crew who visited
these islands every spring in search of the past winter's wrecks.
Most of the sea traffic between Europe and New England came
and went past Cape Sable, and what with snowstorms and fogs
and the surging Fundy tides a lot of ships trying to get around the
Cape were carried to the northward and wrecked. There were
other wreckers working the same grounds, the scatter of reefs
and islands that ran fifty miles past the Cape, and sometimes they
clashed over "partic'ler good pickings" here and there. Hence
Joshooway's precaution with the musket.

He did not say where any of them came from. His own gang
had a schooner, and the game was to hunt among the islands for
what looked like interesting wreckage, and put a couple of men
ashore in each place to gather whatever was of value. Eventually
the schooner came around picking up the men and goods, and
went off to market the stuff. Where that market was he did not say,
either.

"When I got into this game first we used to go out to Sable Island. I don't mean the little island off Cape Sable. I mean another,
a monstrous big sandbar with dunes on it and salt grass and wild
horses, away out in the main ocean, 'bout a hundred mile off Cape
Canso.

"A wonderful place for shipwrecks—even better'n this here. We
lived in huts made o' wreck timber. Lived like kings, too, sometimes. And fought like savages with other gangs. There was some
coves used to toll ships in to the shoals at night, showing lanterns
on spars stuck up in the sand hills, like the masthead lights o'
ships at anchor. I never done that, mind. Never! But what games—
what games we did have, though! Finally some tattle got to Hal'-
fax about robbing dead bodies that washed ashore, including dead
females with rings on their fingers, and the fingers all swole, so
there was on'y one way to get the rings. After that the Gov'nor
at Hal'fax sent a guard o' sogers to Sable Island and the games
there was all over."

The deckhouse was roomy and lighted by three small windows of thick glass. It had a small round stove, a table and two benches. The floor was of loose boards evidently picked up about the shore. Two hammocks lay thrown carelessly in a corner, and Cascamond noted the hooks from which they were slung at night. Along the sides were several sea chests, including one containing the provisions. From spikes driven at random into the walls hung a pair of ship's lanterns, a navigator's quadrant, a cutlass in a leather scabbard, a large silver watch on a chain with a winding-key, a pair of new glazed top hats, and in very odd company a framed print of General Washington and another of the Duke of York in full dress uniform.

"Most of this stuff come off an English merchantman that broke up on a reef towards the Cape. A mixed cargo bound up Fundy to St. John. The tide scattered it here there and everywheres amongst the islands. We got a lot of it stowed outside, under tarpaulins—everything from chests of tea to gentlemen's toppers and bolts of calico. Not George Washington, though. He come off a Yankee fisherman that fetched up here a year ago. Poor pickings, fishermen, as a rule, 'cept for the gulls. I've see this beach covered with codfish, split and gutted and light-salted, and all the gulls and ravens of God's world gathered for the feast. I never *see* so many birds in one place in my life, 'cept on Sable Island when the terns was breeding."

Towards night Jackie boy took an axe into the woods and came back with a backload of brushwood, which he dropped on the floor beside Cascamond.

"There's on'y two hammicks, see? So you sleep on this. There's blankets a-plenty."

For the evening meal Joshooway prepared a pot of what he called "lobscouse," a stew of salt pork, potatoes, onions and ship-biscuit broken into small lumps. Jackie boy lighted one of the lanterns with a brand from the stove, and after eating they sat about the table playing Spoil Five with a pack of cards battered and blackened from use. Joshooway poured a single drink of rum for Jackie boy and "Harry," and went on drinking steadily himself. At last he got up and solemnly wound the watch on the wall, slung his hammock where the cutlass hung, stood the musket in the corner by the head of it, and announced curtly, "Sling your hammick, Jackie boy, and fetch a couple o' blankets for Harry. Then douse the glim."

In this way Cascamond spent the next four days and nights. There was no work to do. Joshooway and Jackie boy had gathered all the goods worth removal and placed them just above the beachhead. Even fuel for the stove was a simple matter of picking up bits of driftwood. "Harry Martock" taught the others how to play *écarté* as a change from their eternal Spoil Five, and carefully he made enquiries about settlements on the mainland. They seemed familiar with villages where the fishermen spoke English, but he had to persist with questions about the French.

Joshooway's answers were always the same. "You mean the Cajuns? Oh, them. They live away up the shore past what they call Cap Four-chew—the place we call Yarmouth. I dunno much about 'em, reely. They keep to 'emselves and mind their own business."

It was from Jackie boy that Cascamond got, at last, something more precise.

"Like Joshooway says, the Cajuns live mostly up the Bay from here, past Cap Four-chew. That means the Forked Cape, see? I know that much. But there's one bunch of 'em right over there." He jerked a dirty thumb towards the east. "Place called Pubnico."

"Pub-nee-co?" repeated Cascamond carefully.

"That's right. 'Tain't a French name. Injun. But they're French people settled from way back. Got a church and all. I seen it once."

At this point Joshooway leaned across the table and tapped "Harry" on the arm.

"How's it come you're so curious about Frenchmen?"

"Just that—I'm curious."

"And how's it come you know all the ins and outs of that French game Ay-carty?"

"I was guarding some French prisoners once, and watched them playing it."

Joshooway's black-whiskered features split in a sly grin. "You ain't on the run from no English frigate. You speak too good for an Englishman afore the mast. You're an ejicated Frenchman on the run from Melville Island, and your name ain't Harry Martock any more'n mine is Jook of York."

Cascamond hesitated, wondering whether to brazen it out or admit the truth. It seemed to him that his only hope of reaching an Acadian settlement was to persuade Joshooway, and through him the leader of the salvagers, to set him ashore on the mainland near this Pub-nee-co. If it lay to the east it could not be far.

"Very well," he said earnestly. "I'm a French prisoner on the run. I don't wish harm to anyone. I've had enough war. All I want is to settle down in this country with people who speak French."

"You're a Crappo?" said Jackie boy, astonished. "A Crappo talking English like a gentleman! Well I never!"

The next day when the tide was on the slack a schooner came into the mouth of the little bay and anchored. Joshooway and Jackie boy waved arms, and a pair of boats put off to the shore. There were three men in each, two rowing and one steering, shaggy fellows dressed in an odd mixture of rags and new clothing. They jumped out and pulled up the boats, with a cheerful greeting to Joshooway and Jackie boy, who had put on their new top hats as if to mark the occasion. Then they noticed Cascamond standing by the cabin door. He could hear them demanding, "Who's that?" and jerking heads and thumbs in his direction. Joshooway replied in a voice too low for him to catch, and after curious stares they set about carrying the salvaged bales and boxes down to the boats.

The boats had to make several trips back and forth, and at the last they took off Joshooway, Jackie boy, and the castaway, whom they addressed as "Frenchie." Cascamond had given up trying to identify them by their speech. They might be New Englanders or Nova Scotians of Yankee origin, like so many in the province. Their schooner bore no name or port, a black-hulled vessel of two masts, with a mixture of new and old sails, like the clothes of her crew. Her condition was what the English would have termed "sound," but with a certain slovenliness that went with the general appearance of her men.

As soon as he hobbled aboard, with Joshooway's hand under his elbow, Cascamond was brought to a man they addressed as "Skipper," a tall fellow with a squashed nose and powerful shoulders. He was about thirty, unshaven like the rest, with sandy hair and whiskers and a pair of cold slate eyes.

"Frenchie, eh? You look like you'd been through a tanner's bark mill."

"Yes," said Cascamond, wondering what that was.

"He was making for one o' the Cajun settlements up the Bay, and his boat sunk in a tide-rip, the one we call The Dancers," Joshooway said.

"Humph! Well, give him a hammock to sling for'ard, and he can mess with the rest of us."

The schooner's hold seemed to be full, for some of Joshooway's bales and boxes were stowed on the hatch covers and the rest on deck. Joshooway took "Frenchie" to the forecastle, gave him a grubby canvas hammock, and showed him where to sling it.

"Where does the schooner go now?" Cascamond asked.

Joshooway rolled his eyes and grinned. "That's up to the Skipper. In this trade we dodge about, like. Account o' excise collectors and tidewaiters and customs officers and such. Never the same place twice hand-running. The Skipper's got a wide acquaintance with small-port merchants that likes to buy goods cheap and ain't fussy where it comes from. Mostly places around Fundy Bay, some on the provinces' side, some on the states' side. If it's any comfort I can tell you one place we sure *ain't* going."

"Where?"

"Hal'fax. All them Army and Navy people, and press gangs, and such."

"Ah! And if you go up the Bay on the Nova Scotia side you'll pass some of the Acadian villages, will you not?"

"We might," said Joshooway.

"It wouldn't be much trouble to put me ashore there."

"It might and it mightn't, Frenchie. Depends on the tides and such."

"What would the Skipper say if I asked him?"

"What I just told you, Frenchie. And you better not ask. The Skipper don't like people—even us—asking nosy questions about where he's going."

When the tide began to flow the Skipper weighed anchor and made sail up the Bay. The wind was cold, and except for the helmsman the watch on deck lay down in the shelter of the bulwark and hatches. Cascamond stood by the foremast gazing towards the mainland, hidden by the ragged sprawl of islands. He could only wish himself there. Jackie boy brought him a pair of duck trousers mottled by tar spots, a faded jacket of blue fearnaught cloth, woolen stockings and a pair of worn shoes. They were meant for a much larger man, and as Cascamond stripped off his rags to put them on he had a queasy feeling that they had been taken from a corpse.

"That's a nasty scar you've got in your leg," observed Jackie boy. "What did that?"

"A bullet. In a fight at sea last year." Cascamond pulled on the trousers. Wherever they came from, it was something to be fully clothed again, and to have both feet shod.

The sky was clouded and the sun showed faintly, like an old worn pewter medal. The sea was the color of the sky, with long streaks of foam created by the rush of the tide. Cascamond stayed on deck as long as there was daylight. As far as he could judge, the schooner was making to the north, keeping well clear of the islands. About dusk the course changed to northeast. Just as he went below for the evening meal it was due east, and far to starboard he could see a long range of hills, the mainland of Nova Scotia. Somewhere over there lay the Acadian villages, with shelter and safety for a Frenchman on the run.

After supper he turned in to his hammock with his clothes on, like the rest of the watch below, and fell asleep at once. He awoke at a shout of "Rouse out there, all hands!" He turned out with the others, and on deck he was startled to see land, a mass blacker than the night, long and high and very close. A faint gleam of water ahead showed that the schooner was entering a sea gap in this black wall. The Skipper himself was at the helm, steering with the confidence of a man who had run the gap many times before. Cascamond found the burly figure of Joshooway at the bulwark with one hand on a stay, gazing at the high mass looming so dangerously close to starboard. He whispered, "What's this?"

Without taking his eyes from the shore Joshooway muttered from the side of his mouth, "Digby Gap. We're going into Annapolis Basin. You'll see it in a few minutes." The names meant nothing to Cascamond. His lost map had not covered much beyond Cape Sable. He could feel Joshooway's apprehension, and he could not help admiring the *sang-froid* of the Skipper, running through this slot in what appeared to be a mountain wall, in the dark, and with the force of a six-knot tide. But now the height on the larboard hand faded away. He could see the shimmer of wide sheltered water. Under the dark shoulder of the range to starboard gleamed a few yellow lights.

"Digby Town," muttered Joshooway. "Most all abed."

"For'ard there!" called the Skipper. "Let go the anchor!"

A splash, and the rustle of the hawser running out. With the ease of practise some of the wreckers were getting a boat ready for lowering. In a few minutes away it went, with four men at the oars and the Skipper in the stern, steering for the lights of the town.

With the grim presence of their leader gone the men chatted freely, like boys when the schoolmaster leaves the room. The schooner swung to her anchor in the tide.

"What happens now?" said Cascamond.

"He's gone to rouse out a merchant in the town and make arrangements. He'll be back in an hour. Then we'll have to work like horses, getting the stuff away. The tide'll soon reach high-water slack, and we got to get out of here on the ebb, and well afore daylight."

When the Skipper returned, his boat was accompanied by a roomy shallop, manned by some mysterious figures from the shore. Behind the shallop, fastened by towlines in a little procession, came two more. Now indeed there was horse-work to be done. The boxes and bales on the deck and hatch covers went first. Then hands whisked the hatches off, and the hold began to give up all the "pickings" of weeks among the islands. The shallops, probably used in the herring fishery, held a large amount of cargo, and as they departed in the darkness the Skipper said, "One more trip'll do it."

Cascamond came to him. "Skipper?"

"Yes?"

"I beg a favor. I want to get to one of the Acadian villages."

"We passed 'em in the night, Frenchie."

"If I could go ashore in one of those shallops I could make my way to them along the coast."

"Well, you're going ashore all right. Depend on't."

With an immense relief Cascamond stepped away to where Jackie boy stood in the dark. "Skipper says I'm to go ashore with the shallops when they return. I intend to walk from there. How far to the nearest village of the Acadians?"

"I dunno, but you can make it. You better skirt around Digby Town. There's only one road out of it and that goes to the west'ard. Foller it two or three mile till you come to a fork. The east fork runs all the way to Hal'fax. You take the west fork and keep a-going till you strike someone talking French. If you make a mistake and foller the east fork you'll be in trouble afore you get far."

"Why?"

"The east road follers the Basin shore to Annapolis town, and there's a fort to Annapolis with English sogers in it. You show up there in the rig you're wearing, and them black whiskers and all, someone'll bring you up with a round turn and ask a lot o' questions. You ain't got a thing to show who you are or how you come here. You speak too good for a common sailor. And them redcoats to Fort Anne is always on the watch for coves run from Hal'fax—sogers, sailors, French prisoners, thieves that's broke lockup, and just plain vagabonds that can't give a good account of theirselves. So, mind, when you come to the crossroads lay your course west. Understand?"

"West. Yes. I shall remember that, Jackie. Would you let me have my money now, please?"

"What money?"

"The money Joshooway told you to keep for me."

"I never seen no money and never heard sich a thing. You was more'n a leetle crazy in the head when you found us, mind that."

"I see."

When the three shallops reappeared there was another busy scramble to transfer goods. Finally a voice from the hold said, "That's the lot."

The men in the shallops prepared to cast off, and the Skipper called out, "Hold on a minute, there's one thing more."

Without warning two men seized Cascamond and fastened his wrists in a pair of rusty manacles.

He cried to Joshooway, "What is this?"

Joshooway said coolly, "We salvaged you too, Frenchie. So you're part o' the lot. As a run French prisoner you're worth a guinea at Annapolis fort, so the Skipper gets five shillings for

you, delivered here over the side. Now go along peaceful and shut
your mouth, or them shallop-men'll shut it for you."

He was pushed to the side of the schooner, and there was nothing for it but to jump down on the bales of cloth in the shallop
below. A voice in the shallop called, "Got a key to them irons?"

"Ay," said the Skipper. "It's a bit rusty but it works. Pass it
down, Joshooway, on a bit o' line."

With that accomplished the shallop-men pushed off. As they
came in to the shore Cascamond found that the goods were not
being landed in the town, but at a small beach outside, where
several horses and wagons waited. The smugglers seemed to be
well equipped and practised. He was given a place on a loaded
wagon and taken on a rough ride that ended at a house and barn
in a cleared patch of woods. The goods went into the barn and
so did he. A lantern hung from a beam, and one of the men
showed him an empty cattle stall and pulled down some clean
hay from the loft.

"You speak English, Crappo?"

"Yes."

"Well, lie down there and get some rest. In the morning one of
the shallops will take you up the Basin to Fort Anne. The Skipper
said you was cast away among the islands down the bay and
come nigh getting drowned."

"Yes."

"Well, you're lucky. In a few more days you'll be back to Melville Island, high and dry, with a good roof overhead and vittles
reg'lar three times a day." The man's voice was kindly enough.
He added, "There'll be someone on watch here all night, so don't
try to slip off. You've had a rough time by the look of you. You
don't want a broke head too."

With that he took the lantern and went out. Cascamond sank
down on the hay and heard the barn doors closing and a heavy
wooden bar falling into place. *High and dry.* He repeated the
words aloud, with a hoarse laugh in the darkness. He could see
himself high and dry at the end of McNab's beach.

19

In any other circumstances the sail to Fort Anne would have been delightful. Annapolis Basin was like a giant horse trough sixteen miles long, and for much of that distance four miles wide, twinkling in the breeze and the warm May sun. A rim of steep wooded hills marched along the north side of it. On the other side marched a lower range, wooded also, with a fringe of farms and salt meadows along the shore. The breeze and tide were fair for Annapolis town, and the shallop, spangled with herring scales and smelling of her usual trade, surged along at a great rate under the soiled canvas hoisted to the wind.

Cascamond was in no condition to admire the beauty of the scene. The night had given him no sleep. His torn nails and raw fingers and toes were agonizing, but more painful still was the trick that fate had played on him. He understood now that Nova Scotia was almost an island; a long peninsula joined by a narrow isthmus to the mainland like a sausage on a fork. All his risks and sufferings had only carried him around one end, traveling in a great loop whose last course lay overland to Halifax. He felt like a lost man wandering in the forest who sees the mocking ashes of last night's fire.

The man at the tiller was a short square person in wrinkled black clothes, with a narrow-brimmed round hat clapped on his head like a chamber pot. He had a tight mouth and eyes as pale and cold as icicles, and Cascamond guessed easily that this was the merchant who bought wrecked goods in the dark and did not scruple to buy a French prisoner for five shillings. The other two men in the shallop were burly fishermen in homespun, and one of them had the key of Cascamond's handcuffs slung about his neck on a loop of spun yarn.

About halfway along its length the Basin narrowed to a bottle shape, and the boat ran up the neck between long green hills with a tidal rim of red mud and a string of farms along the shore.

At last a grassy hillock blocked the view ahead, a peculiar hillock with roofs and chimneys sprouting out of it like a fungus growth, and a flagstaff with the British Union Jack snapping in the breeze. This, then, was Fort Anne, and behind it sat a little town, the entry port of the Annapolis Valley.

The merchant steered the shallop to a high log wharf beside the fort, left it in charge of one fisherman, and with the other, the fellow with the key, marched Cascamond up a steep clay path to the fort gate. There they were challenged by a redcoat sentry in pipeclayed crossbelts and black shako.

"I've business with Captain Sillinger," said the merchant pompously.

The soldier looked over this odd trio with contempt. "Captain's not in the fort. Him and his wife are on a visit up the river." He shifted his musket casually from one shoulder to the other. The long bayonet glittered in the sun.

"Then who's in charge, my man?"

"I ain't your man, Pumpkin," snapped the soldier. "Lieutenant Morgan's in charge, but I ain't fetching him out for the likes o' you."

At this point another soldier came out of the guardhouse, putting on his shako. The brass badge of his regiment and a loop of brass chain, polished like gold, glittered on the front of the shako, and three big white chevrons gleamed importantly on his sleeve. "What's up?" he said.

"I am a gentleman of Digby—name of Hubbs—and I've got here a French prisoner on the run that was arrested by my men. Kindly call the lieutenant and I'll turn him over."

"Gammon! You can turn the beggar over to me. I'll put him in the clink and report him when the lieutenant makes his rounds."

"And what about my money? The reward's a guinea."

"So it is, and a guinea's worth waiting for, so you can wait—outside."

The man in the pot hat made a face of patriotic resignation. "Very well, pass over the key to those irons, Joe."

The sergeant marched Cascamond through the gate and across a parade ground between barracks of white-painted clapboards. The buildings sat in a small bowl of earthen ramparts covered with grass, on which a few cannon faced the water. If Fort Anne had seen any war, it must have been a long time ago. The inner face of the ramparts was studded at intervals with casemates of mortared stone. The redcoat and the prisoner came to one of these, closed by a heavy wooden door and guarded by another sentry. At a nod from the sergeant the sentry put a ponderous brass key in the lock and dragged the door open. Cascamond stepped inside and the door closed.

For some moments he was blind in the quick change from sunlight to the blackness of a cavern. Then things began to emerge from the shadows. The casemate was dimly lit and ventilated by an iron grill above the door. He beheld a low chamber of stone with a vaulted roof and a brick floor, and furnished with a pair of benches, three or four pallets of straw, and an evil-smelling wooden pail. Two other occupants, as shaggy and dirty and poorly clad as Cascamond himself, sat gloomily on the benches.

"*Hola!*" said Cascamond tentatively. At the familiar French hail the two looked up and regarded him. They were swarthy men of about his own age. One said in French, "Who are you?"

"Call me Michel if you like. Are you from Melville Island?"

They were animated at once. One cried, "Yes! Certainly! *Malveillant,* as we call that damned place. My name is Jerome Penthieu, and this one here is Emil Houchard. We have been prisoners at Alfax five years, first in hulks and then at the new prison, *Malveillant.* We'd heard rumors of French people somewhere in the back country—families from the old time when France owned the whole of this damned wilderness. We decided to try to reach them. A month ago three of us skipped from a party working on the road between Alfax and this valley. We had obtained these rags to put on after we threw away the prison clothes, and we'd saved a few biscuits and a chunk of salt beef. *Dieu,* what an affair! Keeping off the road in the daytime, moving only at dark, trembling whenever a farm dog barked in the night. And of course we were lost in woods much of the time. Well, all that *tracas,* just to get pinched outside this town. We had been seen and reported—some farmer I suppose—and when we took the road again after dark a party of soldiers waited for us by a stream, hiding under the end of a bridge. One of us, Thouret, made a dash for the stream. It was not very wide and it looked shallow in the starlight. But the tide runs up into these creeks and makes them

very deep, and when it ebbs, *pardieu,* every one of them is like a
mill race. Poor Thouret could not swim. He gave one cry before
he sank and that was all. *Tiens!* what a way to go—drowned in
the dark like a cat in a sack."

"And you?" said the other man, Houchard. "Are you also from
Malveillant? I don't remember you, but of course among so many
. . . and you have more hair than face, my friend."

"I am not exactly from *Malveillant,*" said Cascamond cautiously. "I was taken at sea and brought to Halifax, but there I
stole a boat and got away down the coast towards the west. I, too,
was hoping to reach places where people speak French in this
country, but my boat foundered and I was taken by some pil-
lagers of wrecks at the mouth of what they called the Bay of
Fundy. They brought me into yonder Basin last night and sold me
to a merchant for five shillings."

"Ah, these damned English!" cried Houchard. "Anything for
money!"

"What happens to us now?" asked Cascamond with a stolid
face.

"In a day or two we shall be marched away to Halifax. The
soldiers don't like that little duty—it's a hundred and fifty miles
they say, the Devil's own promenade."

A silence. Cascamond's mind was busy. He said at last, "That
poor fellow—what was his name, Thouret?—he is dead, you say?"

"Certainly!" snapped Houchard. "When the tide ebbs, this tremendous tide up here, nothing like the simple tide at *Malveillant,*
it drops out of all those deep creeks in the meadows up the river,
and then out of the river itself, a red flood rushing out of the land
as if the bottom had gone out of a great vat of muddy wine. It
makes an eddy in the basin here before the fort and strews the
shore with driftwood from the creeks. The day after we were captured, the redcoats took Penthieu and me down to the shore outside the fort to see a dead man washed up there. It was Thouret,
of course. Just as the redcoats brought us here, that red tide carried poor Thouret to the fort, as if the water itself was in the pay
of King George."

"This Thouret," persisted Cascamond. "An old companion of
yours at Melville Island?"

"No," growled Penthieu. "Houchard and me were messmates

at *Malveillant,* but Thouret was in a mess on the first floor of the prison—the lower deck as the English call it. He had not been a prisoner long, like us. He was there no more than a couple of weeks."

"Then if one gave himself that name, it's not likely that anyone at *Malveillant* would know the difference, *hein?*"

"Tiens!" said Penthieu. "What's the drift?"

"I escaped from the English with difficulties, my friend. For example the theft of a boat. In this country a man or woman can be hanged for stealing anything worth more than five shillings, if the owner can prove the value. That's the English law. I had another embarrassment. Some violence, let us say. So it would go very hard for me at Halifax if the English discovered who I was. Now, poor Thouret is dead and cannot mind if one takes his name, as one might take his hat. Won't you agree to that?"

They looked at each other, shrugged, and turned their eyes back to Cascamond.

"What is your real name?" Houchard said.

"I've forgotten that already, my friends. My surname now is Thouret. What is my first name?"

"Joseph."

"And my ship?"

Houchard shook his head. Penthieu thought for a few moments and said slowly, "As I recall his talk he was in a Bordeaux privateer called *Necessiteux.* He was not of the Navy, I'm sure of that."

"And was he a *Bordelais* himself?"

"No, he was from Rochefort."

"Dark or fair?"

"As black as you."

A rattle at the door, and then a wide swing of it, letting in the flood of light from a fine sunset. The three prisoners jumped up and blinked. Mr. Hubbs was there with his rat-trap mouth, the sergeant bearing pencil and paper, and a tall man in grey, with the nose of an eagle.

Hubbs pointed to Cascamond. "That one there, Cap'n."

The Captain addressed himself to that one there. "D'you speak any English, prisoner?"

"Yes, sir."

"Ah! Take this down, Sergeant. Your name?"

"Thouret, Joseph Thouret."

"And your home?"

"Rochefort, sir." Seeing the sergeant's complete ignorance of French, Cascamond spelt the names for him letter by letter in English.

"Gad!" said the Captain. "You know the language damned well. You were in the Navy, I presume?"

"I was a *corsaire*—a privateersman. My ship was the *Necessiteux* of Bordeaux."

Again he spelt the names for the sergeant's record.

"And you were taken by Mr. Hubbs, here?"

"Let us say that I came into his hands, sir."

"Very well. And speaking of hands, you've got a bad pair there by the look of those filthy bandages. Sergeant, give the surgeon my compliments and ask him to look at this prisoner's injuries. Meanwhile, take off those damned irons. The man's in safe custody."

"And when do I get my money?" demanded Mr. Hubbs.

"Follow me," said the Captain with distaste, "and I'll speak to the paymaster."

The door opened in the grey light of a rainy morning. A glum trio of soldiers, a corporal and two privates, stood outside with a wet shine on their muskets and the black knapsacks strapped to their backs.

"Oo-shar and Pont-you!" the corporal bawled. "Come out! You're off to Alifax. You other feller, what's your name, Turret? —you're to stay."

"Why?" said "Joseph Thouret."

"Cos the surgeon says ye can't march 'alf a mile on that foot o' your'n, that's why. Now come on, you others!" He pointed a thumb at Houchard and Penthieu and jerked it several times over his shoulder. "Allay! Allay! And don't look so bloody sad about it. You're on'y walkin' one way, Crappos. Us poor bloody sogers 'ave got to foot it all the way back 'ere again."

Away they went, and the door closed on "Thouret" alone. For the next two weeks he had the casemate to himself. It was a dreary hole, dim and damp, for moisture trickling down through the earthen rampart made a cold sweat on the stones. However the commander of Fort Anne was a gentleman, and the confinement of this *Crapaud* who spoke English like a gentleman was made as comfortable as possible. The surgeon came to inspect his damaged hands and foot every day, and the surgeon's orderly changed the bandages. At the very beginning the surgeon found the prisoner stinking and lousy, and ordered his hair and beard completely shaven. Then appeared a tub of hot water, a ball of yellow soap, and a piece of old rough towel, with which the orderly scrubbed him down from head to foot. His bedding was taken away and burned and replaced, and the brick floor mopped with a strong solution of lye. His clothes were carried on the end of a long stick to a huge iron caldron by the shore, where fishermen dyed their nets in a solution of hemlock bark and boiling water. The garments came back strangely brown, but without their population.

Thus improved, "Joseph Thouret" was allowed outside the casemate every fine day for air and exercise under the eye of the sentry, limping back and forth across the end of the clay parade ground, or merely sitting on the turf in the sun, with his back against the rampart. He was given the same food rations as the soldiers, and they were free to talk to him. Life in a sleepy little colonial town was dull for the younger soldiers; but most of the garrison were married veterans, and living was cheap and easy here in the fertile farmland by the river. With these conditions the men of Fort Anne had little of the harsh manner that went with duty in the more barren posts of the British Empire. Cascamond found the days as pleasant as a prisoner's could be, and he regarded his healing toes with some regret. He said to them once, "You five little devils may hang me yet."

At last he had company in the casemate, a pair of deserters from a man-o'-war at Halifax. Like most men on the run from Halifax they had taken the main highway out of the town, which plunged through the forest to the Annapolis Valley, and eventually led them to the valley's end, where the watchful soldiers of Fort Anne stood in wait.

Like all of Cascamond's chance-met companions the sailors were astonished to find an apparently well-spoken Englishman who was in fact a French prisoner-of-war.

"Lucky devil!" said one.

"Why?"

"When they catch a run Crappo they just chuck him back in the hulks or wherever they keep 'em. With poor buggers like us, it's . . ." He pouted his lips and made the sharp whistling sounds of a cat-o'-nine-tails in the air.

As "Joseph Thouret's" toes and hands were now well healed, all three of them were ordered off to Halifax, with the usual escort of three young soldiers. The casemate sentry told "Turret" cheerfully, "All sailors bein' slippery coves, and you a French 'un, which makes you a reg'lar greased eel, you'll walk to Alifax between them tarpaulins, in two pair of irons." This seemed an odd remark until they were ready to go, and stood side by side on the parade ground, with Cascamond in the middle. The garrison armorer came out of his workshop with two sets of handcuffs, each pair joined by twelve inches of chain. Cascamond's right wrist was shackled to the left wrist of the sailor on his right side, and his own left wrist to the other's right. They set off, marching three abreast, with a corporal and two privates following at a few paces' distance.

As soon as the town was out of sight the corporal called a halt. The sea breeze off the Basin did not penetrate here, and like a dusty red snake the road wound through the valley in the full blaze of the sun. The soldiers eased their choking leather neck-stocks, unbuttoned the top half of their jackets, and transferred their knapsacks to the backs of the prisoners. When the sailors cursed them cheerfully for "lazy lobster-backs" the corporal chuckled.

"You'll be lively bloody-backs in a few days' time, Jack, dancing to the tune of cat-and-fiddle. Anyhow, why shouldn't you tarpaulins carry some o' the load? Your grub's in there the same as ours—five-days' rations. And we've to carry Old Brown Bess, which you don't. Now, march!"

They struck an easy pace, the soldiers with their muskets slung, and Cascamond found that he could walk very well. They passed farms where men were plowing with horses or oxen, usually oxen. The orchards were in leaf but not yet in bloom, and sometimes between the farms they walked in the dappled shade of birch and maple clumps whose leaves were not far out of the bud. To the

left of the road, now near, now far, they had glimpses of a wide
river with steep banks of rusty-red clay, meandering through
meadows where fat cattle grazed. Beyond the meadows and plow-
lands and orchards ran the two ranges of hills which sheltered
the valley. The soldiers spoke of them as "the North Mountain"
and "the South Mountain."

Each noon and evening they halted at a brook or a spring to
munch their journey rations of biscuit and cold boiled pork,
and at night they slept in wayside barns while the soldiers took
turns on watch. The barns seemed to be accepted night lodgings
for wayfaring soldiers and prisoners, and sometimes this indulgence of the farmers extended to pots of cider and slices of
corn bread thick with butter, and their homespun women and
children came to peer at the travelers.

In places on the road they were overtaken by a farmer driving
horses and a wagon from one village to the next. If the wagon was
empty and big enough all of the party were invited to hop in. If
room was scant the soldiers rode and the prisoners walked behind.
However these breaks in the march were never long. The little
troop covered most of the miles up the valley and across the waist
of the peninsula on their own feet. On the fifth evening they swallowed the last of their rations by the shore of another sea basin,
smaller than the one at Fort Anne, with no trace of the great red
tide, and rimmed by much lower hills. A little river rattled into
it, and in the angle of the river and the basin shore a log fort and
barrack tottered in emptiness, relics of some older time when
Indian war parties came that way.

They slept in the ruin of the barracks and at morning light
took the road again, following the shore of the basin to its southern end, and passing on the way a few summer villas, empty and
shuttered. At the south tip of the basin a lane turned off the highway into the woods, and the party followed it, the corporal grumbling, "Extry miles—extry miles! But that's the orders, boys.
Deliver the Crappo to Melville Island, then foot it around to Alifax with the two Jacks."

When the sun was past noon the party emerged from the woods
into a cluster of tilled fields and wooden houses built in the old
German style, which the corporal called "the Dutch Village."
They were hungry and thirsty. A few words at the nearest farm-

house got them buttermilk cooled in the well, and slices of corn bread and cheese, which they devoured sitting by the road with their backs against a wall of field stones.

Another mile's leisurely travel through more woods in the afternoon brought them to a sudden opening. A brook flowed beside the road and splashed into what seemed the head of a broad river flowing straight away from where they stood. There was a crossroads at this point, and a log bridge carried one road over the brook and into more woods beyond. As they stood on the bridge looking down the "river" Cascamond saw a fringe of wet yellow wrack about the shore, the sure mark of tidewater.

The corporal declared, "We'll stop 'ere and get them knapsacks on our own backs again, boys, and fasten our stocks and button our tunics, and brush the dust off of our trouser legs. From 'ere on we march at parade step, muskets at the slope, 'eads up, chests out, and all the rest of it."

"Why?" grumbled a private. Other than a few small cottages and huts near the head of this long salt inlet there seemed to be nothing but forest.

"Cos inside twenty minutes we'll be under an officer's nose, not to mention sergeants and such that might be on the road from some spit-and-polish regiment at Alifax. This 'ere is the Northwest Arm of Alifax Arbor, and Melville Island is tucked away in a cove in them woods to the right."

Cascamond felt a cold prickling in his skin, despite the heat of the day. The Arm gleamed between wooded ridges like a polished gun barrel, and beyond its muzzle, dim in the distance towards the main harbor, he could see a speck. It was too far to make out clearly but he knew exactly what it was. He was looking at the Thrum Cap, and by turning his eyes a little he could make out the low hump of the island where McNab's house was, and where the hangman's beach ran out into the harbor channel.

They tramped over the little bridge and climbed steeply through woods from which the big trees had been logged, leaving stumps like decaying molars in the flourishing second growth. They crossed another brook, a large one this, rushing down the slope to a sawmill by the Arm shore. Then the road made a sweeping curve, descending at every step, and emerged from the trees on open water, a pretty little cove that had a grim blemish—a cluster of buildings on the island squatting in its mouth.

A fence of high wooden palisades with sharpened tips enclosed the western half of the island, which held the prison and its yard. The prison itself was a long wooden block painted the color of blood, two stories high, with a steeply pitched roof to shed the winter snows. A grassy knoll formed the eastern half of the island, with a signal mast on its crest, and various wooden storehouses and quarters for the guards. At intervals around the prison palisade were sentry boxes, each manned, and others stood around the eastern knoll. Clearly the guardians of Melville Island took no risk of surprise from within or without.

Cascamond noted another precaution. On the shore of the cove, close by the road, sat a formidable cannon under a wooden shelter, with a party of gunners lounging on a bench in the shade. The gun pointed across the water to the west end of the prison, and he noted that it was mounted on swiveled iron wheels and half-moon iron rails, so that it could traverse easily to shoot at any part of the island or the cove.

The little squad from Fort Anne marched past the gun and followed the road to a bridge on pilings stretching out from the cove shore. At the island end of the bridge the palisades were interrupted by a guardhouse and a heavy wooden door braced with iron straps and topped with iron spikes. The sentries watched the party cross the bridge, and invisible hands opened the great door. Cascamond observed that the guardhouse, built of large squared timbers, had loopholes facing inside as well as covering the bridge. A redcoat with a sergeant's stripes came out of it accompanied by a stout man in a black top hat and snuff-brown coat and trousers.

"Escort party reporting from Fort Anne," announced the corporal, standing like a ramrod. The shouldered muskets of the escort party had the exact slope of the drill books.

"All right," the sergeant said. "Take 'em over, Turnkey."

"On'y one of 'em's for 'ere—the Crappo in the middle," said the corporal. "Unlock them 'andcuffs, Parkins. The other two's run men from a man-o'-war. You the chief turnkey?"

"That's right," said the man in brown. "I'll sign for the prisoner."

The corporal unfastened the flap of his cartridge pouch and drew out folded papers. " 'Ere y'are, two copies—one for you and one for the clerk at Fort Anne."

The turnkey read from the papers aloud, "Thow-ret, Joseph. Ship, *Necessitewks,* privateer. Home, Rotch-fort, France. Eyes brown. Hair black. Visage dark. Age about twenty-six. Um! Seems all right."

He signed the Fort Anne receipt with a flourish of pencil. The corporal stowed it in his cartridge pouch and bawled "Squad! Right about face! Quee-ick—march!" Away they went.

The turnkey said to Cascamond, "Parley-voo angly?"

"Yes."

"Ah, that makes things simple. Step into the guardhouse with me."

Inside, the turnkey consulted a huge book like a merchant's ledger, one of several on a shelf above the plain wooden desk. As he flipped over the leaves he said, "When did you run, and how?"

"I don't remember the day, monsieur. I was in a work party on the valley road and ran off with two seamen named Houchard and Penthieu. They were caught and returned here weeks ago. Can you put me in the same mess with them?"

"That depends. The messes change, what with men coming in, and men going out on parole to the town, and work parties—you should know that—or weren't you here long enough? We divide the prisoners into messes of six to ten men, and you'll join some mess that happens to be short. Now let's see. Thouret—Thouret— Thouret. Ah! Here we are. 'Work party returned from a week's labor on the Windsor road, reporting three men run, Houchard, Penthieu, Thouret.' Well, Joseph Thouret, that little game of hide-and-seek'll cost you ten days on biscuit and water in the Black Hole, not to mention no more outside work, and no parole —ever. To make a start, peel off those duds you've got on, every stitch, shoes and all. From now on you wear Transport Office rig, and don't ever let us catch you out of it."

"Thouret" stripped himself under the indifferent gaze of the soldiers of the guard, sitting on benches about the room. The turnkey after looking him up and down went into a storehouse at the rear, and came back with coarse blue denim trousers, jacket and shirt, and a pair of shoes with canvas tops and leather soles. The letters POW were marked large in bright red dye on the breast of the shirt, on each thigh of the trousers, and on the back of the jacket. They were even marked on the shoes. As "Thouret" put them on the turnkey said, "We don't supply no underdrawers nor stockings. You want 'em, you buy 'em, see? I got a shop over there by the gate of the prison palisade, with all kinds of extries for sale, everything from flannel to sugar and the odd bottle of van-rooj, not to mention the odd dram of rum. Cheap, too. Ask anyone in there."

"I have no money," said the prisoner.

"That's too bad. Puts you in a fix, cos you'll want extries. Come cold weather you'll want flannel next your hide and wool on your feet. However that don't signify just now, with summer coming on. As I said, being a run man you won't be allowed outside to work, not even in a road party under guard. So you'll have to figger out some way to earn money on the inside. Lots do. Make things to sell to visitors, and so forth. You'll see. Now step along to the bedding store and draw your blanket and hammick."

At last, glad to be rid of those garments salvaged from some corpse in the Bay islands, but feeling in this new garb like a clown at a country fair, the prisoner put his blanket inside the canvas hammock, rolled up the hammock and lashed it with the spun yarn provided, shouldered the bundle, and followed a lesser turnkey through the gate of the prison palisade.

He walked into an animated scene in which the air was rattling with French tongues in every twang from Artois to Gascogne and from Provence to Martinique. Men in hundreds basked in the sun, squatted over cards or dice or dominoes, strolled aimlessly about the beaten earth of the yard, or paused to chat in little groups. Among them a large cluster of Negroes huddled together in the shabby blue-and-white uniforms of French West Indian regiments, captured in Haiti and Martinique and carried off to this British coop in the far north.

Cascamond's first impression of the white prisoners was that more than half were "run men" like himself, for they wore the same blue denims with the same scarlet POW on breast and back and legs. Then he realised that most of these men, long in prison, had worn out their own clothes or uniforms and had to accept the prison issue.

He followed the turnkey up an outside flight of wooden steps to a large door leading into one end of the second story. The door was open to the air from Northwest Arm, and so was a similar door at the other end of the building, and so were all the iron-barred windows. He could almost hear the voice of the dead Mac-Dougal droning to McNab about "ventilation" and "clean as a bone" and "the health of my poor de'ils at Melville Island."

It was built like an enormous cattle barn. A wide central passage ran the length of each floor from end to end, where the doors were. On either side stood wooden stalls, each stall wide enough to sling a hammock, high enough to hold three tiers and extending to the side of the building. He could see three rows of empty hammock hooks along each side of the partitions.

"Where are the men's hammocks?" he asked of the turnkey.

"Out in the yard to air, along o' the blankets. We run this place like a man-o'-war. H.M.S. Malevoolent, that's what your Frenchmen call it in their own lingo, though I'd call it H.M.S. Benevolent, myself. First thing every morning you'll hear the order 'Lash up and stow.' On'y instead o' stowing the hammicks in nettings on deck you take 'em out in the yard to air—except bad weather o' course. That clears the building for moving about in the daytime too. The next order is 'Wash out!' and all hands turn-to with swabs and buckets o' salt water from the cove, washing down the decks—the floors, I mean. You'll get used to it, Frenchie. They all do."

The inference was the usual English tradition that Frenchmen hated fresh air and cleanliness, and all French ships were floating pigsties. However Cascamond said nothing. If he was to preserve his life in the body of "Joseph Thouret" the less attention he drew to himself the better.

It was not compulsory to remain outside on fine days. Men were drifting in and out, and in each of the long stalls others were sitting on wooden chests, benches, stools, or on the floor, working away at ship models, knitting, weaving long strips of shaved wood into what the English called "chip hats"—a score of occupations. And always and everywhere the chatter of French voices,

sometimes raised in song, and here and there the lively tune of a
fiddle and the sound of dancing feet.

The turnkey halted at a stall on what he called the starboard
side of the gangway, where several Frenchmen were sitting at
work. "Scarron!" he called. A dark fellow with bright black eyes
arose from a bench and came to him.

"Scarron," said the turnkey. "This man—your mess—savvy?"

The man examined Cascamond with the air of one who suspects
the other of everything from laziness to leprosy. Cascamond spoke
up in French. "My friend, I am appointed to your mess. I am
Joseph Thouret, formerly seaman of a Bordeaux *corsaire*. I ran
away from Halifax some time ago and, as you see, I'm pinched
again."

"You ran from here—*Malveillant?*"

It was amusing, this twist of Melville Island on the French
tongues of the prisoners. *Malevolent*. Probably a good name for
it. But Scarron's question was not a bit amusing. It brought up
a problem that Cascamond had considered all the way from Fort
Anne. Taking the name of the vanished Thouret was only catching at a straw in the evil flood of circumstance. It would at least
delay for a time his recognition as the runaway murderer Cascamond.

Now that he was at Melville Island there were two immediate
dangers. One was former shipmates or prison messmates of the
real Joseph Thouret who might encounter the sham one and know
the difference. They might not be so accommodating as Houchard
and Penthieu, and they would have a natural temptation to curry
favor with the guards by denouncing him.

The other was the crew of *La Furieuse*. Presumably the sur-
vivors were here among these hundreds of prisoners. It might be
difficult to recognise the trim lieutenant of *La Furieuse* in this
unshaven and stubble-headed creature in the harlequin costume
of the Transport Office, but there was always the possibility, and
a blurted *"Hola,* Monsieur Cascamond, what are you doing
here?"* would put the hangrope around his neck.

For the moment one thing was certain. He could not conceal
from Scarron his utter ignorance of the prison and its routine,
and it would be foolish to try. So now he repeated the half-truth
he had told Houchard and Penthieu at Fort Anne.

"No, I didn't run from here. I was taken at sea by an English warship bound to Halifax, and there I gave the Englishmen the slip. I got away in a stolen boat along the coast. It's a droll story and someday I'll tell you my adventures. Just now it's enough to say that I was picked up many leagues from here and sold to the redcoats for the bounty money."

"Ah, money! I suppose you have no money in your pocket, M'sieu Corsaire?"

"Not a sou."

"That's bad."

"So the jailer said when he presented me with this elegant costume. But why should that concern you, my friend?"

"We are old hands in this mess, all five of us. And when one joins our mess he is expected to pay his shot."

"For what?"

"For extras from the jailer's shop—fresh English bread, butter, rice, onions, pepper, spice, lemons, a bottle of French wine now and then—things like that. And we buy from peddlers who are permitted to come in here from the town—fruit, sweets, boiled lobsters, pumpkin pies, and what'll-you-have."

"No doubt I can earn money for such things, the same as you."

"On the contrary that's a matter of very much doubt. You took what we call English leave and you've been pinched, so you've lost all privileges. You can't go outside to earn a sou."

"But I'm told I can make things to sell, here, inside."

"Ah, you have a trade? That's different! Here in *Malveillant,* thanks to the Emperor's conscription, we have all trades from goldsmiths to tailors. What is yours?"

Cascamond shrugged. "I am a sailor and that's all. But there must be something I can learn to do or make for money, surely? How do you get money, you others of the mess? And since I've told you my name, tell me yours, if you please."

He looked the man in the eyes with the masterful stare of a boatswain addressing a surly member of the crew. The surly one stared back for some moments in a contest of wills, but the shipboard habit remained in him and at last he turned his eyes downward.

"I am Scarron—Gabriel Scarron. Gunner's mate, and before this damned war a ship carpenter at Brest. The others are Dominique

Hache, sailmaker; Henri Chabray, seaman, wharf porter before the war; Valentin Subiet, seaman, a tailor in peace time; and Georges Laleine, a pastry cook from Toulon, carried off by the conscription to boil salt pork at sea. There were four others in our mess, but they were sickly when they came here from the hulks, and one by one they went to Dead Man's Island. That's the little butte across the cove where we plant the stiffs."

"And how do you earn money, you and the others?"

"All of us go out on work parties when we get our turn. Road-making, woodcutting in the forest for the prison fuel sheds, or for the sawmill up the Arm, things like that. The English pay us at the rate of a shilling and threepence a day, reckoning in the provincial money, which is only worth a shilling in the coin of England. It's droll, but the English here don't seem to have much coin of their own except the gold guineas, which a workman never sees, and the copper tokens of the merchants for small change. Even the soldiers and sailors are usually paid in Spanish silver dollars fetched up here somehow from the West Indies and Mexico. That's what we get, too. They pay us at the rate of five provincial shillings to a dollar.

"Sometimes, when there's a rush job on ships' canvas at Alfax, Hache and other sailmakers here go up to the town on parole and work at their trade. They get good pay for that. Chabray is a clever fellow with his hands; he can do anything from cobbling shoes to knitting stockings for sale. Subiet gets tailor work from officers of the guard and people of the town. Laleine is one of the prison cooks, he gets a shilling a day for that, and for himself he buys extra flour and sugar and prunes and so on from the jailer's shop, and turns out pies and fancy cakes to sell."

"And you, Scarron?"

"I am a maker of ship models. We put them together from meat bones sawn into strips and polished like ivory, and we rig the spars with our own hairs twined into fine ropes. For the cannon we melt down copper coins—we're allowed to use the cook-house fires in summer and the prison stoves in winter."

"A tedious job, all that, *hein?*"

"It passes the time. Especially in winter when there are no outside working parties except to shovel snow and cut wood." Scarron talked with the voluble flow of a man who finds a fresh ear for an old tale. "A really good ship model takes at least three months, but then one gets twenty-five dollars for it. All the Alfax people want a bone ship model for the mantelpiece in the parlor—it's a mania. And of course the prisoners make and sell other things of bone—dominoes, chess pieces, handles for knives and forks, snuff-boxes—you will see the kind of thing. At first we used the bones from our meat rations, but that's a trifle nowadays.

"We do a great trade, I tell you, with visitors from the town. Except for the dockyard, this prison with so many hundreds of Frenchmen at work of all kinds is the biggest industry in Alfax! It's a fact! The chief jailer, Snuff Coat, keeps a shop for the pris-oners, and writes down our orders for things he hasn't got at hand. Once a week he goes up to town with his list and does business with the merchants there. For example, bones. From the butcher shops of Alfax we get ox bones at a dollar a hundred. Then there's the wool for our knitters—our biggest industry of course. Our knitters make all sorts of things from gloves and stockings to Jersey jackets. Last year here at *Malveillant* we used five thousand pounds of wool."

Cascamond felt a guilty red flushing his face behind the beard. He saw in his mind McNab's island and its flocks of sheep, the only large source of wool at Halifax. The turnkey had listened to this outpour of incomprehensible French long enough to guess that the matter of "Thouret's" introduction to the mess had been settled. He now interrupted in blunt English, "Leave your ham-mock and blanket with Scarron. He'll take care of 'em till you come out of the Hole. And come along."

Cascamond followed him along the passage, through the door and down the steps to the ground. The prison was built on a foun-dation of stone masonry, and he now saw a small door there, close to the short flight of steps which gave entry to the first floor. The turnkey chose a key on his big iron ring, opened the door, and said, "In you go!" In the momentary beam of daylight Cascamond saw three or four other inmates of the Black Hole, crouching on straw and blinking. Then the door slammed and the key turned in the lock.

The *cachot* was not entirely black. There had to be some venti-lation, and a small grill in the door admitted a little light with the air. The Black Hole was about the size of the casemate in Fort Anne, and not unlike it.

"What are you in for?" demanded a voice from the straw.

"I slipped away from Halifax several weeks ago, before they had a chance to march me here. And you?"

"I skipped from a work party, and got pinched the next morning. These others are in for missing roll call. If you aren't in the muster to answer your name when it's called, morning and evening, it's ten days in the *cachot,* just as if you'd run away."

Little more was said. The inmates of this cavern under the prison seemed to pass most of the time in sleep or in a state of inertia, like animals hibernating under a winter's snow. The one break in the monotony came each morning, when a turnkey unlocked the door and a prisoner from above, on light punishment duty, made a quaint exchange, delivering two sea biscuits and a pannikin of water to each inmate, and taking away their loathsome wooden bucket to be emptied in one of the latrines by the palisade. From day to day, as the various sentences expired, one or two of the inmates went forth into the light. Others came in, singly or in twos and threes. At one time there were ten men in the *cachot.*

For Cascamond, not gifted with the ability to turn his mind blank and lie as senseless as a log, the ten days were ten years; but there was an advantage in all this. When he faced the full daily gaze of the other prisoners abovestairs he would have ten more days' growth of beard and hair. Since the shaving of his scalp and jaws at Fort Anne there had been time for a thick black stubble to cover them, but he wanted more. Most of the prisoners he saw had clean jaws or the light stubble of men who shave once a week, with their hair loosely cropped as well. Some others had moustaches. A few had beards, and these usually had long hair as well, a mark of eccentrics perhaps, or more likely slovens and half-wits.

For himself there was only one course in this matter of appearance, the natural disguise of long hair and a nest of beard. For he had but one aim. Escape! It was ironical that so long as he could avoid detection by his fellow Frenchmen, this was the safest place to hide. The English authorities, searching up and down the coast for the slayer of Captain MacDougal, would never think of looking for him inside the palisades of Melville Island. But detection

by the prisoners themselves was much too possible, and however
friendly their intentions the word was bound to get out and reach
the guards.

At last the day came for his release to light and air. The morning call of "Lash up and stow!" had been given, and the prisoners
had scurried into the yard and placed their hammocks and blankets
along the inside of the palisade. Just as Cascamond stepped out
of the Black Hole the turnkeys were calling "Muster! Muster!"
echoed by shouts of *"Appel! Appel!"* by French boatswains wield-
ing their old authority for the sake of good order.

In the hubbub as the men trotted into place someone called
"Thouret!" The name at first did not penetrate Cascamond's mind.
Then he turned and saw Scarron beckoning. "Fall in here, quickly!"
Scarron snapped. Cascamond ran, and a rank of men opened and
made a place for him.

"Tiens!" Scarron said. "You look like a black bear. If I hadn't
known you were due out of the *cachot* this morning I wouldn't
have recognised you. Now here comes Snuff Coat with his men to
call the roll. I should say Monsieur Robinson. Be sure to call him
that if he should address you at any time in the presence of the
redcoats. On these occasions he's not the same man as the one
sells you tobacco and onions in his shop."

Cascamond beheld the familiar figure of the chief jailer in his
brown coat and trousers and black top hat. With him came half a
dozen other turnkeys in civilian clothes, and a squad of redcoats
tramping at their heels with muskets shouldered and bayonets
fixed.

Under the direction of their boatswains the prisoners had
formed themselves into companies of about a hundred men drawn
in four lines. Seeing them outside the prison like this, thought
Cascamond, was like seeing the crew of a three-decker swarming
on the quay. You wondered how the deuce the ship contained
them all. Although bare from the constant tramping of feet, the
ground about the prison was rough, with stones jutting out in many
places, and the uneven lines of men would have made a martinet
weep.

Robinson and the soldiers placed themselves along the rear of
the prisoners, watching sharply for the old game of one man answering two names for the benefit of a laggard or a "run cove."

In front, the other turnkeys bawled the names on the rolls. Their pronunciation of the French names was ludicrous but with the ease of custom the prisoners recognised and answered them. At the cry of "Turret, Joseph!" Cascamond was quick to shout *"Ici!"* like the rest. When this was done the turnkeys passed along the lines making a count of heads, an additional precaution that took much time, while the prisoners whispered merry and impolite remarks among themselves.

At last Robinson called, "All present and correct! Dismiss!" and the boatswains' voices arose in the various companies, *"Rompez! Rompez-vous!"* The masses of men broke and hurried away.

"Breakfast!" said Scarron with satisfaction. "Those you see running to the cookhouse are the duty men from each mess, getting the coffee and biscuits for the rest. Soubiet gets ours today. You'll take your turn in a day or two. Come! We go now to our stall to munch the morning fodder."

The long room was swarming with men taking their places in the stalls, sitting on sea chests, benches, and stools that they had made themselves. In the stall of Scarron's mess every one had a chest except, of course, the newcomer. Scarron introduced him to Hache and Chabray, and they accepted him with the chilly reserve of all Frenchmen who have a little money or privilege in the presence of one who may want some of it.

"We shall find something for him to do," said Scarron in an apologetic voice. "Thouret, after breakfast, you must wash yourself thoroughly at the sea pump in the yard, and your clothes as well. You can wrap yourself in your blanket while they dry. That *cachot* is a lousy place. Then I'll lend you two sous for the barber, so you can see out of that damned black muff."

"I'll wash with pleasure," Cascamond answered. "But you may keep your two sous, my friend, as I shall keep the muff."

They looked their surprise. All three were clean-shaven and well kept. Cascamond noted that none of them wore the hideous Transport Office costume but dressed in good blue serge jackets and trousers, leather shoes, and flannel shirts, the unmistakable evidence of taste and wealth.

"Perhaps," said Chabray slyly, "he raises hairs to rig your models, Scarron."

"Hairs!" Cascamond laughed. "In another month I can skin my whole head."

"What for?"

"The Imperial Guard. I've heard the Army contractors get five gold napoleons for one of those hats."

Laughter. Laughter and something more, an almost audible tinkle of breaking ice. And now came Soubiet with a steaming can of coffee and half a dozen sea biscuits, followed by Laleine, away from his cookhouse duty, breakfast being a simple affair. Scarron introduced the new member of the mess, and again there was the momentary reserve.

"He will clean himself, of course," Scarron explained. "But he is growing fur for military purposes. He is a droll boy, this." He glanced at the square biscuits with contempt. "Put away those damned tiles, Soubiet. The English baked them for the royal backhouse roof three hundred years ago. Let us show our new messmate how a Frenchman lives at *Malveillant* when he knows the ropes."

Soubiet looked round their faces and shrugged. Scarron plainly was the leader of the mess. He tossed Soubiet a key to one of the chests, from which the man produced six mugs, a knife, a loaf of fresh white bread, and an earthenware jar of butter. He filled the mugs, cut off a thick slice of bread, buttered it, and sat on his stool. The knife, the bread, and the butter passed from hand to hand.

"I regret the inconvenience of the single knife," said Scarron. "Gentlemen of the sea like ourselves are used to having our own clasp-knives for bread and meat, but the English took those from us. They are suspicious of all these French savages at *Malveillant*, who might arise some night and cut every throat in Alfax. So we are permitted only one flat knife to a mess. The authorized barbers among us are permitted a razor, but only ten barbers have authority. Even so, we are dangerous with our ten razors and our ten dozen table knives. Therefore they keep here a company of infantry, and the soldiers practise shooting at a target on the side of Dead Man's Island, so we can see how well they do it, and to remind us that forever is a damned long time to be sucking the root of a dandelion. And of course there is the cannon—did you observe the cannon, Thouret? They keep it trained on the backside of the prison. That's why they built this big pine coffin for us to live in, so they can rake the thing from stern to stem in case of mutiny."

"Has anyone ever escaped from here?" asked Cascamond carelessly.

"From the prison, never. From outside working parties, yes—it happens almost every week. From parole jobs in the town, very seldom. Only an imbecile would run away from a soft place on parole in the town. The food, the drink, the money, the *jouissance* of the maid or the lady herself when Meester is out of the house—ah! There are prisoners from here, on weekly or monthly parole to the town, who live like gamecocks—nothing but the best. We others, who cannot play the butler, the coachman, the cook, the valet, we can only envy those lucky bastards and go on making stockings and bone corvettes."

"But did anyone ever *try* to escape from here?"

"Once or twice someone, some madman, got as far as the bridge, and then . . ." Scarron put up an imaginary musket, pulled the trigger, and made a rude noise with his mouth.

"Only a madman would try the bridge," Cascamond observed. "But if a man could get over the fence what's to stop him swimming ashore, at night for example?"

"Sharks," said Hache, a blond man with blue eyes, the eyes of a serious child. "The English keep sharks in the cove, it is well known. They feed them with meat."

"In this latitude? *Baste!* We are not in the West Indies."

"But yes, sharks in this latitude," cried Chabray. "Except in winter. All fish go away from this frozen coast in winter. At other times—well, ask any *banquais* in the prison, there are dozens of old codfishers here, and they'll all tell you the same. On the Banks they have known sharks to swallow a hooked codfish and snap the line in one lunge like a bull. And if there are sharks on the Banks there are sharks on the coast."

"Has anyone seen these sharks in the cove?"

"You can't see much through the palisades," Laleine said. "Sometimes, crossing the bridge on a work party, men have seen a dark shape gliding below, a shape as big as a man."

"A stray porpoise, perhaps. There are many fish as big as a man that couldn't eat a man if they tried."

"*Alors!* Who wants to give them a try?" demanded Soubiet.

"How do you know the guards feed them meat?"

"They have told us—the guards. Also Snuff Coat. What's your interest in all this, Thouret?"

"Fairy tales, I've enjoyed them ever since I was a child."

"Listen, *corsaire*," growled Scarron. "If you're dreaming of a run again, you're childish still. There's only one escape from *Malveillant*—over the water to Ile des Morts as a stiff. Even if the redcoats gave you a pass on a silver plate, where else could you go, in all that wilderness? No, no! You've had one experience and that should be enough."

"Oh well," Laleine said, "this damned war can't go on much longer, because they'll run out of money—the English, the French, and everybody else. After all it's been going on for years and years, and there's only so much money in the world."

"There," Cascamond said, "you have reason."

20

To earn money inside the palisades of what Scarron called "H.M.S. Malevolent" the newest prisoner began to learn the art of making ship models. As a boy he had watched shipwrights busy in the yards of Saint-Malo, and as an *aspirant* he had been taught every detail of a ship, the way it was put together, and why it was done in that way. To turn this knowledge to the making of bone toys he had the aid of Scarron and the use of the tools that Scarron kept in his work chest, a remarkable collection of small chisels, saws, scrapers, files, drills, pincers, hammers, and moulds for the casting of midget cannon.

In spite of Scarron's gibes about the knives and razors, Cascamond found that the prison keepers showed a lot of indulgence to the prisoners in their trades and the necessary tools and supplies. As he saw this blend of vigilance and indulgence at Melville Island he heard again and again the ghostly voice of Captain MacDougal in those bygone conversations with McNab.

In the view of the Agent for Prisoners the chief danger always was a mass uprising at night, when the guards might be surprised and overwhelmed. Hence the inmates were separated on two floors or "decks," with no inside stairs from one deck to the other. Iron grills barred the outside of all windows. The only doors were at the two ends. A short flight of steps led from each end of the lower floor to the prison yard, and nowhere else. For quick evacuation in case of fire the upper floor had twin outdoor stairways at each end, rising from the ground in an inverted V to the door landings.

Every night, after the prisoners were counted in, the turnkeys bolted the doors and hung guard lanterns over the landings, so that if the doors were forced any prisoner coming out would be in the immediate sight and fire of the sentries posted about the yard.

Even if the Frenchmen managed to break out of the prison and its palisades, they could not reach the soldiers' quarters to seize their muskets without passing the other stockade, which divided the island into halves. Nor could they reach the bridge without storming the guardhouse at the gate, with its thick walls and loop-holes. And always there was the cannon on the south shore of the cove, menacing everything on the island, including the bridge and the prison itself.

Finally there was the tall signal mast on the knoll beside the officers' quarters. The prisoners could not see past the woods around the cove except at its mouth, where the east landing of the upper deck gave a glimpse of the harbor arm. Even from that viewpoint they could see no more than the farther shore of the Arm, a forest clambering up to a plateau with small farms and villas peeping here and there among the trees. Yet the Citadel of Halifax was only two miles by crow-flight to the east. Signalers on the roof platform of the officers' quarters at Melville Island read by telescope the daily routine messages of the Citadel and replied with signal hoists on their own mast, using flags by day and lanterns at night. Any uprising of the prisoners could be tele-graphed to the Citadel in minutes, and that would bring troops at the quick march, and armed boat crews from the men-o'-war in the anchorage, pulling around Point Pleasant and up the Arm.

Even if the outward prospects for a mass uprising were much better, Cascamond soon discovered that among the French at Melville Island the mass virtues of Equality and Fraternity had gone the way of Liberty. The whites held aloof from the blacks, who lived in one part of the prison with their own mess arrangements. The whites themselves had their cliques who kept aloof from each other. Naval men looked askance at *corsaires,* just as the British Navy considered a privateersman little better than a pirate; and a French seaman (whether naval, privateer, or merchant) had the seaman's natural contempt of a soldier.

Then there were groups drawn together by the trades they plied in the prison or the ways in which they amused themselves. The aristocrats of this little French world were experienced servants who had found patrons in Halifax and got parole to work there as cooks, valets, butlers, coachmen, gardeners, and handymen to well-to-do officials and merchants. At long intervals these were ordered back to Melville Island for a general muster, and they stayed two or three days, regaling the others with tales of the good life in "Alfax." Next in the scale came men with parole to work on farms in the outskirts of the town, returning to the prison in winter. Then came the daily paroles, who did odd jobs for farmers and villa owners near the Arm and for the sawmillers and fish-salters there.

Then came the men who could get no parole but went forth under guard to labor with pick and shovel on the roads out of the town. Beneath these again were the men who never went outside, because they lacked skill or energy for such work, or preferred indoor pursuits, or because they were recaptured "run men" like Cascamond, who were not allowed outside on any terms. The Negro soldiers from the West Indies had none of the restless ingenuity of the Frenchmen. They existed on prison fare, dreaded the cold winters, and moodily waited for something to happen, they knew not what, which might spirit them back to the West Indies again. Last, at the very bottom, were the unfortunate lunatics, who sat in their stalls or at the slits between the yard palisades, staring at nothing, hour after hour, day after day.

So much for the mass of us, thought Cascamond. What about an individual escape? It would have to be at night for the benefit of darkness; but that meant getting through a bolted door or one of those iron-barred windows, and lowering oneself on a rope to the ground, a pretty problem with armed sentries on every side of the prison yard. Then climbing the palisade and swimming the cove. The sharks? Every day, from the upper stair landing, he noted off-duty turnkeys and soldiers amusing themselves with poles and fishlines on the wharf, which was on the eastern half of the island, the garrison's half. They seemed to catch small fish in the clean tides flowing into the cove from the Arm. Even a meat-fed shark would lunge at fish wriggling on a hook, yet nothing disturbed the anglers. When hot weather made the landlocked cove an oven, in which the little island sat like a loaf for baking, Cascamond on the upper landing could hear faint yells and splashes from the east tip of the island, a spot hidden from the prisoners' quarters by the knoll. It faced on the Arm, and the sounds were those of men diving and sporting in the cool Arm tide. All of which proved that the "sharks" were a fable invented by the turnkeys.

But sharks or no sharks, a man could not swim away from the prison until he had passed the stockade. The palings stood twice the height of a tall man, with all the cross beams and braces nailed on the outside, so that nothing within offered an easy hold for fingers and toes. An agile sailor might scramble up and over their sharp tips, but in the silence of night he would make noise enough to waken the stiffs on Dead Man's Island, let alone the live sentries in the yard. So—no climbing. One must get *through* the damned palisade. After all, it had openings.

The prison main gate for one; but that was too well guarded. The chief turnkey's shop had a large slot through the stockade for the sale of his goods, but every night that was closed with a heavy shutter and bolted. In any case the shop was beside the main gate and the sentries there.

The prisoners' cookhouse stood in a corner of the yard with a gate through the stockade for the passage of supplies and fuel. Whenever it was his turn to draw the rations of Mess 127, or to join a fatigue party carrying firewood and food through the gate, Cascamond examined this prospect carefully. The cookhouse had a row of stoves, each with an oven and a big ship's copper for the stew of vegetables and meat or fish which was the chief meal every day. A sentry was always posted there to watch the coming and going of cooks and messmen. When the stockade gate was opened for fuel or supplies the fatigue party worked under the eyes of a group of soldiers and turnkeys, who locked the gate as soon as the work was done. Not much chance there.

What about the *poulaines?* Old MacDougal had overlooked nothing in his concern for the health of the prisoners. The prison yard had three large latrines, all of which extended through the stockade, so that the excrement of a thousand men could fall into the tidal waters of the cove. But it fell through measured holes in those cement floors, holes no larger than the bore of a twelve-pounder. Scarron always referred to his morning trip to the *poulaine* as "firing the sunrise gun."

Well, there must be some way out, and it seemed more and more that the way must be through the garrison half of the island. One advantage of living on the second floor of the prison was that you could see over the stockade on all sides. On the garrison side the officers' quarters and telegraph mast stood on top of the little hill. At the hill's foot by the cove was the hospital, a small red wooden building with a fuel shed behind it, a wharf in front, and sentry-boxes at front and back.

The wharf was a short jetty in the cove entrance opposite Dead Man's Island, and the garrison kept a boat there. Food and other stores came to this wharf every week in a big black ketch which Cascamond had seen from McNab's island many a time on its way to or from York Redoubt, the Point Pleasant batteries, or Melville Island. Smaller matters, such as the mail, usually came by horse and gig along the road around the Arm tip, and so did the wagons that supplied Mr. Robinson's busy shop.

The little cookhouse of the garrison stood on the island shore near the wharf. Then a dwelling for the artillerymen. Then the bridge and its spike-topped gate and guardhouse, always manned by a dozen redcoats day and night. At the foot of the hill where it faced the prison stockade stood wooden buildings of various kinds; the chief turnkey's office, which was also his shop; the living quarters of the turnkeys; the small barrack of the infantry guard; a couple of fuel sheds. Finally what was called "the bell house," where again Cascamond saw the naval touch of MacDougal. A big ship's bell, sounded for musters and alarms, hung under a nicely curved wooden canopy, supported by four pillars, like the belfry of a ship-of-the-line.

Somewhere, somehow, there must be a way off the island from

that side of the stockade. Scarron's grim humor had declared that the only escape from *Malveillant* was to Dead Man's Island. There might be something in it—and not as a corpse. Cascamond asked casually about death among the prisoners.

"It's not so bad as it was in the hulks," Scarron said. "When we were there we seemed to be tipping a stiff off a plank every day, with a cannon ball in a bit of netting at his feet to carry him down. The bottom where the *pontons* lay in Bedford Basin all those years must be stacked with bones and cannon balls. But here on this island one must confess we live better—and longer. Of course among so many prisoners there are always some who sicken of one thing or another, as they would in ships or barracks anywhere. They pass through the stockade to the little hospital by the wharf, and some come back here and the rest go over the water." He jerked a significant thumb.

"Who buries them?"

"Meester Robinson calls for prison volunteers, a party of four. They put the stiff in the boat, with axes and picks and shovels, and a couple of soldiers go along to keep an eye on them. Dead Man's Island is a little butte of stony land covered with trees and bushes. The burial parties don't work any harder than they have to. They chop away a few trees and bushes near the shore, dig a grave just deep enough to stuff the body in, and cover it with stones and earth. Some religious fellow made a wooden cross and stuck it in a pile of stones over there, but they don't attempt to mark the individual graves. You see the mounds and that's all."

The amenities at Melville Island included daily visits by peddlers from the town, drawn by the presence of these hundreds of men, many of whom had money to spend for little luxuries in the way of food. Because no women were admitted to the prison except on Sunday, the regular visiting day, the peddlers were men and youths. Some came by boat, some by road, and they entered the stockade with watchful turnkeys and walked up and down the prison yard, or in wet weather the gangways of the prison itself, crying their wares in rhymes like the market girls of Halifax. "Draw near, draw near, here's good spruce beer!" "Fish ready cooked, and lobsters too, come buy my lobsters, do sir, do!"

"Who'll buy sugar candy, all ready made and handy?" "Here's good apples, they're not high, two for a penny, come who'll buy?"

If few of the Frenchmen understood these rhymes, the wares were plain enough and the peddlers did a bustling trade; and while this was going on the prisoners without money, or not inclined to spend what they had, amused themselves with falsetto imitations of the hucksters.

But Sundays were the great days, especially on fine summer afternoons, when the prison was invaded by townsfolk, male and female, old and young. In the dull round of the colonial port, far from the seat of war, a visit to the French prisoners and their sale of varieties was something the townsfolk would not miss. Fashionable people came in yachts and cutters, sailing around Point Pleasant and up the Northwest Arm. These made a day of it, with picnic meals spread in the shade of the woods about the cove. Others of the quality drove by the road around the Arm in smart horse-and-carriage turnouts. Ordinary townsfolk came in gigs and wagons or walked the three miles from Halifax, a pleasant enough stroll through the farms and woods.

On these days the prisoners were early astir, impatient for the morning rattle of door-bolts, the shouts of the turnkeys—"All out, all out, lash up and stow!" "Muster! Muster!" "All hands wash out!" The barbers had been busy and continued their trade all Sunday morning. An endless file of men shuffled to the washing troughs and the sea-water pump in the yard. Many a prisoner kept a good suit of clothes and a clean shirt stowed away in his chest for these occasions, with a Frenchman's natural desire to look well in the eyes of pretty ladies and a tradesman's instinct to draw the best customers to his wares.

To Cascamond at first the market in the prison was an amazing spectacle. He knew that many of the men made things for sale but to see all their products assembled was another matter. On Sundays the broad passage that ran the full length of each "deck" became a sort of Oriental bazaar, with tradesmen sitting or squatting in the entrance to the hammock stalls and their wares spread out before them in the gangway.

There were toys of all kinds, made from wood and bone, including painted wooden dolls with jointed arms and legs, dressed in fine needlework; chests and sewing boxes with ingenious sliding trays; every kind of knitted goods from caps to brightly clocked stockings and embroidered garters; every sort of needlework from silk embroidery to fine lace. The gold- and silversmiths offered rings and lockets and brooches made from melted-down coins; the workers in bone had their sets of chessmen and dominoes, their inlaid backgammon tables and pieces, their snuff boxes, their exquisite frigates and corvettes rigged with human hair; the picturemakers had prettily painted scenes about the cove, framed in natural birchwood with the bark on; the weavers had carpets and tapestries decorated with ships or flowers in contrasting colors; the hatters had all kinds of headgear from ladies' silk bonnets to summer chip hats woven from dyed strips of wood; the shoemakers had a specialty of list slippers embroidered with flower designs. All of these tradesmen took orders for particular things. The shoemakers would cobble shoes while the customer waited, or make shoes between one Sunday and the next. The gold- and silversmiths would repair any kind of jewelry. The tailors made suits and gowns to order.

Some prisoners had wheels-of-fortune which they kept spinning and clacking through the day. Visitors paid sixpence a whirl, and got prizes that ranged from a bone toothpick and case to a small wooden bust, carved and painted, of "King Chortch," "Admiral Nel-*son*," and "Napoleon," all of whom looked very much alike. One man had a puppet show, where Punchinello and his little troupe capered and chattered in squeaky French for the delight of the children.

Cascamond had looked over the tailors carefully for the merry fellow who came to the hospital and measured him for a uniform —that handsome uniform which was now reposing, he supposed, in his chest on McNab's island. But of course his stay in the hospital would soon be two years past, and the smiling little man from Le Havre was not to be seen. Perhaps he was one of the aristocrats who worked on long parole in Halifax and returned to Melville Island only for occasional musters. Or was he under one of those mounds on the shore of Dead Man's Island? In any case he was not a regular prisoner who would recognise "Thouret" for Lieutenant Cascamond.

Visitors first inspected the goods and services along the passage of the "lower deck," and then went out and climbed the tall stairways to the "upper deck." The air was full of eager sales talk in broken English, and bargaining by townsfolk with a mixture of English and bad French, with much waving of hands, counting on fingers, shrugs, exclamations of despair or pleasure, and a great rolling of eyes. Cascamond made himself useful to Mess 127 as an interpreter, almost his only value to them. As a maker of bone ships he was still very slow, although the long hair brushing his shoulders now supplied the rigging for Scarron's work.

His nickname of *Le Corsaire,* first applied by Scarron ("God knows you look it with that ferocious black mop and beard") was soon adopted by the men of adjoining stalls and messes. Nobody spoke of him as "Thouret" except the turnkeys with their muster roll. When eventually he met Houchard and Penthieu in the daily multitude of the prison yard they passed him without recognition. After many wary days he had seen none of the crew of *La Furieuse* until one afternoon, making the circle of the palisades like a caged bear, he came upon the lunatics squatting in their usual way, staring through the slits between the palisades at the hot glitter of the cove. One of them was *Mousse,* with his blond hair now as long as a woman's and hanging down his back.

Cascamond resolved to put his disguise to the test. He squatted beside the cabin-boy, stared at the water for a full five minutes, and then said, "What was your ship, eh?"

Without shifting his gaze *Mousse* said, *"La Furieuse."*

"That was a bad affair, one hears."

"Yes, it was terrible."

"Your shipmates of *La Furieuse*—are they among these prisoners here?"

"No, the English took them away. To a prison across the sea."

"When?"

A silence while *Mousse* turned the matter in his mind. "It was after the first winter."

"But you were left here?"

"Because I am an imbecile, yes."

"No others?"

"Only some who became sick, very sick. They are over there now." *Mousse* waved a hand vaguely towards Dead Man's Island.

"What is your name?"

"I am called *Mousse,* m'sieu."

"I have a feeling that I have seen you before, *Mousse*. Do you remember me?"

Mousse turned his faded blue eyes and regarded Cascamond for a long minute.

"No, m'sieu, never. You see, I was in a *frégate en flute* on a voyage from the West Indies, and all my shipmates are dead or gone away. Do you wish to make love to me? I have friends here in the prison who stroke my hair and say I am more pretty than a woman and give me sweets and things."

"No," Cascamond said. Among hundreds of men starved of women for years there were bound to be lovers of silly youths with long fair hair. In the prisons they were known as *raffolés*. Like other groups and castes among the prisoners the *raffolés* lived in particular stalls, and there were certain mess numbers that had a ribald significance.

Each day at sunset the prisoners heard the clanging of the great brass bell, the "Muster! Muster!" of the turnkeys, the echoing *"Appel! Appel!"* of the French boatswains. They fell into their familiar companies, answered the roll, and were counted head by head. Then, picking up their hammocks and blankets, they filed into the prison and sat in their stalls while the duty-men brought the evening meal from the cookhouse. Like breakfast it was a frugal one of coffee and sea biscuit, which the energetic and fortunate were able to fatten with white bread, butter, cheese, sausage, smoked herring or salmon, and the pastries of Laleine.

At dusk the turnkeys came in and hung a lantern over the big wooden tub placed in each gangway to serve as *pissoir* for the night. No other lights were allowed. As they closed the doors the turnkeys called out a cheerful "Bonswar messoos!" and the bolts shot home. For their own safety the prisoners kept a rule of no smoking after the doors were fastened for the night. Otherwise, as Scarron said, "we'd all be burned some night like fleas in an old *paillasse*." They climbed into their hammocks and lay talking for an hour or more, and the yawning space above the stalls to the roof was filled with a general babble, giving way slowly to a few drowsy mutterings and then snores.

To Cascamond the sluggish pace of prison life made sleep elu-

sive. There was nothing to tire the body or mind, and he was used
to a daily activity in both. He could only envy the majority, who
passed the days with their trivial hobbies and their evenings in
gambling at keno, Napoleon, Boston, tric-trac, or dice, and then
turned into their hammocks and slipped away to dreamland until
morning and the first cry of *"Dehors! A la porte!"*

He lay awake for hours thinking of Lutine, going over every
moment of those stolen meetings, every word they had said, every
laugh, every touch and caress. Then his mind turned to MacDougal, whose chance discovery had ruined the little idyll and sent
him flying for his life. Again and again he wondered anxiously if
Lutine had been able to save her secret, and what sort of life she
lived now. With her sensitive heart she must have sorrowed for
poor MacDougal as well as for the lover who was gone, and perhaps now she blamed herself for MacDougal's death. The most
painful part of it all was that she lay at McNab's house, undoubtedly thinking of these same things and wondering what had happened to Cascamond, while he was barely more than five miles
off, unable to communicate with her, indeed not daring to try.

Amid these reflections he heard the sighs and snores and dreamy
mutters of the sleeping prisoners, the creak of hammock hooks
as they turned from one side to another, the occasional padding of
naked feet to the piss-tubs in the lantern light. Through the open
window sashes and past the iron grills came the faint lap of the
tide, the hoots of owls in the high woods looming above the south
shore of the cove, and in the prison yard the hourly cry of "All's
well!" going the rounds from one sentry post to another.

One day at muster the little march of turnkeys and redcoats
through the stockade gate was led not only by Mr. Robinson but a
tall old man walking at his side.

"Who is this with Snuff Coat?" asked Cascamond from the side
of his mouth.

"The Agent for Prisoners, Meester Moffit," Scarron said.

"What became of the other you spoke of, Macdoo-*gal?*"

"I don't know. A few months ago Macdoo-*gal* ceased coming
here. After a week or two this old Englishman took his place.
He is not so fussy as Macdoo-*gal* but on the whole he is not so

good. Macdoo-*gal* was strict, like the captain of a ship-of-the-line, but he was also interested in the prisoners and their welfare. This Moffit does not care a damn for us. We are just a lot of names on the muster rolls. He never puts his nose in the cookhouse, for example, to see that we are getting decent meat and vegetables. He never examines bedding, never looks at the latrines, never demands to know if the night-tubs have been rinsed after they're emptied in the latrines. Macdoo-*gal* used to pass along the lines of prisoners looking every man in the face, watching for sick ones, yes, and for dirty ones. Many a time I've seen him point out a man to one of our boatswains and say 'Scrub that man at the sea pump in the yard, or he'll get your whole company lousy.' He spoke very bad French but you knew exactly what he meant, and you did it. Nowadays we have the same privileges that Macdoo-*gal* allowed, but this fellow's only concern is to see that we don't escape."

A few days after that Cascamond heard the cry "*Fossoyeurs! Fossoyeurs!*" passing about the prison yard. Nobody liked the chore of gravedigging, and usually the four volunteers came from the dead man's mess. Making his way quickly through the lounging throng Cascamond reached the gate where Snuff Coat stood expectantly, and was accepted as a volunteer at once. With three others he was led to the hospital, where two armed soldiers awaited them.

The hospital was a single-story building with about a dozen cots, all in demand, for the dead man had been laid on the floor and a live one placed in his cot. As the four prisoners carried the corpse to the boat Cascamond's eyes were busy. The jetty was in front of the hospital, a modest thing of log cribwork filled with stones and decked with plank. It had a sentry box and on one corner at the water's edge a small latrine not unlike the sentry box. The boat was a four-oared thing with a forward thwart pierced for a mast. The mast and sail were probably stowed away in one of the sheds, and taken out only when officers off-duty wanted to amuse themselves on the long reach of the Arm.

After all his time among the English he was at last beginning to measure distances as they did, in feet and yards and miles. Until one could do that one missed a lot of information in what they said. As the prisoners rowed across the cove he estimated the distance to Dead Man's Island at about two hundred yards. When

they stepped ashore and looked for a place to dig the grave he
noted that it was not an island at all but merely a small hill jutting
into the cove mouth. Old sea marks showed that on flood tides,
probably with southeasterly gales, the water almost encircled it;
but any day of the year a man could slip away dry-footed from
this "island" into the woods of the main shore.

The knoll was a rugged little wilderness of trees and rocks, and
the graves were all on the rim just above the tide, where the digging had been easiest. The dead man was a consumptive, wasted
almost to the bones. The hospital attendants had not bothered to
tie his jaw shut and weight the eyelids until rigor had set in, and
as the prisoners put him into the grave his cold eyes stared up at
them and his open mouth seemed to protest against the whole
affair. Cascamond cut some brushwood and laid it over that accusing face before they shoveled in the gravel and stones.

The two redcoats leaned on their muskets and watched with
bored faces. The lone wooden cross that Scarron had mentioned
was tottering in its little cairn, probably because the heaving
frosts and thaws had shifted some of the stones. Cascamond went
over and straightened it, a natural gesture, and the soldiers
showed no concern when he stepped away from the party to do
it. He thought, in thirty steps I could run around the bend of the
shore and into the woods. But in any of those thirty steps the redcoats could slap a pair of bullets through that fat red POW in
the middle of my back, and there would be just another grave to
dig. No, the way of escape has got to be the jetty and the boat. One
must feign illness and get to the hospital, and work out the rest
from there. And how does one feign an illness under the eye of a
surgeon? That must be worked out first!

Apart from the various trades and services in which the prisoners engaged, the devotees of cards and dominoes and dice, and
the peculiar diversion of the *raffolés,* Cascamond found certain
groups like *Les Pantomimes,* who made their own costumes and
practised their silent postures and dances so well that they sometimes got parole to appear in the Halifax theatre. But the group
whose hobby interested him most were known facetiously in the
prison as the Journalists. These were men who sought by every

means to learn what was going on outside the prison, in Halifax and the world.

Most of their information came through the paroles in Halifax, and there was a regular system of communication by word of mouth and by written notes that extended even to the officers far away in the woods of Preston. French servants in the homes of officials and merchants of the town picked up much gossip, and it would have surprised their employers to realise that not only movements of ships and regiments and the details of garrison forts and posts, but much spicier matters in Halifax households were well known to a circle of Frenchmen in the grim prison up the Arm.

There was no ban on English newspapers in the prison, indeed the chief turnkey supplied old copies of London papers for a penny, and occasionally an American newspaper as well. These were read and interpreted by the ones who had a knowledge of English, always watchful for lies about, for example, the exploits of General Wellington. Occasionally an old *Moniteur* turned up, usually concealed in a loaf of bread from the town. Thus they learned that the Emperor's new wife, the Austrian, had given birth to a son—something that the poor Josephine couldn't do. They learned that Napoleon had carried off the Pope and held him a prisoner, another proof of the Emperor's power. They learned that England was bankrupt, living on paper money, with her trade in ruins everywhere. And they learned that war between England and the United States was certain.

Cascamond read the papers himself, and for the sake of argument he would challenge matters accepted by the other Journalists as pure truth.

"If England has nothing but paper money, how does she get the Portuguese and Spaniards to fight for her? How does she stir up trouble among the Prussians and Austrians? Bah! Those people would do nothing without gold and silver, paid in the hand. Would you, yourselves? If there were no conscription and no Emperor, would you go out tomorrow to fight anybody—anybody in the world —without a fat sum of money paid in the hand? You know damned well you wouldn't!

"All this stuff about England's trade. Do you realise that Europe is only part of the world and England trades with all the rest —including the parts that used to be French? Do you understand that France hasn't a single colony left in the world? That the English have them all?"

He tossed these remarks amongst them like bombs and enjoyed the explosion of their replies. One of them cried, imitating him exactly, "Do you realise that the Americans are the only hope for us Frenchmen cooped up like fowls at *Malveillant?* Do you realise that when the Americans enter the war they will come up here and take Alfax and set us all free?"

His reply was rude. "Ah! Have you ever heard of an American fleet? And do you realise how far they would have to march? *Que diable!* If you'd been taught even a sou's worth of history you'd know that the Americans would have lost their own revolution years ago against the English if it had not been for French money, French supplies, the French Army and the French Fleet. I've talked with old Frenchmen who fought there and I know. The battle which ended that affair was fought at a place called Yorktown. Who cut off the English there from all supplies and reinforcements? The French Fleet. Who did most of the fighting on the shore? The French Army. The truth is that the Americans can do nothing to help France in this war against England—England and Spain and Prussia and Austria and Portugal—nearly the whole of Europe. They're all fighting France or awaiting a chance to stab her in the back. And that's where the war will be won or lost. Over there. Nothing on this side of the ocean can change it whatever the Americans do. Put that in your snuff box for a damned good sneeze!"

This kind of thing was always good for an uproar among the Journalists, and then came the yells from neighboring stalls, "Ah, cork it up—cork it up!" and in the storm of epithets he slipped away. Other than these visits to the Journalists, which gave him the latest news and provided some mischief to break the monotony of the day, he had little to do with the prisoners outside of Mess 127. Under Scarron's eye he worked diligently on his model of a frigate, a task that required infinite patience. The beef bones had to be sawn into strips, polished, shaped, and then fitted together with tiny bone pegs. The masts and yards and the little gun carriages were especially tedious work, and so was the twisting of hair into ropes for the rigging. Scarron himself made the cannon, smelting halfpennies in one of the cookhouse stoves with the aid of Laleine and the sanction of the guard on duty there.

At the end of three months, with the summer gone and the cool airs of September blowing down the Arm, he finished the model. It was not as good as Scarron's work but not bad, not bad at all. He could hardly wait for Sunday to come. When it did he was in his place early, squatting on the floor of the stall, with that precious object in the gangway. All through the morning and the afternoon visitors came by, paused to look at the little ship and its hairy vendor, and passed on. When the evening came it remained unsold. He felt crushed. He needed the money so badly, to pay off his debt to the mess, and to obtain warm clothing for winter.

At evening roll call in the yard Scarron said to him, "You asked too much, *corsaire*. Twenty-five dollars! That's what I get myself, for better work. And don't forget there are other makers of ship models selling cheaper. You shouldn't have asked more than fifteen. And here's something else. You may speak English well but you look like a baboon with all that hair. Take a look at yourself in the glass, and see what disgusts your customers."

On his return to the stall Cascamond saw in the little mirror on the partition that Scarron was right. All that bushy black growth made him look a very wild man, if not a baboon. And it was needless now. Except for *Mousse,* who would not know him anyway, whiskered or shaven, nobody in the guard or among the prisoners had ever seen Lieutenant Cascamond. It would be a pleasure to get rid of that savage pelt, to wash his face and head and feel really clean. He decided to get rid of it gradually. He had established himself thoroughly in the identity of the *corsaire,* and too sudden a change might arouse some curiosity. Over several weeks he had a barber trim his beard shorter and shorter, and clip the mop of hair until it was easily kept neat with a few sweeps of a comb. Finally he had the beard shaved away, leaving a magnificent dragoon moustache. The change did not pass without comment, but all of it was humorous, and one of the Journalists probably put it best. "Well, Satan, so now you wear the horns on your lip!"

The following Sunday, as if to prove the advantage of a neat head in the marketplace, a plump woman whose dress proclaimed her the wife of some comfortable merchant paused at Cascamond's stall, asked to examine the little ship, listened to his eager description of the details in perfect English, and paid twenty dollars without any attempt to haggle. Cascamond felt like jumping up and kissing her hands. He could not have been more pleased if he had built an actual ship and sold it for a fortune. With his mess debt paid he had enough money left to buy red flannel from Mr. Robinson's shop, to pay a tailor to make it into two sets of shirts and drawers, and to buy an English pea jacket of thick blue cloth.

He set to work on another model at once; and then, realising that it would take another three months, he exclaimed to Scarron, "Winter! You cannot have a market here in the winter, eh? People won't come all that way through the snow!"

"Nor sail their pretty boats through the ice," added Scarron, with a dour grin. "This cove, and the whole of the Arm out there, freeze over as hard as that." He stamped his foot on the floor. "But have no fear. We get our supplies, and people come to our market, too. After all there's the road, and horses can pull sleighs as well as carriages."

"But after big snowstorms?" Cascamond thought of that winter in the Preston woods, with the road to Dartmouth impassable for months.

"After big snowstorms Snuff Coat turns us out in hundreds, with wooden shovels made for the work, to open the road to town. A guard of soldiers comes along, but there's no need. Who would wish to run away into a wilderness of ice and snow? Ah, I tell you, when winter comes, and the stoves are set up in the gangways, our *Malveillant* is a good snug place to be."

"And you are able to sell things all through the winter?" Cascamond was still incredulous.

"Oh, not so well as in summer, of course. But things are changing. In the summer of last year a rich merchant built a mansion over there." Scarron flipped a hand towards the farther side of the Arm. "It had been a small farm in the woods with a view of the water. Now it is a mansion and a great estate called Joo-bee-lee. What does that mean?"

"I don't know."

"No matter. This merchant turned the farm road into a fine carriage drive through the woods from the town. In Alfax not only the rich but all the fat *bourgeoisie* have fine horses and carriages to drive about the town and to Point Pleasant and along the Basin road. In winter it is fine sleighs painted in all colors of the rainbow, with bells jingling on the harness, and furs to keep the ladies warm. So now it is the fashion on a fine winter day to form a sleigh party and drive out to this mansion Joo-bee-lee. Sometimes as many as forty sleighs—on a frosty day we can hear the *tintin* of the bells. The mansion is only a little way from the shore of the Arm, and last year Captain Macdoo-*gal* set parties of prisoners to work over there, extending the road down to the waterside. So now if our redcoat officers want to go to town they don't have to go around the Arm. They cross over the water in the boat you have seen, and grooms with horses wait for them at the foot of the Joo-bee-lee road. *Voila!*

"Now regard! Those rich Alfax officials and *bourgeoisie* and their families—especially the young ladies and gentlemen—have a new mania. It is not only to form sleighing parties for a drive to Joo-bee-lee. There they dismount and walk down to the shore. They put on skates and glide over the ice to our prison and buy souvenirs from the Frenchmen. Yes! A few young ladies and gentlemen did it one Sunday last winter for a novelty, and soon after that everybody was doing it. It became the great adventure of the week. They even send word beforehand, so that our cooks like Laleine can order special things through Meester Robinson and serve refreshments to them, sitting on benches and stools, as if the prison gangway was a restaurant. Yes!

"So, you see, we are able to trade with *ces fous anglais* on the coldest days of winter as in the warmest days of summer. It's only in the spring and late autumn, the time of the rains and the mud, that our trade falls off. You will see!"

21

Soon came the melancholy autumn skies, the wet gales swooping from the sea, and their massacre of the hardwood leaves; and Michel Cascamond faced his third winter in North America. He still had to find a way of escape, and in this latitude there could

be no hope of escape until another spring, when a man might
survive for weeks under the open sky. As before he must get a
sailboat to make his way westward; but this time he would not
risk those mad tides in the Bay of Fundy for the sake of finding
vague French settlements. This time he would sail on to Cape Cod,
the nearest land of the Americans, regardless of distance, hardship
or anything else. If a man's will was strong enough he could go
anywhere and do anything.

Despite his quips to the Journalists he was convinced of a coming war between England and the United States, recalling the
grave talk in McNab's house about the bygone *Chesapeake* affair,
and later tales of English naval arrogance and increasing American
touchiness. Here in the prison he read carefully the small American
newspapers and broadsheets which came to the hands of the Journalists, all filled with bitter complaints and threats against England,
the unmistakable voices of a people working themselves up to the
pitch of war. The Journalists said firmly that the Americans would
enter the war on the side of the French next year, when the snow
was gone and the backwoods roads to Canada were dry enough
for marching.

What the outcome of that might be he could not guess. According to the Journalists the American armies would overrun Canada
in a summer. But to Cascamond the sailor, Canada was a country
far away inland. Only warships could affect matters here on the
Atlantic coast, and in the course of their long war with France the
English had built the greatest fleet in the world. Trafalgar had
proved that. They were well practised in their blockade of the
coast of Europe, keeping a hard sea-watch on every port from
Copenhagen to Naples, in every sort of weather, summer and
winter, and they could do the same with the chief ports of the
United States. Already without war at all, their squadrons from
Halifax and Bermuda had cruised American waters doing as they
pleased for years.

So he must escape from Nova Scotia no later than the end of
April. That would give time to make his long boat voyage before
the English fleet could fill the American sea horizon with their
sails. Time to find a place for himself somewhere about Cape Cod.
Time to write Lutine that he was free, and where. After that he
could trust in that strange and wonderful intuition of hers, and the

will as strong as his own which would conquer all difficulties, and her courage that would dare anything to be at his side.

For the present he could only count frozen days and months in the person of Joseph Thouret, *corsaire,* fed, warmed, and sheltered by the bitter enemies of Lieutenant Michel Cascamond. The winter routine began at the end of October, when big barrack stoves were set up in the gangways and every prisoner was issued an extra blanket. The prisoners appointed their own daily and nightly watches to feed wood into the greedy stoves, to scrape out ashes, and to raise an alarm in case of danger from the fires. Daily fatigue parties carried fuel from the sheds on the garrison side of the stockade and piled it in the prison gangways. After every snowfall large *corvées* were ordered to clear the muster ground, the paths to the gate, the cookhouse, and the latrines. Beyond the stockade other *corvées* marched out to clear the bridge, the cannon emplacement, and the road, accompanied by a glitter of bayonets.

Washing now was not the easy matter of summer. In this bitter air men could not splash themselves nor rinse clothing at the troughs in the yard, using salt water pumped up from the cove. Indeed the yard pump froze like the water of the cove itself. There was no good well on the island. Shafts had been dug in the past, only to seep full of brackish or bitter salt water. All the fresh water for the garrison and prisoners came from a well on the mainland, fed by a spring under the wooded south ridge of the cove, and pumped through a canvas hose across the bridge. The pump had a small house and stove, tended day and night, to keep it free in the most bitter temperatures. With such a large human company this fresh water supply had to be rationed for cooking and all other purposes, as in a ship at sea.

Whenever snowstorms whistled about the prison and boomed in its iron-grilled chimneys the prisoners' morning tasks of carrying out bedding to air had to be abandoned, and so was the outdoor muster, the swabbing of "decks," the ventilation by wide-flung windows and doors. As the winter dragged on, a reek of unwashed bodies filled the prison like the smoke of their stubby black clay pipes. On visitors' days, and for inspections by the Agent for Prisoners, the doors and windows were thrown open for an hour to get rid of the stench, and that was all.

Few visitors came in November and December, when the road dissolved in mud and then turned to deep holes and ruts moulded by frost for the winter, and the Arm had a skin of ice too thin to cross and too thick to pass a boat. By the turn of the new year 1812 the snows had leveled the road to a smooth way for sleighs, actually a much better road than in summer, and the ice on the Arm and the cove had grown thick enough to bear a regiment.

Corvées working to clear the muster ground around the prison shoveled the snow back to the stockade—there was no other place to put it—and as the winter winds drifted more snow to these sloping heaps there were places where a man could step over the palisades with ease. On a black January night, when the trees in the forest were cracking with frost and every sentry huddled inside his box against what the Frenchmen called "the cold of the wolf," it was possible not only to pass the palisades but to walk across the frozen cove into the woods. However as MacDougal had pointed out to Cascamond long ago, the climate and geography were the best wardens in the world. In those stark forests, so easy to reach now, death would come slower than a sentry's musket shot but just as surely and much more terribly.

With easy travel by horse and sleigh the peddlers and visitors from Halifax flocked to the prison. Visiting was no longer confined to Sundays. Every fine afternoon brought sleighs jingling in procession down the road to Jubilee, and parties of skaters flitted across the ice, the ladies with flying scarves and skirts, and with hands tucked into fur muffs. At the guardhouse they slipped off their skates, and when the turnkeys led them into the prison they entered with sparkling eyes and rosy faces like children out for a lark. Cascamond remembered Lutine skating on the lagoon before McNab's house, and then stealing up the inlet into the wood and entering his cottage with just that look. Did she ever go skating now by the light of the stars?

But to business! He had finally shaved off the ferocious moustache and put his whole face on view; and with his clean looks and straight blue gaze, and his shopman's talk in easy English, he had no trouble in selling a ship model for twenty-five dollars. This in turn got him a decent suit of broadcloth, a pair of thick leather shoes, a cap of raccoon fur, woolen mittens and stockings, and still left some money in hand. When he paid his messmate Soubiet for making the clothes the tailor said with his slow smile, "You are getting rich, my friend. Soon you will be able to join the Misers." Cascamond grinned. *Les Avares* were a distinct group who earned money at all sorts of trades but never spent a sou, and for fear of theft carried their savings sewn into canvas belts next to the skin of their lean bellies. Cascamond thought of his swim for life in the tide-race of Fundy. If he'd had his guineas fastened about his waist then, the fish would have eaten him long ago. The moral was never to let yourself get attached to money.

Les Avares always said they were saving for "after the war," a notion that drew the scorn of easy livers like Mess 127. Scarron declared, "They'll never live to see their precious *àpres la guerre*. Look at those bastards, pale and meagre like tallow candles three for a sou. How much better to put your money inside your belly, where it's not only safe but gives you nourishment. Someday I'll get back to Brest. I won't have a sou but I'll be alive—I'll even have a little fat on my ribs."

"And what then?" asked Chabray, with a wink at the others.

"I'll take my *femme* to bed and prove to her that I'm back, and as good a man as ever. Then I'll stroll down to the shipyard and get my old job back, carpentering real vessels instead of these damned toys. And that will be enough. With my *femme* and my job I wouldn't change places with the Emperor himself. But these *avares*, they'll never get nearer home than Dead Man's Island. And if any of them drop off the hooks before the winter's end they'll be some time getting even that far—they'll be stacked in that old fuel shed behind the hospital, waiting for the ground to thaw."

"This hospital," Cascamond said. "Tell me, do the English keep a regular surgeon there?"

"No, just a surgeon's mate. The butcher's boy. If there are serious matters like putrid fever they telegraph to the Citadel, and on the next fine day a surgeon comes out from Alfax by carriage or sleigh."

"And these surgeons—are they capable?"

"Prisoners who recover say they're capable, of course; but nobody hears what the dead might have to say. One thing I can tell you. The surgeon's mate in residence, the butcher's boy, doesn't know a damned thing more than blue pills and liniment and draw-

ing blood from the vein. If none of those cure your illness he may
send for a surgeon, but your pipe may drop while he's making up
his mind—*crac!* Then you get the little voyage over the water and
your name crossed off the muster book. What's all this interest in
the hospital, *corsaire?*"

"I am interested in everything on the other side of the fence."

"Take your mind off the fence, or you'll wind up with the imbeciles, staring through the cracks."

"The Journalists say the Americans will have us out of this hole
by next summer at the latest, Scarron. What do you think of that?"

"*Zut!* Those fatuous whisperers believe anything they read except an English newspaper, and credit everything they hear from
the *poulaines.* You know what you hear from a *poulaine.* But let
us keep this conversation decent. Long ago I was told by men who
thought they knew—officers of navigation, you understand—that
this place where we are, this *Nouvelle-Ecosse,* was about halfway
between the Equator and the North Pole. But an experience of
seven winters here informs me that it's at the top of the world.
The North Pole is just over there in Alfax, it's the telegraph mast
on Citadel Hill. Yes! And do you think the Americans would struggle to reach that just to rescue a few hundred miserable Frenchmen? Listen! For the Devil knows what reason the Americans wish
to have Canada, a wilderness of forest and savages and a handful
of fur traders back there in the heart of this continent. But this
Nouvelle-Ecosse is not Canada by a damned long shot. It's a little
nothing that juts into the North Atlantic, a male teat on the continent, of no more interest than a male teat anywhere."

"Except the port of Halifax," Cascamond suggested. "England's
one and only naval arsenal on the North American continent. The
place from which English warships reach down the coast of the
United States. Is that of no importance to the Americans?"

"*Peste!* I've been here long enough, listening to the *paroles,* to
know how well this Alfax is fortified and garrisoned. The English
have made it their Gibraltar of America. The Americans couldn't
take it, by land or sea, even if they wanted to. So that notion of
our Journalists is just a whiff from you-know-what. We have no
more chance of rescue or escape than a bear chained to the Pole.
Let us recognise the truth and live out this damned war where we

are, with whatever comforts we can find. All else is folly which can only break the heart—or . . ."

Scarron twirled a forefinger at his temple significantly.

With the hard grip of winter on the landscape the guards and turnkeys could relax their vigilance, and when it came to making up fatigue parties to clear the Jubilee road to town they called the names of "run men" like Cascamond who in summer were never allowed outside the stockade. A small squad of soldiers muffled in scarves and greatcoats was considered enough escort for a hundred or two hundred Frenchmen plying wooden snow shovels. Many of the *corvée* grumbled at such hard work for fifteen pennies a day, but more were glad to get the money, and active fellows like Cascamond rejoiced in a chance of exercise in the frosty air.

Snow always drifted deeply in the pine and hemlock woods between the lone mansion called Jubilee and the town, and it was there that the prisoners did most of their winter road work. On Cascamond's return from the first of these expeditions, Hache asked, "How does it go, this snow *corvée?*"

"Not bad. Not bad at all. Do you know, I always had a horror of the forest in this country. I felt like a man drowning in a dry sea. But now, no. Do you know why? After you pass Jubilee, the rich man's house which looks upon the Arm, you can't see a thing but trees and bushes until you come to the pastures outside the town, at a place the English call Camp Hill. That is where the guards shout the *volte-face* and back we go. In those woods one can't see the prison—one can't even see the Arm. What a pleasure! And the smell of pines is so much better than the stink in here—our dainty French perfume, as Scarron calls it. All that, and fifteen pennies a day. Magnificent!"

In the bright cold of January came another kind of work, the cutting of trees for next year's fuel, which had to be done now while the snow was just right for sledding the logs down to the cove. The Agent for Prisoners hired oxen, sleds and drivers from the farms at Dutch Village, but all the manual labor was done by gangs of prisoners. This, too, Cascamond enjoyed, whether swinging an axe in the woods on the ridge, or rolling the logs with hand spikes on to the sleds, or sawing, splitting and piling the wood by the cove shore, where it could dry hard in the next summer's sun.

With the sun still far to the south, the ridge cast a shadow over the cove and the prison except in the middle of the day. It was like emerging from a cavern as the *corvée* climbed past the stumps of past years' cutting and stood at last in the morning sunshine on the top. The sun had no warmth at this wintry angle, but its bright reflection from the snow changed the pallid faces of the prisoners to red and then a healthy brown, a phenomenon that Cascamond had first discovered in the winter at Preston.

One afternoon, as the *corvée* marched downward into the shadow at the end of a day's work, they saw on the ice of the cove a smart red sleigh piled with furs and drawn by a pair of ponies.

"*Hola!*" someone said. "Here's the Agent and someone else on an inspection. They've driven right across the Arm."

"Those gentlemen don't walk a pace if they can help it," said another.

A soldier had come out of the guardhouse to take the ponies' heads, and Mr. Moffit was helping his passenger down, a man evidently old or lame, and muffled in a thick greatcoat and wool cap. They walked slowly to the mainland end of the bridge and halted there, looking up the slope at the long straggle of prisoners, with the bayonets of half a dozen redcoats bringing up the rear. A French boatswain called out, laughing, "Well, lads, we're to be inspected! Let us do it properly. Close up! Close up the ranks! Shoulder arms!" Nearly two hundred grinning prisoners arranged themselves in a rough column with axes, saws, and hand spikes on their shoulders, tramping down the beaten sled track towards the bridge. When someone demanded, "Where's the music? Give us a march!" someone else began to whistle the exact notes of a flute, and in a moment everyone was singing *Partant pour la Syrie*.

As it chanced Cascamond was in the rear of the column, singing like the rest. He noticed Mr. Moffit solemnly touching his hat in salute at intervals as the prisoners marched past. Cascamond gave no attention to the other man, who no doubt was some visiting official from the Transport Office. The island guards had thrown open the bridge gate. The head of the column passed inside and the frosty bridge was sounding the *boom-boom-boom* of marching

feet as Cascamond drew abreast of the inspecting officers. He
looked at Mr. Moffit. When he flicked a casual glance at the other
man he felt his eyes bulge and his body and blood suddenly cold.
A ghost stood there. What was more, a ghost looking him straight
in the eyes. Desperately he turned his own gaze forward to the
bobbing heads on the bridge and the song died in his throat. His
legs trembled under him.

A voice cried "Halt!" and there was doubt no more. The voice,
the face, the burly figure, the very walking stick with the round
gunmetal knob, all belonged to Old Square-Foot MacDougal, a
living and substantial MacDougal with his familiar rum-blossomed
nose and florid cheeks.

At the word "Halt!" everybody stopped, and there was a busy
turning and peering of heads to see what it was about. MacDougal
beckoned to Cascamond with a wool-mittened hand and said in
English, "Fall out, you!" Mr. Moffit looked astonished but he
snapped to the column, "All right, get along! Marshay! Marshay!
Allay voos ong!"

The last feet boomed across the bridge, the solid wooden gate
creaked shut, and in the clear winter air Cascamond could hear
the guards counting heads and tools, and the sound of axes, saws
and hand spikes being stowed away in the shed.

"Your name, prisoner?" Rory MacDougal said.

Cascamond shrugged and looked at Mr. Moffit.

"*Je ne comprends pas.*"

"*Nom!*" said Moffit. "*Nom, compree?*"

"*Ah, oui, monsieur. Joseph Thouret.*"

"Humph!" said Rory. "Let's go inside and look him up in the
muster book."

In the guardhouse the chief turnkey said at once, "Joseph
Thouret, that's right. Mess 127." He turned up the name in the
muster book and MacDougal and Moffit read the entry together.

"Moffit," Rory said, "I'd like to question this prisoner privately.
It's a little notion of mine."

"Very well, Captain. I'd suggest the chief turnkey's office—eh,
Robinson?"

"Very good, sir."

As he walked the few paces to Robinson's office Cascamond
noticed that MacDougal's limp was much worse than he remem-

bered it. The lame right foot now almost dragged on the beaten snow, and the big right hand on the stick seemed to have lost much of its grip. Also there was something odd about the way he spoke, as if the right side of his mouth had gone a little lame as well.

The chief turnkey's shop was closed for the day and the heavy shutter in the palisade was bolted into place. Robinson and Moffit went on into the prison yard to conduct the evening muster, leaving MacDougal and Cascamond alone amid shelves full of goods for sale to the prisoners. They faced each other across the stove.

"Well, Cascamond, I always felt we'd meet again some day, but never here. I must say you picked a verra canny hiding place."

The Frenchman shrugged. He was bewildered by the resurrection of Old Square-Foot, whom he had left as dead as a clubbed sheep. He had a horrible feeling that he himself had gone insane, that nothing in this encounter was real, that it was all a hallucination of the mind.

"Say something," Rory said with that strange new mouth. "And don't come the *Je-ne-comprends* wi' me. Ye may be Joseph Thouret to these people here, but I can get any of a dozen men and women tae identify ye as Lieutenant Michel Cascamond, late of the frigate *La Furieuse,* who not only broke his parole but broke the Agent's head as weel. And ran off like the sneaking coward he was, leaving a gel tae face the music."

"That is not true!" snapped Cascamond.

"Then what's the truth? Let's have it—all of it."

"When you fell and struck your head, I thought you were dead. So did Lut . . . so did Miss Dewar. I begged her, for her own sake, to go back to the McNab house and say nothing. I knew that your body would be found there by the path to my hut, and I knew that I would be accused. I had no wish to dangle on the hangman's beach, so I stole a fishing boat and made off to the west."

"The muster book says 'Joseph Thouret' was retaken at Fort Anne. That's nowhere tae the west o' McNab's island."

"I was captured by some wreckers near Cape Sable, and through them I was sold at Fort Anne for the bounty money. At Fort Anne I took the name of one Thouret, a prisoner who had run from Melville Island and drowned in the Annapolis River. So I was brought here as Joseph Thouret and I've been here ever since."

They were regarding each other eye to eye, and in MacDougal's eye the Frenchman saw no mercy or charity, nothing but blue ice.

"So ye thought ye'd killed me! And weel ye might! It must ha' been a great shock, there at the bridge, when ye saw the dead man risen!"

"I was afraid I'd gone mad. But now I am relieved."

"Because there can be no murder charge against ye?"

Cascamond nodded. "And because I never had any wish to harm you."

"Ye didna wish me harm, so ye seduced the gel betrothed to me, eh, is that it? Your master Boney would be proud o' ye. It's just the way he says and does himself. Take what ye want, but dinna fight if ye can get it by tricks and lies."

A hard-breathing silence, in which MacDougal kept grinding his stick ferrule on the floor as if he had the Frenchman underfoot. Then he said, "Does Miss Dewar know ye're here?"

"No."

"Ye've made no attempt to communicate wi' her?"

"None."

"Why not? After all, she risked a great deal for ye."

"I am aware of that, sir. You must remember that until a few minutes ago I thought you were dead, and I could do nothing that might connect Miss Dewar with your death or with the man who ran away."

"Verra noble, verra noble indeed! And now see if ye can point your helm a little closer to the truth. To a man like you the world is full o' women made for taking; and a woman taken's a woman done with, like a bottle spent. That's the way ye really feel aboot Miss Dewar, is it not?"

The words were angry but somewhere behind them Cascamond detected a plea. He thought, I know what you want me to say, Old Square-Foot, and it would be easy to say it. Instead he said quietly, "You are quite wrong, sir. I respect Miss Dewar and I love her very much. There's no other woman in the world for me. And because of that I've been very anxious about her all this time. Tell me a little, for the love of God. Is she well?"

"She's weel enough, and nae thanks tae you."

"Have you told the McNabs about Miss Dewar and me?"

A spasm worked in Rory's cheek. "What d'ye take me for—a tattling schoolboy? It may be a surprise to ye but I love and re-

spect Miss Dewar verra much myself, and I'd do naething tae
harm her. For that reason, and for that alone, ye're safe for the
present, my bonnie scoundrel. If it werena for Miss Ellie and the
implications to be drawn by the McNabs I'd tell a story o' that
brawl in the wood. I'd have ye hanged as high as Haman for a
murderous assault upon the Agent for Prisoners."

"And who would be lying then?" said Cascamond steadily.

"Ah! Ye feel bold now, seeing how things are! Well, mark this.
Hanging's what ye desairve. Not for what ye did tae me. For what
ye did tae her. And it's only fair to tell ye here and now that I'll
see ye hanged if ever I can find a charge tae put the rope about
your neck. This war's got a long run yet, and if I know your kind
ye'll make a break to get oot o' prison sooner or later, and ye'll
slit the throat o' anyone that gets in your way. I can bide the time,
Cascamond. I can bide it weel. My moment's in the cards. I felt
that right along, and now that ye've turned up here I know it."

He stumped to the door, threw it open, and beckoned to one of
the sentries at the stockade gate. As Cascamond stepped past him
MacDougal called out in that strange side-mouthed utterance,
which made everything he said peculiarly sinister, "One thing
more! So far as Miss Ellie knows, Michel Cascamond is dead. And
that's the way it's tae remain. Make any attempt to get word tae
her and it'll be the worse for ye. From now on ye'll be watched.
I'll have a parteecular interest in everything Joseph Thouret says
and does." And to the soldier, "Take him inside at once and see
he's counted in the muster."

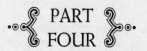

PART FOUR

LUTINE

22

When she saw Cascamond's figure vanishing into the dusk of the wood, Ellen Dewar ran back along the path to the scene of the quarrel. Despite his command she would not flit away to the Mc-Nab house and keep mum, leaving poor Rory's body to the chances of the night and the next day or whenever it might be found. She had seen too often what weasels, wildcats, hawks, and ravens did to a perished sheep. He was lying in the same rigid attitude, with the stick gripped hard in his fist. She hesitated a moment and then scurried away through the gathering darkness to the house.

Supper was ready, the servants waiting in the dining room and the family in the drawing room, when the girl burst in upon them. "Quick!" she cried. "Something awful's happened to Rory!" She turned and ran out again, with the laird, the boys, and a string of manservants and tacksmen trotting along the path at her heels.

"Where is he?" panted McNab. "And what happened?"

"He's fallen in the wood by the path to the hut, with his head against a stone."

It was almost dark when they came to the body. McNab knelt down for a time and arose. "Ay, he must ha' tripped head-on tae the rock. He's bled a lot, and the body's no' cold yet, but there's neither breath nor heartbeat. Pick him up, men, and take him tae the hut, it's only a few steps." And to Ellen, kindly, "Go back tae the hoose, lassie. There's naething ye can do here."

The men found the hut dark and empty, with the door wide open. A few wood-coals still glowed in the grate, and with one of these somebody lit the lamp. They laid the body on the floor and stood about it, shaking their heads and murmuring. In the pool of light from the lamp Rory's face was a horrid sight with its twisted mouth and blind white eyeballs. McNab took the lamp for a look into the bedroom and came back. "Where's Cascamond, I wonder? Yon fire's not out, and the bed's tousled. Maybe he doesna make his bed up every morn. Nae doot he's off on one o' his rambles and o'ertaken by the dark."

An exclamation from Struachan the piper, stooping and putting a finger to the floor by that matted head. "The corp is yet on the bleed, sir!" He held up a red fingertip to the light. McNab fetched the lamp to the floor, and they all bent over and stared.

"It's only a mickle," Struachan said. "I suppose a corp may bleed a bit after daith?"

"Mebbe," the laird said. He opened MacDougal's clothes and pressed a hand over his heart, at the same time putting his ear to Rory's mouth. Minutes passed. He arose, frowning. "I daresay it's my imagination, but whiles I think I feel a faint beat o' the heart, and whiles I think I hear a ghost of a breath at his lips. Try it yourselves."

They tried, and each arose shaking his head and saying much the same.

"There's one thing sure," Struachan observed. "He seems no colder noo than when we came on him first."

"Tach!" McNab cried. "There could be life in him yet. Gahagan!"

"Ay, sor!"

"Take four men and be off tae toon at once in the sloop—the breeze is in the east. I want ye tae get Dr. Haddox. He lives by himself in a stone cottage at the harbor shore, a couple o' hundred yards outside the dockyard gate. It's the only stone hoose on the dockyard road—ye canna mistake it. Ye're tae get him here drunk or sober, or dozy wi' opium or whatever. I don't care how ye do't, either, short o' knocking him on the head. We'll need his brains. He's better qualified for this kind o' thing than any other doctor in Halifax. Be off wi' ye, and don't come back wi'out the man."

In the drawing room Ellen found Jo and Aunt McNab with anxious faces. Supper was forgotten. "He's dead," she said in a

faint voice. Aunt McNab said, "He came here in the afternoon,
looking for you, and we said you'd gone for a walk towards the
Thrum Cap. He set off that way—said he'd saunter along and
maybe meet you coming back. Where's the body?"

"They've carried it to Cascamond's hut."

With that Ellen threw herself on a sofa, shuddering and sobbing,
with tears dripping into the cushion. Jo came and sat by her, stroking her hair, as if to comfort a frightened child. At a sign from Aunt
Frances McNab the womenservants had put away the food and
vanished. She sat now in her habit of an evening, gazing into the
fire.

After midnight McNab came in, saying, "Take that puir gel to
her bed, women, and try tae sleep yourselves. This'll be a long
night and I fear a dowie morn." They obeyed and vanished. The
laird went to the cabinet and poured himself a glass of whiskey.
He was still in his town clothes, and he prowled up and down,
peering at intervals towards the cove.

Just before the case-clock chimed the hour of two he heard a
faint yammer of voices from the wharf, and hurried forth with a
lantern. On the path from the cove he met a strange little group,
the center of which was Dr. Haddox, borne along between two
stalwart Highlandmen. The doctor was in nightshirt and slippers,
with a red velvet dressing gown thrown about him and a red flannel
nightcap drooping on his head like a wilted fool's-cap. In the
lantern light his eyes stared unblinking, the eyes of an owl surprised at night, and his deep protestations boomed in the dark.

"McNab? What's this mean? Here I am trepanned out of my
bed by this party of Scotch ruffians, and carried off in the middle
of the night because 'the laird says he wants ye.' Who in hell d'you
think you are? The Devil himself? And what's all this about?
Think well of your answer, McNab. I'll have you into court for
this, be sure of it."

"Doctor," said the laird earnestly, "I'd no choice in a terrible
emergency. A guid old friend o' mine, and one ye know well, Rory
MacDougal, lies dead or as near it as a man may be, a little way
from here. Ye're the only man in Halifax that's well acquent wi'
wounds aboot the head, and that's what Rory's got. Come this way
if ye please."

They tramped past the house and stumbled in the dark wake of

McNab's lantern to the hut in the wood. The servants on watch there had closed the door against the cold of the April night, and filled the grate of the Franklin stove with blazing wood.

"Here's the mon's tools an' potions," said one of the Highland-men, offering a basket to McNab and jerking his head at the doc-tor. "We gaithered up every damn thing we could find."

"Tools and potions!" Haddox boomed like a gunshot. "If this man's as dead as he looks—if I've been dragged away out here on a fool's errand—I'll use my tools and potions on your own damned heads, if only to let out the sawdust. Bring down that lamp so I can see." He knelt and examined the body carefully.

"How did this happen?"

"As far as we can tell he tripped and struck his head against a stone, back along the path a bit. What d'ye make of him?" McNab demanded.

"Concussion, and possibly a fracture of the skull. But that was secondary. The man actually went down in an apoplectic fit."

"Is there life in him?"

"There may be—there seems to be. Pass me a blanket or some-thing of the sort to slip beneath his head, and another to cover him. Otherwise he's not to be touched in any way, mind that. Gen-tly—gently now! The scalp wound's not important, it's clotted now, though doubtless he bled a lot. MacDougal always had a plethoric look about him, and a bit of bloodletting may have done him good. Well, it's a waiting game. Whatever's going on inside that body will go on or stop, and there's nothing I can do but watch. For that I'll want clothes, McNab—clothes and a bottle of rum."

"I'll see aboot that," the laird said. "But first look among your potions for a drop or two o' laudanum."

"What for?"

"For my ward Miss Dewar, a gel unco delicate in body and mind, and betrothed tae puir MacDougal. 'Twas she found him in this state, a frightful shock tae her. She must ha' sleep, plenty o' sleep, or go melancholy mad; and she'll not get sleep the natural way."

"Ha! Now I'm to deal with a female in hysteria! What the deuce would they say at Surgeons' Hall? But never mind, let's see the basket. Those thoroughgoing Highland thieves of yours tossed in everything from worm powder to opodeldoc plasters, so there must be laudanum—a thing I'm never without. Ah! Now for an empty vial. Bring the light closer. Um. There! Give her this in a glass of wine and she'll sleep like that man on the floor."

Ellen wakened slowly to find Aunt McNab sitting at her bedside dressed for the day, and the room filled with sunlight. The old gentlewoman smiled and put a hand to hers. "How do you feel?"

"Dreadful. What time is it?"

"Nearly noon. No, don't get up. Just lie there till the drug wears off."

"Drug?"

"There were sleeping drops in that wine you sipped. A good thing, too. You'd lain awake hours, trembling from head to foot."

"Rory!"

Aunt McNab hesitated. "There's life in him but you mustn't get your hopes too high, my dear. It seems he suffered a stroke before he fell, or as he fell, and there may be a skull fracture to complicate the matter."

"Then he's suffering! I must go to him!"

She made an attempt to sit up but the firm hand of Miss McNab held her down.

"Rory's not conscious. Anyhow Dr. Haddox wouldn't let you see him. The poor man's still in the cottage in the wood, and mustn't be moved or disturbed in any way." The old lady paused, and then said, "Meanwhile you may prepare yourself for a question from Mr. McNab."

"What question, Auntie?"

"How you happened to find Rory where he was, on the path to Cascamond's hut."

Ellen closed her eyes. "What is the importance of that?"

"Because the Frenchman has vanished. Peter has men looking all over the island for him; and I heard him say it was strange that Cascamond should have left the hut about the time that Rory, and then you, came along the path."

Ellen looked into the calm blue gaze of the old lady. She had no secrets there, she saw at once. "I can't say anything," she said.

"Of course not!" said the mild voice. "So I think you'd best keep your bed and your counsel a few days and let matters take care of themselves. If Rory lives, he can answer questions. The same with Cascamond, if they should find him. Meantime keep mum, Ellie. A still tongue never hurt a woman yet."

On the next day Joanna came into the bedroom with some news. "The fishermen have missed a boat at the Thrum Cap since the evening Cascamond disappeared. And the man is certainly not on the island now—Peter's men and dogs have searched everywhere. So we can put things together. Cascamond's permission here was soon to expire, and he'd have to go back to Preston, a place he hated. He must have planned escape all along—he saved his money so carefully, and young James once peeped in the library and saw him copying one of Peter's charts. So when the time came he broke his parole and went off. I daren't say this in Peter's hearing, but I hope that young man gets away safely to the States. He was always pleasant and polite, and a very good teacher to the boys. We'll miss him."

"Yes," Ellen said, and then quickly, "What about Rory? Tell me the truth, please. Is he alive or not?"

"He's still between life and death, and could go either way. The doctor won't let him be moved, even off the floor. His pulse is very weak and erratic, but he breathes somewhat better, and the doctor managed to get a little spirits of wine down his throat to strengthen him."

"If Rory should recover, how will the stroke affect him, does the doctor say?"

"He said it will affect the right side from head to foot—and poor Rory with a lame right leg to begin with! And he said the paralysis might be partial or complete."

"Would he be able to speak?"

"Peter asked that, and the doctor couldn't say. It remains to be seen. According to Haddox one never knows in these cases until weeks have passed. The man may never utter a word plain again, or he may come to speak quite well, despite a down-drawing on that side of the mouth. And that's enough of that. How are you, yourself? You're still not eating anything, and you can't go on like that or we'll have two invalids on our hands. Let me bring you some Scotch broth at least."

"I have no appetite, Jo."

"Fiddlesticks! You must try."

"Very well."

She swallowed the broth reluctantly and lay back and closed her eyes. It was dreary, lying there thinking, thinking, thinking. She found herself praying devoutly for both Rory and Michel; and in the case of her lover there were visions of him caught by storm in that frail boat, or of him starving, or freezing in these deadly cold April nights, or wandering lost in strange woods. Yet perhaps from the sheer release of prayer she had times of calm, almost of assurance that this frightful tangle would unravel somehow.

On the third day she determined to hide no more from the laird. She arose and washed and dressed, and came down to the breakfast table with a high face and a quick beat of the heart. But McNab was not there. He had risen before daylight and set off for the town in the *Bonnie Jo*. He had urgent business to attend after these days away, and Dr. Haddox had gone along to attend his own neglected patients at the naval hospital. After breakfast Ellen took the path to the hut.

The women of the servants and tenants had arranged a nursing watch among themselves, with a man always at hand in case of need. Ellen found Mrs. Struachan there, and Rory lying on the bed in the inner room.

"I thought he couldn't be moved?" she whispered.

"Och!" said Mrs. Struachan. "I had him moved in there as soon as that rumpot of a doctor was off tae the toon. The idea of lettin' the puir man lie on the floor all this time like a sick dog! It's done nae harm to put him in a decent bed. Come and see."

They tiptoed in, and as she bent over him Ellen noticed that the purple tint had gone from Rory's face, although his mouth still had the twist. His blue eyes gazed up at her, unmoving, but there was something in them for a moment that might have been a glint of recognition. He made no attempt to speak. He was breathing lightly and regularly. Back in the outer room Ellen asked, "What do you think of him, yourself, Mrs. Struachan?" The old woman had a lifetime's experience among folk who seldom or never had a doctor.

"There's strength in sailormen beyond the ordnair and he may pull roond. Just how much he'll be able to say or do after that, I havena the ghost of an idea. D'ye still think o' wedding him?"

"Why do you ask?"

"It's none o' my business I suppose but I might as weel be blunt about it. However weel he recovers he shouldna wed a young wife. A stroke's a stroke. He could have another any time, and the next might be his daith."

Ellen drew her shawl about her suddenly as if the room were cold. "Mrs. Struachan, I want to be doing something. I'd like to take part in looking after Rory."

"Tach! Ye'll no such thing! This is not the task nor the place for a young leddy. He's in guid hands. Be content wi' that."

When the laird returned with Haddox late that evening, Ellen sat at the supper table with the others, quailing a little at every glance from the head of the table but resolved to face an inquisition. It never came. If there was any suspicion in McNab's eyes it was overlaid by the somewhat mystified pity that he had felt for Ellie ever since the affair of the hanged man. The truth was that Aunt McNab had been at work on him with skill, reminding him of Ellie's delicate spirit and the need for letting her alone in this time of shock, lest something worse befall. Such as losing her mind. The laird had been convinced for a long time that there was small margin between fey and daft where poor Ellie was concerned.

As for the missing Cascamond, undoubtedly he was trying what so many paroled Frenchmen had attempted since the war began, an escape to the United States in an open boat. Probably he would perish or give himself up this side of Cape Sable. McNab had warned the Admiral to appoint an acting Agent in MacDougal's place, and handbills had been struck off and sent to every town and village on the southwest coast. McNab fetched one home in his pocket and laid it on the sideboard in the dining room; and Ellen saw it, fortunately at a time when no one was there to see her fingers trembling when she picked it up.

HUE AND CRY

Run from parole, Michel Cascamond, lieutenant of the French Navy, 28 years of age, middle height, person slender but strong built shoulders, black hair, eyes dark blue, visage oval, a few light smallpox marks, deep bullet

scar in right thigh. Believed to have gone to the west-
ward in a stolen boat. Reward One Guinea for his ar-
rest and return.

Tobias Moffit, ACTING AGENT FOR PRISONERS
HALIFAX, N.S. APRIL 30, 1811

When she called at the hut to see Rory the next afternoon she
noticed on a shelf in the outer room Cascamond's toy flagstaff,
with his *tricolore* still lowered in surrender to Lutine, and it was
only with a great effort that she held herself from weeping. Mrs.
Struachan arose with her knitting and cried, "Rory's come roond!
He's not only sensible but he can utter sounds and swallow nourishment. It's a meeracle, like Lazarus up fra the tomb in Testa-
ment! See yourself!"

Ellen walked into the bedroom slowly, forcing every step. She
bent over the bed and saw plain recognition in MacDougal's eyes.
No doubt about it this time. The left side of his mouth moved
and made a sound too indistinct for meaning. She said, "Rory,
you know me?" He made an attempt to blink his eyelids, not altogether successful. The left lid closed well enough but the right
merely fluttered a little, and the result was a grotesque wink.
His mouth moved again, and gave forth sounds like the crowing
and gurgling of a child. From the doorway the watchful Mrs.
Struachan said, "That's enough, Miss Ellie. Ye mustn't let him
tire himself." In the outer room as Ellie withdrew she whispered
to the girl, "He canna talk, but see the rate he's coming on! By another month there'll be a great improvement in the man all
roond."

In a month MacDougal was eating awkwardly but with an appetite very good for an invalid, and by August he could talk with
a slurred tongue, like a man who has taken just enough liquor to
bother his speech but not his mind. Whenever Ellen came to see
him he said "Hello Ellie," and they conversed slowly about news
of the war, of the town, of the island—but never of Cascamond,
or the day of the quarrel. His manner was neither hostile nor
affectionate, a sort of wary friendliness. She was tortured with
her anxieties, first about Cascamond, gone all these weeks, and

next about Rory, and what Rory would say or had said already to the laird about that fateful afternoon.

Her walks about the island were the only relief. For a long time she kept away from the Thrum Cap, but one Sunday she went there and sat, giving herself up to the memory of that first conversation here with Michel, and gazing mournfully into the distance past Cape Sambro where he must have gone in the dark of that terrible night. There was no word of him. Tobias Moffit's hue and cry had fetched no answer whatever from the villages along that shore from Halifax to Cape Sable. Yet if Cascamond survived he must have touched in here and there for food and water and shelter. The laird's own inference, voiced aloud at the table, was that the Frenchman had perished on the very first night, in an unfamiliar boat amongst the Sambro reefs.

By the summer's end MacDougal was well enough that Dr. Haddox permitted his removal to the McNab house. He could even get up for an hour or two each day and walk a little in the garden, leaning heavily on the stick, dragging the right foot, and with one of the women always at his elbow. At last Ellen resolved to put one of her anxieties to the test. She insisted on acting the guardian for one of Rory's walks, and when he sank on the bench in the south rose arbor, where once the McNabs had held a momentous conference on herself, she drew in a great breath like a swimmer about to dive, and then plunged.

"Rory, about Michel—about Cascamond. Have you told Mr. McNab what happened that afternoon in the wood?"

He was leaning forward with his hands folded over the knob of his stick, staring at the ground as if in profound thought or weariness, or both. "Ay, I was wondering when ye'd ask me that. I expected it lang syne. Weel, set your mind at rest on that point, lassie. McNab questioned me aboot how I came tae be on the path to Cascamond's place. I said I'd turned in there tae see the man and remind him of his return to Preston in a few more weeks. But afore I reached the hut I went doon in the fit, I said, and I remember naething more. I must ha' cried out as I fell, I said, and Ellie must ha' heard me from the main path as she came back frae her ramble to the Cap. And so ye found me, and a guid thing too, or I'd be a dead man today."

Tears filled her eyes. "Thank you, Rory. You were always kind
—too kind. I don't deserve it from you."

"Tach! Tach! Let's hear nae more aboot it. What's done is
done, and naething's tae be got frae that." He gave a strange little
chuckle. "Nae more than another dram once the bottle's oot. And
speaking o' drams, the doctor's allowing me a little noo. As medicine, o' course. In a couple more months I may hae it by the pint,
which is the only way I find it does a man much guid. By next
spring, according to Haddox, I can resume my post as Agent for
Prisoners. It looks like sairtain war wi' the Americans within a
twelve-month, and whatever American prisoners come this way
must be housed on Melville Island wi' the French. That'll make a
pretty problem for my rule and pencil tae begin wi', finding room
tae stow 'em, not tae mention the matter o' security. The Admiral wants me at the head o' things, and Moffit can do most o'
the running aboot."

He said all this with his new side-mouthed speech and lopsided
smile.

"I'm so glad, Rory," Ellen said earnestly. "Where could the Admiral find a better man? You've always cared for the prisoners and
treated them like human beings." She paused. "Is there . . . is
there any word of Cascamond?"

"None!"

"What do you think happened to him?"

"Ye canna get him oot o' your mind, can ye, lass? No more can
I, and not for love. Not tae beat aboot the bush, I'd like tae see
the fella hanged. So would any man in my shoes. But I fancy the
sea has taken care of our mutual friend. Otherwise he'd ha' turned
up somewhere on the sou'-west coast, and somebody'd ha' laid
him by the heels for the reward. Being a woman ye'll go on hoping he's got free, I know that. And being myself I can go on hoping
to see him alive and caught. I never did like Cascamond, from the
time I met him in the hospital. A man wi' nae more conscience
than a cadger's dog. But what's that tae a woman dipped in love?
Och! It's time for me tae get back in the hoose for the afternoon
lie-doon, if ye'll gie me a hand."

The Irish priest liked to walk about McNab's pastures talking to
the shepherds. He would say to them, "After all, we're in some-

what the same business, you and I." He was returning from one of the farthest flocks when he came upon Miss Dewar sitting at the wayside, about a mile from the McNab house. She came to her feet at once, with such a set look on her face that he knew she must have come there to speak to him.

"Yes, my dear?"

"May I talk to you in confidence, Father Burke, though I'm not of your faith?"

"Of course. What's troubling you?"

"It's a confession and a request—and you're the only one who can help me."

"I'll do what I can, my dear. What have you to say?"

"It's about the French prisoner Cascamond, Michel Cascamond. We were in love, he and I. And it was I who told him where to find a boat and escape."

"Go on."

"He was hoping to be picked up by an American fishing vessel. Failing that he was going to try to reach one of the Acadian villages on the Fundy shore, where he could shelter amongst French-speaking people. He was to let me know when he was safe, and where I could find him. And it's nearly five months, and not a word of him."

Father Burke reserved his own opinion of Cascamond, which this sad little revelation confirmed. "He may be dead, my child. This coast is very dangerous, and a lone man in an open boat . . ."

"But he's not dead! I'm sure of it!"

"How?"

Ellen looked away. How could she explain the workings of *da-shealladh?* "I . . . just *know,* Father. If he were dead, something would have told me. Unfortunately that's all I know. I'm certain he's somewhere alive, and hasn't been able to get word to me."

"If he's alive, it may be that he daren't write to you, for your sake or his own. Letters get in wrong hands oftentimes. Has that occurred to you?"

"Yes, I've thought of that—I've thought of everything. Father, suppose Michel succeeded in making his way to one of the Acadian settlements. A Frenchman from the old country and obviously a runaway prisoner. Those people are all good Catholics, they'd confide in their priest, and he'd know about it, wouldn't he?"

"Miss Dewar, are you suggesting that I, or any other priest, should assist in a liaison between yourself and this unscrupulous young Frenchman, an infidel, a breaker of parole, and if I may say so, the seducer of a woman betrothed to another man?" His face was severe and so was his voice.

"Oh, please," Ellen cried. "All I want is to assure myself that he's alive. If he doesn't wish to communicate with me, that's the end of it."

"Ah! If I know that young man it *is* the end of it, and it may be just as well to settle the point and get him out of your life. There is only one priest on what's called the French shore, where you say Cascamond was going. He is Abbé Jean Sigogne. Let me tell you something of Jean Sigogne. At the time of the French Revolution he was vicar of Mathelan, in the Diocese of Tours. He was one of the many who refused to sign an oath put forth by the Republic, agreeing to separate themselves from the Church of Rome. Some were jailed, some murdered, the rest had to flee. Jean Sigogne went to England. To earn a living he worked in a wood-turning shop. He learned the English language, and became a teacher of French. About twelve years ago he heard that the Acadian people of western Nova Scotia had no priest, and offered himself. He came out here in a merchant ship, and got a cordial reception from the Governor and from my predecessor here at Halifax, Father Jones. Do you see why I'm telling you all this?"

"Not very well, Father."

"You will in a minute or two. Abbé Sigogne makes his headquarters at Saint Mary's Bay, but he visits all the French settlements on that shore. He is much revered by the Acadian people, and by the Indians. Because of his experiences in the Revolution he has no sympathy whatever for the regime in Paris. This self-styled Emperor Napoleon has no more respect for religion really than Robespierre or Danton or any of the revolutionaries. That is well recognised by all of us. Now, my dear young lady, you have told me something in confidence. I'll tell you something in confidence also.

"During several years past a number of runaway prisoners from

here, single men without wives and families in France, have managed to reach the Acadian villages. Once they arrived and put
themselves in his hands, the Abbé Sigogne helped them to settle
there, to marry Acadian girls, and so forth—but on two conditions.
First, that they make their peace with the Church. Second, that
they make their peace with the British government—in other words
take the oath of allegiance. The Abbé has the confidence of the
Governor at Halifax and perhaps this is a little secret between
them which does no harm to anyone. Poor MacDougal marked
the escaped men off his muster books as Run, and then Dead—
and fully believed it—and the province of Nova Scotia acquired
some new Acadian citizens who wanted only to be free and live at
peace. Now! Do you think for one moment that this infidel
Cascamond, this rabid follower of the Emperor Napoleon, would
submit to anything like that?"

"I don't know," Ellen murmured.

"Well, here's what I'll do. I'll write the Abbé Sigogne asking
him to make discreet enquiry among the villagers and the Indians
for a runaway prisoner who may or may not call himself Michel
Cascamond. I'll give a full description of the man so there can be
no mistake. There will be no mention of yourself, and I shall ask
that Cascamond, if he's there, be kept in ignorance of this enquiry.
And that is all, my dear young lady."

"You are very kind."

"Let us now get along to the house and put our minds on better
things. The boys have been gathering lobsters ever since the tide
went down. There should be a fine chowder for supper."

Father Burke did not come to the island again until a cold rainy
day in November. He supped and spent the evening in the usual
family gathering at the fireside, with music by Aunt McNab and
Ellen, and a visit to MacDougal in his bedroom. Ellen had no
chance of a private talk with the priest until his lean black-robed
figure was on the way down to the boat in the morning.

He said to her quietly, "I have news—and no news. The Abbé
is certain that Cascamond is not in any of the villages on the French
Shore. However, by chance there is word of a sort. A schooner
with some scavengers of wrecks put in to an Acadian harbor

called Pubnico. They were not Acadians but they sometimes went there for fresh water or shelter. In conversation with villagers of Pubnico one of them told of picking up a runaway French prisoner last May, somewhere among the islands. A dark-haired young man who spoke English well and had an old bullet scar in his right thigh."

"What did they do with him?" Ellen said in a shaken voice.

"That's not clear. Apparently the scavengers sell their pickings in various places about the coasts of Nova Scotia, New Brunswick, and Maine. There was just a hint in this fellow's chatter that the Frenchman may have left the schooner at Digby. A few Acadian people live scattered about Annapolis Basin, mostly at the Digby end. The Abbé has sent enquiries there. If I hear further I'll let you know. But don't expect much. My own suspicion is that Cascamond went on with the wreckers to the State of Maine. In other words he's been free in the United States for six months or so, and probably by this time he's found a passage to France."

The one consolation for Ellen Dewar in these empty days and weeks was an occasional visit to the hut in the wood. Since the removal of MacDougal to the McNab house the little cottage stood deserted. The bedding was gone, and the Argand lamp, and indeed everything that had been provided for the comfort of Michel and later Rory. The rooms were cold now, and damp, in spite of the closed door and windows, but to Ellen the spirit of Michel lingered there, as if to watch over the little flagstaff on the shelf and the pine chest in which remained his treasured uniform and hat, his best shoes, and a few odds and ends of clothing left behind in that hurried departure.

She fingered the little flag. She took the blue and white uniform out the chest and held it up before her, as if Michel stood in it, and when she tired of that she sat in one of the cold chairs, rubbing the tarnish from the brass buttons as if she were the Arab in the story of the magic lamp. There was no magic in the buttons, but even to touch what he had touched brought some memory of him. She felt that wherever he was, wherever he went, something of him would remain here always.

On an afternoon in December she left the house for one of these visits. A little snow had fallen in the night, just enough to whiten the ground, and the main track through the wood to the tenant farms was well trampled by human feet as well as the dogs and sheep. When she came to the by-path however, she paused. A lone man's track, dragging the right foot, and accompanied by the dotted line of a walking stick, went in there and returned.

She had a feeling of horror as she followed the tracks to the hut, as if she were living that awful evening all over again. The door stood wide. Inside she found the little flagstaff smashed with a blow of Rory's stick. The lid of the chest had been flung back, and the cherished coat and hat of a lieutenant in the Emperor's sea service had been slashed to rags with a sharp knife. She could fairly see the burly limping figure busy at this destruction, as if the toy and the uniform were Cascamond himself. Or did they symbolize for Rory all the things that had befallen him since the French wars began, the death of his young wife during their long parting, the lame leg and scarred face, the ingratitude of his prisoners in the face of all he had done for them, and finally the Cascamond affair?

She closed the door and came away sick at heart.

Just before Christmas, Father Burke came again. This time he was held three days on the island by a wild gale with snow and then rain. As before it took some contrivance to get a talk with him alone, but at last the chance came.

"Have you news for me, Father?"

The priest looked at her with a solemn smile. "I'm not sure you'll like it, my child. The Abbé's Acadians are an observant people. It is known that a French prisoner of war was brought ashore at Digby by wreckers or smugglers late in May. He was locked in a barn overnight, and the next day taken by boat to Fort Anne. He was not in the boat when it came back. Presumably he had been turned over to the guard at Fort Anne for the guinea reward. But there the information ends. As the Abbé says, there are no Acadian people in the Valley now."

"Does this mean Michel is a prisoner at Fort Anne?"

"It could mean anything or nothing. There's never a summer goes by without French prisoners running away from road gangs and the like, and wandering about the country. One unshaven wanderer would look very much like another. From the description it seems definite that the Frenchman picked up by the smug-

glers was the prisoner Cascamond. It's only a surmise that he was
also the Frenchman taken to Digby and then to Fort Anne. And
from there on we have nothing at all. I still suspect that Cascamond is in the United States or on his way to France. Of one thing
I am very sure, my dear young lady. You'd best forget him. The
man's not worth another thought."

With that he was gone. The conversation had taken place in the
drawing room, apparently empty except for themselves; but after
the priest's departure Ellen heard a stir from a tall wing-chair in
the bay window at the farther end, and she stepped there and found
Aunt Frances McNab with a needle and tambour in her lap, gazing out of the window.

"You heard?" Ellen said.

"Yes, of course. I couldn't help it."

"What do you make of it?"

"Only that Cascamond is in the land of the living somewhere,
probably in the United States, as Father Burke said."

"But mightn't he be at Fort Anne?"

"Heaven knows." Aunt McNab picked up her needle and
worked again at the tambour.

"You really are in love with that man, aren't you?"

"Yes. Father Burke thinks it was a case of seduction on Michel's
part and a momentary folly on mine; but it wasn't like that at
all. We were just passing acquaintances until one day I went to
him in the hut and, well, it happened."

"No seduction?"

"No. Hardly a word was spoken. As if we were both in a
dream."

"And did it seem to you, by any chance, like something dreamed
before?"

"How did you guess?" Ellen cried.

"Once in a long time I walk into a strange room, or meet
strange people, and feel that I've been in that room or seen those
people before. And you—did you feel that you'd seen Cascamond,
or someone very like him, some other time?"

"Yes, he was like the young man I saw on the gibbet, the one
they flogged from ship to ship one day when Jo and I . . ."

"I know, Joanna told me. And so you had a longing to give

your love to this young man, to make up for his sufferings, to save him perhaps from some evil that hung over him?"

"It wasn't quite like that, Auntie. I mean I didn't reason it out like that. If I thought anything it was just that Michel had suffered and was lonely, and I was timid and lonely, and if I'd just be brave a little the loneliness would go away for both of us. Does that sound daft? I suppose it does."

Miss McNab was working away at her embroidery. The needle and the silver thimble flashed back and forth. "I think it sounds quite sensible, my dear. I wish I'd been 'brave a little' at your age. I might have found the world a happier place. But that's enough of that—I hear Jo and the boys returning from the wharf."

23

"Mind those steps, they're a glare of ice," McNab said, handing the ladies ashore at the Market Wharf. "James, gie your arm tae Auntie, and Peter, yours tae Ellie."

All the way up the harbor in the shallop the ladies had sat huddled under a small canvas tilt, the only shelter from a wind that blew wisps of vapor along the water like the wisps of a pot just getting to the boil. The harbor slopes were under a deep white quilt, and here in town the successive snows of the winter had been shoveled into banks at the street sides, now as high as the tops of the shop windows, with passages burrowed through to the doors. Fringes of icicles hung along eaves and gutters, with long fangs like walrus teeth at the corners. Underfoot the hard-trodden snow of Water Street creaked at every step, and people and horses abroad on this bright winter morning breathed forth steam like dragons.

Gahagan held the boat against the landing steps while the boatmen tossed up the portmanteaus and bandboxes of the passengers. "Run for the shop, where it's warm!" called McNab. "I'll hae something doon frae the livery stable in a few minutes." As Miss McNab and Ellen Dewar fled away in a quick swirl of skirts and cloaks he turned to Gahagan.

"Women! Ye never know what notion they'll take intae their heads in a moment and demand it must be done the next. Miss Ellie wouldna come to town at-all at-all the past several years—ye couldna drag her off the island. Nae more would Auntie come away except in summer noo and then. But here 'tis the cauldest part o' winter, wi' the *Bonnie Jo* hauled up till spring and myself content tae bide at home, and all on a sudden they're hotching tae visit the Rosses in toon, and plan tae stay a twelvemonth by the look o' the baggage."

And to young Peter, "Off wi' ye tae Riley's stable, and be sure ye get a closed sleigh and a sober driver—those liverymen are aye nipping at the rum this weather. And you, James, keep an eye on the baggage till the sleigh comes. The boatmen will take the shallop along tae the mooring place."

He set off in the wake of the ladies to the premises of Peter McNab & Sons. In the big store, cheated of daylight by the banks of snow and lit by a few frugal candles, McCrea the factor regarded this astonishing visitation of females from McNab's island. They did not have long to wait. A closed sleigh arrived in a cloud of vapor and a jangle of bells, with the luggage fastened to the back. The driver jumped down to hand the ladies inside, where a small brazier of glowing charcoal gave a token of warmth. The two horses stamped and fumed until a crack of the whip sent them off at a great rate towards Argyle Street.

Ellen turned to Miss McNab at once. "Now we're really alone, Auntie, tell me for heaven's sake what it's all about? You were so urgent about seeing a poor gentleman, and you put off all my questions with that look in your eyes . . ."

"Ah! I'm a sly one, Ellie, am I not? The Poor Gentleman is just the title of a play. The officers of the garrison are acting it at the theatre this week. There's to be a musical farce besides, and some French prisoners from Melville Island are to perform a pantomime between the acts. All in all it should be fine entertainment, and maybe we'll have a chance to congratulate the players afterwards."

"And is that all?" Ellen cried.

"Of course not! Maybe my notion's a false one and we're on a goose chase, but it seems to me I have a dash of *da-shealladh* myself. It came to me the other evening, drowsing by the fire the way

I do when the hour's getting on. Some chatter of one of Peter's officer friends last year, about Fort Anne, where he'd been posted some time back. He'd found it pleasant enough in the mild weather, what with hunting and fishing and all, but a terrible bore in the winter. 'Why,' said he, 'we were worse off than the dodgers we picked up—deserters from the Halifax regiments and warships, and runaway Frenchmen, and jailbirds. *They* were sent back to Halifax, begad, while we poor devils had to stay the long winter in that tumbledown coop of a fort!' It was just like those lightheaded young officers of course. Three dull days in a row— worse than death."

"But what has that to do with us?"

"Where's your mind, girl? Don't you remember what Father Sigogne's people told? A runaway French prisoner answering Cascamond's description was picked up near Cape Sable and taken to Digby. Then a Frenchman of no description was taken by boat from Digby to Fort Anne. Mightn't he have been the particular poor gentleman you'd like to see?"

"Then he'd be here now!" Ellen's face was radiant for a moment. Then it fell.

"But they'd poke him back into the woods at Preston!"

"No, they wouldn't. When an officer breaks his parole he forfeits his privilege of rank. I've heard Rory say it many times. So if the man's retaken he goes to Melville Island like a common sailor."

"And you think that's where Michel is?"

"It's worth a look, don't you think?"

Ellen considered, as the sleigh turned past St. Paul's into Argyle Street. "If Michel's there, then Rory must be aware of it. He's lately taken over his duties as Agent again. And I've told you how Rory hates Michel. He'd kill him if he could."

"Pshaw! I doubt if Rory moves about much these winter days. Even before he had that stroke he spent most of the cold weather in his lodgings. Nowadays I venture he lets Moffit do the weekly prison inspections, and Moffit wouldn't know Cascamond from a thousand others."

At the mansion on Argyle Street they were welcomed by Mrs. Ross, delighted with company in mid-winter when except for the sleighing and skating parties of the young most of the townsfolk stayed close to their fires. Mrs. Ross confessed herself quite satisfied to be house-bound in the frosty months, and she and her busy merchant husband were no admirers of "those silly plays the military young gentlemen put on." Consequently Miss McNab and Miss Dewar had the Ross sleigh to themselves on the way to the Theatre Royal the next evening.

There was nothing grand about the theatre except its title. It was a former warehouse, heated by army stoves and furnished with hard wooden seats like low-backed pews. A railed enclosure before the stage made a "pit" for the orchestra. The stage was lighted by Argand lamps suspended overhead, and by a row of small footlamps burning whale oil, with tin reflectors screening them from the audience and throwing their full light at the players. A painted landscape of Prince Edward's lodge and grounds at Bedford Basin covered the curtain, the painting done with skill by a military artist long before and now much cracked and patched.

A procession of sleighs decanted their passengers at the door, and the theatre was filling up rapidly when the ladies from McNab's island took seats as near a stove as they could get. Soldiers passing up and down the aisles presented each party with a printed handbill setting forth the evening's entertainment.

THEATRE ROYAL

By permission of His Excellency Sir George Prevost, Bart.

The comedy of THE POOR GENTLEMAN
also
THE WAGS OF WINDSOR
a musical farce in two acts

SONGS:

Captain Beaugard:	"When the lark in aether singing."
Lucy:	"A poor little gipsy I wander forlorn."
Phoebe:	"A merry tight soldier I'll swagger away."
Looney McTwalter:	"O whack! Cupid's a mannikin."
William and Phoebe:	"And will my love contented be."
Quotem:	"I'm parish clerk and sexton too."

Characters by gentlemen of the garrison.
Pantomime between acts by the French troupe from Melville Island
Music under the direction of Captain Carter, 8th Regiment.

Miss McNab, reading it over, exclaimed, "Looney McTwalter! Why, why, when they play a fool or a clown, must he always have a Scotch name or an Irish one?"

A laughing Irish voice beside her said, "Never fear, ma'am, the English make fools of themselves well enough. These young officers playing female parts in wigs and gowns, and looking as much like a woman as a horse in petticoats!"

The musicians filed into their seats amid a great stir of the audience. They were chosen from regimental bands, with some added civilians, and in the pit they made a mixed show of sober mufti and brilliant scarlet. When they struck up the overture the music was remarkably good, and it was evident that Captain Carter of the 8th Regiment had practised them with care.

The somewhat haggard scene of Bedford Basin rolled up and discovered the cast of *The Poor Gentleman* in frozen attitudes on stage. Suddenly the actors sprang into their parts with voice and verve. It was a one-act play, mostly nonsense, and Ellen watched the players with impatience. It seemed an age before the curtain slid down in an uproar of applauding hands and stamping feet. The winter night sent cold drafts along the floor in spite of the stoves, and any chance to coax some warm blood into the feet was not to be neglected.

Up went the curtain again, and the ladies from McNab's island sat forward intently. Here were the French pantomimes in their quaint costumes—Harlequin especially notable in his patchwork colors and spangles, his mask, and his shaven skull. The others had their faces covered with a white paste, probably made of flour and water. Their show was a little ballet in which Harlequin and his companions moved to the music of piano and violin, posing, gliding, grimacing, fluttering arms and hands, telling a story without saying a word.

When they skipped off into the wings there was some polite applause, and once more the audience regarded the cracked summer scene on the curtain. When it went up again the stage held *The Wags of Windsor*. Again the music was good, especially the truly male voices—even "Looney McTwalter"; but the chief amusement came from the young subalterns in paint and powder and elaborate false curls, in gowns borrowed from fashionable lady friends and suitably padded fore and aft. In a storm of laughter, especially from the ladies in the audience, they minced about the stage and paused to sing separately or together in falsetto.

Between the acts of The Wags the French troupe appeared again with their ancient art, the graceful leaps and glides and poses, the mobile facial expressions, the eloquent hands. It was, said a female voice behind Ellen, the sort of thing that Frenchmen did quite naturally—"They talk mostly with their hands and eyebrows anyhow."

Although most of the patrons of the Theatre Royal had brought cushions, the wooden seats were making their angles felt long before the entertainment came to an end. It was a somewhat uncomfortable and rather thankful throng that saw the curtain roll up for the last time with the entire company on the stage, the Frenchmen forming a little group at one side, to receive the final applause. The orchestra played God Save the King, and the audience dissolved. Most headed for the doors and the waiting sleighs, but an opposite stream of young ladies made for the stage to lavish personal congratulations on the officers in the cast.

"Come!" said Miss McNab, grasping Ellen by the hand and striding forward. The military young gentlemen were surrounded by laughing and chattering females in furs and cloaks. Les Pantomimes stood almost ignored near the right wing, where a pair of dour redcoats with muskets waited to escort them away to the town barracks for the night.

"Gentlemen," Miss McNab said to the prisoners. "Do any of you speak English?" Harlequin had taken off his mask and revealed himself as a thin young man with the sombre face and earnest gaze of an artist consumed with his art. He said diffidently "I speak English, madame. And all my friends have some."

"Ah! Well, this young lady and I wish to tell you how much we enjoyed your performance. The pantomime was excellent, the dancing beautiful. I haven't seen anything like that since I was a young woman in Edinburgh and saw a troupe from your country perform Cupid and Psyche."

"By Noverre? Thank you, madame."

Les Pantomimes were delighted at this appreciation by English ladies who evidently knew something of their art. And now Miss McNab steered her conversation artfully to something else. "Monsieur Harlequin, until you took your mask off you resembled an-

other young prisoner at Melville Island. His name is Cascamond
—Michel Cascamond. Do you know him by any chance?"

Harlequin pursed his mouth, shook his head, and threw out his
thin expressive hands, as if he were still in performance. He looked
about the other members of his troupe and they answered in the
same way.

"Oh?" the lady said. "Perhaps I've got the name wrong. This
young man was taken at sea, and had a bad wound in the thigh.
Black hair, blue eyes. He speaks English extremely well."

Still no sign of recognition by *Les Pantomimes*.

"Naughty fellow," Miss McNab went on lightly. "He ran away
last spring, and was taken again in the Bay of Fundy, if you know
where that is. He was brought back to Melville Island last summer. In the month of June, I think."

One of the white-faced dancers said something at that, and
there was some rapid French conversation. Harlequin turned to
the ladies politely.

"There is a man named Thouret who speaks your language
like an English gentleman and sometimes interprets for our prisoners at the bazaar. He was brought to the prison last summer
from Fort Anne. Is that near this bay you speak of?"

"Yes, it is. Well, it's not a matter of importance. We may visit
the bazaar some day, and then perhaps we shall see the man.
What is his name again?"

"Thouret, madame. We do not know the number of his mess,
but it is on the upper deck of the prison and one has to climb the
stairs outside. He is a maker of ship models, I believe."

"Thank you—thank you all. I hope we may see you perform
again."

Les Pantomimes bowed gracefully in unison as the ladies withdrew.

For two days after the performance in the Theatre Royal a high
wind blew snow about the streets in stinging clouds, and the Misses
McNab and Dewar stayed by the drawing-room fire with Mrs.
Ross, who knew everything and everybody in the town and gave
them the season's chatter. It took some time and patience for Miss
McNab to steer the conversation towards the Northwest Arm.

She found an opening when Mrs. Ross made mention of the carrying trade in American goods to Portugal.

"Ross has made some money at it, and so has Mr. McNab no doubt; but the shipping man who's really getting rich is Enos Collins, and next to him I'd say John Pryor. Pryor's only forty-three, and already they say he's worth a hundred thousand pounds."

"Ah!" said Auntie. "Now what on earth possessed a shrewd man like John Pryor to build a mansion away out in the woods by the Northwest Arm?"

"The same reason Peter McNab built his at the harbor mouth," returned Mrs. Ross. "To get away from the town, although why anybody would want to live far out of town in this kind of weather is beyond me, I confess. Pryor began in a small way, like McNab. He bought a little farm in the woods by the Arm for a summer home, a nice place for his wife and that brood of young Pryors in the hot weather. The farm lane went down to the waterside and he kept a pleasure boat there, for sailing about the Arm and over to Melville Cove. That was before the prison was built, of course. Melville Cove was such a pretty little place before they stuck up that great ugly red box on the island and filled it full of Frenchmen."

"But the Arm itself is still a lovely place?"

"Oh yes indeed—in summer, mind you. I'd as soon live in Labrador in winter. After he closed it up for the winter Pryor's farm used to be snowed in for weeks on end. However, Pryor's a shrewd man, as you say, and when the prison was built three years ago he saw his chance. The foot of his farm lane at the Arm shore made a handy place for a ferry to Melville Island, and at his suggestion Captain MacDougal had a gang of prisoners improve it. It didn't take very long to make Pryor's road run straight from the Arm to the town just back of the Citadel, by Camp Hill. It made a handy route for officers and men of the prison guard, and when the Arm was frozen it was the shortest for supplies. So MacDougal saw to it that his prison gangs kept the road open all through the winter, and kept it in good repair in summer. What more could Pryor want? He began to build his mansion and clear his park and estate the very next year. That was 1810 you'll remember, when our poor mad king celebrated his fiftieth year on the

throne. So Pryor called the house Jubilee and everyone in Halifax knows the way to it as 'the Jubilee road.' I doubt if the poor
prisoners see much of a jubilee about it, though."

Ellen spoke up. "Mr. McNab says it's a favorite route for sleigh
parties nowadays."

"So it is. For the young people, especially. If I were a giddy
young girl I daresay I'd enjoy that kind of thing as they do. They
drive well muffled in furs and robes, of course. And at the Arm
they put on skates and go gliding on the ice, and visit the prison
and buy gewgaws from the Frenchmen, and stop at Jubilee for
hot chocolate and cakes—the Pryors love company. Years ago
the fashion was to go sleigh-driving along the Basin road to Prince
Edward's lodge. He used to order the troops out to shovel the
snowdrifts after every storm—just the way MacDougal's prisoners
do on the Jubilee road nowadays. Quite a come-down when
you stop to think of it—socially, I mean—from calling on a Prince
to visiting a lot of smelly prisoners. But that's the way things go.
Change! Change! And young people doing whatever they like,
wherever they like. It's the war, of course, going on all these years;
and now Ross tells me the Americans may soon be fighting us on
the side of Napoleon, as if the world's not mad enough."

"Well," said Miss McNab, "I for one am mad enough to enjoy
a sleigh drive and a visit to Melville Island, and so, I'm sure, is
Ellen here. Could that be arranged, do you think?"

"Nothing's more easy." Mrs. Ross flapped her hands. "The
sleighing's at its best now—in a few more weeks we'll have the
March thaw—and there's a party driving out to Jubilee every few
days. You can have our turnout—the coachman likes to exercise
the horses; and I'll find out who's going next, and when—it's more
fun with a crowd."

The sleigh party gathered on Grand Parade, a dozen turnouts,
every sleigh with two horses in tandem and dozens of small bells
jingling on the harness. The Ross turnout was typical of them all;
the sleigh painted a bright blue, with its in-curving prow like a
wave of the sea about to break into the passengers' laps, the warm
robes of buffalo and bear skins, the fine horses prancing and
snorting in the cold air. They formed a procession, and in the lead-

ing sleigh an amusing young gentleman from time to time produced a key-bugle and sounded a few notes of "Rule Britannia,"
apparently the only tune he knew. Away they went up the slope
past Citadel Hill, across the snowy common, around the low hum-
mock of Camp Hill, and then into the Jubilee road.

The sunshine splashed on the snow until they entered the blue
shadow of the woods towards Northwest Arm. The sleigh runners
whined and squealed on the white road, the bells tinkled like the
whole chorus of Fairyland, the bugle tootled, the lively young
faces chattered and laughed. At last they emerged from the dense
wild woods into the "park" of the Pryor estate, where the finest
trees had been preserved and all the rest cut away with the undergrowth. Here the land dropped steeply and the horses ran
like mad. Suddenly the mansion appeared on a broad terrace
of lawn. The ladies in the Ross sleigh scarcely saw the house at
all. They were looking down on the ice of the Arm, shining in the
sun, and across the ice, directly opposite Jubilee, the roofs and
smoking chimneys of Melville Island.

Now the passengers leaped down, leaving the sleighs in charge
of grooms and coachmen. The big front door of Jubilee flew open,
and the lady of the house with her brood of young Pryors waved
and called out greetings, urging everyone to stop in for chocolate
on the way back. The party set off, skates in hand, down the lane
to the little wharf where in summer the Army ferryboat plied to
Melville Cove. Aunt McNab and Ellen wore blue cloaks with
deep fur collars, very much alike, and as they had covered their
heads with similar blue wool tammies and carried black otter-fur
muffs they might have been a pair of fashionable sisters.

At the shore the ladies sat on the wharf and the young gentlemen moved about swiftly and gallantly, strapping on the skates.
Then, with another blast of "Rule Britannia" they were gliding on
the ice, pair by pair, arm in arm.

"Keep a good hold on me, Ellie," said Miss McNab, "till I see
if I've forgotten how. I don't think I've skated once the past twenty
years."

"Of course you've not forgotten, Auntie. It's like breathing—you
don't even have to think about it. See now?"

"All right, but I'm a bit on the wabble, so let's not go fast like
those others."

The party, still led by the gentleman with the bugle, were turning now to skate along the middle of the Arm, moving in long zigzags of nimble legs and flying skirts. The ice boomed like cannon in an irregular salute and the sound went echoing along the wooded slopes.

"I know it's pressure of frost and a sign the ice is thick," said Miss McNab, "but whenever I hear it roar like that I have a feeling the whole thing's about to break up under me. Where are they off to?"

"Just down the Arm. They want to stride about and get warm after sitting in the sleighs."

"Well, my legs aren't young enough for anything like that. We'll just make our way across to the island, and take our time. I suppose you'd rather fly along like those other young things but you can do that at home, my dear. There goes the ice *woomping* again. My heart flops every time. It seems a very long way across, now that we're out on the ice. Think of all that deep water under us! From Jubilee it looked no wider than the cove at home."

"It's not half a mile, Auntie."

"Dear, dear, I hope all this is worth it. If it's not I'll blame myself for an old fool and you may call me worse."

Well down the Arm the skaters had turned, and now were making long tacks back like ships reaching in a head wind. They arrived at the mouth of Melville Cove at about the same time as the sedate ladies of McNab. The flat notes of the key-bugle rang about the cove, and brought military heads popping out of sentry boxes, and from the doorways of the barracks and officers' quarters. The tides, lifting and lowering the heavy ice sheet, kept it broken about the shores, and two of the young gentlemen skated ahead to find a good place to land. They found it quickly, right at the island wharf, and then there was a business of unstrapping the skates and depositing them with the gate guard. The chief turnkey's door opened and Theobald Robinson bustled out to greet them. "Old Snuff Coat" was always quick to recognise people of "the Quality" and was very obsequious with them. Apart from anything else these well-to-do young people were the most generous patrons of the prisoners' bazaar, and a lot of their money found its way eventually into Mr. Robinson's shop.

A few Frenchmen were walking briskly in the yard. The rest

were indoors. The jingle of many sleigh bells on the Jubilee road
had carried across the frozen Arm, and if the prisoners needed any
further notice to set up their bazaar they could thank the merry
gentleman with the bugle. When the visitors entered the "lower
deck" they found its gangway lined with souvenirs for sale and the
salesmen squatting hopefully in the stalls.

One of the party said to Miss McNab, "Don't buy anything right
away. The thing to do is to look over all they've got, first on the
lower deck and then on the upper, before you make up your mind.
They're clever at making things, but some are better than others;
and often you can make a better bargain between one deck and
the other."

They passed along the first floor gangway slowly, pausing to
examine the souvenirs for sale and to chaffer gaily with the Frenchmen over prices. Ellen looked eagerly for Michel's face. The salesmen sat in the entrance to their stalls, and peering past them she
could see the other prisoners, standing or lounging in the half-
shadow, all watching the visitors with a lively curiosity. Only one
looked familiar, and he only because his head was shaved and
white as a peeled egg. It was Harlequin of *Les Pantomimes,*
glimpsed for a moment in a long stall filled with men.

Although the windows and doors had been opened briefly for
a change of air there was a thick smell of unwashed flesh, strongly
male, eddying with the warmth of the roaring wood stoves. Ellen
was reminded of that other visit with Joanna to the Frenchmen in
"the fish shed," only this time she herself felt the hunger in these
watching eyes. Having traversed the length of the gangway, the
party went out by the great door at the other end, a quick plunge
into the cold and a laughing dash up the stairways to the upper
deck. Then again the slow saunter, the pauses to examine this and
that, to compare opinions, and to chaffer in broken French and
English over prices.

When she reached the farther end Ellen's hope was gone. None
of the men selling ship models or anything else resembled Michel
Cascamond. She missed Aunt McNab, and looking back saw her
coming away from a stall about halfway along the gangway. The
old gentlewoman's blue eyes were as bright as a girl's. As she came
up to Ellen she said casually, "I think I've found the stall where
Joseph Thouret is. He has a ship model but it's only half finished,

so he wasn't offering it for sale. He was sitting on a chest, back in the stall, working on the model, when I enquired. Do come and look. If the work is good it may be well to put in a bid for it when it's finished."

They walked back to the stall. Three Frenchmen sat in the entrance, offering knitted things, a carved wooden bijou box, a set of bone dominoes. Beyond them, in the depths of the stall, with its rows of hammock hooks, was the usual cluster of men lounging or busy at their little manufactures. Ellen looked for a man on a chest, working at a ship model, and there he was. He had lifted his gaze from the model as if by instinct and their eyes met. Slowly he arose and came to the entrance of the stall.

"Madame is looking for something?"

She felt herself tingling and flushing. It was a harsh effort not to throw her arms about his neck and cover his face with kisses.

"I was told that a prisoner named Joseph Thouret made very good ship models here. Are you the man?"

"Yes, madame. But I have nothing finished."

"May I see the one you're working on?"

He fetched it. The bone hull was almost complete but there were no masts, no rigging, no cannon.

"It's beautiful. Just what I want. How long will it take to finish?"

"About two weeks, madame."

"And what is your price?"

"I cannot sell for less than my friend Scarron here, who also makes good models. The price is twenty-five dollars, madame. No —no money now, please. You will wish to come again, to see how it goes, will you not, before you buy?"

"Yes! Yes, I should like to do that."

"Very well, madame. I shall look forward to another visit. I notice that your party has gone down again to the lower deck. Let me escort you to the landing—you and the other lady."

As they stepped out on the landing and closed the door they were for a few moments beyond the hearing of the other prisoners, but well aware of glances from the sentry boxes in the yard below. To all appearances a persistent salesman of ship models had followed the two ladies to the landing, and the older one, evidently immune to his persuasions, had gone down several of the steps, drawing her cloak about her against the February air.

"Lutine," Cascamond said in a low voice, "how wonderful to see you."

She started to speak and found her voice choked, and her eyes full of happy tears. She blinked and swallowed and gave him a tremulous little smile.

"We have only a minute," he said. "And you mustn't come here often, or there may be trouble with Captain MacDougal. He knows I am here under this name of Thouret. But we can write to each other."

"How?" she said, surprised.

"By the prisoners' post. Don't write any names. Give your notes to a man named Claviere, a coachman at the house of the merchant Cunard in town. You may trust him perfectly. Simply tell him who the note is for. I shall answer in the same way. Claviere will see that you get mine. And now, dear Lutine, you must go. God bless you and keep you for me till this war is over. *Au 'voir!*"

She nodded, turned, and ran down the steps to Aunt McNab, and then went sedately on with her to the young ladies and gentlemen busy bargaining on the lower deck.

24

Ellen, writing a small letter in the seclusion of her bedroom in the Ross house, glanced out of the window upon the soiled and trampled slush of Argyle Street. The spring thaw had come and ruined the sleighing, and now for a month the roads outside the town would be deep in mud and impassable for anything but an ox-wagon. Already the ice on the Northwest Arm was too rotten to cross, although still too thick for the passage of boats. Aunt Frances had gone home after that first visit to Melville Island and the discovery of "Joseph Thouret," but Ellen had stayed on in town for three weeks. In that time she had made a discreet weekly visit to the prison in a sleigh-and-skating party. There was never more than a minute alone with Michel on the upper landing, a time for a few whispers and for looks more eloquent than talk. Inside, in the presence of so many ears and eyes, their conversation always had to do with the little bone model, which now sailed a dry sea on the windowshelf at Ellen's elbow.

The only possible intimacy came in their notes exchanged by the prisoners' post, in which there was no salutation or signature, no mention of names at all, and no address on the outer fold. The notes were simply sealed with wax and passed from hand to hand. This one under her pen said, "The posts will be difficult, if not impossible, until the snow and ice are gone and the roads begin to dry. So I shall go back to the place you know, lest I draw suspicion by my long absence or outstay my welcome here. Remember, my dear love, you have promised not to do anything rash and that you will stay where you are, where I know you are safe. I shall come back here in about a month's time, when it should be easy again to visit you. Until then do not send any notes unless the matter is urgent. If so you can write in care of the lady here, whose name I have told you, and she will address the note to me in her own hand. Meanwhile do be patient. The war cannot part us for ever, and it may end suddenly. All my love."

At a certain hour each day the coachman Claviere always paused at a pump and horse trough in George Street, and there in the jostle of foot and horse traffic he gave or received certain notes and verbal instructions. He was only one of the couriers used in the prisoners' post, so that he had few to handle. Each note went into a separate pocket, with shrewdly noted detail of the seals, the kind of paper and the shape of its folds, so that despite a complete absence of written address on the outer fold there was never any mistake in delivery.

Before leaving for McNab's island, Ellen took the romantic Mrs. Ross into her confidence, partly at least. Mrs. Ross remembered McNab's quaint effort to find suitors for the hand of his ward, and its failure, and the resulting chatter that the Dewar girl, poor thing, was doomed to old maidery. Now the lady was agog.

"But you must tell me something about him, girl. Is he someone in the garrison? The fleet? The town? I'm dying to know!"

"I can't say more than that he's a young officer, in very poor circumstances at present, but honest and tender, and we love each other very much. Mr. McNab wouldn't consider it a good match at all, so for the present we can't see much of each other and we must be careful with our little messages. And so, if anyone should leave a sealed note and say it's for me, please address it to me in your own hand, and send it by one of your servants to Mr. McNab's office in Water Street. In that way it will reach me safely, and no one the wiser."

"But you're coming back to town, Ellen?"

"In about a month's time, if you'll put me up."

"Shooks! You know very well I'll be delighted. I just hope you know what you're doing. But why do I say that? You're in love, and you're loved—what else matters? All the rest of life is just a lot of shooks and barrel hoops. Goodbye, my dear, and give my best wishes to Joanna and the boys."

Cascamond read the note several times, and at last walked down the gangway to one of the stoves and dropped it into the flames. He returned to the stall and stood watching Scarron busy with gun-carriages for his greatest effort, a wooden ship-of-the-line two metres long, commissioned by a wealthy merchant in the town. The March thaw was in progress, with warm sunshine after heavy rains. Each day at noon the sun reached higher above the south ridge of the cove, the piled snow sank inside the palisades, and patches of ice on the cove and the Arm turned dark like bruises on a white skin. The prison windows stood open through the afternoon, and most of the inmates lounged about the yard, enjoying the mild air and the feel of the sun.

"It's not my affair," rumbled Scarron, without looking up from his work, "but these little messages you've been getting lately have the air of *billets-doux*."

Cascamond made no answer. "Except to shovel snow, you haven't been out of this stranded Ark of Noah since they brought you here last summer," Scarron went on, "so these *billets* may be from someone you knew outside, before you went on the run, or some visitor you met here in *Malveillant*. Putting one and one together I'd say they're from the *demoiselle* who came in here three weeks ago with her mother and arranged to buy your model. She came back twice afterwards, without the mother; and each time you had a little moment with her on the landing."

"You are very observant," said Cascamond calmly.

"I can see lightning and hear thunder, my friend. And what's to become of this delicate affair? Do you still have that mad dream of escape from here?"

"It's no dream. It's a good plan to get away. However I have set it aside. I have decided to stay here till the war ends, like you."

"And when that happens, when you go back to France, what becomes of this *chère amie?*"

"I intend to marry the lady and live wherever she wishes, which may not be France at all."

"*Que diable!* You're not serious!"

"Yes! Don't look so astonished, Scarron. The Journalists can tell you of at least a dozen paroles from here, even some officers at Preston, who intend to marry and stay in this country when the war ends. They would marry now if they could. So would I."

Scarron sucked fiercely on the little black pipe tucked in the corner of his mouth. "This is what comes of being away from France so long, and learning to speak English well, and seeing these pretty English women on visiting days. You forget the pretty women at home."

"I have none to forget, Scarron."

"What about your family—father, mother, brothers, sisters?"

"None. Understand, I tell you all this in confidence as a messmate and a friend. I am a man without attachments except the one I speak of. I am not a romantic but I feel it was not chance that brought me to this country and this *demoiselle*. It was destiny. I have had little affairs—who has not? For a sailor the world is wide. But one day it shrinks to a spot beneath the feet of one woman, and all the rest is emptiness."

Scarron arose and prowled along the gangway peering into the stalls. He came back and seated himself on his work chest. "They're all outside, except those damned Journalists in Mess 58, twittering away to each other like winter sparrows in a hedge. *Eh bien,* you are wise to trust a messmate and nobody else. Now, my friend, perhaps you will tell me something more in confidence. You are no mere *corsaire*. You speak too well, and you have the knowledge and the manner of a naval officer. You say you

learned to speak English as a prisoner in England. Shall I tell you
what I think?"

"Yes."

"I think you are a naval officer, that you learned your English
on parole in Alfax or Preston, where you must have met this marvelous *demoiselle,* and that for God knows what reason you ran
away last year and got pinched and thrown in here. Am I right?"

"In part, yes."

"And now you say you've shoved up the spout a good plan to
escape from *Malveillant. Tiens!* I've been here ever since the English built this ark, and I tell you nothing bigger than a rat has ever
escaped from it. Nothing! So you shove away nothing but a fool's
dream."

"On the contrary, Scarron, to escape is a simple matter, wanting only a bold stroke, the last thing the enemy would expect.
That's how the Emperor wins his wars. And believe it or not, the
idea came from you, yourself."

"Baste! I never had any idea."

"Of course not. It was something you said in that rough humor
of yours. After I'd gone over everything, and rejected everything,
I came back to that."

"What?"

"Someday I'll tell you, Scarron. For the present I keep it to
myself. I trust you well enough, but I don't trust these walls and
stalls even when they seem empty. The Agent for Prisoners has
ears in here as we well suspect, and this plan of mine is something
that a whisper could destroy."

Joanna kissed her and said, "Did you enjoy your holiday? But of
course you did! It shows in your face, I haven't seen you look so
happy in a long time. Auntie's told me something of the gay doings
—the theatre, the sleighing, and the skating. And of course the
town society always amuse themselves indoors with dinners and
whist parties and so forth—I daresay you had a lot of that?"

"No," Ellie said. "The Rosses don't go in for the social whirligig,
and as you know I'm not greatly taken with dinners or cards."

Jo was tempted to ask if she had met any interesting young men,
but of course that was a closed subject. "How is Rory?"

"I'm told he's recovered quite well from his stroke. He's more lame than before, but he gets about well." Ellen paused, seeing the question in Joanna's eyes. "I should have told you, Jo. Rory and I—we dropped our notion of marriage."

"When?"

"Months ago."

"What happened?"

"We both came to realise it was impossible. And now it's best to see no more of each other."

"I see," murmured Jo, although she did not. She had given up trying to fathom the black deeps of Ellie's eyes long ago.

A few days later a fisherman's shallop rounded the gibbet point and put a passenger ashore in McNab's cove. It was Malachi Sparling. In spite of a rough passage from Cape Sable in the unclean cuddy of the little craft he looked as if he had just stepped out of his office in New York. McNab and his sons were away in town, and Joanna engaged the visitor with small talk and refreshments. She knew Mr. Sparling from previous visits, and was aware that he and Peter were engaged in some mysterious business of ships and cargoes to the westward.

When Peter and the boys arrived home in the *Bonnie Jo* there was no word of business however, and dinner was a stately affair with a great regale of food and wine, and then the brandy and the march of the piper up and down the room. The American, with his thin intellectual face, maintained his part of a conversation that played over the gentler matters of the times and made no mention of the wars. Not for the first time he noted the quiet elegance of this family living in what he had always considered the northern wilds of the continent. The shrewd and amiable Highland gentleman, the intelligent youths, the remarkable face and mind of the old aunt, the shy young woman with the mysterious eyes, and the beautiful golden-haired wife who was the serene goddess of the household. Were there many more like these in the British provinces of North America? He was touched with a feeling of sadness, as if he were looking at flowers before a frost. Later, behind the closed door of the library, he spoke his mind.

"McNab, the storm we've feared so long is about to break on us all in North America, whether we call ourselves Americans, Yankees, British, Canadians, Nova Scotians, or whatever."

"You don't mean war?" blurted the laird.

"War, sir, and no mistake about it. Our War Hawks are determined on it—and this year. They won their way to power at Washington in the elections last fall. Now they're pushing President Madison. And they have a trump. Something else happened last fall. An American army destroyed the Indian confederation in the west, at a place in the Indiana Territory called Tippecanoe. Those Indians have long been allies of the British. So the western flank is now clear for an American march into Upper Canada. Another American army will march into Lower Canada from the tip of Lake Champlain, where the border's only forty miles from Montreal."

"When is all this to happen, Sparling?"

"The militia of the border states and territories will be called out next month. That's to give them a couple of months for preparation. War's to be declared in June, when the backwoods roads are dry and hard, with four months' good campaign weather ahead. I guess you know the military situation. For the past three years the British have been pulling their troops out of the Canadian provinces and shipping them to Wellington in Portugal. In fact pretty well the whole of the British Army is there now, tied up in the wrestle with Napoleon. I have it on good authority that there are now less than five thousand redcoats to guard the whole of the Canadian provinces from Halifax to the head of the lakes. None of them can shoot like Americans. None of them know anything about fighting in the forest, as Americans do. And in any case they'll be outnumbered ten to one. You can see what's going to happen."

"But Upper and Lower Canada—all that country's verra far frae here, on the coast, Sparling. Even Québec's a guid six hundred miles if it's an inch. Six hundred miles o' forest, most of it lacking the vestige of a road. And the Royal Navy guards the sea approach."

"Ah, you'll be safe for a time, sir, away down east here by the sea. But mind, there'll be a swarm of American privateers snapping up your merchant ships—the Royal Navy can't stop that, whatever else it may do. And your West Indies trade, which is so important to you Halifax merchants, has to pass up and down the whole length of our coast, with no friendly port but Bermuda, a speck in the western ocean. When the American armies have taken Upper

and Lower Canada they'll come this way next. Mr. Clay, our chief
War Hawk, declares he's not for stopping at Québec, he's for taking the whole continent and no peace until it's done. He says we
have the land of North America as much at our command as the
British Navy has the sea. So naturally the War Hawks won't leave
this naval arsenal at Halifax in British hands—they'd be crazy if
they did. You think you're safe because Québec is six hundred
miles away? You're not half that from the State of Maine, and
what's two or three hundred miles to hardy men in summer
weather? A ten-days' walk. Don't delude yourself, Mr. McNab.
These are facts."

McNab put out a hand absently. His fingers encountered the
globe on its stand. He gave it a whirl and a profound gaze, as North
America came and went in the merry-go-round.

"Our people will fight," he murmured. "Those few redcoats in
Canada won't be alone. And when it comes tae fighting in yon
frontier wilderness our Canadians will be as nimble and can shoot
as straight as yours. They may be o'erwhelmed at last, but it'll be
a bloody affair. And it won't be done in a summer." He was net-
tled by the bland assumption of Mr. Clay, and his Highland blood
instinctively defied any fact in conflict with his loyalty.

A silence followed in which the two men regarded each other
gloomily. Sparling broke it. "Please understand, McNab, I didn't
come here to brag and boast. I merely repeat what I've heard from
good sources. Personally I'm sick at heart, and so are a good many
others like me in the States. Starting a war's like setting a fire in
the forest in hot weather. No telling what winds may blow or where
it'll go before the rains come; just one thing sure, a lot of black
destruction and a lot of innocent creatures killed. You take a brave
view, sir, and it does you credit. No doubt many Canadians feel
the same. Like a porcupine, when they smell an enemy they're inclined to bristle and stand their ground. Porcupines act just the
same when they scent a forest fire. Ever seen what happens then?
I did, once, as a young man on a visit to the Adirondacks. Taught
me a lesson I never forgot. Courage has its time and place, but
not with the woods afire. It'll just get you frizzled, quills and all."

McNab gave the globe another spin and watched it settle to a
stop. "What becomes of our present concern, American supplies
to Wellington?"

"It must end. I myself won't continue longer than another month. This shift of affairs changes everything. I didn't care a rap for the Embargo Act. Unjust and stupid—proposing to ruin American sea trade for a mere illusion. I cared no more for the Non-Intercourse Act. Bonaparte's the greatest robber and tyrant in the world today and I'd ship supplies to any enemy of his, English or whatever. But now I must put my opinions in my pocket. I'm first of all an American, and when my country's at war I cannot serve her enemy. There are some—I'll go further and say there are many Americans in the seaboard states who will probably go on trading with the British under some disguise, war or no war. They hold their own convictions, they have no use for the War Hawks or for Madison, and of course there's the profit, in spite of added risks and penalties. But I won't be one of them. I say this with pain, sir, considering our long and friendly dealings in the past, and of course this present trade to Portugal, which we might have continued to our mutual profit if the war hadn't cropped out here in North America."

"Then I take it your last cargo will be delivered to Cape Sable towards the end of April?" McNab said quietly.

"That's right, sir. And for you and me personally, I fear this must be our last meeting until the end of hostilities in North America." Mr. Sparling hesitated. He wanted to say, "It's a tragedy, but it can't last more than a few months—six at the outside." But he refrained.

Strolling about the beaten earth inside the stockade Cascamond sniffed the warm breath of the forest like a chained animal. He forgot his dislike of its green shadows. After the long winter in *Malveillant* it was like that other time, when the scent of pines, distilled by a summer sun, came through an empty gunport of *La Furieuse* like a breath of paradise. As he passed the imbeciles staring between the palisades at the calm water of the cove he missed the thin figure of *Mousse* with its spread of fair hair. He paused. It was of no use to ask the lunatics. A few moments later one of the *raffolés* walked by, a man with debauched eyes and a complexion of soiled wax. He had a gift of music with the violin and played for *Les Pantomimes*. Lest someone harm the instru-

ment he carried it with him wherever he went, even to the latrines,
where he was going now.

"*Hola!*" said Cascamond. "Where is *Mousse?*"

The man gave him an insolent look. "What do you want with
Mousse?"

"Answer my question, scum, or I'll cram that violin down your
throat!" Cascamond stepped towards him with ready hands.

The fellow cringed. "He is in the hospital. He coughed blood all
the winter, and now he is dying. One must learn to live without
Mousse."

Cascamond walked on to the turnkey's shop and made a purchase of tobacco. Mr. Robinson was not there, and his wife was
attending the shop.

"Madame, I believe one of my former shipmates, a cabin boy
named Chardin, is ill in the hospital. Can you tell me what is being
done for him?"

"Yes, and I'm afraid there's nothing much. Consumption, you
know. The galloping kind according to the surgeon's mate. Carries
off a lot of people nowadays, even amongst the quality in town,
young gals especially."

"Thank you."

On the way back to Mess 127 he stopped on the stairway landing and surveyed the scene. The prisoners sprawling and smoking
in the sunshine, the weathered grey timbers of the stockade, the
guardhouse, the officers' quarters, the telegraph mast, the bell-
house, the hospital, and wharf. The dance of sunlight on the
water, pricking the eyes with a thousand sparks at every glance.
Across the cove the long stacks of firewood, cut last winter and
now drying by the road. The stumps on the slope above, and the
chopped brushwood turning brown, and then the forest on the
crest, the green wall that surrounded everything. The ice and snow
were gone, and the frost had melted in the ground, leaving the
road a narrow slough winding around the cove and into the woods.
This was the season of laziness, "spring fever" as the turnkeys
said, when all work was hateful and even the smoke of the chimneys curled into the air with a slow indolence.

He marked a stir of soldiers on the island wharf, and saw the
garrison supply ketch appear around the point of Dead Man's
Island, nosing her way into the cove. There seemed to be an un-

usual number of men about her deck. After she had tied up to the
wharf a group came ashore, moved to the guardhouse, and then
to the chief turnkey's office and stores. So it was a new batch of
prisoners, the sure sign of another fighting season, like the north
flight of wild geese and the whistling of the frogs.

Soon they were coming through the stockade gate into the prison
yard, thirty or forty men carrying their small belongings and the
issued hammocks and blankets. The familiar cry went up from the
yard, "Fresh meat!" and the sardonic laughter of the old hands.
Cascamond went inside and seated himself in the stall of Mess 127
for another bit of work on his new model. Scarron was there, and
Subiet and Hache, all busy with their manufactures, and after a
time Laleine came in with Chabray.

"Who are the new ones?" Scarron said.

"The crew of a *corsaire* picked up on the Banks of Newfoundland."

"What's their news?"

"Not much chance to talk with them so far. Old Snuff Coat is
busy with his muster list and mess numbers. Someone said there's
no news really. In France more conscriptions—nobody left at home
now but women and children and old men. The Emperor seems
to have changed his mind about invading England, and the armies
are marching to Pomerania and Poland, what for, nobody knows.
On the sea it's the same old affair—no fleet, everything left to
cruisers and *corsaires*—like fleas attacking an elephant."

There was a tramp of feet on the stairway outside, and then
through the east doorway. Peering from the stall Scarron and Cascamond saw Mr. Robinson coming along the gangway at the head
of a score of new prisoners, stopping at one stall and then another
to allot the men to their messes.

When he came to Mess 127 he touched the shoulder of the nearest prisoner and said, in what he liked to think was French, "Ici
vote mess, compree?" He nodded to Scarron. The inmates of
the stall glanced at the newcomer, a stocky red-faced man with lively
black eyes. He wore white pantaloons with thin stripes of blue, a
grey shirt, blue pea jacket, and a knitted blue cap. The hammock
and blanket were slung over one shoulder, and in the other hand
he carried a small canvas sea bag.

"Welcome to His Britannic Majesty's Ship Malevolent," Scarron said. "Your name?"

"Fargeau—Emil Fargeau. A seaman in the privateer *Renard,* out of Nantes, like these others. An English frigate caught up with us off Newfoundland and popped us in the sack."

Robinson and the others had moved on.

"*Eh bien,* put down those things," Scarron said. "You may sling your hammock there when the time comes." He pointed to a pair of hooks well back in the stall. The privilege of living near the gangway was the property of old hands.

He went on, "My name is Scarron, Gabriel Scarron. Here are your messmates. This is Dominique Hache, that's Henry Chabray, that's Valentine Subiet, that's Georges Laleine, and that's Joseph Thouret."

Fargeau gave each a nod and a grin. He was obviously a happy-go-lucky fellow of the ebullient kind, as full of talk as a parrot. He looked back at "Thouret," narrowed his eyes, and then burst into laughter, dropping his burdens, rushing over to him, and slapping hands on his shoulders.

"*Hé!* God's thunder! It's Cascamond! After all this time thinking you were dead!"

Cascamond remained tense and silent, staring with his steel blue gaze into the merry eyes of the newcomer.

"Cascamond! My old *aspirant!* Don't you know me? It's Fargeau!"

The eyes of Mess 127 flicked back and forth, inspecting the two faces. Laleine said, "You are mistaken, *matelot,* his name is Thouret."

A delighted smile. "Ah, bah! This is Michel Cascamond, and the last time I saw him was in a top of the old *Redoutable,* in the fight off Trafalgar. She went down, the night after the battle, and I thought everyone was dead but me. I floated on a grating, you see, until some Spanish fishermen picked me up."

Cascamond turned his head and glanced at his messmates. Their faces showed surprise and interest as much as doubt, except for Scarron. There was no doubt in Scarron's. "Well?" Scarron said. His tone, his whole expression, declared, "So that's your name! Why deny it? *Que diable!*"

Old Snuff Coat, having disposed of the last of his batch, had passed through the west doorway down the stairs. Fargeau's voice rang loudly in the empty space between the stalls and rafters, the common atmosphere of the upper deck.

"Of course it's Cascamond! Senior midshipman of the old *Redoutable* and captain of the *artimon* top. *Parbleu!* Has he never told you? But he was never one to talk much. This messmate of yours is the brave lad who killed the English admiral, Milor Nelson."

"Comment?" cried Mess 127 in one voice. Cascamond raged within. Already the voice of this fatuous windbag had caught the attention of other stalls. The air prickled with a growing silence, as if the whole upper deck of *Malveillant* held nothing but hundreds of ears.

"It's the truth, I tell you! I was there. It was magnificent. *Boom-boom-boom.* Smoke and flame and thunder. And we up there in the top like a nest of rooks in a hurricane. All of a sudden the smoke parted below and there was the English admiral, as near as the toss of a hat. A moment in the history of France, of England, of the world! And in that moment our brave *aspirant* here aimed his musket and fired. Without hesitation. As if he had been waiting for that moment all his life. And down went Milor Nelson to the deck—*crac!* He'd lost his mess number at last."

Out of the silence men began to emerge from the stalls into the gangway, and to crowd about Mess 127. Fargeau, flattered by this audience, rose to the occasion. His voice blared like a trumpet. His arms and hands flew out in gestures. He went over the battle of Trafalgar in general and the fight between *Redoutable* and *Victory* in particular. When he mentioned orders he put his hands to his mouth like a speaking-trumpet and shouted them. When he described the sounds of battle as the noise of all the devils in hell he gave a passable imitation of the devils, roaring and thumping his fists on the stall partition and stamping his feet on the floor. He tucked an arm inside his coat, dangling the empty sleeve, when he was "Milor Nelson" walking the deck; he aimed Cascamond's musket with a cocked thumb for the hammer and snapped the thumb down, crying *"paf!"* for the flare of the priming and *"boum"* for the sound of the shot. At last he threw himself down on the floor and became "Milor Nelson" again, this time falling on his knees and putting out his left hand to the deck; and then slowly the lone hand giving way, and the body falling on its left side. It was all done with such verve, and with such exactitude, that it was obviously not the first performance, indeed it was plain that ever since a wild October day in 1805 Fargeau had been telling his tale in taverns and forecastles and fixing every word and gesture in his memory.

He arose and almost bowed to his audience, which now broke into a vast chatter. He tipped a generous hand towards the silent Cascamond, sitting on his clothes chest and glowering.

"He is too modest, this brave boy. He always was. One seldom knew what he thought. One only saw what he did."

After a time the prisoners began to drift away to their stalls, seeing that the *brave garçon* was not disposed to talk, while Fargeau was only too willing to repeat his performance. But they were excited. A high buzz of conversation sounded under the roof and it had one theme—the slayer of the great Nelson here in *Malveillant!* When the last visitor had departed Scarron said quietly, "This is true, Cascamond—that is your name?"

"That is my name, yes."

"And is it true, what this fellow says?"

"You may believe as much as you wish."

"But you were the senior midshipman in *Redoutable,* in charge of the *artimon* top?"

"Yes."

"And Fargeau, here, was with you?"

"Yes."

"You see?" cried Fargeau with his delighted grin. "He is modest, this boy Cascamond. But he cannot avoid the fact that he is one of the greatest heroes of France in this war. When he returns home the Emperor will make him a *chef d'escadre* at the very least, and give him a sword of honor, maybe even the Order of the Legion, and . . . and . . . a purse of gold, of course, so that he may regale his old shipmates and messmates, like you and me."

"Shut your mouth!" snapped Cascamond. He was trembling with fury, and the members of Mess 127 noted it, with more interest than ever.

"But why?" demanded Fargeau in a tone of injured friendship. "It's all true—the battle—and Milor Nelson—and you with your musket . . ."

"And you with your mouth. *Pouah!*" Cascamond leaped up and Fargeau cringed. The hero of France had evidently gone mad in long confinement. However Cascamond strode along the gangway and down the stairs to the yard. Scarron alone followed, and came upon Cascamond standing with his head bent and pressed against one of the palisades, an attitude of despair familiar enough in *Malveillant*. He felt the touch of a hand on his shoulder, and heard Scarron's voice.

"What's so bad, my friend?"

Without turning Cascamond said, "You heard."

"Certainly. The fellow chatters like a monkey, but what's the harm in a monkey?"

"The harm of the devil, Scarron. That affair at Trafalgar—it has been my secret, all this time. Or so I thought. Now it's *secret de polichinelle*. Listen! After the battle I was taken with the other prisoners to England. I saw none from *Redoubtable*. I thought I was the only survivor. As a midshipman I was placed on parole in a village where one mingled with the gentry as well as common people, and I learned their language. I soon came to know that the English, all of them, worshipped their admiral Nelson like a god, and at his death they wept as if a god had fallen. More, they were in a rage because he was killed by what they called a cowardly shot from the French rigging. The English don't shoot from their own tops, that is an order in their fleet, and they talk of it as if it were the law of all mankind. There was a lot of English nonsense about Tyrolese chamois-hunters placed with rifles in the French tops, with orders to watch for the admiral Nelson and shoot him down. I heard it said, in drawing rooms as well as taverns, that the man who fired the shot was a criminal who should be hanged if he survived the battle. So I kept my mouth shut."

"*Soit,*" Scarron muttered.

"Finally I was sent home to France in an exchange. I returned to the naval service and got my rank as a lieutenant. Nearly three years ago I was captured again, and taken to Halifax with a bad wound in the leg. When I was discharged from the naval hospital I was sent to Preston on parole. Then I was offered a position as schoolmaster, teaching French to the sons of a Scotch merchant."

"In Alfax?"

"His place of business was in the town, but he lived on the island at the harbor mouth—you must have seen it when you came in there yourself. It has a long stone beach like a mole in the channel."

"Where the dead men hang?"

"Yes. I was there nearly a year. That is where I met the *demoiselle* you have seen here. She lived with the merchant's family, *en tutelle*. And this is the part you will find incredible—one of those tricks of fate which happen as if God or the Devil were amusing themselves in an idle moment. The lady was affianced to a man much older than herself, a man for whom she had respect but not love."

"And so she fell in love with you. *Tiens!* What's incredible about that? It happens all the time."

"Her affianced was Captain MacDougal, the Agent for Prisoners."

Scarron pushed out his lips and made a low whistle.

"Exactly!" Cascamond said.

"And he discovered the affair and that's why you ran away?"

"There was more to it than that, but yes, I took a fishing boat and went off to the west. I hoped to reach one of the old settlements in this country where people still speak French."

"*Hein?* Those are all up the other way, towards Québec. A number of prisoners from here, working on the road from Halifax towards the Gulf of St. Lawrence, have run away and tried to reach those settlements. None did. It's too far through the forest."

"No doubt. But there are some settlements on the western coast of this *Nouvelle-Ecosse* also. They are a people who call themselves *acadiens,* not *canadiens.* Their ancestors came from my part of France—Bretons, Normans, Vendeans. One could live amongst them without feeling a foreigner. Well, those are the people I was looking for, but my boat sank on the way. I had to swim for my life, and I fell into the hands of some rogues who sold me for the bounty money. So I was brought here."

"And this name of Joseph Thouret?"

"Belonged to a prisoner who ran away from a road party and was drowned."

"And the Agent for Prisoners, Captain Macdoo-*gal*—he does not know who Joseph Thouret really is?"

"Ah yes, he does, Scarron. He recognised and questioned me,

one day in the winter, when he came in a sleigh across the ice."

"And he did not break your head? *Parbleau,* that's not like those damned English!"

"He is old and lame, but that's not the point. He retains his jealousy for the lady's honor, and he would do nothing to me that might set tongues wagging in her direction. But he told me, between ourselves, in cold blood, that he would hang me if he got the chance. He has a fanatic belief that he will have his revenge, and when he found me here he was sure of it. Now, understand this, my friend. It is a law of this country that anyone who steals anything of the value of five shillings or more may be hanged. Anyone! Man or woman, old or young. And I stole a boat worth all of that."

"But surely you'd have been hanged before this, Cas—what is it, Cascamond? You'd have got the hemp cravat as soon as the Agent found you here!"

"No, not at all. Even the English have some idea of justice, and the Agent would find it hard to persuade a court that a prisoner of war should be hanged merely for the theft of a boat. Every year French prisoners break their parole and steal a boat for their escape. Most are caught, but none are punished with anything more than a few days in the *cachot.*"

A light came into Scarron's puzzled face. "Ah! Ah! I see now! Just like those damned English! They wouldn't hang a poor prisoner of war for stealing a boat. And it would make a great scandal in the world if they hanged one for shooting Milor Nelson in battle. But if they knew they had in court the man who killed Nelson . . ."

"They could hang him for stealing the boat. Exactly! And now here is this ass Fargeau braying his news all over the prison. Old Snuff Coat does not understand much French, but there are many tongues in *Malveillant* that can wag a little English, and we know there are informers. Eventually Snuff Coat will know what sort of prisoner he has got in Mess 127, and after that it won't take long to advise Captain MacDougal. Then a farce in the court and the hemp cravat, and the perfect revenge for MacDougal. His rival on a gibbet at the hangman's beach, naked and tarred, in sight of the lady herself."

Cascamond said all this with an earnest and compelling look straight into Scarron's eyes, as if it were a demand.

"*Dieu!*" Scarron said. "What is there to do?"

"You can help me to escape."

"Ha! This wonderful plan! Well, what is it?"

"Understand, Scarron, it will take you and three others of the mess. And you will be punished for helping a prisoner to escape."

"Ten days in the *cachot*. What's that compared to hanging? Get on with it."

"First, find out about the prisoner called *Mousse*. His real name is Chardin and he is dying in the hospital, if not already dead. We need a corpse."

"I can find that out from one of the prisoner-attendants who take turns at duty there, day and night."

"Find out also the routine of the surgeon's mate. When does he sleep, and where, and at what hour does he make his morning rounds."

"That won't take long. Stay here, I'll be back in a few moments."

Scarron sauntered off casually amongst the groups of prisoners in the yard. Before long he came back in the same manner. "*Mousse* is dead. He dropped off the hooks this afternoon and they'll bury him tomorrow. The surgeon's mate sleeps in the officers' quarters on the hill. He goes off duty about four in the afternoon, spends the evening drinking rum like a hole in a cask, and doesn't show up for morning rounds till about ten hours."

"Good! First I must send a note to a lady in town, this afternoon if possible. I know how to arrange that. This evening, at muster, I shall be taken ill. Whoever is standing near can call the turnkey and get me to the hospital. Not you, nor anyone from our mess, must have a hand in that. Your job comes in the morning. Now listen carefully."

The prisoners were in their ranks in the yard, the soldiers as usual watching from their places at the rear, and Mr. Robinson and his turnkeys making their round of the companies with muster lists. At the call of his name, "Joseph Thouret" answered *"Ici!"*, waited a moment or two, and then uttered a loud groan and sank to the ground clutching his stomach. A babble of prisoners broke out around him at once, and at the repeated cry of *"malade! malade!"* a turnkey came, and then Mr. Robinson himself.

"What's wrong here?" demanded Old Snuff Coat. More babble. Cascamond was giving forth dismal moans with his knees bent up to his chin. "Well, don't stand about chattering," Snuff Coat roared. "Pick him up, some of you, and get him over to the hospital." For translation he made elevating gestures, and jerked a thumb towards the main gate in the stockade.

Cascamond was carried like a log past the stockade gate, and then, accompanied by a turnkey and an armed soldier, through the second palisade to the little red hospital beside the wharf. There he passed to a cot, where the French prisoner-attendant stripped away his faded and shabby POW denims and shoes and covered him with a blanket.

"You going to call the surgeon's mate?" the soldier asked the turnkey.

"Him! Can you picture that rum-boozer coming down here in off-duty hours just to see a Frenchman with a bellyache? Not him. Whatever this frog's got wrong with him will keep till tomorrow forenoon." And out they went, taking his carriers back to the prison stockade. Cascamond groaned now and then for the benefit of the *infirmier,* who sat at the end of the room in a chair comfortably padded with a blanket from the hospital bedding stores. Cascamond's fellow invalids lay on the row of cots as still as the dead youth on the covered bier by the door. At dark the *infirmier* was relieved by another French attendant for the night. The night man passed once along the cots, lit a candle in the guard lantern hanging by the door, devoured bread and cheese provided by the garrison cook, a perquisite of the hospital attendants, and settled himself in the chair.

As the night went on Cascamond could hear the sentinels, one outside the hospital door, the other on the wharf at the rear, shouting "All's well!" in the hourly chant that began at the main guardhouse and passed from sentry to sentry, stamping about in a small circle to warm their feet, and then stepping back into the shelter of their boxes. All the sentries were relieved at midnight and again at four o'clock in the morning. Sunrise would come about half-past five, and the morning would be well advanced when the next relief came at eight.

At each relief he heard the approaching tramp of redcoats from the guardhouse and the stamp of their feet at the cry of "Halt!" Then the command, "Sentries, pass!" and the movements of men exchanging places in the boxes before and behind the hospital. In the ritual of his round the sergeant of the guard opened the hospital door for a perfunctory glance about the room. The *infirmier,* with the instinct of long experience, came out of his doze at exactly the right moment and stood to give the soldier a nod. When the door closed he put another chunk of firewood in the stove and settled down to snore again in the chair. At each of these visitations the *malades* stirred in their sleep but remained with heads muffled in their blankets against the drafts that stabbed the room from the chill April night.

The wind was in the east, and drops of rain pecked at the window panes. The windows had no curtains or blinds and it was possible for the sentinels to see inside the dimly lit room whenever they stepped outside of their boxes. When all was quiet after the four o'clock relief Cascamond slipped out of the bed with the crouched and silent movements of a cat stalking prey, and kept well below the level of the windowsills as he moved across the floor. The *infirmier* slept soundly in the chair. The bier stood in the wide pool of shadow cast by the lantern's bottom. When Cascamond reached it and drew the blanket aside he had a spasm of nausea. Here lay all that was left of poor *Mousse,* wasted like that other corpse which Cascamond had helped to bury, and

with the same gape and the same blind stare. But it was no time
to be squeamish.

He had planned to drag the body slowly across the floor, keeping well below the window level until the unavoidable moment
of risk at the bedside. But now, hearing the rain again, he decided
to be bold. Except for their hourly shout and stamp of feet the
sentries were content to huddle in the shelter of their boxes. He
picked up the frail and rigid burden and in a few steps he was at
the bed, rolling *Mousse* into the blankets and drawing them about
his head, like those of the other inmates. Cascamond's prison
clothes hung on a peg by the head of the bed, and his shoes lay
on the floor. Quickly he put them on and crept away to the bier,
where he stretched himself at full length and covered himself from
head to foot with the blanket.

The bier was a simple litter made of poles and canvas and fitted
with four short legs. He told himself, "You have slept on worse
beds, my boy," but his mind was taut in expectation of what was
to come, and his body found no rest. The hours that remained
of the night were like years. From time to time one of the sleepers
uttered a groan or a cry, and the attendant stirred in his chair.
When sunrise brought a grey stain to the windows the candle
in the lantern had already expired.

Eight o'clock brought the new sentries, and the *infirmier* of
the day arrived to change places with his comrade of the night.

"How did it go?" he grunted.

"All slept like the dead."

"And you, too, *hein?*"

A dry laugh. The night man's worn list slippers shuffled to the
door and paused by Cascamond's blanketed head. "We must get
this carcass out of here before the butcher's boy comes in for the
morning rounds. It should have been buried yesterday, but Old
Snuff Coat said it was too late in the afternoon to call volunteers
and furnish a guard. I'll order a call for gravediggers as soon as I
pass through the gate."

The day attendant took a broom and made a casual round of
the floor, belching with the loud satisfaction of a man who has a
good breakfast under his belt. In the distance Cascamond could
hear the shout of *"Fossoyeurs! Fossoyeurs!"* The morning muster
would be over now, and prisoners would be swabbing the "decks,"

but because of the wet weather the hammocks would remain indoors, rolled up and lashed to give room for moving about the stalls.

Most of the prisoners would stay indoors too, and Scarron and his comrades would have no difficulty in getting the gravedigging job. They were to loiter near the gate, looking over the goods displayed in Robinson's shop, ready for the call. The only hazard was that some of the cabin boy's *raffolés* might insist on burying him, out of sentiment. However Scarron was confident on that score. *"Baste!* Those? They're too damned lazy to lift a hand in honest work. Anyhow, as far as they're concerned he's something devoured and gone like yesterday's *ragoût*."

Nevertheless it was a relief to hear Scarron's familiar growl at the hospital saying, *"Hola! Fossoyeurs ici!"* As the attendant opened the door the same voice said, "Grab those handles, boys, and let's get on with it." The party consisted of Scarron, Chabray, Subiet, and Hache, wearing their English pea jackets against the rain, with an escort of two soldiers in greatcoats. As usual in wet weather the soldiers had pulled little covers of oiled cloth over their musket locks to keep the powder dry, and their bayonets remained in the scabbards.

The Frenchmen lowered the bier into the boat with the stolid care of messmates tucking away an old comrade. The soldiers climbed in. Then began the slow dip of oars across the cove to Dead Man's Island. The air was a grey drizzle with occasional heavy showers that rattled on the boat like a kettle drum. When they reached the farther shore and beached the boat, the soldiers stepped out and sat against the gunwale, with coat collars turned up against the rain, and water dripping from the glazed peaks of their shakos. They had no intention of following the Frenchmen step by step while they searched for an easy place to dig the grave. They simply watched and kept their muskets handy.

Scarron and his fellows laid the pick and shovels and axe on the bier with the covered "carcass" and set off with it along the shore, passing the old graves and the lone wooden cross, which leaned sadly after another winter's frost and thaw. Beyond these they paused and looked about, putting the bier down in the bushes and pointing here and there with a lot of gesticulation and argument. *Les Pantomimes* could have done no better on a stage.

Gradually they moved on from place to place and from argument to argument until they reached a point of the shore about sixty paces from the soldiers.

"This is as far as we dare go," Scarron muttered. "Set him down, lads. Take off your jackets, and one of you start cutting away the brushwood."

The thin man Subiet, wearing Cascamond's pea jacket over his own, took them off as one coat, slipped Cascamond's under the blanket, and set to work briskly with the axe. The spot was the usual sort for tenants of Dead Man's Island, as near the shore as possible, to save work in felling trees and hacking tough roots, and just far enough above an ordinary tide that salt water could not flood the hole. The soil was a mixture of coarse gravel and yellow clay, with a few large stones.

When the grave was at knee depth Scarron cast the pick aside. "That's enough!" And in a whisper, stooping over the bier, "Are you all right in there, *corsaire?*"

"Yes!"

"You still wish to go through with it?"

"Yes!"

"Dieu! It will be cold and wet in that hole. This damned rain! We can't even leave you this miserable blanket, which must be returned to the prison with the tools."

"I know all that, Scarron. Cover me in the grave with my English jacket and then the brushwood, as we arranged. And get on with it quickly, or those redcoats will be suspicious."

They placed a layer of brushwood on the floor of the grave, lowered the "carcass" down to it, drew away the blanket, and covered Cascamond's head and torso with the blue pea jacket. All this was hidden from the soldiers by the dwarf bushes of laurel and bayberry and sweet-fern around the hole. Hache had been busy cutting branches of fir from a tree nearby, and now Scarron, working swiftly, wove the branches and the cut bushes into an arch over the "carcass," thrusting the butts into the grave sides. When he had finished Cascamond lay in an aromatic basket, with a little chimney of latticed twigs rising from his head to the level of the ground.

Now they shoveled in the earth they had dug out of the hole, leaving aside the larger stones. When they had finished, the grave

looked like any other, a long mound of clay and gravel. Even the
breathing chimney was covered with carefully placed pebbles. The
soldiers had been grumbling to themselves, and now one of them
came striding through the wet bushes to see what was taking the
Frenchmen so long. He gave the mound a careless glance.

"Finny? All right then! Allay voos ong!"

The Frenchmen nodded, picked up the tools and the hospital
blanket, threw them on the empty bier, and filed off to the boat
without a backward glance.

Now came the worst part for Cascamond. Even with these careful preparations the sensation of being buried alive was horrible.
He had a fear of suffocation. The downpour of rain soon drenched
the crumbled earth above him and dribbled in cold runlets about
his body. He had a growing illusion that the tide of the Northwest Arm was rising and seeping into the grave, and that he would
be drowned like a bilge rat caught in some blind corner of a sink-
ing ship. He had to restrain a wild impulse to hurl off the brushwood and earth and breathe the sweet air of life again. What made
it worse was the darkness and silence, especially the silence. He
could not hear the party getting into the boat, nor the slow beat
of oars which meant that all was going well. For all he knew the
redcoats had guessed his game and remained nearby, with sardonic grins under their dripping shakos, waiting for the "corpse"
to arise.

He clenched his teeth and forced himself to lie still and breathe
lightly of the thin air. He dared not wait too long, however. Soon
the hospital attendant would begin his round of the beds with
breakfast bowls of hot gruel. If he found one of the sick men apparently fast asleep he might not disturb him, but it would not
be long before he had to smooth the bedding and prepare the invalids for the morning inspection of the surgeon's mate. Then
the body of *Mousse* would be revealed—and the fox would be out
of the sack.

Cascamond had not dared to take the *infirmiers* into his confidence. As Scarron had warned him, these fellows prized their
easy job at the hospital and were not likely to risk it, and ten days
in the Black Hole, for the sake of an escapade by some rash fellow from another mess. The day attendant was bound to raise the
alarm when he discovered the substitution of a dead *Mousse* for

the live invalid from Mess 127. The sentry outside the door would run to the belfry and set the bell clanging, the soldiers would dash out of their barrack like angry red ants, and in a few minutes Dead Man's Island and the adjoining forest would be alive with tramping feet and prickling with bayonets.

So it had to be not too soon and not too late. A nice calculation for a man buried alive, in sight of the prison, and slowly drowning in cold water! He tried to soothe his mind with other things, and succeeded in one only. There were twigs of bayberry and sweet fern in Scarron's careful basketwork and the freshly cut stems gave off their pungent scents. How many times, strolling the path in the wood with Lutine, or on the way to the Thrum Cap, she had paused to pluck leaves of these plants and rub them in her hands. She would put her face down to sniff the aroma and then hold out the hands so that he could enjoy it also. He could see her now, the pert nose drinking in the scent, and then the black eyes, eager and luminous, watching his face as he bent to her hands, and the lips smiling as if she were holding forth a casket filled with the luxurious perfumes of an empress. It was so like Lutine, her utter pleasure in things that a woman of the world would have taken casually or ignored. That was why, when she had found love in his arms, it was such a tremendous discovery, something that could never become jaded or spoiled.

Ah, Lutine, Lutine, to have you in my arms again!

The time for his resurrection came at last, and he made a tentative movement that accomplished nothing. Scarron's careful vault of woven twigs and branches, with their butts driven into the sides of the grave, now formed a cage weighted with earth, from which it would not be easy to break free. In a rush of panic he struggled wildly, realising that his plan had been faulty after all. Lying in the chosen position on his back in this narrow slot, with hands crossed on his breast under the covering jacket, he could neither get room nor leverage enough to force his way up through the mound. It was a frightful sensation. He was now drenched with cold sweat as well as the drip of wet earth, and as he struggled it seemed that Scarron's little chimney of twigs above his head had collapsed under the weight of the stones.

At last something moved. He had worked a branch loose from its socket in the side clay. Then another. Another—another. In a supreme effort, with strained lungs and the last of his strength, he pushed his hands through that dank shroud of sticks and earth. At once he could breathe fresh air. With new strength he scrabbled at the cocoon like a grub turning into a creature with wings. Finally he could grip the edges of the hole and heave himself upward, bursting through the last of Scarron's handiwork into the open. He was free, lying in the dwarf bushes and ferns by the graveside, panting and drenched and exhausted. Drops of rain fell on his face and he welcomed them. They had the blessed touch of holy water in those far-off days when his mother had taken him to church, dipped her hand in the stoup, sprinkled his face, and made the sign of the cross.

He had no idea of the time as he lay there. How long had it been since the gravediggers and soldiers departed? He arose on hands and knees and peered through the bushes. Two hundred yards away across the water he could see, dim in the rain, the wharf, the hospital, the bulk of the garrison knoll and the roof of the prison beyond. There was a distant buzz of voices but nothing out of the ordinary. He shook the pea jacket free of dirt, put it on, and felt in the pockets. His food was there, a dozen sea biscuits of the prison issue and a chunk of cheese from the private larder of Mess 127. His money was there, ten silver dollars. He looked into the grave with a curious feeling as if he had indeed risen from the dead, with a completely new life before him.

He crawled away through the bushes until he reached the thick growth of firs and birches which covered the little hill of Dead Man's Island. Here he could safely stand upright, and he walked over the crest and down the other side. In a few minutes he passed over the shallow ravine where sometimes in flood tides a wet finger crept over the neck that joined the "island" to the mainland. Now he was in the forest itself. He turned his steps southward, aiming for the distant point where the Northwest Arm left the body of Halifax harbor. Fearful that he might lose his bearings in this green wilderness he kept the water in sight through the trees.

By his reasoning the soldiers would search first about Dead Man's Island, then the woods towards the Arm tip and the Dutch Village. Then the hue and cry would pass along the roads to Windsor and Truro, the usual routes of fugitives from Halifax. Possibly Old Snuff Coat would send the prison's boat to prowl along the

Arm shore, and for that reason he must keep his movements hidden in the trees.

It was rough going, a land of Cain in which the trees grew among fantastic boulders, with tough bushes of huckleberry breast-high in the open places, and sometimes thickets of bramble that tore at his clothes and skin. Streams rattled down the slope to the Arm, none very wide or difficult to cross, and sometimes he went down on all fours and drank like a thirsty beast. In about half an hour he came upon a round cove in a dell of birch trees, with a cool spring running through a strip of brown gravel beach to the tide. He recognised it from the chatter of summer visitors to the prison. This was the Dingle, where people in pleasure craft put ashore to dabble bare feet on the beach and to eat refreshments in the shade. He remembered something else they had said. From the steep knoll by the Dingle you could look across the Arm and see high in the woods on the other side the rooftop of "Studleigh," the mansion of His Lordship Alexander Croke, Judge of the Vice-Admiralty Court. According to *Les Journalistes* this man Croke was an example of the English devil in person, clever, arrogant, cold, pitiless, hated by everyone in Halifax. One would not wish to make his acquaintance!

Cascamond scrambled on. From prisoners who had come to Melville Island by boat he knew that this side of the Arm was a stretch of forest unbroken except at the entrance, where a few fishermen lived in a cove. The distance from the prison to the main harbor was about four kilometres according to *Les Journalistes;* but a man traveling the woods and following the windings of the shore would find it much longer.

Several times he thought he heard the distant clang of the alarm bell. He paused and heard nothing but the beating of his heart and the drip from branches overhead. It was doubtful if he could hear the bell at this distance and in these sodden woods. He stopped by a little brook for a drink and a rest. Sitting with his back against a boulder he began to gnaw one of his biscuits. Then came a sound unmistakable. The cannon at Melville Cove, a heavy thud and then echoes rumbling like thunder along the Arm slopes. He threw the biscuit away and fled as if the redcoats were at his very heels, and did not stop until he tripped over a fallen branch and fell breathless to the ground.

As his breath came back so did a calmer sense of things. He drew another biscuit from his pocket and ate it hungrily, reflecting that these things, which the contemptuous Scarron called "those tiles," were the same hardtack on which Wellington's army marched in Spain, which carried the British fleets about the world. While he sat there munching and musing, three moose came out of the woods to drink in a pool a few paces downstream. The rain, now in one of its drizzling moods, killed all trace of scent and they did not notice him. A calf and two adults, one of them probably a bull who had dropped his horns last winter and had yet to grow a new set. They were lean from the hard months in the snow, and now in springtime their thick black pelt was falling away in patches like the hair of a mangy dog.

"*Hola!*" he called softly. "We do not look our best, you and me, but at least we are free, *hein?*" They threw up their heads when he spoke, and then wheeled and trotted off into the green silence from which they had come.

In the afternoon the wind shifted to the west, and the sky was clearing when Cascamond reached a bight in the shore and saw beside it the flakes and stagings of a fishing village. This then must be Purcell's Cove, the armpit of the Northwest Arm. Beyond lay the main harbor, and by climbing a tree he could see McNab's island across the water, at a distance of not more than two miles.

Much nearer, indeed just across the Arm itself, rose the woods of Point Pleasant, where the English had several batteries. *Les Journalistes* said that two of the batteries covered the entrance to the Arm, lest some invading force try to slip in behind the town. The main one was on the tip of the point, with guns on traversing iron carriages and rails, so that it could shoot across the Arm, or the harbor itself, or straight towards the harbor entrance by Hangman's Beach. There was a much smaller battery farther up the Arm, built long ago to cover a chained boom that barred all movement in or out. Cascamond could see it clearly. The boom was gone and there was no sign of life in the battery, only a few gulls drifting like flakes of snow against the dark mass of the woods.

The battery on the point itself was another matter. Smoke arose from the barrack chimney and a flag fluttered on the staff. Again he considered the gossip of *Les Journalistes*. There had

been a great stir four or five years ago when an English warship
fired on an American and seized some deserters. These poor devils
had been executed at Halifax. Everyone at Melville Island thought
the United States would declare war at once. So did the English
government, apparently, for they sent out a General Prevost with
several regiments, and this Prevost had made a great *bruit* about
Halifax, repairing and manning the defenses. Then it all died
away. Prevost had gone. So had most of the redcoats. The Citadel
and the outermost fort, York Redoubt, were still well manned,
but each of the batteries at Point Pleasant had little more than
a corporal's guard.

Nevertheless, thought Cascamond, they must be artillerymen
and they must have heard the warning gun at Melville Cove. They
will be on the lookout, then. One must wait for night. In any case
one dare not try to steal a boat in daylight. From his tree, looking
down into Purcell's Cove, he could see several shallops of the
sturdy kind built for the fishery in these seas. They were sloop
rigged, with a small cuddy for shelter at the stern. In a pinch one
man could handle them.

During long wakeful nights at Melville Island, evolving his plan
for escape, he had considered asking Lutine to come away with
him, but he had soon rejected that. However willing she might
be, he could not take her on such a passage, remembering what
had happened on the other. No, it was best to go on alone and
hope to make a rendezvous somewhere in the United States. How
Lutine could manage to join him there he did not attempt to guess.
It was bad for one's resolution in a bold enterprise to consider
all the chances beforehand. There were so many to go wrong. The
only way was to take them one at a time, like stairs in the dark,
each separate achievement leading to the next. Already he had
achieved what Scarron had declared impossible, an escape from
Malveillant. What else was impossible?

In the shadow of the woods he found a spring, and there he
supped on biscuits and cheese and awaited the fall of night. After sunset the panes of the fishermen's cottages glowed with can-
dlelight, but not for long. These frugal folk went to bed early to
save fuel and candles as much as to rest from the long day's work.
When all was dark Cascamond crept down from the woods to
the shore. A dog barked suddenly and he froze. More dogs

aroused themselves and growled, but evidently they were tied, for
none came near. At last a door opened. There was a shouted
curse and something thrown, and the noise subsided.

During the afternoon he had marked the shallop he wanted.
It was moored in the cove with a small flatboat conveniently pulled
up on the shore nearby. When he reached the flatboat he found
the thole pins in place and a pair of stubby oars tucked under the
thwarts. Launching was easy. Alongside the shallop he pulled
himself over the gunwale and tied the flatboat to a cleat. The shallop was moored with a single anchor, and he knew what sort of
anchor it would be. None of the inshore fishermen could afford
iron ones. They made wooden "killicks" with four flukes, and
weighted them with a heavy stone caught between four sticks
lashed together at the top. It took a violent effort to drag it free
from the bottom, to raise it, and to get it on board without making
a sound. At last he felt the craft moving adrift. He dared not
hoist the sails here in the cove, for the blocks were sure to squeal
like pigs. He fumbled for one of the shallop's long sweep-oars,
put it in the stern slot, and sculled the craft slowly towards the
entrance.

Outside the cove the westerly breeze caught the hull and carried it into the harbor channel. He glanced back towards the cottages. All remained dark and silent. Across the Arm a single
lantern showed in the Point Pleasant battery. Behind those dark
ramparts a bored redcoat would be on sentry duty but he could
not see a shallop at half a mile. Cascamond walked forward to
the mast and hoisted the sails. As he had expected the blocks
shrilled but that did not matter now. He shipped the oar and fitted
the tiller in the rudder socket. Far astern as the shallop moved on
its new course he could see over his shoulder the masthead lanterns of ships at anchor off the town, scattered lights in the town
itself, and one lofty gleam which must be the lantern on the telegraph mast of the Citadel—Scarron's "North Pole."

High on the black mass of rock to starboard shone the guard
lantern in York Redoubt, the watchdog of the harbor entrance.
On the other side of the channel and much lower he could make
out the loom of McNab's island, without a light of any sort. The
shallop went along well and before long he was able to discern
the tip of McNab's beach, where the dead men swayed in their

rusty chains in the dark. Then he was watching for the white wash about the Thrum Cap. The light on York Redoubt was behind him now, hanging in space like one star in a deserted sky. He shifted his course to give the Cap and its shoals a wide berth, but even so he could hear the light surf on them as he passed.

Now it was time to haul the wind for a run up the eastern side of McNab's island. He put the tiller hard over and held it there with his knee while his hands were busy with the sheets. There was a great flurry of old canvas before the shallop came about. It was clumsily done—the fishermen would have known exactly where to put a hand on any rope in the dark—but done anyhow. Already he could make out the loom of Lawlor's island. He steered in cautiously, marking the shores by the sound of the sea and an occasional glimpse of white foam.

At last he was deep in the lee of McNab's island, where the westerly breeze perished and the sails went slack. He dropped the killick from the bow. The splash, the pause with the rope slithering out, then the drag-slack-drag of the wooden flukes catching the bottom. Finally the anchor was firm. He furled the sails, pulled a biscuit from his pocket, and gnawed at it. His nerves were still too taut for proper sleep, but as the night went on he found himself nodding.

When daylight came he examined the cuddy with interest. It was not so much a cabin as a kennel and one had to stoop to enter. His first clear look showed him a brass boat-compass, battered and green with verdigris but in good working order. He could hardly keep from shouting, like a pauper finding gold in the street. There was little else to shout about. A narrow berth held an old soiled quilt whose goose feathers were escaping from rents in the fabric. A badly worn tarpaulin jacket and sou'wester hat. A demijohn of thick glass encased in wickerwork, originally containing five litres of smuggled Martinique rum, but now holding a little fresh water. Rusty fishhooks and a bait knife in an old candle box.

He now took the sweeps and worked the shallop well into the Back Cove, where the woods of Lawlor's island hid the craft from fishermen using the Eastern Passage. He set himself to watch the break in the woods where the path came across from McNab's house. This was where MacDougal, in his strange diffident courtship of Ellen Dewar, had watched for her slim figure to emerge from the trees. There on the shore was the old mast where they sat. *Il est un bien triste aspirant, le capitaine MacDougal.* Cascamond smiled at the memory. He was feeling anything but *triste* himself. Everything had gone so perfectly that he had an enormous confidence in himself and his luck.

Nothing could go wrong now.

26

McNab and his lads tramped up from the home wharf in the welcoming clamor of dogs, and Joanna was at the door for her tribute of kisses as they entered the light and warmth of the house. The laird threw off a wet cloak and hat.

"There's a few letters—one for Ellie, that Mrs. Ross sent doon at the last minute." Ellen took the note with what she hoped was a casual air and turned away to the stairs.

"Och," said the laird, "I thought 'twas only love letters a gel went off tae read by her lee-lone."

Ellie flashed her widest smile. "Oh, it's not all that important. Just the latest gossip from Argyle Street, I suspect."

"Ah! For a woman no' greatly given tae social doings herself she has a fine ear for the clack of 'em, has Mrs. Ross." McNab was moving on to the cabinet, where he poured himself a dram of whiskey to offset the damp of the voyage from town. Aunt McNab appeared now, and seeing one or two newspapers with the letters asked, "What's new from the old country? Something good, I hope?"

"Naething verra late nor verra guid, Auntie. The Parliament opened, and somebody read the Prince Regent's speech for him, mainly consairned wi' more money for Prinny and the royal tribe o' brothers and sisters. Money-money-money! It's a' they think aboot. As if the country werena fair staggering under the burthen o' this long war, and facing worse tae come. Meanwhile the puir auld king clings tae life like a wreck tae a reef, stone blind and

mad's a March hare. There was high praise in Parliament for
Wellington and his army, and quite right, too. Still and all, there's
nae blinking they havena given Wellington force enough yet tae
venture far intae Spain. If he did, Boney'd come thundering doon
wi' masses o' troops as he did on puir Johnnie Moore a few years
back. For the present Britannia seems content tae rule the waves
and doesna fear invasion, forbye the French are just across the
Channel. There's a rumor Boney's on the outs wi' Rooshia, but
I put nae stock in't—Boney's been verra cosy wi' the Rooshian
emperor these past five years. In the Hoose o' Lords, Grey and
Grenville got verra hot aboot the ill conduct o' the war in general,
and in parteecular the conduct o' the Admiralty wi' Yankee ships
and seamen. Sir Francis Burdett also took that view, and for
the matter o' that so did everyone in the Opposeetion—foretelling
war wi' the Americans, as if we hadn't enough wi' Boney on our
hands. Not a cheerful note anywhere that I can see. Castlereagh's
back in the government. Foreign Affairs. As far's he's consairned
that means entirely the affairs o' the European alliance against
Napoleon. The rest o' the world can gae tae the de'il."

When the laird went on with this, Ellen stole away to her
chamber and with trembling fingers broke the seals of the note
addressed to her by Mrs. Ross. At once she saw the handwriting
of her lover as if it were his face, and the words coming from his
lips.

> *Something has happened, dear Lutine. I must leave
> here at once. My plan is made and with luck I shall
> come to the place where our lame friend used to meet
> you on the shore. I shall watch for you there. Bring
> some food if you can. But it is you, yourself, Lutine,
> that I wish to see more than anything in the world.*

She was astonished and dismayed. How could he leave Melville Island "at once"—as if it were just a matter of walking past
the gate! She knew that a "run man" like Cascamond was not
allowed outside except on work parties in winter, when escape
was hopeless. It was springtime now, and all too often she had
heard Rory boasting of his security measures. Cascamond's plan,
whatever it was, must mean some desperate hazard in getting

out, and stealing another boat, and further hazards all along the coast. He had described his other boat voyage in a few light phrases, as if it were simply a string of merry misadventures, but she was not deceived. She had not lived all this time on Mc-Nab's island without being dreadfully aware of the perils of the sea.

And what had happened so suddenly? Something to do with Rory for a certainty—Rory and his vow to hang Cascamond on any charge that would hold water in the Vice-Admiralty Court. Somehow he must have found one, and Michel must run for his life. But run where? And how? A train of questions shot across the darkness of her mind like rockets in a night sky, each flaring and then fading as the next came along. And never an answer.

A long uneasy night, with a frequent pelter of rain on the slates of the "muckle hoose." By morning a sea mist drowned the fields and woods and shut out the sky. She put on a grey gown of home-spun, made from the wool of McNab's sheep in mingled black and white yarns. It was the common wear of the island women, warm, almost proof against damp, the best wear for this kind of weather.

At breakfast she was silent but that was usual, and there was nothing strange about her going into the kitchen afterwards and filling a basket with scones, bread, butter, cheese, and a shoulder of cold roast mutton. She and Joanna often took food to one or another of the tacksmen's cottages where the wife was ailing or had many young mouths to feed. With the hood of her Canadian cloak drawn over her head she went out through the garden as if to take the track to the south farms. After a few steps the house vanished in the mist.

She turned away then, flitting through the trees until she came to the path across the island to Back Cove. With her feet on that familiar strip of brown fir needles she began to run. She emerged from the trees upon the cove wildly expectant, and found nobody. Not even a boat. Nothing but the loom of Lawlor's island in the fog beyond the cove mouth. She sank down on the old mast where she had sat with Rory in the days of their strained and awkward courtship. Time crawled. An hour. Two hours. Three? She had no timepiece and could only guess. At last she arose, chilled and stiff. To avoid enquiry she must appear at the noonday meal.

Amongst the raffle cast up among the bushes at the beach head lay an oak cask and a scrap of old sail. She placed the contents of her basket in the cask and covered its top with the sail.

In the afternoon she returned with another basketful and again kept an empty vigil with no change except a clearing of the weather. As the fog drew off she could see the trees on Lawlor's island and then the flicker of surf on Devil's Island. Again she stowed the food in the cask and covered it. She had hopes of another message when the laird brought the mail from town but she was disappointed. The talk at the supper table was the usual thing, Joanna and Aunt McNab reciting the day's little doings on the island, and the firm of Peter McNab & Sons going over the day's affairs in Halifax. When the coffee and brandy appeared however the laird turned and chuckled to the table at large.

"One o' Rory's Frenchmen got away frae Melville Island yesterday or the night afore—the fairst that ever did. MacDougal will be in a fine wax. He was aye bragging on his guards and precautions. I daresay by noo he's drummed up half the garrison o' Halifax tae scour the woods aboot the Nor'west Arm."

Ellen's nerves sprang into a tight knot. She all but screamed aloud, and the silent screaming within her reached at least one person about the board. Aunt McNab's eyes met her own, and question and answer flashed back and forth in the mysterious telegraphy of women. And now Struachan came in with his bagpipes, received and swallowed his dram with the reverence of a monk at communion, and began to strut up and down filling the room with *Hey Johnnie Cope Are Ye Waukin Yet?*

In the morning, when the McNab males set off for the town, Ellen decided not to raid the kitchen again, lest she arouse the curiosity and probably the indignation of the cook. As she went out of the house she found Frances McNab waiting at the bottom of the garden.

"So it's your Michel?"

"Yes."

"How did you know?"

"That note from Mrs. Ross. It was really from Michel, and he said he had to get away at once."

"Rory?"

"Yes, I'm sure. He's trumped up something to take Michel

into the Admiralty Court for his life—and you know Judge Croke."

"And does Michel purpose to see you?"

"Yes."

"That means he must steal another boat."

Ellen shrugged. "I'm to watch for him at the Back Cove, and I've already taken some food there for our journey."

"What! You don't mean you're going off with him in some cockle of a fishing boat? Where?"

"I don't know and I don't care, so long as I'm with him. I'm sick of all this time apart."

"Hmmm! It's natural that he'd dare anything to see you again. But take you with him on some wild voyage down the coast? No! If he loves you he won't hear of it. Come now! Did he say a word about going with him?"

"No, but I'm going just the same."

Aunt McNab sucked her lips in and pushed them out, and said no more.

Ellen stepped away along the path to Back Cove with the high face of a woman who is certain that love will conquer the world and all. When she reached the cove she saw a fishing shallop at anchor, with a ridiculous little flatboat tugging at a rope alongside. She walked along the beach to the old mast and seated herself as if it were a magic chariot of some kind waiting to convey her to paradise. For some moments nothing moved. Then a man emerged from the cuddy of the shallop, put off in the flatboat, and came with quick oar-strokes to the shore. He wore an unfamiliar pea jacket but there was no mistaking the head and shoulders. She ran to the water's edge as the boat touched, and in a moment, without a word, they were in a rapturous embrace. First a long kiss, a marriage of mouths with eyes closed, breath held, the whole being given up to it; and then the little kisses and nuzzlings and murmurs going on and on in the language of lovers long parted.

For a time they were unaware of anything but each other—not even aware that the rising tide was lapping about their feet. Then, each with an arm about the other's waist, they moved to the head of the beach and sat on the mast, turning their heads from the sea instinctively as if to shut away all thought of it. Their minds came at last to the boat and the sea, however, and when Ellen declared she was going with him Cascamond cried, "No, Lutine! No, no, it's quite impossible! That little shallop is well enough for me. I am a sailor, I am used to rough weather and what the English call hard lying—and this voyage will be very hard. You see, this time I am going for the United States."

"That's a long way, Michel."

"I know," he smiled in a whimsical way and flipped a hand towards the shallop. "I'm told that some of the first Frenchmen, exploring this coast long ago, made voyages in craft not much better than that, and they went as far as Cape Cod. And if they did it, I can, too."

"Very well. Then I shall go with you, like the first French women."

"No, Lutine. Please listen to me. Here is the way it must be. You shall remain here, in the McNab house, while I go on alone. I hope to be picked up by an American fishing vessel, but anyhow I shall steer for Cape Cod, which is the nearest point of the United States. When I am safe among the Americans I shall write to you in the care of Mrs. Ross. Then perhaps, dear Lutine, you can join me there—I don't know how but surely there will be a way."

"There's only one sure way, Michel, and that's to go along with you. I've brought some food—it's in that cask over there—and I'll fetch more. You'll be safe here for another day. Nobody ever comes over the path at this time of year, and the Back Cove's well hidden from the Eastern Passage. What about water—drinking water?"

"I have what the fishermen call a demijohn, and I'll fill it in the pool where you used to pick the blue lilies in summer."

"Ah! And when you've done that, Michel, stay in the cuddy, just to be sure no one sees you. I must go back to the house now. Tomorrow I'll come with my basket and a few clothes."

"I tell you, Lutine . . ."

"And I tell you, monsieur, that I am coming with you."

She put her arms about his neck and kissed him firmly. It was not love alone. She was escaping from something just as he was. They were one in their adventure. In her own case there had been no guards and bars, only the tender hooks of long kindness and custom which had held her all this time in McNab's domain, haunted by sorrowful ghosts of the past. And now she was being rescued by a brave young man out of nowhere, like a prince in a fairy tale.

Cascamond did not feel anything like a prince. He was well aware of his tangled black hair and stubbled jaws, the worn and dirty clothing of His Majesty's Transport Office, and the telltale red POW on back and breast and thighs which made him a hunted animal. But his mind refused to question any more the gift in his arms, this Lutine of the generous mouth and the great black eyes lit with a mysterious glory just for him. With this charming sorceress he could go to the end of the world, and the Devil himself could not stop them.

A slight sound from the mouth of the cove caused him to take his lips from hers and turn his head. The stolen sloop bobbed peacefully at anchor. The sunlight sparkled on the water. The little flatboat was safely pulled up on the foreshore. But something else was adding itself to the scene, a blunt little sloop with a familiar hull and sails coming into the cove. There was no mistaking anything about it. The *Rob Roy* swam into full view with several redcoats for passengers, the sun glinting on their muskets and brass badges, and with Roderick MacDougal at the helm.

Cascamond and the girl sprang up, still with arms about each other, and the voice of Rory came like a crackle of muskets in the silence.

"There! What did I tell ye? I knew he'd make for here—and there's the gel as I suspected—and there's Purcell's shallop that he stole."

Ellen shuddered and caught Cascamond's hand, crying "Come! Run!"

Run where? he thought glumly. Remembering that other flight MacDougal would have men posted at the Thrum Cap. There was no escape by the path across the slim waist of the island. That led only to McNab's house. Yet he ran along the path, with Lutine ahead clutching his hand as if he were a child being dragged away from danger. As they fled through the fir wood they could hear shouting from the Back Cove, and Cascamond guessed what was afoot. A soldier or two would be left at the cove to guard the boats in case the Frenchman doubled back that way. The rest were dashing up the beach and into the path, while MacDougal hitched himself along furiously in the rear, thumping the ground with his stick and dragging the lame foot.

The fugitives came to the place where the woods opened on the tacksmen's cottages and gardens, and fled on past them to the garden of the "muckle hoose." Lutine still held Cascamond's hand and ran like the wind towards the house. There was no time to pause and think. He had a quick glimpse towards the harbor and saw the *Bonnie Jo* at the little wharf, and recognised the figures of McNab and his sons, the sailor Gahagan, and a black robe or soutane which must be that of the Irish priest.

As the panting girl and man entered the drawing room they came upon Joanna and Aunt McNab sitting by the fire, their usual place at this time of an April day, when the sea air was chill however bright the sunshine. The older women looked up startled at this sudden incursion, and their eyes widened at the frantic state of the girl and the savage apparition of the once neat teacher of French.

"What on earth . . ." cried Joanna.

"It's Michel—Michel Cascamond," Ellen gasped, as if they did not know. "He's run away and they're after him, Rory and the soldiers!"

Joanna arose and put out a finger as if to test an illusion. "But Cascamond ran away a year ago!"

Aunt McNab spoke then. "Jo, we've been keeping a secret from you, Ellie and I. It's too long a story to tell now. Cascamond has been shut up at Melville Island and now he's on the run again."

"And we must hide him!" Ellen cried.

Joanna read it all then, in the girl's face. So that was it! All that strange business of a year ago. A love affair between Ellie and the Frenchman, and Rory finding out, and a quarrel that left Rory with a cracked head. And now the lovers together again, and Rory after them again, like a little procession popping out of a German clock whenever it struck noon and midnight. It was all so mad that Jo nearly broke into a fit of nervous laughter. But at this point the door was flung open and in came four soldiers, a sergeant and three privates, all out of breath and with their muskets at the ready, as if they were storming a French fort. Jo drew herself up like a queen confronting a rabble.

"Stop where you are!"

The sergeant pointed at Cascamond with his musket. "That there's a Crappo run from Melville Island, ma'am." He was puffing too hard to say more at the moment. Suddenly the laird appeared, in a leaping of dogs, with his sons and a priest behind. He took in the scene with a quick gaze around the room—the rigid figures of Jo and Aunt McNab, the young woman clinging to the man in prison denims, the redcoats with their muskets advanced. His astonishment turned to fury in a second.

"Put doon those guns!" he roared. "And take off your caps! This is a gentleman's hoose, no' a barrack yard!"

The redcoats obeyed in haste, drawing together in a little knot by the door, with the dogs sniffing and growling about them. McNab advanced into the room, his eyes all dark fire.

"Noo, Jo, what's all this?"

"Just what you see," she answered with spirit. "Cascamond was caught after he left here last spring, and has been in prison since. Now he's away again, and he came to see Ellie."

McNab marked the attitude of Ellen, with her arms about the Frenchman and her great black eyes fixed on himself in appeal. Cascamond stood erect and his gaze met the laird's firmly, the look of a man doomed but not afraid.

"Weel, Cascamond, and what ha' ye tae say for yourself?"

"Not much, sir—Captain MacDougal will be here in a few minutes. Miss Dewar and I, well, we were in love, and Captain MacDougal found out. That was why I had to leave the island. After a time I was caught, and last winter Captain MacDougal discovered me among the prisoners at Melville Island. He promised to hang me at the first excuse. Now he has found one. So I had to run away again. I took a boat over there"—a wave of hand towards the Northwest Arm—"for another attempt to reach the United States. And, well, on the way I stopped here to see Miss Dewar—to say au revoir."

"And where d'ye hope for this au revoir?"

"In the United States, sir."

"D'ye mean she'd follow ye there?" McNab looked at Ellen.

"Yes. I'd go with him if I could," she said.

"If ye could! Weel, my lass, I've information for ye there. War's aboot tae break betwixt ourselves and the Americans, and God knows what will be the end of it. Britain's been at war wi' the

French nigh twenty years, off and on, so a bit more war doesna seem tae make much deeference tae those gentlemen in London, 'specially those in the Admiralty. It's we on this side the ocean who must bear the brunt o' the bit more. The Americans are a strong people, and sharp, so we may look for trouble in the brawl. One thing's sure, Ellie. Wi' a war on there'll be a puir chance o' meeting Cascamond in the United States—assuming he gets there, which seems verra unlikely at this moment."

And at the moment there was a stir outside, and Rory Mac-Dougal came in with his face purple and the breath wheezing in and out of him, tapping the floor with his heavy stick and scraping his right foot over the boards. He wore what had become his uniform of office, the squat black top hat, the brass-buttoned blue coat, the white shirt and black cravat, the yellow nankeen trousers.

"Ha!" he gasped, taking in everyone and everything with a sweep of fierce blue eyes. "Well, Muster McNab, here we are again, and naebody blind this time. Yon's your ward, Miss Ellie . . ."

"Ward!" snapped the laird. "Miss Ellie's past the age o' one-and-twenty. She's her own mistress, a guest in my hoose, and mind that carefully, Rory Mac!"

"Aweel, sir, there's Miss Ellie, auld enough tae know right fra wrong, let us say. And there's the sneaking Frenchman that made love tae her and tairned her head, though she was plighted tae me. Plighted o' her own accord, mind ye—o' her own accord. But weesht! That's a pairsonal matter, and my pairsonal feelings dinna matter here. I'm here as Agent for Prisoners of War, appointed by the Transport Office o' the Board of Admiralty, and my business is the care and custody o' the said prisoners, and the matters o' discipline and punishment."

"Tach!" said the laird. "We know a' that." He turned to look at the badge on the shako in the sergeant's hand. "So ye're men o' the 98th, eh? Colonel Dunning's regiment. Suppose I were tae inform my friend Dunning how ye'd come intae my hoose, intae the presence o' these ladies, wi' a brandish o' muskets as if 'twere a den o' thieves, and a' wi' no warrant of any kind! Ye know verra weel what'd happen. He'd hae the skin off your backs at the triangles the next morning sunrise! Keep that in mind and let's hear what ye hae tae say for yourselves. Fairst, how did ye get here?"

MacDougal spoke up, still breathing hard. "Wi' me, on His

Majesty's sairvice. It's like this. When the word finally got tae me in toon that yon prisoner had escaped, he'd been on the free foot a guid four-and-twenty hoors. Weel, I guessed right off what he'd be up tae. He'd be bound tae see Miss Ellie afore he flitted far. That meant he'd steal a boat and make for the Back Cove yonder, where he'd be well hid and in close touch wi' the gel. So I picked up this squad o' the 98th at the King's Wharf and sailed oot here in the *Rob Roy*. And when we entered the Back Cove, there they were, him and her, on the shore, and the stolen boat at anchor in the cove. They flitted here, we followed 'em, and I needna say more."

McNab addressed himself to the sergeant. "Get oot o' my hoose, and take these fellows wi' ye. A hangdog lot, the four o' ye, and I don't doot ye hae the drummer's receipt on your backs for past misdeeds. Be off, the way ye came, and smart aboot it!"

The sergeant looked at MacDougal but the Agent's face was of stone. The man jerked his head at his fellow soldiers and they went out quickly, brushing past the McNab youths and the priest. There was a murmur of oaths from the garden as they clapped on their shakos, slung their muskets, and tramped away towards the Back Cove.

"Ye're carrying things wi' a high hand, McNab," growled Rory, "but nae matter. Yon's my prisoner Cascamond, alias Joseph Thouret, and I want him. I intend tae charge him in Judge Croke's court wi' breaking his parole as a naval officer, and subsequently breaking oot o' His Majesty's custody at Melville Island. Also two items o' marine theft, to whit, a boat fra the Thrum Cap last year, and noo a shallop frae Purcell's Cove, all of which makes it a hanging matter."

"What!" snapped McNab. "Croke's a harsh judge, but even he'd no' hang a prisoner o' war for making off wi' a boat. Else he'd be hanging Frenchmen by the score, and—depend on Boney—there'd be reprisals on our own prisoners in France. Na, na, MacDougal, it wouldna do, and Croke knows it."

"And what," cried Rory triumphantly, "if I produce clear witness, in addeetion tae his other crimes, that this is the villain who murdered Lord Nelson wi' a skulking shot from o'erhead?"

"Gammon!"

"Ah, but it's true, McNab. And Cascamond canna deny it.

There's a Frenchman noo at Melville Island saw him do it—he's been telling it all roond the prison—I can bring a dozen men tae testify. If it comes tae the fine point I can put the witness himself in the dock."

Cascamond was silent, and in his unflinching eyes the laird saw the admission of this astonishing charge. He uttered a succession of *humphs* and *ha's,* as if to tune his vocal pipes. Then he roared, "Trafalgar was nigh seven years ago—a dog's age. What the de'il faith would any o' His Majesty's courts put in such a witness at this late time? And on such a charge! Whate'er the feelings o' the Fleet or the British people on the daith o' Nelson, there's no law in the world that says in war ye may shoot a man sideways but no' doonwards. Hoot, man, Croke may ha' nae more heart than a grindstone but he's no' a fool."

"Say what ye like, Muster McNab. I intend tae haul this rascal intae the Vice-Admiralty Court on all those charges I mentioned, and taken taegether—taken taegether, mind—I can bet ye gold on the vairdict. As ye say yourself, Judge Croke's a hard man and nae-body's fool."

McNab made a sour mouth at that. "Rory, I never thought I'd see the day ye werena welcome in my hoose, but here it is. Be gone, then, and take your redcoats back to toon."

"And what aboot the prisoner?"

"Cascamond bides here, whiles I thresh the matter oot in private wi' my family. When I've got tae the bottom o' this affair I'll make my own deceesion."

Rory thumped his stick on the floor impatiently two or three times, as if to summon up the spirit of Lord Nelson himself. Then, "Verra weel. I leave the prisoner in your custody. And I warn ye, sir, that I hold ye responsible for him. I hae my duty tae pair-form."

"Hoot-toot! You and your duty, MacDougal! 'Twas your duty tae keep your prisoner under lock and key at Melville Island, and the government spends a pretty sum for the establishment. If ye drag this matter intae the Vice-Admiralty Court it'll be your duty tae explain why he was able to break oot as if your fine prison was nae better than an auld wife's hen-hoose. Mark that, and a guid day to ye!"

MacDougal gave a stiff nod, and without a further glance at

Cascamond or Ellen shuffled away out of the house and through
the garden.

Now the laird dropped his voice to the size of the drawing
room. "Jo, my dear, we have a guest for the night. Father Sigogne
—my wife."

Like Ellen and Cascamond, Joanna had seen the priestly robe
beyond McNab and the boys, and expected Father Burke. They
now beheld a short man with a sallow face, large dark eyes, and a
smile that did not erase a suggestion of melancholy about the eyes.
The face of a saint who had suffered. His voice was mild, speaking
fluent English with a French accent.

"Madame, I was about to return to my parish from some church
business in Halifax, and your husband very kindly offered me
lodging in your house and a passage to Cape Sable in his sloop."

"We're honored, Father," Jo murmured pleasantly, and put her
head into the kitchen. "Make ready a bedchamber, Mairi, please.
A reverend gentleman will be spending the night with us."

The priest had heard the strange conversation which occupied
the McNabs from the moment of his arrival, and he had given
Cascamond a searching gaze while it was going on, but he remained
aloof in a polite silence.

"Ellie, the truth noo," McNab demanded. "Am I tae believe
ye'd run off wi' this man, whatever he's done or hasna done?"

"Yes," she said almost in a whisper. Cascamond had tried to
withdraw his hand from her clasp, but she clung to it.

"And what if the Court o' Vice-Admiralty sentences him tae
daith?"

Ellen pinched her lips in her teeth and then cried out, "I wish
they'd hang me with him! Live or die, it's all one to me, so we're
together!"

"And, Auntie, what aboot you? What's your mind on this?"

"Ah, Para, they're so deep in love, the two of them . . ."

"Love! Love! D'ye women think o' naething else? What aboot
these crimes o' Cascamond? Ye heard Rory Mac. Everything frae
shooting an admiral to stealing a puir fisherman's shallop!"

The old gentlewoman tossed her white head. "To my mind
Cascamond's done little wrong. And what has Rory Mac done
right? Whatever troth there was between Ellie and himself, Rory
must have known she didn't love him. Rory has common sense

enough for that. But it stung his pride to find the girl in love with
Cascamond, and jealousy's addled him ever since."

"And what's tae be done?"

"Let them go," Jo said. "What else?"

"Go? Go where?"

"To the American ship at Cape Sable. The one your men are
unloading there—her final voyage, isn't it?"

"And what, may I ask, d'ye know aboot that?"

Joanna glanced at Aunt McNab and made a little gesture as if
to brush aside the pretences of a mere male mind. "I'm neither
blind nor deaf, Peter. Nor is Auntie. All these comings and goings
to Cape Sable, and by times the American merchant or his captains
calling here. You're not sending your sloop to the westward only
to set Father Sigogne afoot in his parish. You're sending the
papers for one last twist of the Americans' law of Non-Intercourse
before they go to war with us. So, as I say, let Ellie and Cascamond
go along in the *Bonnie Jo*. At Cape Sable they can transfer to the
American ship—you've only to scratch a pen to the captain—and
in that way they'll reach the States in safety, instead of taking a
mad chance in an open boat."

"Tach! Non-Intercourse indeed! D'ye really think I'd let these
two run off wi' nae more ceremony than a pair o' sheep turned
loose in the pastures? Where's your moral sense, Jo?"

"Well in hand, like your sense of duty, Peter. Do you realise
you're discussing a young man and woman right before their faces
as if they were a pair of sheep? You've heard what Ellie said. Now
let us hear from Cascamond."

The prisoner hesitated, with his gaze fixed on Ellen's face, as
if there were no other people in the room. "I suppose I am what
your English preachers call an infidel. Certainly I am a French
officer whose duty is to the Emperor. But more than all that I
am a man—just a man—and I love Miss Dewar. For her I would
go anywhere and do anything."

"Ah!" said Jo. "That's the most sensible remark I've heard
this afternoon, from anyone. Now Ellie, dear of my heart, what's
your opinion of all this? Do you want your Cascamond to fight
again, as he must if he reaches the States? Duty to the Emperor
and all that? Or would you rather he went with you in care of Fa-

ther Sigogne to the Acadian settlements, where you will both be
far removed from the wars and all that has to do with war?"

Ellen held Cascamond's hand so tightly that her own slim
knuckles were white, a fact well noted by Jo and Aunt McNab.

"All I can say is I love Michel and whatever happiness there
is in the world for me will be with him—just him. Oh, I'm grateful, do believe me, for all you've done for me, the love you've given
me, the care you've had for me. But you understand—of course
you do—that any woman's happiness depends on someone else
eventually. A man. A man you may not know much about. In my
case you've known the man as a teacher of the boys, and a good
one, you'll admit. You know he's polite and intelligent. And brave,
too. Oh, very brave! I myself have known Michel in all those ways,
and still another. And I want to be with him in that other way,
wedded or not. And anywhere."

"Well?" said Jo to the laird.

"Weel what?" grumbled McNab. "Here's a bonnie pot o' chowder. Everything's in't. Ye want me tae connive at the escape of a
prisoner of war. That's treason. Ye want me tae connive at an
elopement wi'oot even the whisper of a marriage. That's . . ."

"Never mind," Joanna said. "Here's someone else who may
have a word on the subject. Father Sigogne!"

The priest made a deprecating gesture. "My dear sir and madame, I am your guest, not your adviser. I serve my church and my
flock. In affairs of the world I gave my allegiance to the British
crown and government when I was driven out of France and found
a sanctuary in England. With those things well understood I
can say a word or two, perhaps. Monsieur Cascamond—my people,
my *acadiens,* are industrious fishermen and farmers living on the
edge of the forest by the Bay of Fundy. Their people suffered
cruelly during the old wars of the French and English in this country, so they know the blessing of peace, which they have enjoyed
more than half a century. They are a devout people, they trust
in God, and I am their only priest, in a parish that stretches nearly
a hundred miles along the coast. Not one in twenty of them can
read or write his name. I would like to see a school in every village but we have only two or three, for lack of teachers."

"What has this to do with me?" said Cascamond.

"You are a Frenchman of education, it seems. If Monsieur Mc-

Nab permitted, I would like to offer you a post as schoolmaster. The pay would be small but you would be provided with food and lodging. Or if you chose, you could have a house to yourself." He paused and turned his face to the laird and Joanna. "Of course we would prefer a married man. If you should agree to let this young lady depart in my care, I can perform the marriage. First, however, Monsieur Cascamond would have to make solemn undertakings to the Church and to the government of this country. All of these things can be done at Saint Mary's Bay, where I am going, and where there will be a proper time for everything."

Sigogne spoke in English throughout, but Cascamond replied instinctively and rapidly in French, "There is a guinea on my head. Someone there would inform the Agent for Prisoners."

Sigogne spoke again in English. "There is no danger of that. We have several escaped prisoners of war amongst us now. Let us say that I have an understanding with the Governor at Halifax. To settle among us I require these men to give up, under the most solemn oath, their allegiance to France. Each of them is now a citizen of Nova Scotia, a peaceful subject of King George, entitled to every protection that the law gives to His Majesty's subjects anywhere."

"No redcoats? No press gangs?" snapped Cascamond, with the aggressive air of a man who finds his prejudices crumbling and feels obliged to make a last thrust in their defense.

"None. We have our militia, under our own officers, but these are for our own defense in case of war." The priest smiled slowly and added, "We call our part of this country Acadie and ourselves *acadiens*. But I like to think of it as Arcadie, the land of simple plenty, of innocent pleasures, of peace without end. If Monsieur McNab agrees, I invite you to become one of us."

Cascamond turned to Ellen with a whimsical face. "And you, Lutine—would you wish to live on a schoolmaster's pay in this Arcadie?"

For answer she put her arms about his neck and kissed him.

The laird harrumphed and found his business voice. "Weel, then, let's get doon tae brass tacks. Ye'll sail, all three, in the *Bonnie Jo,* as soon as it's dark tonight. I'll follow astern in my own shallop as far's Chebucto Head, just in case Rory may be lurking aboot the Thrum Cap wi' that gang o' His Majesty's hard bargains. Father Sigogne will take Miss Ellen in his care. He'll also take in his care the sum of a hundred and feefty poonds, which is Ellen's dowry, Cascamond, tae be paid the day she becomes your wife. Na, na, don't interrupt me—ye may thank my Jo some time. Meanwhile, Ellie, ye must promise tae write and say how ye get on. And some day, when a' this damned fighting's over, ye must come wi' your husband and bairns and visit us here. Take care o' her, Cascamond. I'll be frank and say ye're not what I'd hae wished for Ellie, though I grant ye're quite a man. If the Father here can make a guid Catholic o' ye, and a subject o' the King besides, I don't doot I can make an honorary Scotsman o' ye bye-and-bye. And here's my hand on't."

"But you, sir," Cascamond said as he took the hand. "What about you? Captain MacDougal will complain to the Admiral . . ."

"The Admiral! The Admiral! I've had a deal tae do wi' admirals the past ten years and more, admirals guid, bad, and so-so. And I can tell ye the present one's got too much on his mind tae care a docken aboot a missing prisoner o' war. The Americans will declare themselves at war wi' Britain any day noo, and on the heels o' that will come a swarm o' Yankee privateers, right tae the Admiral's door—here! They ken this coast as weel as we oorselves. They'll be snapping up merchant ships under the Admiral's verra nose, and all too nimble for his frigates and ships-o'-the-line tae catch. He'll be in the poseetion o' trying tae kill mosquitoes wi' a sledgehammer, and he knows it. As for Rory, I've a notion he'll tuck his tongue in his cheek and swallow a leetle mixture o' rum and philosophy. He kens he's beat, and that will be all o' that. Och, there's other things tae think aboot. Cascamond, ye need a wash and a scrape of the razor, and I'll find ye some clothes more sober than that fine raiment o' the Transport Office." And to Jo and Aunt McNab, "A' this havering! I'm dry's dust and starved besides. When the de'il is supper?"

The *Bonnie Jo* slipped away into the night with McNab's shallop in her wake, manned by a party of burly islanders hoping for "a touse wi' Rory's sogers." Other than these, the whole population of McNab's island stood on the shore, and all the women, and even young Sheamus and Para, had wet eyes. Joanna linked arms with Aunt McNab at last and turned back to the house, sighing, "God keep them happy always."

"Don't ask God to do what's not his business," the old High-landwoman said, and blew her nose. "I've lived long, and if I learned one thing along the way it's that men and women make their own joys and sorrows in this world. People don't marry and live happy ever after except in children's tales. Cascamond's got a dour temper behind that quick French face of his, and being a man there'll be times when he's difficult anyhow. He'll wish him-self free, he'll wish himself back in France, or the West Indies, or any place but where he is. And as for Ellie, you know her moods, and she can use a sharp tongue when she's a mind. They don't fully know each other yet, and perhaps they never will. But what a flat world this would be if we all really knew each other! All an-swers and no questions. What would happen to the nations? The religions?"

"Ah!" said Jo. "And speaking of that, do you think Cascamond will really make a good Catholic?"

"No more than I think he'll make a perfect husband. The Church and Ellie will have their heartburnings over Cascamond at times. Look what's behind him. An orphan of that horrible revolution. Then the life at sea—sailors don't make saints. And then so long a prisoner, with a natural hatred of anything that shut him in or tied him down. I'll say this—call it *da-shealladh* if you like—Ellie will come as close to taming him as anybody can this side of Judg-ment Day. She'll have a time of it, mind. And so will he, for that matter. After all a fey woman's not to be fathomed by any mere man. There'll be times when he'll feel he's married to a mermaid or some other fabulous creature not made for breathing plain air. But on the whole there will be love to butter the scone, and I seem to see a fine little troop of children."

"What else do you see, Auntie?"

"Cascamond won't be satisfied long with teaching school. He's made for action, like a frigate or a corvette or whatever the Frenchmen call those things. A man of that kind must be up and doing or go daft. From all I've heard, those Acadians are clever men with tools, and a man like Cascamond could turn their hands to building ships, just as he learned to build models in the prison. Here on this coast, with a forest behind and the ocean in front,

with half the world at war, and ships wanted everywhere . . .
well, that's not *da-shealladh,* it's just my born Scotch business sense
. . . maybe I should have been a man!"

There was no sign of Rory off the Thrum Cap or anywhere
else, and McNab's men were disappointed. At the harbor headland there was a last calling of farewells as the shallop turned back.
The laird was at the helm, and opposite the black cliff where York
Redoubt held its lone guard lantern high in the dark he shifted the
tiller sharply.

"Och," said Struachan beside him, "wipe her off a bit, Para, or
we'll fetch upon the stones wi' the hanged men."

"Ay, so we will."

"What! A-purpose?"

"Ay. We've a wee job o' logging and launching tae do there tonight. If ye look in the cuddy ye'll find axes and saws for't."

As the shallop drew in to the point they could hear the creak and
groan of gibbet chains. "Here's an eerie business!" Struachan said.
"Couldna we put it off till day?"

"Wi' the soldiers keeking at us yonder in York Redoubt? This
must be done in the dark and I'll no' wait another night—I've waited
years for this. By morn the Admiral's orchard will be gone fra
the point, and all of us the better for a guid night's work."

"The Admiral will put up more, Para."

"Wi' an American war in the offing? Not he! The Admiral weel
knows what Prevost obsairved tae the Board of Ordnance—that a
bold sea raider could slip in under the verra guns o' York. And
he knows the remedy. A battery here on the point, tae cover the
channel at sea level."

"Cannons and sogers here? What aboot hurricane weather?"

"They'll need a Martello fort, built roond as a thimble, wi' walls
seven or eight foot thick, strong enough tae stand any bombard-
ment, let alone tides and weather. And a garrison o' living men
won't stand for dead ones under their noses."

The shallop swung alongside the outer stones of the point, and
the tacksmen doused the sails and tossed a grapnel to the shore.
They had heard the conversation. An uncanny business, ay, but
if the laird wanted it the business must be done.

"There's whiskey in the locker," McNab said as they prepared to go ashore. "Fetch oot the jug. There's naething like a guid stiff dram all roond tae bring luck at a launching."

Forth came the jug and down went the drams, and bye-and-bye down went the Admiral's trees with their rusty chains and Dead Sea fruit, and the ebb tide carried them away past the Thrum Cap to the oblivion of the sea.